D1295344

BEYOND SOCIOBIOLOGY

JOHN D. BALDWIN

and

JANICE I. BALDWIN

University of California, Santa Barbara

Exclusive Distribution
throughout the World by
Greenwood Press, Westport,
Ct. U.S.A.

ELSEVIER
New York · Oxford

Elsevier North Holland, Inc.
52 Vanderbilt Avenue, New York, New York 10017

Sole distributors outside the USA and Canada:
Elsevier Science Publishers B.V.
P.O. Box 211, 1000 AE Amsterdam, The Netherlands

Library of Congress Cataloging in Publication Data

Baldwin, John D.   1941–
    Beyond sociobiology.

    Bibliography: p.
    Includes index.
    1. Sociobiology. 2. Nature and nurture. I. Baldwin, Janice I., joint author. II. Title.
GN365.9.B34   304   80-28032
ISBN 0-444-99086-0

Desk Editor   John Molyneux
Design   Edmée Froment
Design Editor   Glen Burris
Mechanicals   José García
Production Manager   Joanne Jay
Compositor   Maryland Composition
Printer   Haddon Craftsmen

PERMISSION
P.6: Reprinted from *The Mountain Gorilla* by G.B. Schaller by permission of the University of Chicago Press. © 1963 by the University of Chicago. All rights reserved. **P.27:** Mori, U. 1979. Inter-unit relations. In M. Kawai (ed.) *Contributions to Primatology: Ecological and Sociological Studies of Gelada Baboons,* Vol. 16, pp. 83–92. S. Karger AG, Basel. (Photo by M. Kawai.) **P.40:** Kawai, M. Director and Professor of the Primate Research Institute, Kyoto University. **P.53:** Charles-Dominique, P. 1974, Ecology and feeding behaviour of five sympatric lorisids in Gabon. In R.D. Martin, G.A. Doyle and A.C. Walker (eds.), *Prosimian Biology,* pp. 131–150. Gerald Duckworth and Co., London. **P.80:** Yukimaru Sugiyama: *Primates* 12(3–4):247–266, 1971. Characteristics of the social life of bonnet macaques *(Macaca radiata).* **P.84:** Saayman, G.S. 1971 Behaviour of the adult males in a troop of free-ranging chacma baboons *(Papio ursinus).* Folia Primat. 15:36–57. S. Karger AG, Basel. **P.88:** Tattersall, I. 1977. Ecology and behavior of *Lemur fulvus mayottensis* (primates, lemuriformes). *Anthrop. Papers Am. Mus. Nat. Hist.* 54, part 4:421–482. **P.101:** Kosei Izawa and Akinori Mizuno: *Primates* 18(4):773–792, 1977. Palm-fruit cracking behavior of wild black-capped capuchin *(Cebus apella).* **P.99:** McGrew, W.C., Tutin, C.E.G. and Baldwin, P.J. 1979. Chimpanzees, tools and termites: Cross-cultural comparisons of Senegal, Tanzania, and Rio Muni. *Man* 14:185–214. **P.109:** Mason, W.A. 1960. The effects of social restriction on the behavior of rhesus monkeys: I. Free social behavior. *J. Comp. Physiol. Psychol.* 53:582–589. © 1960 by the American Psychological Association. Reprinted by permission. **P.107:** James Loy: *Primates* 12(1):1–31, 1971. Estrous behavior of free-ranging rhesus monkeys *(Macaca mulatta).* **P.117,126:** Eaton, G. The Oregon troop of Japanese macaques. Reprinted with permission, from *Primate News* (Oregon Regional Primate Research Center) 9(9):2,3,7, October 1971. **P.121:** H.F. Harlow, University of Wisconsin Primate Laboratory. **P.123:** Mason, W.A. 1968. Early social deprivation in the nonhuman primates: Implications for human behavior. In D. Glass (ed.), *Environmental Influences,* pp. 70–101. The Rockefeller University Press, New York. **P.124:** Mason, W.A. and Kenney, M.D. 1974. Redirection of filial attachments in rhesus monkeys: Dogs as mother surrogates. *Science* 183:1209–1211. © 1974 by the American Association for the Advancement of Science. **Pp.125,167:** Mori, U. 1979. Individual relations within a unit. In M. Kawai (ed.) *Contributions to Primatology: Ecological and Sociological Studies of Gelada Baboons,* Vol. 16, pp. 93–124. S. Karger AG, Basel. **P.142:** de Waal, B.M. and van Roosmalen, A. 1979. Reconciliation and consolation among chimpanzees. *Behav. Ecol. Sociobiol.* 5:55–66. **Pp.150,189,208:** Oppenheimer, J.R. 1977. *Presbytis entellus,* the hanuman langur, pp. 469–512. In *Primate Conservation* (HSH Prince Rainer and G.H. Bourne, eds.). Academic Press, New York. **P.152:** McGrew, W.C. and Tutin, C.E.G. 1978. Evidence for a social custom in wild chimpanzees? *Man,* 13:234–251. Reprinted by permission of the Royal Anthropological Institute of Great Britain and Ireland. **Pp.154,187:** Hladik, C.M. 1972. L'Atele de Geoffroy, ce singe-araignée. *Science et Nature* No.111, mai-juin. **Pp.188,210:** Symons, D. 1978. *Play and Aggression.* Columbia Univ. Press, New York. **P.194:** Figure 14.1 (p.429) from *Foundations of Physiological Psychology* by Richard F. Thompson. © 1967 by Richard F. Thompson. Reprinted by permission of Harper & Row, Publishers, Inc.

Manufactured in the United States of America

To our parents
Helen and Herman Baldwin
Elizabeth and Walter Whiteside
who gave us balanced gifts of both nature and nurture.

CONTENTS

PREFACE

During the past several years, sociobiology has become a very visible and prominent theory of animal behavior. Several scholarly books and numerous journal articles have advocated, promoted, and/or advanced the theory. In addition, various books have attempted to apply sociobiology to human behavior, and others have attempted to popularize the theory for the general reader. The rapid rise of this new theory of behavior has caught the attention of many and generated much debate. Advocates believe that sociobiology represents a major advance in knowledge about animal behavior—with astounding implications for human behavior. Opponents see it as an overly zealous attempt to force all behavior into the mold of genetic determinism.

There is reason to believe that sociobiology is not the last word in behavioral theories. There are serious flaws in the theory, which many of its practitioners freely admit. The strong emphasis on evolutionary analysis neglects too many other variables that should be built into a comprehensive theory of behavior. Yet many people cannot see where to go next, and sociobiology looks like one of the better alternatives available in spite of its flaws. In this book we suggest the next step—beyond sociobiology.

Sociobiology has taken an unreasonable position in the nature–nurture debate. Its extreme emphasis on natural selection leads to unbalanced theories of behavior, especially when dealing with advanced species. We need to replace sociobiology with balanced theories. This becomes particularly important when dealing with humans. Unbalanced theories can easily misinform us and misguide our efforts to improve the human condition. Given the enormous problems facing us in the coming decades, we cannot afford to use unbalanced theories in making decisions about human behavior or social planning. Instead, we need to develop new theories that produce a balance of both nature and nurture. In this book we present one approach to balanced theories of behavior, demonstrating how nature and nurture can be interwoven into a unified model of animal and human behavior. Balanced biosocial theories are within our grasp. They allow us to go beyond the problems of sociobiology. The time has come to develop them.

NATURE AND NURTURE

Why was Beethoven so creative? Did he have special genes? Or was it something special about his environment? Was it nature or nurture?

People have loved to speculate about such matters, and many have not realized that they were being misled by a loaded question. The question—was it nature or nurture—biases one to think in terms of black and white categories. The answer must be either one or the other. Because many people have been willing to take sides on this type of question and argue extreme positions, the nature–nurture controversy has had a long and heated history.

Throughout the 20th century there has been a growing awareness that black and white answers are seldom adequate for explaining behavior. Neither nature alone nor nurture alone explain behavior. The entire nature-nurture controversy has distracted people from the more complex question: How do nature and nurture interact to produce behavior? This question is more difficult. It demands that we leave behind simplistic black and white answers, venture into the gray area in-between, and create theories based on an appropriate balance of various causal factors. All behavior reflects the joint contributions of both nature and nurture. The goal is to arrive at balanced theories that give proper weighting to all the determinants of behavior and weave them together in the correct relationship.

Since the 1950s, many students of behavior have agreed that the black and white approach of the nature–nurture controversy is dead and that we must move beyond black and white arguments to more balanced theories of behavior.[1] However, an interesting thing has happened. In the late 1960s and early 1970s, a new scientific theory emerged that argued forcefully that the total pattern of behavior produced by any individual results from evolutionary and genetic causes.[2] Sociobiology is the rigorous application of evolutionary theory to the study of behavior, and its proponents claim that the theory will explain all types of behavior. Evolutionary theory is one of the most successful and powerful theories in the biological sciences. The application of this influential theory to behavior has caused many to forget the dangers of black and white argument, and return to an extreme position in the nature–nurture debate.

It is understandable that sociobiologists have espoused their new theory with great enthusiasm. Their theory brings order to an enormous body of data. Sociobiology offers a parsimonious theory that is well founded in evolutionary principles. The theory is fertile with suggestions for research topics, and in many domains these research questions have paid off with exciting new discoveries about behavior. Finally, the theory promises to unify all the behavioral sciences in one grand synthesis.[3]

However, there are anomalies: not all the pieces fit together. In this book, we will discuss some of the anomalies and suggest a way of producing balanced theories that avoid both extremes of the nature–nurture controversy.

In this chapter, we will present a basic overview of the issues to be considered: evolutionary interpretations of behavior, the anomalies, and possible future directions. The remainder of the book is divided into four parts. Part I contrasts balanced theories of behavior with sociobiology. Part II describes the data and theories that sociobiology has neglected. Part III gives a concrete example of a balanced synthesis of nature and nurture, as an illustration of the type of theory that goes beyond extreme nature–nurture arguments, and beyond sociobiology. Part IV points to future possibilities.

WHAT IS SOCIOBIOLOGY?

According to one of its founders, E.O. Wilson (1975:4), "sociobiology is defined as the systematic study of the biological basis of all social

---

[1] Lehrman (1953); Schneirla (1956); Anastasi (1958); Lorenz (1965); and Crook (1970b).
[2] For example, see Wilson (1975:4, 255).
[3] Wilson (1975:4).

behavior." Sociobiology is an attempt at a very rigorous application of evolutionary theory to the topic of social behavior. Biologists have been generously rewarded for applying evolutionary theory to almost every domain of biological research. Sociobiology has attempted to extend evolutionary principles to the last domain of biology to be subsumed under Darwinian theory, the domain of animal social behavior.

Ethology—the biology of behavior—is a school of animal behavior that began developing decades before the advent of sociobiology. The research and theories created by Lorenz, von Frisch, Tinbergen, Hinde, and other ethologists helped set the stage for sociobiology by analyzing many behavior patterns seen in the animal kingdom. Classical ethology studied innate patterns of animal behavior and then explained them as functional adaptations for survival. For example, Lorenz's book, *On Aggression* (1963), attempted to show that aggression has many functions in promoting survival. Species-typical patterns of aggression, dominance, or territoriality evolve in each species; the survival of the species in its unique niche depends on the effectiveness of these strategies. Some birds will establish mating territories and fight off all same-sex intruders; whereas others will coexist in flocks, but regulate access to food and sex via hierarchies based on fighting. Each strategy is suited to certain types of species adaptations and ecological niches.

Sociobiology built upon this analysis, by assuming that behavior is controlled by "behavioral genes"[4] and that, in the final analysis, all behavior patterns evolved due to the survival of the fittest genes. The thesis of Dawkins's book, *The Selfish Gene* (1976), allows one to grasp sociobiological principles easily. If each gene were selfishly motivated to insure its own survival, what kind of behavior would it program in the animal that carried it? Selfish genes that caused an animal to compete for scarce resources and to reproduce at the maximal rate would be passed to the next generation in abundance. Genes that caused an individual to be noncompetitive or unconcerned about reproduction would have less chance of being passed on to the next generation. Clearly the selfish genes that program competitive and reproductive behavior have an advantage over other genes and would be expected to dominate in the gene pool. In laying the foundation for sociobiology, Williams (1966:251) wrote: "a gene is selected on one basis only, its average effectiveness in producing individuals able to maximize the gene's representation in future generations." According to this logic, the individual animal merely behaves according to the program established by the selfish genes, in order to maximize the transmission and multiplication of the genes.

This theory made it very easy to understand selfish behavior, tooth and claw competition, and aggression. According to Williams (1966:193),

[4] Wilson (1978).

"these self-seeking behavior patterns, which are widely prevalent in the animal kingdom, are easily attributed to selection for competitive efficiency in genetic survival." Natural selection produced genes that compelled each individual to compete ruthlessly for its own survival, for the survival of its own offspring, and hence for the survival of the controlling genes. The challenge for sociobiology was to explain the benign, cooperative, and even altruistic behavior that is also seen in the animal kingdom. Why would one individual help another, if helping in any way jeopardized the genetic fitness of the first individual? According to Wilson (1975:3–4), "the answer is kinship: if the genes causing the altruism are shared by two organisms because of common descent [i.e., kinship], and if the altruistic act . . . increases the joint contribution of these genes to the next generation, the propensity to altruism will spread through the gene pool." Because each individual shares genes with kin, the selfish interests of the genes can be served by having animals programmed to help kin, especially close kin. An individual's own personal fitness (the ability to transmit its genes to the next generation) is less important than its *inclusive* fitness—the ability of all individuals with similar genes to transmit those genes to the next generation. Altruistic sacrifice may decrease an individual's personal fitness but increase its total inclusive fitness if the benefits to gene-sharing kin outweigh the costs to its own fitness. The individual may make a sacrifice that jeopardizes its own reproductive capacity but promotes the reproductive success of several brothers and sisters; and this increases its inclusive fitness by enabling its siblings to pass on the shared family genes.

After developing the principle of inclusive fitness in the abstract, Hamilton (1964) used the principle to explain one of the perplexing problems of animal behavior: the extraordinary altruism of the social insects. The mode of sex determination in the social insects is unusual. All the workers are more closely related to each other (with a degree of relatedness of ¾) than they would be related to their own offspring (a relatedness of ½). All workers cooperate altruistically in the care of the hive and the next generation of workers because they "may increase their inclusive fitness more by care of their younger sisters than by an equal amount of care given to their own offspring" (Wilson, 1975:416). Other researchers were soon able to extend this type of sociobiological analysis to explain other aspects of social insect behavior that had never been understood.

The major breakthrough was this: Sociobiology could explain *both* competitive and altruistic behavior in strictly evolutionary terms. Both competition and altruism were consequences of natural selection operating on behavioral genes. Competition with nonkin and altruism with close kin both increase the likelihood of the controlling genes in being transmitted to future generations. The problem of altruism at the level of individual behavior was "solved" by analyzing the best "strategies" of the selfish genes for guaranteeing their own transmission.

The parsimony and elegance of the solution were compelling arguments in favor of the new theory. Darwinian principles had been successfully extended to the arena of social behavior to explain both the obvious (competition) and the obscure (altruism). Natural selection—the "organizing principle of biology"[5]—had triumphed to bring order to yet another area of biology. It is easy to appreciate the enthusiasm with which such a breakthrough was welcomed in many circles.

MONKEYS AND ANOMALIES

Understandably, sociobiologists have not actively sought out the anomalies that all theories must eventually face. In the first stages of the development of any theory, the theory's advocates tend to focus attention on data that fit the theory, attempting to explain as much as possible and trying to expand the boundaries of the theory's domain. A good theory provides numerous rewards for this strategy because a good theory, by definition, is one that succeeds in explaining a large body of data. Because the theory of sociobiology can explain both self-seeking behavior and altruism—and everything in between—it virtually cries out to be applied to all behavior at all phylogenetic levels. The large number of cases in which the animal data appear to confirm sociobiological theory have convinced many of the theory's power.

However, not all the data fit the theory. There are anomalies at many phylogenetic levels. Some are minor and may be resolved within the framework of sociobiology. Others present major problems that cannot be easily resolved without an extensive revision—or perhaps an abandonment—of the basic assumptions of the sociobiological position. It is the major anomalies that have motivated many to look beyond sociobiology for alternative theories.

In this early phase of the critique of sociobiology (and given the brevity of a book of this nature), we cannot review all the major anomalies. Having spent 14 years involved in primate research, we will focus on the data with which we are most familiar.[6] The emphasis on primate behavior is not intended to imply that anomalies occur only among the primates. The alternative theory proposed in this volume predicts that anomalies will be common elsewhere in the animal kingdom.

Primate field research began to gain momentum around 1960.[7] There

[5] Mayr (1978:47).

[6] Although most of the data on primates presented in this volume appear in the primate literature and are referenced to it, some statements are based on unpublished personal observations on squirrel monkeys, howler monkeys, and capuchins.

[7] Altmann (1967:xi).

PLATE 1.1. Gorillas were among the first primates that were well studied in the wild in the early 1960s. Schaller (1963) reported considerable within-species variability in gorilla behavior. *(Courtesy of G.B. Schaller.)*

had been a few field studies in the 1930s and after World War II; but the real deluge of data has come in the past two decades. Many of the early primate studies of the 1960s were heavily influenced by the classical ethological theories that behavior and social organization are genetically fixed and adaptive. It was expected that both physical morphology and behavior would reflect the evolutionary adaptations of a species to its species-typical ecological niche. Not surprisingly, the early researchers often reported that primate behavior and social organization *were* fixed and adaptive. The major concepts of classical ethology—dominance, territoriality, stereotyped displays, fixed action patterns, ethograms, releasers, and so forth—were taken to the field and data were often reported in these terms.

Some of the early field studies seemed to fit genetic models very nicely. A famous and frequently cited study by Irven DeVore (1963a,b)[8] was based on 11 months of field observations on olive baboons in Kenya. These baboons live on the open grasslands, and observations could be made without the problems that face observers in forests or swamps. DeVore reported that baboons lived in closed societies: Different groups

[8] Data from this study were also reported by Washburn and DeVore (1961), DeVore and Hall (1965), and Hall and DeVore (1965).

seldom came near each other and only two individuals were ever seen to change groups. The core areas of their home ranges rarely overlapped. Within each group, the social order was controlled by the dominant adult males. These adult males were the focal point of attention: When the males ate, other group members ate; when the males moved, the others moved. Baboons have a conspicuous sexual dimorphism: The males weigh about twice as much as the females, have larger canine teeth, and are considerably stronger. It seemed only natural that these morphological features which equip the adult males for effective fighting were accompanied by the behavioral correlates of male assertiveness, aggression, dominance, and autocratic control over the group.

The male baboons maintained a salient dominance hierarchy. The high-rank males had first access to food and sex. They gave conspicuous threat and warning displays—such as the yawning display, in which the male flashes his canines—that functioned to keep dominance relations visible even in the absence of fights. The hierarchy of the central males was more complex than the linear "peck order" seen in chickens. The older males formed coalitions that enhanced their power and prevented any single younger male from successfully challenging them. High-rank males traveled in the center of the group, surrounded by the adult females and their young. Low-rank males were excluded from this central social position by the high-rank males and were forced to travel at the fringe of the group, where they served as sentinels and first line of defense in case of danger. This social structure, in which the mothers of young infants were sheltered in the center of the group and expendible young males were exposed to the dangers at the outer edge of the group, was often cited as having obvious survival value. The powerful central males played the most important role in protecting the entire group from predators. In times of danger, the adult males formed a bodyguard between the source of danger and the rest of the group. "When baboons are away from trees, foraging in open country, the powerful muscles and large canines of the adult males are the group's only protection" (DeVore and Hall, 1965:49). The central males also maintained order within the group. They stopped squabbles between other group members. If an infant was frightened or endangered, the high-rank males would rush to defend it.

The early picture of baboon adaptation was simple. A central cluster of autocratic males controlled the group. They provided protection and order; and in return, they received first rights to food and sex. Only the strongest and most aggressive males reached the top of the hierarchy. As a result, the genes for male-chauvinistic behavior, fighting skills, and large canines were passed to the next generation, guaranteeing the strength and vigor necessary for survival on the savannas. The adult females specialized in reproductive behavior and were usually pregnant or occupied with infant care. Given the high infant mortality—due to injury, disease, and predation—this female reproductive specialization also appeared very adaptive. Because of the "obvious survival value" of the baboons' behavior and social organization, it was easy to infer that their behavior reflected honing and tuning by natural selection, that their behavior had evolved to be a close fit to the demands of their environment.

Since humans also evolved on the savannas of Africa, the next logical step was to infer that we shared a "biogrammar"—an underlying genetic deep structure—that impelled us to behave in similar ways.[9] Thus, the aggressiveness and chauvinism of the human male were viewed as having a genetic base. The domestic interests of the human female were assumed to result from the survival value of such traits. It was only natural for males to leave domestic duties to females and turn their attention to the politics of leadership, coalition formation, and power plays. Literally dozens of writers rushed their books and articles into print with variations on these theories of human behavioral evolution.[10]

ENTER: THE ANOMALIES

The simple picture that emerged from the early field studies on baboons began to dissolve as additional studies were conducted on them at different times and in different places. Comparative studies on other primates tended to alter the early generalizations about those species also. The comparative data on most species revealed a surprising level of variability in the behavior and social organization of primates—a level of variability that had not been predicted by genetic theories.[11]

For example, Thelma Rowell (1966a) studied a population of olive baboons in Uganda, about 480 miles west of DeVore's site. A major difference between these two studies on olive baboons is that Rowell's baboons spent most of their time in forests rather than on the open savanna. "Baboons are usually regarded as animals of open country, yet this population spent 60% of its time in forest, though open grassland was available to them" (p. 363). The preference is striking because only 12% of the animals' home range was forest. Rowell's study revealed considerable variation in baboon behavior and social organization and called into question the notion that field observations on primates in a single location could be used to infer the "species-typical" behavior and adaptations of the species.

The adult males in Rowell's study did not display the aggressive,

---

[9] Tiger and Fox (1971).

[10] For example, Ardrey (1961, 1966), Lorenz (1963), Morris (1967), Tiger (1969), and Tiger and Fox (1971).

[11] Jay (1968); Crook (1970b); and Bernstein and Smith (1979).

dominance-oriented behavior DeVore reported. In fact, dominance relations "could not be observed" (p. 362). Threats, fights, and displacements—from which dominance is inferred—were "extremely rare" (p. 362). The males showed mutual cooperation as they policed the environment; and their "remaining social interactions chiefly involved mutual grooming with females and acting as focus of juvenile play" (p. 362). The groups were not closed societies. The males drifted in and out of groups, joining other groups without commotion or social disturbance. Groups showed tolerance toward new members. The adult females did not change groups, but rather formed the cohesive core of each group. The infants and juveniles organized themselves around the adult females, and the fact that these females did not change groups gave stability to the social organization. The adult males did not monopolize the central areas of the group or force the young males to travel at the fringe of the group, as DeVore described. Rather, the young males traveled with the main group. Pregnant females were most often at the fringe of the group. Adult males often waited at the end of group processions—until all the group members were ahead of them—before following group movements. The entire group waited for stragglers, "even those with injuries that made walking difficult" (p. 362). The adult males sometimes served as group protectors, if the source of danger was not too alarming. But the males were the first to flee—leaving the females to fend for themselves—if the danger stimulus was too frightening.

Why were the adult males not more aggressive? Why did the biggest and strongest males not seek to maximize their genetic fitness by dominating the other males, by excluding the low-rank animals, and by monopolizing food and sexually receptive females for their own selfish ends? If behavior is actually under strong genetic control, how can one reconcile the tremendous variation in baboon behavior with the static nature of genetic information? Although DeVore's baboons were used by many as an example of the adaptations produced by primate evolution on the savannas, Rowell concluded that "whatever the baboons' adaptation to life in grassland, they do not seem any less competent as a forest animal than other primates" (p. 361). "Until we know more about the general effects of environmental differences on primate behaviour, we may also be misled about evolutionary mechanisms in the group, especially since knowledge of past environmental changes is also inadequate" (p. 364). Rowell's work indicated that caution was needed in inferring, from a small number of field studies, the existence of presumably fixed, species-typical behavior. Because olive baboons behave so differently in forests and savannas, she concluded that "direct environmental effects may be responsible for many differences at present regarded as specific, so that caution and intraspecific comparative studies are needed before behaviour is described as species typical" (p. 344).

As other scientists began to study baboons in other environments, the variations in behavior and social organization that they observed justified Rowell's call for caution. Altmann and Altmann (1970) reported on the yellow baboons at Amboseli, Kenya, in a grassland setting similar to DeVore's. They too reported unexpected variations which demonstrated that savanna living did not always produce behavioral patterns like those DeVore reported. Dominance relations were not conspicuous at Amboseli. Home ranges overlapped completely. And the "adaptive" group structure reported by DeVore—in which the high-rank males traveled in the group center with the adult females and young, while the low-rank males traveled at the periphery—was not observed. "The progressions that we observed . . . did not reveal any invariable order of progression, nor was it true that the front and back of the progression invariably consisted of adult males and older juvenile males" (p. 188). In a subsequent analysis of 11 hypotheses about group geometry, Altmann (1979) found that group progressions were "essentially random."

Paterson (1973) studied olive baboons in two different ecological conditions—a thicket savanna and a forest edge. "Each troop of baboons examined showed very different mannerisms, attitudes, and, to some extent, variations in social structure" (p. 646). For example, the group in the thicket savanna had a hierarchical group structure, with a rather linear dominance structure, and a high level of aggression. The forest group did not have any type of dominance hierarchy among the males or the females; and fighting was virtually nonexistent. Patterns of sexual interaction and courtship were also quite different in the two groups.

Hamilton, Buskirk, and Buskirk (1975, 1976, and 1978a,b) conducted a comparative study on chacma baboons living in either desert or swamp environments. There was considerable within-species variation in behavior and social organization. Much of this variation could be traced to intergroup differences in past experiences, local traditions, habituation, motivational states, resources, economics of resource utilization, and social organization.

Harding (1977) observed olive baboons near Gilgil, Kenya, for one year. The spatial arrangement of group members described by DeVore was not observed during the study, "nor has it been reported by other field workers since its original description" (p. 349). Instead, variability is the norm. "In short, baboons change their dispersion patterns in response to past experiences in different parts of their range" (p. 352).

The new data make it clear that past experience, local traditions, the local economics of resource utilization, and other nongenetic factors have a significant effect on primate behavior. Any theory that neglects these types of influence on behavior and that focuses undue attention on evolutionary variables is likely to be misleading and inaccurate.

CONCLUSION

Over the past two decades literally thousands of studies on dozens of primate species have appeared in the scientific literature. Some fit the evolutionary model beautifully. Others do not. Those that do not fit have caused many primatologists to be skeptical of extreme evolutionary theories of behavior. In addition, studies on other mammals and on birds reveal that the evolutionary model is not always appropriate for explaining the behavior of many advanced species.

A new picture of animal behavior is emerging that stresses the behavioral flexibility of advanced species. Theories that the behavior of advanced species can be traced directly to evolutionary and genetic causes are extremely misleading. There is an increasing awareness that direct environmental influences on behavior must be studied in order to account for the enormous variability in behavior.

The main thesis of this book is that sociobiology has taken an unreasonable position in the nature–nurture controversy. Its extreme evolutionary bias may produce reasonably good explanations of the behavior of primitive species. But the theory fails to do justice to the data on those species where nature is not the predominant determinant of behavior. Neither extreme in the nature–nurture controversy is ever truly defensible, since all behavior at all phyletic levels is influenced by both nature and nurture. Therefore, we need to abandon behavioral theories that espouse either extreme. We need to construct theories of behavior that recognize the importance of both nature and nurture and weave both together into a meaningful synthesis. This book presents one possible method for accomplishing this goal. Such balanced integrations of nature and nurture will allow us to go beyond sociobiology.

THE CENTRAL ISSUES

The two chapters in this section will examine the most fundamental issues involved in creating adequate theories of animal behavior. Chapter 2 outlines the basic criteria that any behavioral theory should meet in order to have general utility in explaining the broadest range of behavioral phenomena. Theories that conform to these criteria will be designated as "balanced biosocial theories." Chapter 3 evaluates sociobiology in light of the basic design features of balanced biosocial theories and asks: Does sociobiology pass the test? Several core problems in sociobiology are identified, and their pervasive influence suggests that sociobiology is an unlikely candidate for becoming a balanced biosocial theory.

PART

I

BALANCED BIOSOCIAL THEORY

Current theories of behavior are fragmented and compartmentalized. Each academic discipline that deals with behavior—biology, psychology, anthropology, sociology, economics, and political science—has its own theories of behavior. Each discipline has erected barriers that have impeded communication among the disciplines. Due to limited interdisciplinary work, few have tried to pull together the various compartmentalized theories to create a unifying synthesis. One of the attractive features of sociobiology is the fact that it *has* attempted to produce a comprehensive, unified theory. Even if sociobiology is not the ultimate synthesis, the sociobiologists have hastened the development of all-encompassing theories by having made a serious attempt at creating a synthesis, and by stimulating criticism and efforts to produce alternative unified theories.

If the behavioral sciences are finally embarking on the search for comprehensive theories, it would be wise to establish the criteria for evaluating such theories. Here we suggest several basic design features that many behavioral scientists would agree upon as desirable criteria for comprehensive theories of behavior that are suitable for all phylogenetic levels, including humans. We have selected the most basic design features in order to increase the likelihood of consensus among behavioral scientists from different disciplines. Some may disagree with our selection. Others may wish to include several additional design features. Certainly there is room for debate. At this point, however, these basic features will establish criteria against which to evaluate sociobiology (Chapter 3). Later in the book, we will utilize these design features as guidelines for constructing an alternative to the sociobiological theory. This alternative will provide concrete examples of a type of theory that adheres to the basic guidelines proposed in this chapter and will provide detail about the ways in which the basic design features can be realized in actual practice.

THE DESIGN FEATURES

A comprehensive theory of behavior should provide an empirically defensible interweaving of multiple causal factors—involving both nature and nurture—that are adjusted to fit the species and behavior under analysis. Because the goal of such a theory is to give a balanced weighting to all components of nature and nurture, we will designate the goal as *balanced biosocial theory*.

Although this name, balanced biosocial theory, is new, the ideas encompassed by a balanced biosocial approach are not new. Many competent behavioral scientists, working in a variety of disciplines and on species at many phylogenetic levels, have conducted their research and constructed their theories with goals similar to those presented here.[1] These researchers have never been grouped as a single school with one label. There is no pre-established name to capture the core ideas discussed here. Therefore, the term balanced biosocial theory is introduced to help unify and focus the work of researchers in diverse areas.

There are at least four major criteria that must be met in producing a balanced nature–nurture synthesis. First, a central criterion for a balanced biosocial theory is that it not be biased toward either nature or nurture. For example, at the human level, a balanced biosocial theory must avoid the extreme environmentalism of Watson's (1924) behaviorism, and likewise, the extremism of those contemporary writers who fail to recognize the biological nature of *Homo sapiens*, the animal. On the other hand, an adequate theory of human behavior must avoid the other extreme of biological determinism, such as James's (1890) or McDougall's (1908) instinct psychology and other theories of genetically programmed behavior. An adequate biosocial theory must be balanced

---

[1] So many people have done balanced biosocial research that we cannot acknowledge them all here. However, many of those who have contributed balanced work (especially in the field of primatology) are gratefully cited, where appropriate, throughout the text.

to contain an empirically defensible mixture and interaction of genetic and environmental factors. This is not easy. Although scientists have been warned since the 1950s to avoid extreme nature–nurture positions and to seek a balanced synthesis of both genetic and environmental variables,[2] this goal still eludes many researchers and theorists.

Second, a balanced biosocial theory will necessarily involve multicausal models of behavior, with room for interaction effects among the numerous causes. The multiple causes fall into two main categories: phylogenetic and ontogenetic, i.e., nature and nurture. The phylogenetic causal factors are those that shape the evolution of each species; the ontogenetic factors are those that shape the development of each individual from the moment of conception through the remainder of life. These two sets of causes will also be designated the distal and proximal causes of behavior, since the phylogenetic causes are distant in time and the ontogenetic ones are proximate.[3]

The distal causes include a multitide of factors that also divide into two broad categories: phylogenetic inertia and ecological pressures, which are the two primary determinants of evolution.[4] A species' phylogenetic history of specialization and generalization imposes constraints on the direction and speed of its present evolution. Superimposed on this phylogenetic legacy are the mutations and genetic recombinations that help produce variety and individuality in each new generation.[5] This variety, in turn, is the raw material for natural selection. Variations that are adaptive for an individual vis-à-vis the multiple demands of the current environment, social and nonsocial, confer competitive advantages and a statistically greater probability of surviving and leaving offspring. Differential survival and differential reproduction are the mechanisms that continuously sort the genes of a population, selecting in favor of genes that encode the information that produces an adaptive fit to a multitude of ecological pressures. Thus, the information stored in the genes reflects the long phylogenetic history during which distal causes produced and selected the currently surviving genes.

The proximal causes of behavior shape the development of each individual from the moment the individual's genetic endowment is fixed at conception.[6] Whereas the genetic information represents a "blue-

---

[2] For example, Lehrman (1953), Beach (1955), Schneirla (1956), Anastasi (1958), and Hebb (1958).

[3] Sociobiologists usually refer to these causes as ultimate and proximate causes (Wilson, 1975:23; Barash, 1977:37). The unfortunate implications and biases involved in labeling evolutionary causes as the "ultimate" causes of behavior lead us to prefer the more neutral terminology of distal and proximal causes (page 50).

[4] Wilson (1975:32f).

[5] Dobzhansky et al. (1977) and Mayr (1978).

[6] To a small degree, an individual's development can be affected by environmental influences on the egg and sperm before conception.

print" for physiological development, the environment provides the building blocks from which the developing organism is constructed. In mammals, for example, the manner in which the genotype is expressed in the developing fetus is influenced by numerous proximal causes, such as the mother's diet, exposure to poisons or drugs, disease, stress, hormone titers, and anoxia. After birth, each individual interacts more directly with the environment, since it is less protected by the mother's biological systems. Postnatal physical development is affected by nutrition, poisons, injuries, diseases, parasites, exercise levels, and so forth. In addition, the central nervous system is in part structured and modified by general levels of sensory stimulation, patterned sensory input, and specific learning experiences.[7]

During the life of each individual there is a continuous interaction between genetic and environmental influences; hence, a balanced biosocial theory must attempt to integrate both, including the often complex interaction effects among the multiple factors.

Third, a balanced biosocial theory must adjust the weighting of genetic and environmental effects according to the phylogenetic level of the species being studied. When analyzing the behavior of honeybees, for example, a heavy weighting is attributed to genetic influences and nutrition; a small but crucial weighting is attached to the special chemicals given to the developing larva during the critical time-period that determines its caste as queen or worker; and a small weighting is allocated to learning. (Other weightings would be affixed to the remaining causal variables.) In contrast, an analysis of chimpanzee behavior would reveal a much reduced relative impact of genetic information along with corresponding increases in the weighting of environmental variables, especially in the area of learning. Ideally, mathematical weightings would be associated with each variable; but at present it is often only feasible to indicate the approximate importance of each variable by the relative emphasis given to it in the overall explanation of behavior.

Fourth, the relative influence of the various distal and proximal determinants of behavior can be different for different behaviors in an individual's repertoire and can change at various stages in the development of behavior. Thus, a balanced biosocial theory must adjust the weighting of various genetic and environmental factors involved in explaining a given behavior to reflect their changing influences throughout the life cycle. For example, the activities of crawling and walking, in primates, are explained differently at different developmental ages. Prenatal development and movement of the musculature are largely determined by genetic and nutritional inputs that establish mechanisms for reflexive limb movement. Early postnatal crawling is largely reflexive, but operant conditioning begins to have its effects in the early days

[7] Hebb (1972).

of life. During the pre-adult period, crawling, then walking and running, become increasingly influenced by exercise and operant conditioning. Genetic and nutritional factors continue to influence these behaviors, but relatively less than before. Injury, disease and other factors can enter the picture at any point in time to produce major or minor effects on locomotor activity. Differences in local environmental conditions can cause the weightings to vary within species for individuals of the same age and sex.

Balanced biosocial theories will include the large number of behavioral variables that influence behavior. Instead of representing an *a priori* position about the importance of any of these factors, they will be flexible and open to empirical methods for weighting each factor involved in the production of any given behavior pattern in any given species. When analyzing a certain behavior in different species or at different developmental stages, the empirically established weightings would be expected to change. Since neither genetic nor environmental inputs to an individual's behavior are ever zero at any phyletic level or at any phase of the life cycle, extreme nature–nurture arguments never supersede balanced theories. As behavioral scientists pursue comprehensive theories, the basic design features of balanced biosocial theories can be used to guard against genetic and environmental extremes and establish general guidelines for adequate theory.

INTEGRATING NATURE AND NURTURE

Many theories do an inadequate job of integrating nature and nurture. Clearly, a primary goal of balanced biosocial theories is the integration of the multiple facets of both the proximal and distal causes of behavior. In this section we will outline the multiple factors and present a generalized model that integrates them in a balanced manner. This generalized model provides a broad overview of balanced biosocial theories and criteria against which to evaluate sociobiology in the next chapter. More concrete examples of balanced biosocial theory will be presented in Chapters 7 and 8.

All behavior is the product of a behaving organism. Behavior is produced by the organism's physiological mechanisms of behavior: the nervous system, hormonal system, muscle system, cardiovascular system, skeletal system, etc. Thus, as a first generality, behavior is a function of all relevant physiological mechanisms.

BEHAVIOR = f(PHYSIOLOGICAL MECHANISMS)

This approach serves balanced biosocial theories well because it focuses attention on the biological structures where nature and nurture interact. The physiological mechanisms are clearly a product of the combined influences of genetic and environmental factors. Physiological mechanisms—e.g., muscles and nerves—are not the product of genes alone, nor are they the product of the environment alone. Genetic blueprints must interact with environmental building blocks in order for these mechanisms to be constructed. Therefore, the structure of the physiological mechanisms is a function of "GENES × ENVIRONMENT," i.e., a function of *genes* in *interaction* with *environmental factors.*

$$\text{BEHAVIOR} = \text{f(PHYSIOLOGICAL MECHANISMS)}$$
$$= \text{f(GENES} \times \text{ENVIRONMENT)}$$

Genetic information is always being decoded in the cells to guide cell operation; but this genetic information always has to interact with the building blocks provided by the environment.

The fact that the physiological mechanisms of behavior are all biological structures makes it obvious that *all* behavior has a "biological base." However, the statement that behavior has a biological basis does not begin to solve the more complex problem of analyzing and integrating the multiple genetic and environmental factors that are involved in constructing and modifying the mechanisms of behavior. Thus, the expression "such and such behavior has a biological base" says little. In order to evaluate the biological basis of behavior, one must investigate the multiple interactions represented by the expression "GENES × ENVIRONMENT." Numerous variables are involved in this interaction, and they can have different importance or weighting at various phylogenetic levels, and even within species (due to differences in developmental age and local ecology).

Let us begin with the genes. No organism can begin life without genetic information. Genetic information serves as a proxy variable that represents the effects of countless mutations and innumerable selective pressures that have accumulated through the phylogenetic history of the species. The genes are a proxy variable passed to the present as a concrete product of the distant causal influences of natural selection. Multitudes of distal causal factors have created one summary statement—the genes inherited by the individual—that enters the current behavioral equation "GENES × ENVIRONMENT."

The *interaction* between genes and environment occurs all during life (Figure 2.1). Genetic information is continually being decoded within the cells to guide the metabolism, function, growth, and division of those cells. The decoded information can only produce development and change in biological mechanisms if the appropriate *constructive* environmental inputs are present with which to build and modify these mechanisms. In addition, *destructive* environmental inputs may be present that hamper normal development, prevent the full realization of the

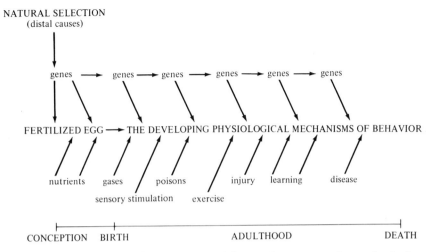

FIGURE 2.1. Genetic and environmental factors interact continuously during the development of the individual.

genetic potential of the individual, hence handicapping an individual's behavioral capacity. Once the physiological mechanisms have developed part way, they can allow learning to further modify the behavioral output of the individual.

The interaction between genes and environment begins at conception. Table 2.1 summarizes the major environmental factors that are involved in forming and molding the physiological mechanisms of behavior. Environmental factors influence behavior all through life, though the weighting of different factors varies from species to species and from individual to individual.

The following paragraphs will outline the major types of interactions between genetic and environmental factors involved in structuring the physiological mechanisms of behavior.[8] The environmental factors are grouped in three main categories: constructive inputs, destructive inputs, and learning. To minimize the confusion created by drawing examples from many phylogenetic levels, we will only use examples from primates and certain other mammals.

Constructive Inputs

Nutrients, calories, vitamins, minerals, and *oxygen* from the environment must be present for the fertilized egg to proceed to develop into a behaving organism. The physiological mechanisms of behavior—nerves,

---

[8] Similar models have been proposed before, e.g., Hebb (1958:120f).

glands, muscles, bone, and so forth—can be constructed only if sufficient quantities of these building blocks are available for actualizing the genetic blueprint. If the environmental raw materials are lacking, growth is stunted and the resultant physiological mechanisms are defective. Although the genes may encode information for the production of perfectly adequate physiological structures, a suboptimal supply of environmental raw materials can impair the development of an individual's behavioral mechanisms, resulting in environmentally induced behavioral handicaps. Not surprisingly, the genes carry information that helps bring individuals into contact with the critical raw materials, such that each new generation may be provided with the correct sustenance, both prenatally and postnatally. In primates, the prenatal, intrauterine environment is well buffered from external environmental perturbations and provides the fetus with a relatively well balanced supply of constructive raw materials under most conditions in which the mother would find herself. After birth, mother's milk continues to provide a relatively well balanced supply of raw materials until the infant has developed considerable independence and skill at locating its own sustenance. Later, group living provides the young with a social environment

TABLE 2.1. Major Environmental Determinants of Behavior[a]

CONSTRUCTIVE INPUTS
nutrients
calories
vitamins
minerals
gases
exercise
stimulation
DESTRUCTIVE INPUTS
poisons
wastes
drugs
thermal extremes
desiccation
disease
parasites
injury
LEARNING
habituation
Pavlovian conditioning
operant conditioning
observational learning

[a] The list is not intended to be exhaustive.

that usually directs the young toward useful foods and away from less desirable ones.[9] Although natural selection has provided most species with various systems for obtaining adequate sustenance, these systems do not always appear and are not foolproof, even though they are often "overdesigned" with redundant backup safety systems. Malnutrition, vitamin deficiencies, and other problems can cause considerable behavioral handicaps.

Exercise and *stimulation* are needed for the normal development of several components of the physiological mechanisms, especially in advanced species with complex behavioral mechanisms. Exercise promotes muscle growth and the development of strength.[10] Certain environmental conditions are more conducive to exercise than others. Olive baboons living in a group that regularly travels 6 kilometers a day are likely to exercise more than conspecifics in a group that travels only 3 kilometers a day. Individuals that do not receive enough exercise can be handicapped in performing activities requiring strength, speed, or endurance. Nerve cells require sensory input to activate them (or "exercise" them) so that they develop and interconnect into fully functional units.[11] Individuals living in environments that are deficient in certain types of sensory stimulation will suffer incomplete development of the central nervous system and hence be handicapped at activities requiring fuller development of the affected structures. The genes of most advanced species carry information that helps produce a variety of mechanisms that normally lead the young to exercise and expose themselves to sensory stimulation (especially during the developmental periods when muscle and nerve growth is most rapid). However, not all environments allow the full development and operation of these exercise mechanisms, hence handicaps of the muscular or nervous systems can appear in certain environments.

Destructive Inputs

Poisons (including metabolic wastes and deleterious drugs) can damage an individual's physiological mechanisms of behavior at any point in development. If metabolic wastes are not removed from the individual's system—either prenatally or postnatally—these self-created poisons can damage healthy structures. All through development, poisons from the external environment can damage the physiological mechanisms—temporarily or permanently—and handicap an individual's behavioral capacity. Given the dangers of poisons for the realization of the individ-

---

[9] van Lawick-Goodall (1973a).
[10] Fagen (1974, 1976).
[11] Riesen (1961, 1965); Volkmar and Greenough (1972); and Rosenzweig (1976).

ual's genetic potential, it is not surprising that natural selection has favored genetic information that helps produce mechanisms that minimize the risk of damage from poisons. Natural taste aversions often keep animals from eating potentially poisonous foods. In many species, individuals are reluctant to try new foods, and they may sample only tiny bits of new foods before adopting them—if no sickness is experienced. Primate groups pass on learned food traditions from generation to generation, helping the young avoid foods that caused sickness to their predecessors. These behavioral systems cannot guarantee that poisoning never occurs, but they clearly indicate that evolutionary processes have selected genes that help produce mechanisms for protecting individuals from many deleterious interactions with the environment.

Thermal extremes and *desiccation* can damage the physiological mechanisms of behavior at any point in an individual's life. Again, evolutionary processes have produced genetic information for mechanisms that minimize this damage. Primates have mechanisms for both physiological and behavioral thermoregulation. In dry environments where desiccation is a problem, primates engage in a variety of specialized behaviors for acquiring water, such as digging holes to find water and checking areas where water has been found in the past.[12]

Disease and *parasites* can also produce temporary or lasting damage to an individual's physiological mechanisms of behavior. Minor effects on behavior include slowed response time, lethargic movement, decreased wakefulness, and impaired learning. Major impairments include paralysis, loss of coordination and balance, and early death. Natural populations are often significantly affected by disease and parasites. There are cases in which primate populations have been reduced by 40–60% by epidemics.[13] Of course, the genes carry information for producing biological defense mechanisms against disease—antibodies, leukocytes, phagocytes, etc. There are behavioral protections, too. Primates groom themselves and each other, removing parasites and dirt and cleaning infected areas, thus promoting health.

Injury due to falls, fights with conspecifics, or close encounters with predators can damage the physiological mechanisms of behavior and handicap an individual behaviorally. Injury can vary from slight to major. Primates with one eye, a broken leg, or missing tail are not uncommon in nature.[14] Again, there have been selective pressures favoring genetic information that makes possible various mechanisms for avoiding injury: extra strong bones in vulnerable areas, antipredator mechanisms, signals for minimizing fights with conspecifics, ability to learn controlled aggression, and so forth.

[12] Kummer (1971) and Hamilton et al. (1978a).
[13] Southwick (1963).
[14] Berkson (1970, 1974).

Learning

The major modes of animal learning are *habituation, Pavlovian conditioning, operant conditioning,* and *observational learning*.[15] All modes of learning are clearly dependent on the individual's experience with the social and nonsocial environment in which it lives. Some environments provide greater opportunity for an individual to learn important survival responses than do other environments. Even within a group of primates, each individual lives in a different microenvironment that provides unique experiences and causes the individual to learn a unique set of skills and information. For example, the offspring of a high-rank primate mother is usually protected by its mother if it explores dangerous situations or gets into fights. The offspring of a low-rank mother does not receive as much protection and is often punished during social exploration or when getting into fights. As a result, the offspring of low-rank mothers explore a smaller subset of the environment, have more limited experiences, and learn fewer skills than the offspring of high-rank mothers. Because each individual has different experiences and skills and information, there can be considerable within-species variation in primate behavior. Individuals with inadequate learning experience may not be well prepared to cope with danger, hardship, competition for scarce resources, or other problems. Not surprisingly, the genes carry information that helps produce mechanisms to facilitate learning. Behavior that is crucial for survival and reproduction can often be learned with the minimum of practice, indicating that there is a genetic "preparedness" to facilitate this type of learning.[16] Behavior that is less important for survival often does not reflect this genetic preparedness; and there is often a counterpreparedness for learning counterproductive behavior, which retards the learning of these activities. In some advanced species, the genes provide for a large learning potential, thus allowing rapid acquisition of an extensive repertoire of highly differentiated behavior under precise discriminative control. There are also behavioral mechanisms that make exploration a high probability behavior for immature individuals (and even for adults if novel conditions are present to be investigated). These mechanisms for exploration help insure that individuals will investigate their environment and learn a repertoire of skills for coping with it (Chapter 7). Naturally, these behavioral mechanisms do not always guarantee that individuals will learn everything necessary for dealing adequately with the environment, hence for surviving and reproducing.

This brief sketch of the interactions between genes and environment should make it clear that the physiological mechanisms that produce

---

[15] Variations on these major modes of learning will be explained in Chapters 4 and 8.
[16] Seligman and Hager (1972) and Hinde and Stevenson-Hinde (1973).

behavior are influenced by a complex integration of genetic and environmental factors. Balanced biosocial theories must not only interweave the multiple factors, they must seek an empirically defensible weighting for each factor involved in any particular behavior under study.

PROXIMAL AND DISTAL CAUSES: SIMILARITIES AND DIFFERENCES

There are some striking similarities in the distal and proximal processes that mold behavior. These similarities help point the way toward a unified theory that integrates both types of causes into one larger system (Chapter 9). However, the similarities can also be misleading. Because both distal and proximal determinants of behavior reflect ecological pressures or conditions—and both tend to produce adaptive modifications in behavior—it is possible to mistake the effects of one determinant (either distal or proximal) for those of the other. This can cause considerable confusion when trying to establish the relative weighting of the distal and proximal factors involved in any given behavior. An observer may locate similar and adaptive behavior at two phylogenetic levels and infer similar causal factors. Yet, the behavioral similarities in two species may result from very different weightings of distal and proximal factors, making the behaviors far from comparable. For example, division of labor in termite societies may result largely from distal factors. Yet analogous behavior at another phylogenetic level—e.g., division of labor in primate societies—may result from a very different weighting of factors. In order to minimize the errors which arise from confusing the similar features of proximal and distal processes, it is necessary to point out the differences in these two processes.

We will review both the similarities and differences in the distal and proximal processes that influence behavior. An awareness of the differences makes it possible to appreciate the similarities without confusing one set of causes for the other.

Distal Causes of Change

Ecological factors play an important role in the process of natural selection. In the evolution of any genetically controlled trait, it is the environment that selects which individuals survive and reproduce and which do not. Either an animal breeder, conspecific, predator, disease, or some other environmental factor determines whether any given individual will live, die, or reproduce at a given point in time.

The role of the environment in natural selection is most easily seen in the modification of traits in which genetic factors are more heavily

PLATE 2.1. The large canine teeth of adult male baboons help the males cope with predators and conspecifics during fights or during conspicious displays, shown here. (*Courtesy of M. Kawai.*)

weighted than proximal factors.[17] For simplicity, let us consider the process of natural selection as it might have operated in the evolution of the long, sharp canines of male baboons.[18] Because canine length is under strong genetic control, it is safe to assume that an individual's canine length correlates closely with the individual's genetic information for canine length, unless severe disease, malnutrition, or injury has

[17] The process is more complex with traits in which genetic factors play a minor role, since variations in proximal environmental conditions can confound the relationship between genotype and phenotype and make the natural selection of phenotypes less likely to assure the survival of the relevant genotypes.

[18] We are not attempting to give an exhaustive explanation for the evolution of baboon canines. The example is being made artificially simple to emphasize the main features of natural selection.

prevented the normal expression of the genetic information. Let us trace
the evolution of long canines from a time when baboons had considerably shorter canines. At that early time (t_1) there might have been a
moderate amount of variation in tooth length—with length B being
more common than lengths A or C—as shown in the top frame of Fig.
2.2. The evolutionary modification of any trait is possible only if there
exists variation in the genetic information for that trait. Presumably the
individuals with longer canines (C) were more successful in coping with
their environments than conspecifics with the other variations in canine
length. Longer canines probably gave their possessors a selective advantage for coping successfully with predators and conspecifics—either
during fights or threat displays—hence gave them a better chance of

FIGURE 2.2. The natural variation in male canine length in a population of
baboons at an initial time (t_1) becomes modified as differential reproduction
causes the less adaptive variations (A and B) to become less common (*downward
arrows*) and the more adaptive variation (C) to become more common (*upward
arrows*). Without mutations, the trait could not evolve (at times t_2 and t_3) further
than the limit of the initial variation (*dotted line at x*).

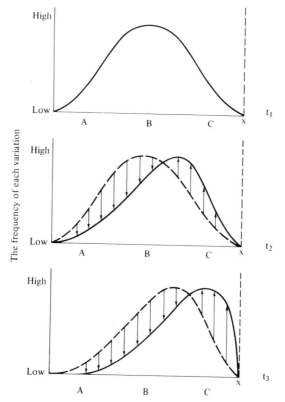

living to reproduce their own kind. Through this process of *differential reproduction*, the genes for longer canines were passed to the next generation at a higher rate than genes for shorter canines. At a later evolutionary time (t_2), short canines (A) would have become less common in the population (downward arrows in Figure 2.2) and the longer canines (C) would have become more common (upward arrows). In essence, the presence of predators and competitors created ecological conditions that favored the reproductive success of the possessors of longer canines. The predators and competitors were the environmental agents of selection.

If there were no mutations for even longer canines (type D), natural selection would not be able to increase the length of canines beyond the limits of the original variation in the population (dotted line "x" in Figure 2.2). Continued selection could increase canine length toward this natural limit "x," but no further, as is shown at t_3.

Mutations serve as the primary source of novel genetic variation in a population and are needed to provide the raw material for the evolution of new forms that were not present in the original population. Sexual reproduction and diffusion mechanisms spread mutations through the population and to neighboring populations. Due to random genetic mutations in individuals with canines of length A, B, and C, new variations would appear in the population. For example, mutations in individuals with type C canines might encode information for shorter canines (type B) or longer canines (type D). If individuals with type D canines were more successful in coping with predators and competitors than were individuals with shorter canines, they would have a better chance of surviving and reproducing. Figure 2.3 depicts selection in which the original variability in tooth length (A–B–C) is augmented by mutations. Beginning with the same A–B–C distribution at t_1 as was shown at t_1 in Figure 2.2, mutations allow evolutionary change to go beyond the limit "x" at later evolutionary times (t_2 and t_3 in Figure 2.3). If the mutations for longer teeth of type D increase the probability of survival and reproduction, type D teeth would become more common by t_2 and become the most common type by t_3. By t_3 individuals with short teeth (type A) have ceased to be represented in the population, and new random mutations (type E) have appeared, providing the raw material for even further evolutionary change.

The natural selection of progressively longer canines might continue until any of a variety of limiting factors made the cost–benefit ratio of the longest canines less advantageous than that of somewhat less extreme canines. The different costs and benefits of long canines for males and females should explain why the canines of females are only about half as long as those of males. Because female baboons are smaller than males, they are less likely to do battle with predators than are males.

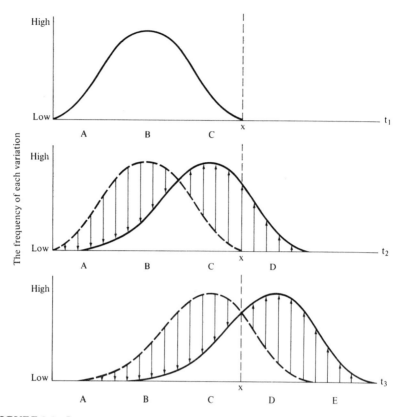

FIGURE 2.3. In contrast to Figure 2.2, this figure shows how mutations (D and E) augment the original variation in tooth length. If they confer adaptive advantages, these new forms become more common (*upward arrows*), allowing tooth length to evolve well beyond the limits of the initial variation (*dotted line at x*).

Because females have no scarcity of sexual partners, hence no reason to compete for mates, they are less likely than the males to fight among themselves in ways that influence the survival of their genes. Therefore, the selective advantages (or benefits) of long canines are less pronounced in females than in males.

Because the environment is the agent of selection, ecology has long played a key role in explaining the phylogenetic history of highly heritable traits. Natural selection usually favors traits that are well adapted to the species-typical ecology. This is true because individuals with more adaptive traits are more likely to survive and reproduce than are conspecifics with less adaptive traits. However, *optimally adaptive traits need not appear*. First, if there are no mutations for optimally adaptive traits, natural selection cannot produce a better fit to the environment than is possible from the available genetic variations. Second, adaptiveness is relative, not absolute; and suboptimal forms may survive quite satisfactorily if no better competitor appears. Third, the environmental agents of selection operate on the phenotype (which is the product of "GENES × ENVIRONMENT"), hence only indirectly change the frequency of relevant genes.[19] Because proximal environmental factors introduce nongenetically caused variations in phenotypes, the phenotypes that are selected do not correlate 100% with the optimal genetic information. Fourth, entire individuals—not separate traits—are selected. Because the genes for some adaptive traits may not appear in individuals with enough other adaptive traits to survive, the most adaptive genes may not be passed effectively to the next generation. Even individuals carrying desirable genetic information may lose their lives due to accidents and these random events counteract the processes for producing adaptive adjustments to the environment and prevent natural selection from creating optimal adaptations. Fifth, if there are variations within the species-typical environment (and there usually are), selection may not produce traits that are optimally adaptive in all subsets of the species-typical environment. Sixth, many species live in environments that undergo changes and impose new ecological conditions on the individuals. Since natural selection is a slow, conservative process, the genes are always behind the times. As they are modified to suit one set of environmental conditions, the environment is changing to produce new and different conditions for which the genes are not adapted. Seventh, even if a certain individual carried an optimal set of genetic information, when the genes interact with the environment to produce the phenotype, suboptimal constructive inputs, destructive inputs, and maladaptive learning can impair the full expression of the genetic information.[20] All seven of these phenomena can prevent actual traits and behavior from being optimally adaptive.

Proximal Causes of Change

During the development of each individual, the environment influences its physiological mechanisms—and therefore influences its behavior—though these environmental influences operate on a different time scale and through different pathways than natural selection. An animal's genetic inheritance establishes the potential range of physiological

---

[19] Thus, genes are neither pure causes of behavior (as discussed on page 19f), nor are they selected directly by the evolutionary processes.

[20] Even if the physiological mechanisms for learning are adequately developed, certain contingencies of reinforcement will cause animals to learn maladaptive behavior: for example, seeking repeated exposure to aversive stimuli that could easily be avoided (Kelleher and Morse, 1968; McKearney, 1969; and Byrd, 1972).

mechanisms and traits that may develop; but in many species, there are numerous degrees of freedom open for proximal environmental influences. Let us divide these proximal environmental influences on behavior (from Table 2.1) into two broad categories: (1) constructive and destructive influences on the physiological mechanisms of behavior, and (2) the various forms of adaptive and maladaptive learning.

Constructive and Destructive Influences. First, many of the environmental determinants of behavior listed in Table 2.1 influence behavior by their differential effects—either constructive or destructive—on the physiological mechanisms. These differential environmental influences on physiological development determine which subset of a species' genetic potential will be realized and which will not (Figure 2.4). There

FIGURE 2.4. Early in an individual's developmental history (t_1), a broad range of the individual's potential is open, though not well developed. Good nutrition, exercise, sensory stimulation, and other constructive inputs (*upward arrows*) favor continued development. Injury, disease, thermal extremes, and other destructive inputs (*downward arrows*) progressively restrict the range of traits that can be realized from the individual's potential.

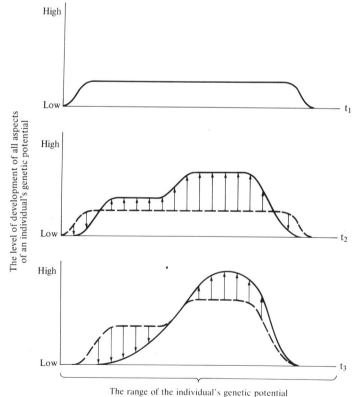

The range of the individual's genetic potential

is some parallelism with the selection resulting from differential reproduction (shown in Figure 2.2). Abundant nutrients and other building blocks are constructive environmental inputs that increase the likelihood that the genetic potential will be fulfilled (upward arrows in Figure 2.4); but deprivation of any of these constructive inputs can limit development of the physiological mechanisms and decrease behavioral capacity (downward arrows). In a similar manner, abundant environmental sensory stimulation and opportunity to exercise facilitate nerve and muscle development, hence the realization of behavioral potential (upward arrows); whereas environments that deprive an individual of sensory stimulation and opportunities to exercise have adverse effects (downward arrows). Injury, poisoning, disease, and other destructive factors all add further constraints on behavioral capacity. Thus, each individual is clearly a product of a multitude of differential environmental inputs that determine which subset of the individual's genetic potential will be realized and which will not. Whereas the environment causes natural selection via differential reproduction, it influences the development of the physiological mechanisms via *differential exposure to constructive and destructive inputs.*

During the development of the individual, physiological mechanisms and behavior outside the individual's genetic potential cannot appear. There is no process equivalent to the mutations of natural selection for producing new forms outside of prior genetic limits. However, novel combinations of proximal environmental inputs can produce new forms—within the genetic potential—that have never been realized before.

Learning. Second, there are several modes of learning through which current environmental conditions can modify an animal's behavioral mechanisms and behavior. The four most important modes of learning are habituation, Pavlovian conditioning, operant conditioning, and observational learning.[21]

(1) *Habituation* is a simple form of learning in which an individual ceases responding to repetitive stimuli. Habituation reduces the likelihood that an individual will respond to stimuli that appear frequently but are of no functional significance. For example, young monkeys often startle, stare, or make other responses when a nearby bird gives a loud call. In most cases, the bird call is irrelevant to the monkeys' lives; and after hearing many repetitions of the call, the monkeys usually cease responding. (If the stimulus is relevant, individuals usually learn to respond to it due to one of the other modes of learning, below).

---

[21] See Nevin and Reynolds (1971), Houston (1976), and Fantino and Logan (1979) for detail and references on the various types of learning.

The effects of habituation are reversible. If a stimulus ceases to appear for a period of time, the effects of habituation are reversed. After such a period of nonexposure, the individual will show a partial or complete recovery of responding when the stimulus reappears. Thus, a monkey that had not heard a parrot's call for several months might startle if a nearby bird gave a loud call.

The particular stimuli to which an individual habituates are determined by the individual's *differential exposure to environmental stimuli*: Frequently repeated stimuli cause habituation; infrequent stimuli do not. Habituation is usually adaptive because it helps an individual conserve energy, avoid distraction, and minimize behavioral disruption by not responding to irrelevant stimuli. Habituation produces a decrease in responsiveness within an individual's potential behavioral range, hence the environmental conditions that produce habituation have an effect similar to that indicated by the downward arrows in Figure 2.4. Recovery produces the opposite effect.

(2) *Pavlovian conditioning* allows biologically wired-in reflexes to come under the control of environmental stimuli that have been paired with the reflexes in the past.[22] For example, bad food in the stomach elicits the unconditioned reflexive response of sickness and regurgitation. If a monkey has eaten some small red berries before becoming sick, the individual will learn a food aversion elicited by the stimuli of small red berries. In the future, the sight or taste of similar berries will elicit aversive emotional responses and incipient responses related to nausea and regurgitation. Due to a different pairing of stimuli and reflexes, a conspecific living in a different environment may learn a food aversion elicited by large green fruits. The local environment determines which stimuli become associated with the reflexive responses to bad food. The stimuli that become associated with all the reflexes depend on an individual's *differential exposure to stimuli*. Stimuli that are paired with a reflex become conditioned stimuli; those that are not paired with a reflex do not become conditioned stimuli. When conditioned stimuli cease to be paired with reflexes, they usually lose their ability to elicit conditioned responses: This process is called extinction.

Not all stimuli can be conditioned with equal ease to any reflex. There are species-typical variations in conditionability. Animals often display considerable preparedness to learn certain associations, and considerable counterpreparedness to learn other associations.[23] This variability in preparedness is often adaptive and reflects evolutionary modification of the learning mechanisms to fit the species-typical environmental con-

---

[22] More technically, Pavlovian conditioning is based on stimulus pairing, as a neutral stimulus is paired with stimuli that already have the ability to elicit reflexive responses. See Chapter 4 or Terrace (1971) for further elaboration.

[23] Selgiman (1970).

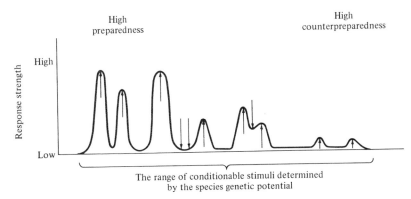

FIGURE 2.5. Pavlovian conditioning (*upward arrows*) and extinction (*downward arrows*) modify the strength of a given conditioned reflex in response to various stimuli, depending on the individual's differential exposure to environmental stimuli and the degree of preparedness for learning various associations.

ditions. For example, some species that find food by smell have a preparedness to learn food aversions elicited by the odor but not by the sight of bad food. In contrast, some species that select food by visual properties have a preparedness to learn food aversions elicited by visual input.[24]

Figure 2.5 shows how one reflex may be conditioned in one individual to appear in response to a variety of stimuli. The stimuli are located on a continuum from high preparedness to high counterpreparedness. Upward arrows represent Pavlovian conditioning and downward arrows represent extinction. The precise form of the curve is a function of the degree of preparedness for learning various associations and the individual's differential exposure to stimuli that were paired with the given reflex.

(3) *Operant conditioning* modifies behavior via *differential reinforcement*, as certain response variations are reinforced and others are not. As an example of operant conditioning, let us consider the process by which young squirrel monkeys learn to catch insects, which are an important part of their diet. Adults can make rapid, accurate grabs that catch flying insects in midair or as they rest between flights; yet young squirrel monkeys do not display these skills even after they have gained a great deal of dexterity at other activities. The rapid, accurate grabs needed to catch flying insects apparently require extensive practice and differential reinforcement to be learned. The insect-catching skills of the yearling contain variations in speed and accuracy. For simplicity, let us describe these variations in speed and accuracy on one continuum. The yearling

[24] Wilcoxon et al. (1971).

(at t_1 in Figure 2.6) may perform a variety of responses, A, B, and C. Response A is slow and inaccurate; response C is moderately fast and moderately accurate. The intermediate response, type B, is the most common. Because type C responses are more likely to result in the capture of a flying insect than are type A and B responses, there will be more food reinforcers to strengthen type C responses than for the other responses. After sufficient months of practice, this differential reinforcement will modify insect grabbing behavior to become faster and more accurate, the pattern shown at t_2 in Figure 2.6. Type C responses become more frequent due to reinforcement (upward arrows); responses of type A and B become less frequent due to nonreinforcement (downward arrows).

FIGURE 2.6. The natural variation in an operant performance at an initial time (t_1) becomes modified as differential reinforcement causes the nonreinforced variations (A and B) to become less frequent (*downward arrows*) and the reinforced variation (C) to become more frequent (*upward arrows*). Without a source of extra response variation, the final operant performance could not be shaped further than the limit of the initial variation (*dotted line at x*).

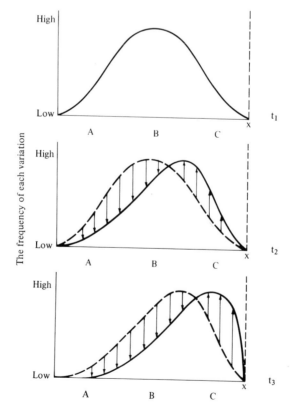

One might say: "The monkey is learning to use faster and more accurate grabs to catch insects." However, it is the environment that determines which grabs will be reinforced and which will not: The environment provides the reinforcement of insect food contingent upon fast, accurate grabs, and these responses become more common. The environment provides little reinforcement with insect food for slow, inaccurate grabs, and these responses become less common. Thus environmental patterns of differential reinforcement mold learned behavior (Figure 2.6), much as environmental selection by differential reproduction molds highly heritable traits (Figure 2.2).[25] Differential reinforcement determines which operant responses become more frequent and which become less frequent at a later time; differential reproduction determines which genes become more frequent and which become less frequent in evolutionary time.

Figure 2.6 depicts a hypothetical case of operant conditioning in which there is no mechanism for creating new variability in responses. Because the most rapid and well targeted grabs produce the greatest amount of reinforcement, there is a progressive strengthening of these responses and extinction of the slower, less accurate responses. Without a source of new response variation outside the limits of the original response range (A–B–C), there would be no opportunity for new responses to appear that were faster and more accurate than the limits of the original response variation (dotted line "x" in the figure). Prolonged differential reinforcement could condition response speed and accuracy closer to this natural limit "x" (as is shown at t_3 in Figure 2.6), but no further. However, there is considerable variation in the performance of any operant behavior. No two replications of a given operant are identical. Differences in general muscle tension, posture, deprivation state, concurrent activities, and so forth cause variability in operant performances. This phenomenon is called induction. Induction can produce novel variations outside the original A–B–C range.

Figure 2.7 depicts operant conditioning in which the original variability of the operant behavior (A–B–C) is augmented by new variations resulting from induction. As differential reinforcement conditions greater skill for type C grabs at insects, some of the imperfect replications of type C responses will be even more rapid and accurate than the norm (these being newly induced type D responses). The type D responses provide the raw material for the shaping of new performances by further differential reinforcement. As long as the environment provides more reinforcement for increasingly rapid and accurate grabs, any induced variation in that direction will be reinforced and brought to higher frequency, until the limits of the species behavioral capacity are neared.

[25] Rachlin (1976:73f).

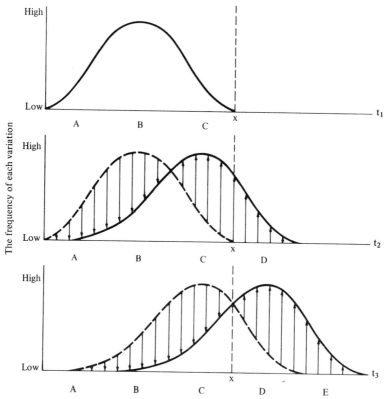

FIGURE 2.7. In contrast to Figure 2.6, this figure shows how newly induced response variations (D and E) are superimposed on the initial range of variation. If they are reinforced, these new variations become more frequent (*upward arrows*), allowing the behavior to be shaped well beyond the limits of the initial variation (*dotted line at x*).

Induction results from imperfect replication of operants much the same as mutations result from the imperfect replication and storage of genes. Induction is responsible for producing new response variation much the same as mutation provides the raw material for the selection of new genetic traits (compare Figures 2.3 and 2.7). Natural selection favors the evolution of physiological mechanisms that introduce moderate levels of response variations into operant behavior because this increases an individual's behavioral flexibility and ability to learn new operant responses.

Operant conditioning usually produces adaptive responses to current environmental conditions. If flying insects require rapid responses to be captured, food reinforces rapid grabs. If a species of soft berry must be picked gently to prevent it from disintegrating and falling to the

ground, the properties of the food create patterns of differential reinforcement that condition gentle manipulation of the berries. The adaptiveness of most operant conditioning can be traced to the selection of
genes for physiological mechanisms that make food reinforcing for hungry animals, make certain tastes more reinforcing than others, establish
a preparedness for learning certain operants, and set limits beyond
which operant conditioning cannot produce further modification of behavior. However, the mechanisms for operant conditioning do not always produce adaptive response patterns. Failure to discriminate subtle
but important changes in environmental conditions may cause an individual to perform an operant behavior at the wrong time or in the
wrong place. When induction fails to produce adaptive variations in
operant behavior, the raw material for the shaping of adaptive behavior
is absent, and an individual continues to produce suboptimal performances. Punishment in a certain context may cause an individual to learn
strong avoidance responses that prevent the individual from returning
to the situation and learning how to respond appropriately in that context.[26] Not only does operant conditioning occasionally produce suboptimal or maladaptive behavior, the physiological mechanisms that mediate conditioning may be suboptimal due to (a) selective processes that
fail to produce optimal adaptations (page 30f) and (b) suboptimal combinations of constructive and destructive proximal inputs that prevent
the complete realization of the genetic potential (page 20f).

(4) *Observational learning* occurs when one individual observes the
performance of a second and acquires information that allows imitation
of the performance. Observational learning is affected by the environment in two ways. First, the observer is influenced by those individuals
in the social environment who provide models of behavior that the
observer may imitate. Second, the patterns of reinforcement that follow
the imitative performance determine whether the imitative response
will become a high or low frequency operant in the observer's repertoire.[27] For example, if a juvenile howler monkey imitates an adult
male's jump across an especially wide arboreal gap, the juvenile may
take a serious fall. This aversive event will partially suppress (a) the
response of jumping at this and similar wide gaps, and (b) future imitation of similar adult male behavior. Thus, any individual's observational learning is influenced by two features of the environment: *differential exposure to models* and *differential reinforcement*. Although observational
learning is usually adaptive, it need not be (for reasons similar to those
discussed in the preceding section on operant behavior). The major
advantages of observational learning are that it allows an individual to

[26] Sidman (1966).
[27] For further details on observational learning see Bandura and Walters (1963) and
Bandura (1969).

PLATE 2.2. A juvenile Japanese macaque looks on while its mother washes a sweet potato. Sweet potato washing is a group tradition that is passed on by observational learning. (*Courtesy of M. Kawai.*)

learn many types of responses more rapidly and effortlessly than is usually possible through differential reinforcement alone. Primates learn many important survival skills by observation, and each new generation can benefit from the learning of its predecessors.

Traditional behavior is a subset of observationally learned behavior and is also shaped by environmental reinforcers. Japanese macaques imitate the habits of other monkeys who have learned to wash sweet potatoes before eating them.[28] Young chimpanzees imitate the methods used by experienced older animals for fishing termites out of their mounds and eating them.[29] If sweet potato washing or termiting produces more reinforcement (in the quality or quantity of food) than other feeding behavior does, the animals who imitate the response are likely to acquire and perform the response, hence to perpetuate the tradition. If the environment changes so that an old tradition ceases to produce reinforcement, the behavior will be extinguished and under most circumstances completely disappear from the group's repertoire of tradi-

[28] Kawamura (1954).
[29] van Lawick-Goodall (1968).

tions. Because observers rarely if ever produce flawless replications of a model's behavior, random variation is introduced into imitative responses. Some of these variants—if reinforced—will serve as the raw material for improved traditions, while others will be eliminated by extinction or punishment. Human traditions and culture depend in part on observational learning and reinforcement for transmission,[30] but many additional variables are involved that make the process considerably more complex than the cultural transmission seen in other species (Chapters 8 and 9).

(5) *Other types of learning*—such as imprinting, insight, rule-use, and prompting—will be discussed in later chapters. The current data indicate that all of these are merely subsets of or variations on operant and Pavlovian conditioning (Chapters 4 and 8).

COMPARING THE SIMILARITIES AND DIFFERENCES

Table 2.2 summarizes the similarities and differences between the distal and proximal determinants of behavior. First, the primary similarity between distal and proximal processes is that the environment plays the primary role in selecting and molding behavior. Evolutionary theory has long recognized that ecological factors are the main determinants of differential reproduction. It is important to recognize that ecological factors play a similar role in molding the physiological mechanisms and behaviors of the individual throughout development. Each individual has a unique history of interactions with its environment during which its behavior is molded by differential exposure to multiple proximal inputs. Differential exposure to constructive and destructive environmental inputs (nutrients, disease, injury, etc.) is a crucial determinant of much of the development of the physiological mechanisms. Differential exposure to stimuli is the major determinant of all conditioning, establishing which stimuli become associated with a given response and which do not. Differential reinforcement is the prime mover of operant conditioning, creating changes in behavioral patterns much as differential reproduction creates changes in gene frequency. Thus, behavior is a function of the environment, through *both* distal environmental selection of genes and proximal environmental influences on the mechanisms of behavior.

Second, both distal and proximal processes involve mechanisms of imperfect replication that introduce random variations from which new forms can be created. Mutations arise from imperfect storage, replication, and transmission of genes; and these genetic variations provide the raw material for the natural selection of new forms. Induction—

---

[30] Bandura (1969, 1977).

TABLE 2.2. Similarities and Differences in Distal and Proximal Processes

Similarities	Differences
1. Ecological factors mold the distal and proximal determinants of behavior by differential reproduction, differential exposure to constructive or destructive inputs, differential exposure to stimuli, and differential reinforcement.	1. The time scale on which distal and proximal processes modify behavior are very different.
2. Novel, creative traits and behavior appear as a result of imperfect replication and transmission mechanisms, i.e., due to mutations, induction, or imperfect imitation.	2. The mechanisms by which information from distal and proximal influences is encoded and stored are very different. 3. The transmission routes by which the information is passed to others are different, being limited to kin transmission in one case but not limited to kin transmission in the other.
3. Both distal and proximal mechanisms produce relatively adaptive (but not optimal) adjustments to environmental conditions.	

resulting from the imperfect replication and performance of operants—produces novel response variations that serve as the raw material from which new, creative operants can be shaped. When behavior is passed to others by observational learning, imitative responses are rarely perfect copies of the modeled behavior; and imperfect imitation introduces additional variation into operant performances.

Third, natural selection and learning both tend to produce adaptive adjustments to environmental conditions; but adaptation need not be optimal. Natural selection frequently fails to produce optimal adaptations due to phylogenetic inertia, absence of well suited mutations, constraints imposed by selection of phenotypes and entire individuals (rather than genes), recent changes in environmental conditions, and so forth (pages 30–31). Evolution has produced a variety of adaptations for minimizing destructive environmental influences on the physiological mechanisms of behavior and promoting adequate constructive influences; but these, too, are not perfect and do not ensure optimal development of the physiological mechanisms in all environments. Learning tends to be adaptive; but enough cases of maladaptive learning exist to demonstrate the imperfections in learning mechanisms.

In spite of these similarities, there are major differences in the various processes by which ecological factors mold and modify behavioral mechanisms. First, the time scales involved in the evolutionary modification of genetic information and proximal modification of physiological mechanisms are considerably different. It may take dozens or hundreds of generations for a species' genetic inheritance to be modified in ways that significantly affect behavior; yet proximal causes can produce radical behavioral changes within seconds (e.g., injury or observational learning), hours (e.g., disease, poisoning, or conditioning), or longer (e.g., nutrition, exercise, or sensory stimulation).

Second, there are major differences in the mechanisms by which information from distal and proximal environmental influences is encoded and stored. As mutations and natural selection modify a species' phylogenetic inheritance, the effects of environmental selection are stored in the surviving genes. The genes serve as a very conservative storage mechanism that remains unaffected by most short-term environmental perturbations. In contrast, proximal influences that shape the development of each individual's physiological mechanisms produce effects that are not stored in the genes. In many advanced species, the brain is especially constructed to allow continuous modification and remodification of behavioral output via learning, in response to ever-changing environmental influences. The differences between genetic and nongenetic storage mechanisms are so enormous that argument by analogy from one species to another can be hazardous if the species do not have similar mechanisms for responding to distal and proximal factors. Careful attention must be paid to all the mechanisms that integrate distal and proximal inputs in order to avoid the misleading interpretations of behavior that can arise from arguments based on simple analogy (Chapter 8).

Third, transmission routes for genetically encoded information and learned information are different. After genetic information is produced by mutations and modified by environmental selection, it can only be passed directly to offspring or advanced indirectly by aid to kin. Thus, coefficients of genetic relationship play a central role in explaining the transmission of genetic determinants of behavior. Social learning mechanisms are not restricted to kin transmission lines. Once a response has been acquired from the nonsocial or social environment, it can be passed to others—kin and nonkin alike—via observational learning. The social effects of operant conditioning—when one individual's behavior reinforces or punishes the behavior of others—are also not limited to kin. The infant primate's early learning is highly influenced by its mother (and sometimes by other close kin); but with increasing age and independence, it broadens its social environment and becomes increasingly influenced by nonkin.

CONCLUSION

Balanced theories of behavior must consider all relevant variables—both distal and proximal—that influence behavior, and interweave them in an empirically defensible manner. Behavior at all phylogenetic levels is influenced by *both* distal and proximal causes, though the weightings vary considerably between species. Because the distal and proximal influences on behavior operate in different manners, the failure to separate and analyze the various causal determinants of behavior can result in serious errors when comparing and explaining the behavior of different species. These errors can destroy much of the validity of any science of behavior that does not give adequate attention to all the distal and proximal determinants of behavior and weight their influences appropriately.

IS SOCIOBIOLOGY
A BALANCED BIOSOCIAL THEORY?

Numerous scholarly criticisms of sociobiology have already appeared.[1] The goal of this chapter is not to provide a comprehensive summary of all the criticisms. Rather, we will focus on the question of whether or not sociobiology is a balanced biosocial theory. The answer is not black and white. At some phylogenetic levels, sociobiology comes close to being a balanced theory. However, at many phylogenetic levels, sociobiology fails to produce a valid balance of distal and proximal causal factors.

A brief review of the central tenets of sociobiology reveals a strong bias in favor of strict evolutionary explanations of behavior. In addition, the logic of sociobiology makes it likely that many behavior patterns that are strongly influenced by proximal causes will be misidentified and presumed to result from distal causes. Thus, sociobiology is prone to Type II errors—accepting evolutionary and genetic hypotheses that should not be accepted. This propensity blinds sociobiologists to the inadequacies of genetic theories, obscures the importance of proximal influences on behavior, and thus creates a

[1] For example, Waddington (1975), Allen et al. (1976), Sahlins (1976), Miller (1976a,b), Gould (1976), Blute (1976), Burian (1978), Reed (1978), Washburn (1978), Quadagno (1979), Lewontin (1979), and Busch (1979).

deeply engrained bias in favor of nature over nurture. If we wish to escape unbalanced nature–nurture arguments, we must go beyond sociobiology.

THE CENTRAL TENETS OF SOCIOBIOLOGY

Sociobiology is based on modern evolutionary theory. Many biologists find it only logical to use evolutionary principles as the cornerstone of their theories of behavior. Evolutionary principles have been so successful in analyzing the impressive diversity of forms in the biological world, that evolution has become "the organizing principle of biology."[2] Classical ethology—or the biology of behavior—led the way in applying evolutionary principles to the analysis of behavior. Sociobiology has extended ethological work by coupling it with behavioral ecology and population biology to strengthen the evolutionary foundations of the study of animal behavior.

A brief history of the emergence of sociobiology from ethology will help clarify the degree to which sociobiology relies on evolutionary principles to explain behavior. A central objective of classical ethology has been to apply the evolutionary perspective to the study of behavior. Ethologists trace their science to the work of Darwin, who made several significant contributions to the explanation of behavior in light of evolutionary ideas. "Darwin's procedure could be characterized by saying that he treated behaviour patterns as *organs*—as components of an animal's equipment for survival."[3] Heinroth (1910) continued in this tradition, with a strong emphasis on "innate" behavior, i.e., behavior that shows little or no modifiability by the environment during an individual's life. Subsequently, Lorenz advanced the experimental and theoretical development of ethology so much that he has been called "the father of modern ethology."[4]

Lorenz and others of his contemporaries stressed the importance of observing animals in their natural habitats, determining the adaptive value of behavior, and comparing the behavior of various species. Lorenz's interests lay primarily in studying instinctive responses (both their mechanisms and their survival value) and the maturation of innate patterns under internal biological control. According to Lorenz (1937a [1970:281]), *"the instinctive behaviour pattern has the same properties as an organ . . . [and] . . . in the ontogeny of the instinctive behaviour pattern factors operate which are very similar to those operating in the ontogenetic development of organs."* Since the physiological development of most organs is under rather strong genetic control, the *assumption* that behavior can be treated *as if* it were an organ introduced into classical

---

[2] Mayr (1978:47).
[3] Tinbergen (1969 [1973:130]).
[4] Huxley (1963).

ethology an automatic bias that favored genetic rather than environmental explanations.

Lorenz's early position elicited criticism from many students of behavior because of its lack of concern for proximal determinants of behavior.[5] By the 1960s, the ethologists showed clear signs of increasing interest in proximal influences on behavior. In answer to his critics, Lorenz (1965) described ethology as a theory with a relatively well balanced integration of distal and proximal causes. However, most of his subsequent work reflects a continued commitment to the evolutionary perspective, to models of unmodifiable behavior patterns, and to a conviction that traits that are crucial for survival are biologically determined.[6]

Tinbergen's central interests have been the study of instinct, hierarchies of instincts, social communication, and the evolutionary adaptiveness of behavior in its natural environment. Tinbergen (1972 [1973:211]) follows "the time-honoured comparative method . . . [and] . . . interprets differences between allied species in terms of adaptive evolutionary divergence; and similarities between otherwise dissimilar species in terms of adaptive convergence." British ethology has tended to be less unbalanced than classical ethology. When summarizing the major questions to be dealt with in ethology, Tinbergen (1963a) repeated three research problems listed by Huxley, "that of causation, that of survival value, and that of evolution—to which I should like to add a fourth, that of ontogeny." Tinbergen has focused considerable attention on the ontogeny of behavior, recognizing that "behaviour patterns can be placed, according to their development, on a scale ranging from highly resistant to variations in the environment to highly modifiable."[7] But Tinbergen never abandons the evolutionary doctrine that behavior has evolved to be adaptive, hence even modifiable behavior is under genetic control: "Even learning [the most modifiable behavior] is not random, but its occurrence, what is learnt and how it is learnt, are prescribed internally within relatively narrow limits" and each species "is 'programmed for learning' in its own, and adapted way." Thus, Tinbergen's interest in the ontogeny of behavior reflects an interest in "the genetic instructions for the development of behaviour."

Tinbergen and several other British ethologists have clearly attempted to bring balance to ethology.[8] However, perusal of the ethological journals clearly demonstrates that the majority of ethologists are much more interested in the traditional biological topics of evolutionary adaptation

---

[5] Lehrman (1953); Hebb (1953); and Schneirla (1956).

[6] Lorenz (1974, 1977).

[7] This and the following two quotes are from Tinbergen (1972 [1973:214f]).

[8] For example, Hinde (1970, 1974) and Hinde and Stevenson-Hinde (1973, 1976) have attempted to create a synthesis of ethology and comparative psychology in order to balance the phylogenetic perspective of ethology with an emphasis on learning from comparative psychology. Crook (1970a,b) has been critical of Lorenzian ethology and has attempted to create a new branch of ethology—called social ethology—to better cope with the social behavior of birds and mammals. Among other things, Crook sees primate behavior "as

(continued)

and genetic control than they are in evaluating proximal environmental influences on behavior. After all, if even learning and modifiable behavior are presumed to be programmed within narrow limits by genetic instructions, it is only rational for the researcher to focus most attention on evolutionary causes.

The evolutionary perspective is often well balanced when explaining behavior that is under strong genetic control. Ethologists have made excellent contributions to the analysis of both the behavior of primitive organisms and of the more stereotyped, invariant behavioral features of advanced organisms (e.g., stereotyped signals, constraints on learning, and preparedness to learn certain associations). Much of their research can serve as a solid foundation for either sociobiology or other biosocial theories.

While some ethologists were attempting to integrate the study of behavioral ontogeny into their overall program in the 1960s, changes in genetic theories of behavior were setting the stage for the rise of sociobiology. Wynne-Edwards (1962) attempted to utilize ethological ideas in conjunction with theories of group selection to demonstrate that animals cooperate to produce adaptive levels of population density. For numerous reasons Wynne-Edwards's theory caused quite a reaction among animal researchers. Of relevance here is the fact that Wynne-Edwards strayed from the strict Darwinian logic that natural selection throws individuals into reproductive competition, which in turn makes cooperative reproductive restraint and group selection very unlikely. Many biologists were challenged to explain cooperative social behavior in strict Darwinian terms. Williams (1966) was among the more influential of the critics of group selection, arguing that "We must take the theory of natural selection in its simplest and most austere form, the differential survival of alternative alleles, and use it in an uncompromising fashion whenever a problem of adaptation arises" (p. 270). Hamilton (1964, 1970, 1971a,b) set the stage for modern sociobiology with his theory of kin selection. By assuming (a) that selection operates on the genes (rather than on individual animals)[9] and (b) that there could be genes for altruism, selfishness, and related behavior, Hamilton could demonstrate that altruistic behavior directed to close kin was in many

(continued from previous page)

being largely 'shaped' by the environment. The habitat, physical and social, is, as it were, nature's Skinner box providing locally characteristic types and frequencies of natural learning trials in complex schedules that interrelate to pattern individual behaviour as a whole" (1970b:130). More recently, Bateson and Hinde (1976:536) can point to numerous "examples of the eclectic manner in which ethologists are now straying even farther from what could be called classical ethology."

[9] Hamilton (1964), Emlen and Oring (1977), and several other sociobiologists assume that selection operates on the genes rather than on the phenotype. This differs from the standard biological assumption that phenotypes, not genotypes, are selected (Mayr, 1978; Ayala, 1978). By assuming that genes are selected, these sociobiologists sidestep the issue of ontogeny and proximal causes of behavior. Phenotypes are neglected. Proximal control of behavior is deleted from the model. Genes are selected; and genes cause behavior.

cases a rational evolutionary strategy. Self-sacrifice that benefits one's brothers and sisters—or other close kin who share similar genes—helps the shared genes, even though the altruist suffers losses. Altruism pays off *for the genes* if the loss of fitness of the altruist is less than (a) the benefit to the recipient, (b) times the coefficient of relatedness (the fraction of genes that they share in common due to common kinship). Thus, helping close kin pays off more than helping distant kin. Since the altruist's kin benefit, the genes for altruism toward close kin then spread through the population.

Wynne-Edwards was refuted and a new system based on a pure, austere genetic theory had arisen to fill the gap. This new perspective on behavior suggested fresh interpretations for numerous forms of social behavior and generated a host of new topics for research. Attracted by the promise of exciting research and potential breakthroughs, many climbed on the bandwagon and sociobiology gathered momentum.

Wilson's lengthy book, *Sociobiology: The New Synthesis* (1975) consolidated sociobiology's contributions and greatly increased the visibility of the new discipline. In the 1920s and 1930s, population genetics and Darwinian selection had been merged to form what is called the "Modern Synthesis." The sociobiologists have extended this neo-Darwinian view of evolution to include the analysis of behavior and social organization. Sociobiologists believe this extension of evolutionary theory represents a major breakthrough in the development of evolutionary theory, hence the subtitle of Wilson's text, "The New Synthesis." Although ethology in the 1960s showed signs of de-emphasizing natural selection and directing increased attention to ontogeny and proximal causes, sociobiology has pulled away from this trend and returned to a more purely evolutionary point of view. The discovery that austere genetic theories could explain both competitive and altruistic behavior (page 4) strengthened the sociobiologists' conviction that any behavior could be explained in terms of evolution and genetic causes.

According to Wilson (1975), the "central dogma" of sociobiology asserts "the pervasive role of natural selection in shaping all classes of traits in organisms" (pp. 21–22). (In contrast, a balanced biosocial theory states that *both* natural selection *and* proximal factors shape behavior.) Since sociobiology claims that "natural selection is the agent that molds virtually all of the characteristics of a species" (p. 67), little attention is paid to proximal, ontogenetic causes for behavior. Socialization is reduced to a "multiplier effect" (pp. 11–13) which is claimed to multiply small genetic influences into large effects on behavior and social organization. Sociobiologists affirm the classical ethological position that

---

Simple! But not balanced. Phenotypes are never 100 percent determined by genotypes; and natural selection cannot operate on genes alone. Denial of these facts is clear evidence of sociobiologists' bias on the issue of nature vs. nurture.

"behavior and social structure, like all other biological phenomena, can be studied as 'organs,' extensions of the genes that exist because of their superior adaptive value" (p. 22).

The sociobiologists' preoccupation with phylogenetic and genetic explanations can be seen throughout their work. For example, only one chapter out of the 27 in Wilson's (1975) lengthy book deals with proximal causes of development; and even this chapter begins with a debatable six-page argument that claims "All social traits of all species are capable of a significant amount of rapid evolution at any time" (p. 145).[10] A scattered sampling of proximal mechanisms receives only cursory attention in the remainder of the chapter. In sharp contrast to the brief coverage of proximal mechanisms, Wilson devotes entire chapters, lengthy mathematical explanations, and numerous graphs and tables to explaining the details of heritability, polygenes, coefficients of inbreeding and kinship, gene flow, changes in gene frequencies, r and K selection, reproductive strategies, population growth, extinction rates, and other details of evolutionary theory. Genes are in the limelight, while the complexities of behavioral development and proximal environmental causes are given little serious attention. The powerful forces of natural selection are presumed to program the physiological mechanisms of behavior such that everything important is taken care of by genetic control. The proximal "machinery carries out the commands of the genes" (Wilson, 1975:23). Even the brain, the organ of thought and learning, "is an extension of the gonads" (Ghiselin, 1973:968), geared "to favor the maximum transmission of the controlling genes" (Wilson, 1975:4).

Sociobiologists refer to the distal and proximal causes of behavior as ultimate and proximate causes. This use of words serves them well. Interwoven into many different sentence structures, they transmit the message that natural selection provides the *ultimate* explanation for behavior. Therefore, proximal causes need not be studied as autonomous influences on behavior (Wilson, 1975:23). We believe that the terms distal and proximal are less likely to produce the misleading impression that evolutionary causes provide the *ultimate* explanation of behavior; therefore the terms distal and proximal are more compatible with the goals of balanced biosocial theories.

It is true that sociobiologists do research and discuss proximal mechanisms to a certain extent. The data on proximal variables, however, are usually presented to demonstrate how behavioral development is programmed by natural selection and is under command of the genes.

---

[10] An examination of the data that Wilson presents to support his assumption of "rapid evolution" reveals that most involve advanced species where rapid change could easily result from learning. Enamored by a genetic theory of behavior, he apparently did not entertain this ontogenetic hypothesis.

There is generally little interest in proximal causes that are not under strong genetic control.[11]

Humans receive a full chapter in Wilson's text and an even higher percentage of space in most other sociobiology texts. In addition, human examples are intermingled throughout sociobiological theories to "clarify" genetic principles, though empirical evidence is rarely given that the human behavior being discussed is genetically determined. Nowhere in Wilson's (1975) book do we get the impression that he thinks his system could be unbalanced for humans. The introduction tells us that "sociology and the other social sciences . . . are the last branches of biology waiting to be included in the Modern Synthesis" (p. 4). A selfish, nepotistic morality rooted in genetic survival is seen as the underlying force in human moral thinking (pp. 3, 129, 563). Because spite, selfishness, altruism, family chauvinism, blind faith, self-righteousness, and other human qualities are described as universal,[12] they are presumed to be species-typical behavior in the service of the genes. The kind act of the first Good Samaritan is described as resulting from an "altruist gene" which was at first a "rare mutant" (p. 120).[13] Only evolutionary variables are considered when discussing whether altruistic behavior could survive in a genetically competitive world (p. 120–121). Wilson apparently is unaware of or uninterested in the empirical data and theories concerning the proximal causes for altruism. (The reader might wish to contrast Wilson's genetic speculations about human altruism with Mussen and Eisenberg-Berg's [1977] summary of the empirical data on human altruism.)

Sociobiology may come close to providing a balanced biosocial theory of behavior that is under strong genetic control; but the theory grows ever more unbalanced as we turn to behavior that is not genetically programmed. Although some sociobiologists claim that they are not overly biased toward evolutionary explanations, their actions speak louder than their words. The vast majority of their written work reveals their enthusiasm for applying genetic theories to behavior at all phyletic levels. They are not reluctant to extend totally genetic "explanations" to the domain of human behavior, even though their ideas frequently fly in the face of well documented psychological, anthropological, and sociological findings.

---

[11] Some sociobiologists are critical of E.O. Wilson's claims that explanations in terms of distal causes have priority over other explanations (Daly and M. Wilson, 1978:321). But the only proximal causal mechanism that receives much attention from these authors is hormonal control, a proximal control system that is highly programmed by genetic information.

[12] See Allen et al. (1976) for greater detail.

[13] Few behavioral geneticists believe that single genes control single behavior patterns in humans. A multitude of genes are needed to encode the information that guide the development of the physiological mechanisms that mediate human behavior.

Our conclusion is that sociobiology does not meet any of the four basic criteria for a balanced biosocial theory (pages 16–19), although it comes closest to doing so for primitive species. Sociobiological theories are strongly biased toward explaining behavior in terms of distal causes. They consistently neglect the multiple proximal causes that a balanced theory must contain.[14] And they attempt to apply the same mixture of explanatory variables to problems at all phylogenetic levels.

FUNCTIONAL LOGIC AND TYPE II ERRORS

Not only is sociobiology biased toward an overemphasis on distal causes, certain features of sociobiological logic tend to blind its practitioners to those biases. In particular, the emphasis on function, design, and adaptiveness often lead evolutionary thinkers to infer genetic causes when the inference is unwarranted. Inferred genetic causes for behavior frequently lead sociobiologists to overestimate the role of genetic control, and this creates a risk of Type II errors—accepting genetic hypotheses that should not be accepted. Overestimating genetic causation only reinforces the sociobiologists' conviction that natural selection explains most behavior. These problems create an inherent imbalance in sociobiology that its practitioners are not likely to correct.

The concepts of adaptiveness and function have long played an important role in biology. For example, it is functional for animals to have some type of light detector or eye; and one can trace the evolution of various types of eye spots and eyes, demonstrating their adaptiveness. The vertebrate eye represents a model of form and function. Light enters through a lens that focuses an image on the retina, where specialized cells respond to light and pass their messages along through the nervous system. Many nocturnal vertebrates have a relatively large lens—which creates a small, bright image—and a reflective layer behind the photoreceptors of the retina reflects the light back past the photoreceptors to stimulate them a second time (Plate 3.1). Diurnal vertebrates have smaller lenses that create larger images and allow finer resolution. These highly functional structures are clear demonstrations of adaptive evolution. Other organs usually reflect similar functional design.

The mechanisms of natural selection allow biologists to explain how such functional structures arise. Given the variation in genetic information for eye structure in a population at any point in time, some individuals will carry genes that encode information for eyes that produce sharper than average vision, and others will carry genes which

---

[14] The fact that sociobiology uses dozens of intervening variables to explain natural selection may give the impression that the second criterion of balanced theory (that it be a multifactor model) has been fulfilled. However, virtually all of the multiple variables that sociobiology uses are from the domain of evolutionary biology and very few focus on independent proximal causes for behavior.

PLATE 3.1. Nocturnal primates—such as this Demidoff's Bushbaby (*Galago demidovii*)—have a reflective layer behind the photoreceptors of the retina that increases the total stimulation to the photoreceptors. The animal's eyes shine brightly because the photographer's flash is reflected back to the camera. (*Courtesy of P. Charles-Dominique.*)

encode information for eyes that produce inferior vision. In those habitats where sharp vision is adaptive, the individuals with the genes for sharper eyes will have a competitive advantage, hence a better chance of surviving and reproducing their own kind. When mutations arise for still sharper vision and confer additional competitive advantage, they will tend to be retained and become more frequent in the population. Thus, natural selection tends to produce adaptive, functional traits.

Having seen countless examples of the evolution of adaptive structures and organs, many biologists feel very comfortable in concluding:

PROPOSITION 1: *Natural selection produces functional, adaptive traits.*

The converse seems equally logical to some:

PROPOSITION 2: *Adaptive, functional traits reflect the operation of natural selection of relevant genetic information.*

If a given trait, structure, or organ has a functional design, the logical groundwork is available to "demonstrate" that individuals with the genes for such a trait had a better chance of surviving and reproducing their own kind than individuals with genes for less adaptive, less functional, less well designed traits. Proposition 2 can be so nicely embedded in evolutionary logic and genetic theory that evolutionary thinkers often forget that other causes than natural selection and genetic control can be involved in producing adaptive traits. In addition, many of the traits studied by biologists develop so automatically and regularly in a wide variety of different environments that biologists are often used to neglecting proximal environmental influences. The eye of the rhesus monkey develops much the same in the forest-living monkey as it does in the urban monkey or the laboratory monkey. No one will dispute that nutrients and other environmental building blocks are needed for the construction of the eye, but the invariant structure of the eyes of most rhesus monkeys makes it easy for biologists to neglect proximal causes in most circumstances. In addition, the practice of inferring genetic causes for adaptive traits (Proposition 2) has often been reinforced when, in fact, fossil evidence later demonstrates the evolutionary development of the modern form from earlier, more primitive forms.

Sociobiology has adopted the practice of inferring evolutionary causes for organs and behavior that appear to be adaptive. Proposition 2 can be applied at any phylogenetic level. For example, in a discussion of the primate literature, Clutton-Brock and Harvey (1976:195) state that "A primary aim of primate socio-biology (or socio-ecology) is to explain variation in social behaviour in terms of biological function." If it can be shown that it is functional for male squirrel monkeys to compete for access to females during breeding season, evolutionary logic makes it easy to conclude that the competitive behavior has been produced by natural selection. Some say that male aggression "has evolved" to increase reproductive success, as if evolution were the only cause.[15] Since sociobiologists often cannot reconstruct the evolutionary history of a behavior—whereas morphologists can sometimes use fossils to reconstruct the evolution of physical structures—arguments for the evolutionary causes of behavior are based more heavily on evidence of adaptiveness than are arguments for the evolution of physical structures.

The Problems with Functional Arguments

Anyone who is eager to "demonstrate" evolutionary causes for behavior by using Proposition 2 need only locate one or more plausible functions for the behavior. This turns out to be a relatively easy task. People can

---

[15] Klopfer (1973) asks, "Does behavior evolve?" and concludes that this unfortunate phrase only obscures the importance of nongenetic influences on behavior.

invent numerous functional interpretations for almost any behavior (even nonfunctional or dysfunctional behavior). This creates a risk of erroneously inferring selective and genetic causes for any behavior that can be made to appear adaptive. It is not difficult to devise plausible theories for the evolution and possible functions of acne, migraine head-aches, ejaculatory incompetence, vaginismus, child abuse, and so forth. For example, acne could function to elicit grooming, which then in-creases the likelihood of sexual interaction, hence the propagation of the genes that cause acne. The number of imaginative "explanations" is amazing. Proof by adaptiveness can be used to "prove" anything, even things that should not be "proven." As the sociobiologists Daly and M. Wilson (1978:109) point out, adaptive "theories certainly have some validity, but they are disturbingly *post hoc*: Ingenious explanations could surely be devised for chimp monogamy or for great herds of orangs had they been discovered to occur! The problem of hindsight is the bane of all socioecology, but it is particularly acute here."

The ease with which functional "explanations" can be invented cre-ates a risk of Type II errors—accepting genetic hypotheses that should not be accepted—since even nonfunctional and dysfunctional behavior can be interpreted as functional. One might argue that truly functional behavior cannot be confused with nonfunctional or dysfunctional be-havior. However, many observers of animal behavior have found that it is extremely difficult to obtain any kind of evidence for evaluating or rejecting functional hypotheses about behavior.[16] As Rowell (1972, 1979) points out, many statements about the adaptiveness of a given primate behavior are mostly speculative, since there is presently very little direct evidence available with which to evaluate them. Welker (1971) notes that it would be so difficult to evaluate many of the speculations about the adaptiveness of specific behavior patterns that the status of the "explanations" as untestable hypotheses makes them virtually unscien-tific. Lewontin (1979:11) states that the absence of data on past evolu-tionary parameters makes arguments about adaptiveness "an exercise in plausible story telling rather than a science of testable hypotheses."

Three Automatic Explanations

Three central propositions of sociobiology heighten the risk of Type II errors. Sociobiology has developed three different strategies for explain-ing behavior as an adaptation for enhancing reproductive fitness. First, if a behavior can be seen as providing a direct selective advantage for

---

[16] When we realize that there is a continuum of adaptation from the optimal to subop-timal to nonfunctional to dysfunctional, it becomes clear that the black and white logic of calling a trait either adaptive or not adaptive obscures much of the complexity that may lie between the extremes.

the individual, then it is adaptive because it advances the individual's own personal fitness. Second, if the behavior can be seen to provide a selective advantage to kin, then it is adaptive because it advances the individual's inclusive fitness, i.e., the fitness of kin who carry the family genes. Third, according to Trivers's (1971) theory of reciprocal altruism, if a behavior provides a selective advantage to nonkin who reciprocate the favor, the behavior is adaptive because it advances the initiator's fitness. Thus, these three fundamental sociobiological propositions provide ready-made and "legitimated" explanations for demonstrating the adaptiveness of any behavior that appears to benefit the individual, related kin, or anyone who may engage in reciprocal altruism. With these three bases covered, almost nothing remains that cannot be subsumed under at least one of these genetic explanations.[17] The ability to pigeonhole behavior into any of three tidy genetic explanations increases the risk of Type II errors. If virtually *everything* can be explained as an adaptive, functional product of natural selection, then almost all behavior—even learned behavior—will appear to confirm genetic hypotheses. This, in turn increases the risk of accepting genetic explanations that should not be accepted. Such systematic biases in the core assumptions and logic of sociobiology tend to produce unbalanced theories at any phyletic level where proximal causes play a significant role in influencing behavior.[18]

Learning

There is a third problem associated with functional interpretations of behavior. The behavior repertoires of many species have enough behavioral plasticity that individuals can learn either adaptive or maladaptive behavior. Thus, holding species genetics constant, one individual may learn an adaptive pattern while a conspecific learns a maladaptive pattern, depending on current environmental conditions. For example, depending on the schedules of reinforcement, individuals of various species will either learn operants that avoid painful stimuli or learn operants that produce painful stimuli.[19] The ability to learn is genetically programmed; but the precise nature of any individual's learned responses depends on the individual's past history of learning experience. Thus, an individual's response of avoiding pain or self-inducing pain is determined by proximal variables and is not programmed by distal causes. The avoidance of painful stimuli is usually an adaptive response; and if only the adaptive behavior were studied (without attention to

---

[17] Allen et al. (1976) and Sahlins (1976:84).

[18] Hinde (1975) and Lewontin (1978:217f) give several other problems involved in creating functional explanations.

[19] Kelleher and Morse (1968); Stretch et al. (1968); McKearney (1969); and Byrd (1972).

learning or the possibility of maladaptive responses), evolutionary logic would allow the observer to conclude that this adaptive behavior had "evolved" and was under genetic control. (Even if the maladaptive behavior were observed, it is likely that an adaptive "explanation" could be invented; and this in turn would allow the observer to conclude that the behavior had "evolved" to cope with special conditions and was also under genetic control.)

These errors become most problematic in species where behavior is strongly influenced by proximal factors, yet still appears to fit the functional logic that "demonstrates" that behavior results from natural selection. Even the presence of substantial data to document the adaptiveness of a given behavior does not prove the existence of a strong genetic base for the behavior. Thus Proposition 2 is incorrect: Even if a behavior were proven beyond a shadow of a doubt to be adaptive, it does not follow that the behavior is genetically programmed. Learned behavior often appears to be adaptive and functionally related to local environmental conditions (though there is no genetic guarantee that it must be). Even if a behavior appears to be invariant and universal in a species, this is not evidence that the behavior is genetically determined. Cooking with fire and driving cars are not genetically programmed; yet these activities can be observed in all countries. Any environment where fire or cars are readily available and rewarding to use provides the proximal causes for the learning of these activities.

Because behavior that is predominantly influenced by proximal causes can be erroneously attributed to genetic design, the risk of a Type II error is further increased. Wilson (1975:254–255) provides a clear example of such a Type II error. In spite of abundant data that human aggression is highly influenced by learning,[20] Wilson's reliance on adaptive logic leads him to emphasize evolutionary explanations:

> Is aggression in man adaptive? From the biologist's point of view it certainly seems to be. It is hard to believe that any characteristic so widespread and easily invoked in a species as aggressive behavior is in man could be neutral or negative in its effects on individual survival and reproduction. It also does not matter whether the aggression is wholly innate or is acquired part or wholly by learning. We are now sophisticated enough to know that the capacity to learn certain behaviors is itself a genetically controlled and therefore evolved trait.

It does not matter to sociobiologists whether or not aggression is learned because they are not interested in studying proximal causes. Their logic says: If a behavior exists and appears to be adaptive, it is an evolved trait. Balanced biosocial theory takes a different approach: The capacity for humans to generate behavior lying anywhere along a continuum

[20] Bandura (1973).

from friendly to aggressive is genetically established; but the unique behavior patterns that each individual displays are, for the most part, learned. Thus, one person commits murder, another beats his wife, and a third is never aggressive. Sociobiology can, of course "explain" this within-species variability, too, since everything can be made to look adaptive. Wilson (1975:255) asserts that "the aggressive responses vary according to the situation in a genetically programmed manner. It is the total *pattern* of responses that is adaptive and has been selected for in the course of evolution." (Presumably, if a man learned to stop beating his wife, this would be a consequence of genetic programming, too.)

Sociobiology provides an armarmentarium of methods for analyzing behavior in terms of adaptiveness and natural selection. Because it has neglected proximal causes, it gives us no way of disentangling distal and proximal influences on behavior. The fact that there are many similarities between distal and proximal influences (pages 26–42) makes it easy for sociobiologists to confuse the two and to overestimate the contribution of genetic causes. Functional logic and Type II errors make most sociobiologists blind to these biases.

THE QUESTION OF OPTIMAL DESIGN

Sociobiology has carried the issue of adaptiveness to an extreme that clearly demonstrates the inherent bias of sociobiology toward explaining behavior in terms of distal causes. Sociobiologists claim that not only should behavior be adaptive, it should be maximally adaptive and optimally suited to ecological demands. Even the most basic outline of a balanced biosocial theory makes it clear that natural selection is unlikely to produce optimal genetic adaptation (page 30f). Because proximal causes must intervene between the genes and the production of behavior, we would not expect to observe optimal behavior, even *if* the genetic information were optimally adapted.

The sociobiologists' assumption that behavior will be optimally adaptive results from carrying the logic of natural selection to an extreme, making selection the sole cause of behavior, and totally neglecting proximal influences on behavior. If one disregards the effects of proximal factors, natural selection can be seen as a process that always favors better adaptation over poorer adaptation, such that suboptimal forms will be replaced by better adapted forms until (presumably) the optimum is reached. In the field of ethology, McFarland (1976:57) calls this the "principle of optimal design," and explains that "biological structures, subjected for a sufficiently long time to a specific set of selective pressures, will tend to assume characteristics which are optimal with respect to those circumstances."

Sociobiology has elaborated on the principle of optimal design by stating that traits will be selected to produce optimal inclusive fitness. According to Barash (1977:63) the "fundamental hypothesis that seems to underlie the discipline of sociobiology . . . states: When any behavior under study reflects some component of genotype,[21] animals should behave so as to maximize their inclusive fitness." And: "An animal's behavior can thus be said to be designed by natural selection to maximize fitness" (Daly and Wilson, 1978:24). This analysis lends itself to an economic model of investments and returns. "For a given reproductive season one can define the total parental investment of an individual as the sum of its investments in each of its offspring produced during that season, and one assumes that natural selection has favored the total parental investment that leads to maximum net reproductive success" (Trivers, 1972:139). Naturally, sociobiologists put limits on the principle: They conceive of adaptations as being the "optimal feasible solution" rather than the "optimal conceivable solution" (Oster and Wilson, 1978:304). The optimal will be the best possible adaptation, given the constraints of the situation, i.e., the constraints of phylogenetic inertia, the limits of the species' behavior capacity, compromises or trade-offs in maximizing other traits, and so forth. All of these constraints are drawn from evolutionary theory, thus, the theory incorporates no junctures at which sociobiologists would need to introduce proximal variables into their equations. (A balanced biosocial theory would never adopt central theoretical principles that did not provide for an interplay of both distal and proximal causal factors.)

Once optimality is assumed, it is possible to "demonstrate" optimal design in many patterns of behavior. Trivers (1972, 1974) uses economic models to calculate optimal parental investment strategies and optimal offspring strategies that allow individuals to maximize their reproductive success. Wilson (1975) includes additional discussions of optimal population growth and density, optimum reproductive yields, optimal longevity, optimum group structure and size, and so forth. Wilson attempts to buttress the idea of optimal design with questionable data on "rapid evolution," claiming that 10 to 15 generations is sufficient for a new optimal equilibrium to be reached when evolutionary pressures change.[22] Oster and Wilson (1978) devote an entire book to analyzing the caste systems of social insects with the mathematics of vector optimization and make "optimization theory the cornerstone of caste theory" (p. 315).

---

[21] Since all behavior reflects "some component" of genotype, all behavior becomes fair game for sociobiological analysis by optimal design.

[22] See footnote 10, this chapter.

Problems

When it comes time to test the theory of optimization, sociobiologists admit problems. Natural selection should produce maximal fitness, they say; yet fitness is difficult to measure. Indirect measures are used to argue the case, though different types of indirect measures are often difficult to compare. The animal is seen as an economic investor, allocating time, energy, reproductive effort, and parental care in presumably optimal combinations to maximize fitness vis-à-vis all relevant risks; but the various investments and risks are hard to measure and to compare.

Next, no single behavior can be studied in isolation from all the other activities that it may influence or cause to be compromised. Because "there are generally many fitness 'components' to be simultaneously maximized if the 'overall' genetic fitness is to be maximized" (Oster and Wilson, 1978:301), a large number of variables would have to be measured in comparable terms in order to determine which compromise solution was optimal. Usually too few indirect measures are available to determine whether a trait is actually optimal when judged vis-à-vis the costs and benefits of all the possible evolutionary compromises that could be involved. According to Daly and Wilson (1978:33), "It must be admitted that the economic theory, although elegant and compelling, is difficult to apply with precision to carefully measured data on real behavior." In their attempt to apply mathematical models of vector optimization to insect behavior—where evolutionary causes should have a heavy weighting—Oster and Wilson (1978) encounter enormous problems. Without introducing any of the problems caused by proximal causes, the authors encounter virtually insurmountable difficulties in advancing beyond the simplest of models for local optima (pp. 292–315). If proximal causes had been entered into the equations and if advanced species had been studied, the problems with the optimal models would have increased dramatically.

Thus, it is unlikely that the optimality theory can ever be tested. Oster and Wilson (1978:315) "conclude that the mathematical techniques of the theory cannot be used to make long-range predictions of evolutionary processes. Indeed, the concept of lone optima toward which many species can be said to be moving along certain trajectories appears to be an unsupportable metaphysical notion." In fact, the basic "assumption, frequently made, that 'sufficient genetic flexibility exists to realize the optimal ecological strategy' is an assertion of pure faith. Rather like the concept of the Holy Trinity, it must be believed to be understood" (p. 307). In spite of these problems, the theory of optimal design has not lost its appeal to those who think primarily in terms of genes competing for survival.

Suboptimal Realities

Are the assumptions of optimal design and maximal fitness warranted? Sahlins's (1976:74–75) critique of sociobiology points out that the process of natural selection does not automatically guarantee that organisms will be maximizers or optimizers. The more traditional approach to the theory of natural selection assumes that animals may well be sufficiers rather than maximizers. Lawton (1979) notes that "Fitnesses are relative, not absolute, and as long as no better competitor appears the suboptimal may survive perfectly well." Biological researchers are discovering that suboptimal traits are extremely commonplace in biological systems. Not only is natural selection not producing optimal designs and adaptations, natural selection *tolerates*—and even *generates*—a substantial amount of suboptimal variation in biological systems.[23] Kummer (1971:90) sums it up nicely: "Discussions of adaptiveness sometimes leave us with the impression that every trait observed in a species must by definition be ideally adaptive, whereas all we can say with certainty is that it must be tolerable since it did not lead to extinction. Evolution, after all, is not sorcery."

On the molecular level, biologists are discovering far more variability in biochemical systems than optimal design predicts and far more non-adaptive evolution than most biologists would have guessed several decades ago.[24] Because biochemical synthesis is under strict genetic control, the existence of substantial suboptimal variation at the molecular level indicates that genetic information itself—in very old, conservative protein systems which have had hundreds of millions of years[25] to be "perfected"—is far from optimally designed. "Large numbers of alleles are stored in populations even though they are not maximally adaptive"; and this is guaranteed by five mechanisms[26] "that actively maintain diversity in spite of selective forces tending to eliminate it" (Ayala, 1978:63). In addition, the fact that the environment is constantly changing means that evolutionary adaptations are always behind, therefore always slightly ill adapted at best.[27]

The suboptimal variation was not expected by advocates of optimal design because it creates a costly genetic load in terms of suboptimal

[23] Clarke (1975); Lewontin (1978); Kimura (1979); Bernstein and Smith (1979); and Cohen and Shapiro (1980).
[24] Kimura (1968, 1979); King and Jukes (1969); Lewontin (1974); Ohta and Kimura (1975); Clarke (1975); and Ayala (1978).
[25] If hundreds of millions of years cannot produce optimal design, free of suboptimal variability, it seems unlikely that Wilson's "rapid evolution" could do better in 10 to 15 generations.
[26] These five mechanisms are heterozygote superiority, diversifying selection, hybrid vigor, frequency-dependent selection, and selective neutrality.
[27] Lewontin (1978).

traits, inefficiency, infertility, and so forth. Biologists have concluded, however, that the load can be seen as acceptable when one appreciates that it is "the entire individual organism, not the chromosomal locus [that] is the unit of selection" (Ayala, 1978:64). The individual's strong points compensate for its weak points. Sociobiologists are aware of these facts, but prefer to exclude nonadaptive evolution from their concern.[28]

If there is suboptimal variation in the genetic information, it should be obvious that when the genetic blueprints are interfaced with countless proximal environmental factors during development, many extra levels of variation (which are not genetically controlled) can be introduced into the final product. This is especially true in the advanced species, where learning is a well-developed mechanism for modifying behavior according to current environmental conditions. The data on primate behavior indicate that far more behavioral and social variation is present than the principle of optimal design would predict.[29] In a review of primate social organization, Eisenberg, Muckenhirn, and Rudran (1972:873) state that:

> Although we can generalize about the selective advantages of primate social structures, we must remember that the history of the population under study, its particular adaptation to local environmental conditions, and the idiosyncratic nature of its dyadic relations (which have been ontogenetically established within the particular group) can result in a great deal of variability in social structure, even within the same species when it occurs in widely differing habitats.

Spuhler and Jorde (1975) conducted a multivariate quantitative analysis on 19 primate variables across 29 population samples and found that phylogenetic and/or genetic factors accounted for less than one half of the variance. They conclude (p. 398): "In general, local ecological settings, and probably local social traditions transmitted by learning, are equally, if not more, important determinants of primate social behavior" than phylogenetic or genetic determinants. In addition, it is likely that the studies analyzed by Spuhler and Jorde underestimate primate variability. Because a species must be studied in several different environments before the extent of social variability can be estimated, and because many species have not been adequately researched, it is not possible at present to ascertain how much more variability actually exists.

Needless to say, the variability in human behavior is enormous; and not all the variability can be optimal. The species' genetics clearly establishes certain limits and predispositions, which set human behavior

---

[28] Barash (1977:33).
[29] Bernstein and Smith (1979) and Baldwin and Baldwin (1979:90).

apart from the behavior of other species.[30] However, within that species-typical range, there is enormous behavioral plasticity and variation. Sociobiologists themselves have admitted that biological factors may explain only a small portion of human behavior. In an interview with the Harvard *Crimson*, Wilson estimated that perhaps only 10% of human behavior could be traced to biological causes.[31] (People less enthusiastic about sociobiology than Wilson might estimate an even smaller weighting for genetic factors in humans.) The problem is that sociobiologists do not change their theoretical strategies when dealing with humans (and other advanced species). They continue to generalize about human behavior directly from their idealized models of natural selection, in which distal causes are given primary weighting.

GENETIC IDEALISM

If our analysis is correct, sociobiologists are guilty of genetic idealism. By trying to push the logic of natural selection to the limits, as the ultimate explanatory model, sociobiologists have allowed an idealized model of genetic causes to obscure the importance of suboptimal realities. Suboptimal variation is neglected, along with the distal and proximal causes of suboptimal conditions.

Idealism has often blinded scientists to the realities of our fair but imperfect world. For example, prior to Darwin, many biologists had difficulty perceiving and comprehending within-species variation.[32] One of the major intellectual obstacles that hindered the development of evolutionary thought in the 1800s was that of idealism, or "essentialism." Plato was a very influential advocate of idealism, and his impact has not ceased resonating through Western thought. "The observed vast variability of the world has no more reality, according to this [idealist] philosophy, than the shadows of an object on a cave wall, as Plato expressed it in his analogy" (Mayr, 1972:984). Only the unchanging "ideas" behind the flux are important. Idealism made it easy for early biologists to believe that each species was perfectly adapted to its environment, as if a benevolent Designer had maximized each species' fit to its ecological niche. Operating within this paradigm, the scientist could observe a real lion but be thinking of an idealized lion, the invariant form located in a Platonic heaven. This type of idealism hinders the perception of variability, and was a major obstacle to the discovery and acceptance of the variability of the species, and hence of evolutionary theory, in Darwin's time.

---

[30] Seligman and Hager (1972) and Hinde and Stevenson-Hinde (1973).
[31] Sahlins (1976:65).
[32] Mayr (1972).

When sociobiologists describe behavior in terms of strategies[33] for maximizing fitness and optimizing adaptiveness, they draw attention to idealized, formal models to the point that suboptimal variation becomes invisible. In fact, variation is often described as merely "noise" that is superimposed on finely tuned survival strategies, a nuisance that clutters or confounds otherwise lovely mathematical equations. In his valedictory as president of the International Congress of Genetics, Curt Stern captured the leitmotif of genetic idealism succinctly: "The eggs or sperm of a lion are the lions themselves, stripped of all ephemeral attributes."[34] This form of genetic idealism allows one to forget all the "noise" and imperfections that are encountered in the real world when the developing lion has suboptimal nutrition, a serious infection that retards development, an injured paw, or unique learning experiences. Genetic idealism is attractive to those who wish to believe that genetic causes will explain everything important about behavior. The suboptimal variations are dismissed as unimportant, ephemeral imperfections; the Platonic essence is explained by the genes. The "selfish gene" (to use Dawkins's term[35]) can be seen as the designer, director, and choreographer of the great pageant of life. However, when the variation that is not accounted for by genetic factors is substantial, disregarding it may be unwise. The Platonic lion, even if it were to be "realized" under conditions of optimal nutrition and exercise, along with minimal injury and disease, would not be able to survive in its natural habitat. The genetic code does not provide it with the ability to stalk prey, kill, and coordinate with conspecifics, for these skills are dependent in large part on learning.[36]

IS EVOLUTIONARY THEORY WRONG?

Advocating a balanced biosocial theory does not imply that evolutionary theory is wrong. Natural selection is a major determinant of physiological structure, and in some cases of behavior. But no behavior can ever be explained by natural selection alone. As Beach (1955) pointed out in a criticism of the instinct theories of the time, "No bit of behavior can ever be fully understood until its ontogenesis has been described."

Among insects and other primitive organisms, behavior is highly programmed by the genes with relatively few degrees of freedom for prox-

---

[33] The term "strategy," though commonly used by many biologists, is objectionable because of teleological and anthropomorphic overtones. The concept of strategic behavior suggests an unwarranted level of rational, cognitive planning that biases one subtly toward idealism.
[34] Douglas (1973).
[35] Dawkins (1976).
[36] Adamson (1960) and Schaller (1972:165).

imal environmental control; thus evolutionary theories can be fairly accurate in predicting and explaining behavior at these phylogenetic levels. However, as one turns to the more advanced species, proximal environmental conditions have increasing influence on behavior, and pure evolutionary theories can explain fewer of the particulars of behavior (though evolutionary considerations must be present in the explanations of these behavioral patterns). Naturally, there will be some behavior patterns of advanced species that fit—or appear to fit—purely genetic models. This is true because (1) a certain portion of any species' behavioral repertoire is under strong genetic control, and (2) many responses that are under strong proximal control will *appear* to be adaptive, and hence seem to fit a pure evolutionary model. Thus, sociobiologists will be able to gerrymander the data on advanced species, locate patterns that fit the predictions of their model, and thus claim to "demonstrate" evolutionary causation.

In species with considerable behavioral plasticity, much of the within-species variability results from learning. Although the ability to learn—along with specific preparednesses and counterpreparednesses—is determined by natural selection and genetic information, there are many degrees of freedom in the behavioral system that are not under genetic control. Thus, behavior cannot be predicted from distal causes alone (nor can distal causes be inferred from the behavior). In various species, the ability to learn confers selective advantages. Phylogenetic controls are extremely conservative and slow to respond to environmental changes; whereas learning in response to proximal environmental conditions allows rapid adjustment to current ecological situations.

In addition, innate responses are usually tied to simple cue stimuli, which makes them error-prone when the environmental stimuli are complex, variable, or unusual.[37] Learning permits rapid behavior change and more subtle discriminative capacity. Opportunistic species and species living in variable environments would be especially handicapped if the species' behavior repertoire were under strict genetic control. In these species, the evolutionary advantage would go to those individuals with genes for physiological mechanisms that allowed their behavior to be rapidly shaped by current environmental conditions, to learn by observing other group members, and to accumulate traditional responses associated with positive consequences. Thus, in many species, the genes have relinquished their hegemony over behavior, allowing increased control by the current environment. In these species, the genes' control over behavior has become increasingly *indirect*.[38] For example, the genes make it possible for humans to have advanced nervous

[37] Moynihan (1976:217).
[38] Anastasi (1958).

systems, extensive cortical capacity, language-processing centers, a responsiveness to certain stimuli as reinforcers, etc. But knowledge about the phylogenetic and genetic factors alone will predict only a small fraction of the actual behavior observed in a given individual (except at the most general level).

The evolution of behavioral plasticity and learning capacity involved an evolutionary compromise. When natural selection began to favor behavioral plasticity, many features of genetically programmed behavior were sacrificed. The ability of the genes to produce highly controlled behavior was gradually lost as the current environment gained more influence. As the genes lost their hegemony over behavior, there was less guarantee that any particular behavior pattern would approach optimal adaptation. Although insects may produce behavior that conforms closely to genetically optimal patterns, there is less guarantee that animals with considerable behavioral plasticity will always behave according to optimal evolutionary patterns. The advantages of flexibility allow the advantages of genetic programming to be compromised. The disadvantages of behavioral inflexibility—slow change and errors in responding to stimuli that are complex, variable, or unusual—hasten the decline of strong genetic control. These compromises lead us to expect that many species will behave in ways that deviate considerably from the patterns seen in insects and other species where behavior is under strong genetic control. Therefore, models that analyze only distal causes for behavior are likely to make serious errors in interpreting malleable behavior.

Increases in behavioral plasticity create additional evolutionary compromises. Although it has been recognized that biological factors put constraints on learning,[39] it is important to realize that increased specialization for learning also puts constraints on natural selection, closing certain evolutionary options while opening others. Species that have been selected to have a high learning capacity can no longer have as much of their behavior directly controlled by strong genetic programming. Also, the capacity to learn increases the probability that certain evolutionary directions will pay off well while others will be counterproductive. For example, as less behavior becomes genetically determined and more degrees of freedom enter a species' repertoire, it becomes advantageous for the young to have a longer dependency period in which they are protected by others and can learn from their groupmates and from the nonsocial environment.[40] Since environments in which the young must learn to survive and be social may be variable,

---

[39] Hinde and Stevenson-Hinde (1973).
[40] Washburn and Hamburg (1965:613).

there would be a selective pressure to favor diverse and redundant learning mechanisms in order that behavior patterns could be acquired under any of a variety of different circumstances.[41] Because of the advantages of minimizing interference between fixed action patterns and learned responses, there would be evolutionary pressures for dropping fixed patterns from the species' repertoire or making them amenable to conditioning. For example, various human stereotyped signals—such as the eyebrow flash or smile[42]—can be easily brought under proximal control, as can many other human reflexive responses.

Balanced biosocial theories do not discard evolutionary principles. However, they must avoid the problems that result from a heavy reliance on evolution as the primary organizing principle in behavioral explanations for all species.

CONCLUSION

At present, ethology is less distant from the goal of balanced biosocial theory than is sociobiology. Many ethologists are interested in the ontogeny of behavior, comparative psychology, integrations of proximal and distal influences, and within-species variability. The sociobiologists with their newly formulated, "austere" genetic theories have shown less interest than ethologists in ontogeny and proximal environmental causes. As long as sociobiologists continue to use genetic causation as the central organizing principle of their discipline, the extreme emphasis on genetic factors will produce unbalanced theories that do not fit the data for many species. Yet the calculus of genetic fitness lies at the core of sociobiological theory and gives it an identity distinct from that of ethology. In addition, sociobiologists have an enormous amount of sunk costs in the study of other biological variables that bias them to focus their analytic attention on phylogenetic and genetic variables rather than on proximal causes. After investing a great deal of effort in the study of population biology, reproductive strategies, and numerous other technical biological theories, sociobiologists are unlikely to cast these aside and admit that they play a small role in the explanation of the behavior of many species, including that of humans. Indeed, they stand to profit most by suggesting that their biological variables explain a larger proportion of behavior than they can empirically demonstrate. Because Type II errors blind sociobiologists to the inadequacy of their theories, it seems likely that the sociobiologists will continue to overstate the case for genetic causes of behavior. Finally, the sociobiologists' lack

[41] Baldwin and Baldwin (1977:389f).
[42] Eibl-Eibesfeldt (1975).

of contact with other behavioral sciences (partly due to the artificial boundaries maintained by the traditional disciplines) may continue to retard their learning material that has been well documented in psychology, anthropology, and sociology. Thus, we conclude, that not only is sociobiology not a balanced biosocial theory, it is unlikely that it will become one.

NEGLECTED ISSUES

It is clear that sociobiology has neglected several major topics that play central roles in balanced biosocial theories. In the next three chapters, we will deal with three of the most important neglected issues: (1) *natural learning*, (2) *behavioral development*, and (3) *the influence of learning on social organization*. A demonstration of the importance of these neglected topics will further document the inadequacies of the sociobiological position. More importantly, it will underscore the need for analyzing proximal variables if we are to produce balanced theories of animal and human behavior.

Chapter 4 focuses primarily on the principles of natural learning as they appear in primate behavior. Chapter 5 deals with the behavioral development of the individual primate. Chapter 6 presents a model of group structure that builds from the data on individual behavior presented in Chapters 4 and 5.

Because these three chapters focus special attention on issues that are neglected by sociobiology, they are not in themselves balanced biosocial theories. They overemphasize proximal causes of behavior rather than natural selection. However, the proximal causes are important elements that must be woven into balanced theories; thus the discussion in Part II lays the groundwork for Part III, in which an attempt is made to produce a balanced theory. Throughout Part II, every effort has been made to present the proximal causes of primate behavior in ways that dovetail with evolutionary considerations in order to facilitate the later construction of balanced models of behavior.

THE FUNDAMENTALS
OF NATURAL LEARNING

In Chapter 2, we presented a general outline of the distal and proximal causal variables that must be incorporated into balanced biosocial theories. Although sociobiology does an excellent job in developing the distal variables in its model of behavior and social organization, it neglects many of the proximal causes, especially those that are least constrained by genetic factors. There is no question that species genetics and maturation play an important role in explaining behavior; and sociobiology has little difficulty incorporating these factors into its evolutionary model. Even the constructive and destructive environmental inputs (e.g., nutrients, poisons, exercise, injury) discussed in Chapter 2 could be incorporated into sociobiological theories as factors that facilitate or hinder the biologically programmed development of physiological mechanisms and behavior patterns. Learning stands as the single most important determinant of behavior that has been neglected by sociobiology. Since recognizing the importance of learning threatens genetic theories of behavior by endangering the sociobiological view that genes are the primary determinant of behavior, learning is seldom seriously considered in evolutionary models of behavior. Nowhere in Wilson's (1975) lengthy text is there a discussion of operant conditioning, Pavlovian conditioning, or social learning theory. Few other sociobiology texts make any mention of these proximal determinants of behavior.[1] However, conditioning and social learning play a crucial role in explaining much of the behavior of advanced species; and any theory that neglects learning when analyzing the behavior of humans or other advanced species cannot produce a balanced model of behavior.

Learning does not exist in isolation, separate from genetic and biological factors. Animals are capable of learning only if they inherit the genetic information for the physiological mechanisms that mediate learning. Each species has species-typical patterns of preparedness and counterpreparedness to learn, along with species-typical sensitivities to the reinforcers and punishers that are the prime movers of learning. Genetic information is a major determinant of the complexity of learned behavior, the speed of learning, and a species' potential for operant conditioning, Pavlovian conditioning, observational learning, insight, and other modes of learning. Balanced biosocial theory requires that these biological variables be integrated into theories of learning in order to facilitate the eventual synthesis of learning with data on natural selection and other determinants of behavior. In addition, an adequate theory of learning must deal with natural behavior patterns seen in natural environments. Thus the goal is a theory of *natural learning* that explains natural behavior in a way that is compatible with the data on natural selection and other biological variables. Much as Darwin utilized data on artificial selection to construct his theory of natural selection, contemporary scientists can utilize laboratory data on learning[2] to develop theories of natural learning (Chapter 9). This chapter presents the most basic principles of learning in a way that should facilitate the integration of natural learning into balanced biosocial theories.[3] The next two chapters expand this view of natural learning by exploring the role of learning in natural behavioral development and social organization. Most examples will be drawn from primate behavior.

OPERANT CONDITIONING

By far the greatest amount of overt behavior that primates generate in the natural environment is operant behavior. Operant behavior operates on the environment and is instrumental in producing rewarding out-

---

[1] In a review of a recent sociobiology book, Miller (1979) made a criticism that holds for sociobiology in general: "No contributor adequately addresses what may be the greatest conceptual flaw of sociobiology—a lack of concern for the role of experience in the development of species-typical behavior."

[2] The learning principles developed in laboratory research are explained in greater detail by Nevin and Reynolds (1971), Houston (1976), Honig and Staddon (1977), and Fantino and Logan (1979).

[3] A related description of natural learning in humans is presented elsewhere (Baldwin and Baldwin, 1981).

comes. Walking, running, playing, grooming, feeding, consorting, mating, and most other overt behaviors consist of long chains of operant behaviors, with reflexive responses or fixed action patterns interspersed at various points in the chains.

As explained in Chapter 2, the single most important determinant of operant behavior is differential reinforcement—though observational learning and related processes have their influences. Differential reinforcement occurs when certain responses are followed by reinforcement and others by nonreinforcement or punishment. Every operant behavior contains natural variations, and some of the variations may be followed by higher levels of reinforcement than others. The differential consequences increase the probability of the reinforced variations and decrease the probability of nonreinforced variations. Totally new operant behavior may appear in an individual's behavior repertoire due to induction, imitation, or related factors; and these new responses serve as raw material from which new operants can be shaped by further differential reinforcement. Operant conditioning is usually adaptive in producing skills that help an individual adjust to changes in local environmental contingencies; therefore, in species that live in changeable environments, natural selection often favors those individuals with the physiological mechanisms for operant learning.[4] Selection also explains patterns of preparedness and counterpreparedness for learning certain operants.

The analysis of operant behavior involves a description of the threefold relationship between antecedent stimuli (A), and operant behaviors (B), and consequences (C).

$$A \rightarrow B \rightarrow C$$

This threefold relationship is called the *contingencies of reinforcement*. The antecedent stimuli are stimuli that precede a behavior and set the occasion for the behavior to appear. Operant behavior can be followed by any of three types of consequences: reinforcement, nonreinforcement, or punishment. Although these three types of consequences are sometimes complexly intertwined, we will discuss them separately in order to minimize confusion. The consequences are the prime movers of operant conditioning: They influence both the future frequency of the operant behavior and the ability of antecedent stimuli to control the occurrence or nonoccurrence of the behavior in the future.

Reinforcement: When an operant behavior is followed by a reinforcer, the reinforcer increases the probability that the operant will be emitted in the future in similar stimulus settings.[5] The antecedent stimuli become discriminative

---

[4] Rachlin (1976:75).

[5] Although operant conditioning is most rapid when reinforcement occurs within a second of the operant (Grice, 1948a,b), delayed reinforcement can be effective if internal or external cues are present that correlate with delayed reinforcers (Perin, 1943). These

(continued)

stimuli (S^D's) associated with reinforcement, and they help set the occasion for future performances of the reinforced operant. For example, when an infant monkey is hungry, its approach to mother and nursing are followed by the reinforcement of milk. After several conditioning experiences, the sight of mother becomes an S^D that sets the occasion for the behaviors (B) of approaching mother and nursing when the infant is hungry.

$$S^D \rightarrow B \rightarrow REINFORCEMENT$$

The next time the infant is hungry, the sight of mother will serve as the S^D that sets the occasion for the operants of approaching and sucking, which, in turn, produce the reinforcing consequence of milk. Each operant in an individual's behavior repertoire comes under the control of its own S^D's. S^D's are the cues that control when and where an operant will appear in the future, based on past reinforcement in the presence of those S^D's.[6]

Responses may be strengthened by either *positive reinforcement* or *negative reinforcement*. If a response is followed by positive reinforcers— such as milk, food, water, or sex—it becomes more probable due to positive reinforcement. Thus the hungry infant learns to approach mother due to positive reinforcement. If a response is followed by escape from or avoidance of an aversive stimulus—such as a cut, fall, sting, or hard blow—it becomes more probable due to negative reinforcement. Thus, an infant may learn to balance carefully while crossing tiny branches to reach mother, since skills at balancing are negatively reinforced by the avoidance of falls.

Nonreinforcement: When a small infant is off its mother, exploring the environment, it may easily come across other adults besides its mother. If an infant is hungry and happens to approach an adult who is resting nearby, its approach may be met by nonreinforcement. The infant may crawl onto the adult's body, move toward the nipples, and be gently brushed away by the adult. *When operant behavior is followed by nonreinforcement, the nonreinforcement causes the future probability of the operant to decrease in similar stimulus settings.* This process is called extinction. Any stimulus that sets the occasion for nonreinforcement becomes an S^Δ (*ess delta*) or discriminative stimulus for *not* responding.

$$S^\Delta \rightarrow B \rightarrow NONREINFORCEMENT$$

In the example, the hungry infant will learn to discriminate that approach to adults other than mother is not followed by milk reinforcers;

(continued from previous page)
cues become conditioned reinforcers that help bridge the time gap between the response and the delayed reinforcer. Advanced species are capable of learning with reinforcers delayed one hour or more (Wolfe, 1936 and Kelleher, 1958).
   [6] Nevin (1971a) and Rilling (1977).

thus these adults become S^Δ's for not approaching for milk, because in the past these cues correlated with nonreinforcement.

Punishment: If an infant happens to approach a group of rowdy, playing juveniles, the juveniles may playfully swat at the infant or wrestle with it. Because the juveniles are larger, stronger, and more skillful than the infant, they can easily hurt the infant or unbalance it, causing it to fall. These aversive consequences function as punishers that are contingent upon the infant's approach to the juveniles. *When an operant is followed by punishment, the punishment causes the future probability of the response to decrease in similar stimulus settings.*[7] The antecedent stimuli that correlate with punishment become discriminative stimuli, S^Δ's, for not emitting the punished response in the S^Δ context.

$$S^\Delta \rightarrow B \rightarrow PUNISHMENT$$

After the infant has had a few aversive contacts with juveniles, punishment will suppress its approaches to juveniles, and the sight of the juveniles will become an S^Δ that controls not approaching.

Discrimination: Animals learn to discriminate the differences between stimuli due to differential consequences. The infant in the above examples learned to discriminate between mother, other adults, and juveniles: As it learned discriminations, the infant learned to direct its approaches to mother (an S^D) and to avoid the rowdy juveniles (S^Δ's). As reinforcement creates S^D's and nonreinforcement or punishment creates S^Δ's, individuals learn the differences between antecedent stimuli and respond differently to them. Thus, reinforcers and punishers are the prime movers that cause the learning of discriminations.[8]

Generalization: Once an individual has learned a certain behavior in one stimulus context, the individual will often emit the operant in the presence of similar stimuli. This is called generalization. Generalization allows an individual to respond to new settings with responses that were effective in similar settings in the past. Thus, new stimuli that are similar to either S^D's or S^Δ's can function much as S^D's or S^Δ's themselves. The more similar a new stimulus context is to the past contexts in which learning took place, the more likely the new stimuli will be to evoke the response. Generalization helps individuals respond to im-

---

[7] Although punishment is most effective when it appears within a second after the response, advanced species are capable of learning even when there is a considerable delay in punishment (Walters and Grusec, 1977).

[8] The genes for the innate discrimination of releaser stimuli are *selected* much as operants are reinforced. The antecedent stimuli (A) that precede an innate behavior (B) that favors adaptive consequences of reproduction (C) are called releasers. Releasers gain the ability to elicit behavior only because the behavior leads to the consequences of increased reproduction. Any stimuli (A') in whose presence an innate behavior (B') would lead to lowered fitness (C') should take on the ability to suppress the innate response. Thus, the analysis of innate responses also requires attention to A–B–C contingencies, except that the consequences are differential reproduction rather than differential reinforcement.

portant cues, even if the cues are not exactly alike on two separate occasions. It is adaptive for the hungry infant to approach mother even if she is sitting in an unusual position and does not present exactly the same stimuli as on past occasions. Because her present appearance is similar enough to the S^D's the infant has seen in the past, the infant will recognize her and approach. It is adaptive for the infant to avoid rowdy juveniles, even if they are engaging in new forms of play that are different from the old activities that are S^Δ's for the infant's not approaching.

The effects of past learning experience on generalization and discrimination can be seen nicely in experiments with infant bonnet macaques.[9] Infants were raised in one of two types of situation. Some infants were raised in cages with mother only. These "mother-only" infants learned to approach mother for contact, nursing, and other positive interactions, hence mother became an S^D for approach. Other infants were raised in groups with mother and several other females who also had infants. These "group-reared" infants had more extensive social learning experience in which mother became an S^D for approach due to reinforcement, and other adult females became S^Δ's for not approaching due to nonreinforcement, and perhaps punishment. All the infants were tested at various ages during the first year of life to see how they responded to the sight of mother and the sight of a strange adult female.

The "mother-only" infants had never interacted with strange adults. How would they respond to the strangers? The strangers were the same species as mother and thus looked somewhat like mother. Because of generalization, the "mother-only" infants should respond to the strangers much the same as they did to their own mothers. Because the infants had never experienced nonreinforcement or punishment with strangers, the strangers would not be S^Δ's for not approaching. As is shown in Figure 4.1, the "mother-only" infants showed few differences in their preferences for the two stimuli, though they did approach the strangers slightly more than they approached their own mothers.

In contrast, the "group-reared" infants did not approach the strangers nearly as much. During their history of social learning experience, they had learned to discriminate between mother and other adults. Because only mother provided many reinforcers, only mother became an S^D for approach. Due to nonreinforcement or punishment, other adults became S^Δ's for not approaching. As shown in Figure 4.1, the "group-reared" infants discriminated between mother and strangers, showing increased preference for mother as they had increased experience. Physiological measures indicate that group-reared infants find contact with the

[9] Rosenblum and Alpert (1977). Similar results have been reported for squirrel monkeys (Kaplan and Schusterman, 1972).

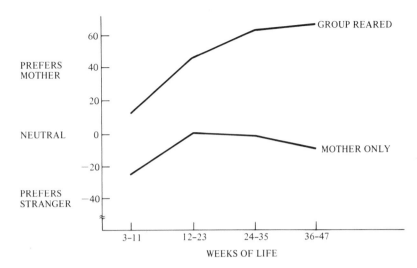

FIGURE 4.1. The relative preference for mother or stranger shown by infant bonnet monkeys who were raised with mother only or group reared. (Adapted from Rosenblum and Alpert, 1977:468.)

mother's body much more comforting and arousal-reducing than contact with other adult females.[10]

Physical similarities in the appearance, texture, sounds, or other properties of two stimuli can cause generalization. However, differential patterns of reinforcement and punishment cause discrimination, as one set of stimuli become S^D's and another set become S^Δ's. Animals can often learn to make very fine discriminations between stimuli, especially if there is genetic preparedness for this type of discrimination. Much as humans can learn to discriminate the differences between different people's voices, primates can learn to discriminate the differences between the "voices" of groupmates. For example, some group members may be reliable watchguards whereas others are alarmists. If alarm calls of a reliable watchguard regularly predict the presence of danger, they become S^D's for being alert to danger (since being alert has been negatively reinforced by escaping danger in the past). If another individual frequently gives alarm calls when there is no real danger (hence no real source of aversive stimuli for being inattentive), alarm calls from that individual are less likely to serve as S^D's for being alert to danger.[11] Thus, the effect of any given stimulus—such as an alarm call—can be modified by differential reinforcement, such that a call functions as an

---

[10] Coe et al. (1978) and Reite et al. (1978).
[11] Even brids learn to discriminate between the alarm calls of reliable watchguards and alarmists (Tinbergen, 1963b).

S^D for alertness when given by one individual but not when given by another.

THE BIOLOGICAL FOUNDATIONS OF REINFORCERS AND PUNISHERS

Each species is biologically programmed to respond to certain stimuli— such as food, sex, water, cuts, and blows—as reinforcers and punishers. These stimuli are called *unconditioned reinforcers* and *unconditioned punishers*, since no conditioning is needed to make these stimuli effective. Although each species responds to slightly different stimuli as unconditioned reinforcers and punishers, most primates respond to somewhat similar types of stimuli. Table 4.1 lists some of the basic unconditioned reinforcers and punishers that influence primate behavior.

The ability of any given stimulus to serve as an unconditioned reinforcer or punisher can be traced to natural selection.[12] If hungry individuals did not respond to food as a reinforcer, they might starve and thus fail to pass on the genes that were responsible for their unresponsiveness to food as a reinforcer. In contrast, any hungry individuals who were biologically predisposed to respond to food as a reinforcer would be likely to eat, since searching for food and eating would be reinforced by food. Because they would be less likely to starve, these individuals would be more likely to survive, reproduce, and transmit the genes that make food a reinforcer. Likewise, individuals who responded to genital stimulation as a reinforcer would be more likely to engage in sexual interaction and reproduce their own kind than individuals who did not. All the unconditioned reinforcers—food, water, genital stimulation, optimal temperature, and so forth—are important for survival and reproduction, hence natural selection favors those individuals who find access to these stimuli to be rewarding. Although the stimuli that serve as unconditioned reinforcers in any given species are in large part genetically determined, the behavior that a given individual of that species will learn due to these reinforcers is not genetically determined. Chimpanzees in one environment may learn to hunt

---

[12] Breland and Breland (1966); Glickman and Schiff (1967); Dunham (1977). A second type of definition of reinforcers and punishers involves circular logic: e.g., if it reinforces, it is a reinforcer. Circular definitions can be defended because they are useful (Kaplan, 1964). It is possible to escape the problems of circularity by turning to either of two independent, noncircular definitions of reinforcers and punishers—the Pavlovian hypothesis (that reinforcers and punishers are US's or CS's) and the Premack principle (Dunham, 1977). The Pavlovian hypothesis is used in this book because it is best suited to a balanced theory of natural learning. Interestingly, the simple definition of evolutionary fitness and survival is also circular (Lewontin, 1978:222); yet the circular definition is still a useful tool.

TABLE 4.1. Partial Listing of the Unconditioned Reinforcers and Punishers That Are Effective in Primates [a]

Reinforcers	Punishers
Food	Starvation
Water	Dehydration
Normal body temperature	Extreme temperatures
Optimal levels of sensory stimulation	Over- and understimulation
Rest after effortful activity	Exhaustion, fatigue
Sleep	Stress
Gentle skin contact, scratching, grooming	Strong contact, cuts, blows, stings
Nipple stimulation (especially in lactating females)	Sore nipples, sore skin, wounds
Genital stimulation	Strong stimulation to the genitals
Certain tastes and odors	Certain tastes and odors
	Effort above certain thresholds
	Poisons or diseases that cause nausea, sickness
	Interruption of nonplayful behavior
	Suffocation
	Overly full stomach or bladder

[a] Stoffer and Stoffer (1976) have identified 31 aversive stimuli that can serve as punishers or negative reinforcers in primates; and they index 582 sources that demonstrate the effects of these stimuli. Unfortunately, we know of no such well documented analysis of positive reinforcers in primates.

for ants and eat them, whereas conspecifics in another forest do not.[13] Proximal environmental variables must be studied to predict which behavior a given individual will learn.

The ability of certain stimuli to serve as unconditioned punishers can also be traced to natural selection. All the unconditioned punishers are stimuli that are potentially dangerous. If individuals did not respond to cuts, falls, stings, broken bones, bad food, and other dangerous stimuli as punishers, they might not learn to avoid the situations that exposed them to these dangers; and the failure to avoid dangerous stimuli decreases the probability that these individuals would survive and reproduce their own kind. In contrast, any individuals who were biologically predisposed to respond to dangerous stimuli as punishers would learn to avoid situations that were associated with dangerous stimuli in the past, and this would increase their chances of surviving and reproducing their own kind. Again, the fact that the unconditioned punishers are in large part genetically determined does not imply that the behavior learned under the influence of these punishers is geneti-

[13] McGrew (1977).

PLATE 4.1. Primates—such as these bonnet macaques—often stand bipedally when standing is reinforced by such things as better visibility of food, conspecifics, or predators. (*Courtesy of Y. Sugiyama.*)

cally determined. After experiencing several painful falls when jumping a wide arboreal gap, some monkeys may learn to avoid jumping at this gap, whereas others may learn to avoid falls by jumping more vigorously. Data on proximal environmental conditions are needed to predict which operant behavior will be learned.

Because each species has evolved to live in different ecological situations, it is only to be expected that natural selection would produce species differences in sensitivity to reinforcing and punishing stimuli. For example, nocturnal species would be expected to find dim light more reinforcing than diurnal species do. In fact, when various species are allowed to control the light intensity in a closed compartment by pressing on levers that increase or decrease light levels, nocturnal primates learn to adjust the light to very low levels that correspond to conditions for which they are suited in the wild.[14] The level of illumination that is most reinforcing clearly reflects adaptive selection.

The ability to respond to tastes as a reinforcer also varies from species to species.[15] Macaques are more sensitive to a variety of sweeteners than are many other species that have been tested. Squirrel monkeys

[14] Kavanau and Peters (1979).
[15] Patton and Ruch (1944); LeMagner (1967); Sato et al. (1977a,b); and Dua-Sharma and Smutz (1977).

show a preference for bitter tastes. Schaller (1963) tasted the various foods preferred by gorillas and found many to have tastes that were not appealing to him. It is reasonable to assume that species differences in responses to various tastes as reinforcers or punishers result in part from natural selection. For example, if protein was scarce in a species' natural environment, the individuals who responded to protein-rich foods as reinforcers would have a higher probability of seeking out foods containing protein than individuals who did not. This would increase their chances of surviving and reproducing, hence increase the frequency of those genes that predisposed individuals to respond to protein as a reinforcer.[16]

The mechanisms underlying *deprivation* and *satiation* also reflect the operation of natural selection. Primates who have been deprived of food respond to food as a reinforcer, but satiated individuals do not. It is adaptive for hungry animals to seek out food and eat, and it is adaptive for satiated animals to stop eating. Thus, there is a selective advantage for individuals with behavior mechanisms that make food reinforcing only after periods of deprivation and nonreinforcing after satiation. There are deprivation and satiation mechanisms for several of the other reinforcers—such as water, rest, and to some degree sexual stimulation, skin stimulation, and nipple stimulation.[17] Naturally, the amount of food, water, sex, or other reinforcers required for satiation would be expected to vary from species to species, depending on past selective pressures in the environment.

In contrast there are no mechanisms for satiation and deprivation of punishers. A punisher is always effective. When an individual is cut several times in a row, the last cut is not less aversive than the first one (as would be the case if satiation were operating).[18] The reason is that the last cut in a series can potentially be as dangerous as the first cut; and adaptive selection favors individuals who find the last cut as aversive and punishing as the first one. Thus, punishers motivate learning and behavior at all times, not just after periods of deprivation (as is the case with reinforcers).

To summarize, primates respond to many stimuli that favor their survival and reproduction as positive reinforcers. They respond to many

---

[16] Richter (1954) demonstrated that rats respond very sensitively to the nutrients needed to balance their diets.

[17] Optimal levels of sensory stimulation and warmth are always reinforcers, showing neither satiation nor deprivation effects.

[18] This effect can be confounded by other variables. After the first cut, an animal may become more active and the competing stimuli from high activity level responses may make the next cuts relatively less obvious, since their presence may be somewhat masked by the other competing stimuli. At other times punishers may become more aversive after several repetitions (holding other factors constant), reflecting the operation of sensitization mechanisms (Catania, 1971:36).

stimuli that endanger their survival and reproduction as punishers.[19] Thus, reinforcers and punishers function as proximal causes that shape operant behavior in ways that are usually compatible with the distal selective forces of differential survival and differential reproduction. In primates the genes have given up most of their direct control over behavior because reinforcers and punishers are much more effective in producing rapid adjustments to changing environmental conditions than are genetic adjustments due to differential reproduction. During the evolution of primates from prosimians to monkeys and apes, there has been a general trend for behavior to become increasingly under the control of reinforcers and punishers. The percentage of behavior that can be explained without reference to reinforcers and punishers has become progressively smaller. Even the unconditioned reinforcers and punishers themselves can be modified by conditioning.[20] If one of these unconditioned stimuli is paired with other reinforcers or punishers, it can be modified to a new position on the continuum from extremely reinforcing to extremely punishing stimuli. For example, if a very nutritious food is regularly paired with sickness in a given environment, even this unconditioned reinforcer will take on conditioned aversive properties.

PAVLOVIAN CONDITIONING

The second major form of conditioning seen in primates is Pavlovian conditioning. Pavlovian conditioning builds from biologically established reflexes—called unconditioned reflexes—and allows new stimuli to gain control over reflexive responses. An unconditioned reflex is a stimulus–response unit in which an *unconditioned stimulus* (US) elicits an *unconditioned response* (UR). Table 4.2 lists some of the unconditioned reflexes typically found in primates. All the reflexes involve biologically significant responses that facilitate survival and reproduction. For example, bad food elicits regurgitation; genital stimulation elicits sexual responses.

When a neutral stimulus is paired with the US of one of the reflexes, the new stimulus usually becomes a *conditioned stimulus* (CS) with the ability to elicit certain features of the reflex.[21] Rapid Pavlovian conditioning occurs when a monkey sees and tastes a new food before the US of "bad food in the stomach" elicits the UR of nausea, regurgitation,

---

[19] Various schedules of reinforcement can create exceptions to this generalization (Kelleher and Morse, 1968; Barrett and Glowa, 1977; and Barrett and Spealman, 1978).

[20] Pavlov (1927).

[21] The conditioned reflexive response usually differs from the unconditioned reflexive response in several ways, typically being slower to appear, less complete, and less intense (Terrace, 1971).

TABLE 4.2. Partial Listing of Unconditioned Reflexes

US	UR
Digestive system	
food	salivation
bad food	sickness, nausea
objects in esophagus	choking, vomiting
Reproductive systems	
genital stimulation	vaginal lubrication, penile erection, orgasm
nipple stimulation	milk release (in a lactating female)
Circulatory system	
high temperature	vascular dilation leading to sweating
sudden loud noise	vascular constriction leading to pounding heart
Respiratory system	
irritation in the nose	sneeze
throat clogged	cough
Muscular system	
low temperature	shivering
blows or burns	withdrawal
touch to eye	eyeblink
light to eye	pupil constriction
novel stimulation	reflexive orienting
sudden stimulus onset	startle
strong aversive stimuli	attack, bite
Infant reflexes	
touch to the cheek	head turning
object touches lips	sucking
food in mouth	swallowing
object in the hand	grasping
mild aversive stimuli	squirm, vocalize

and aversive sensations. After one or two pairings, the sight and taste of the new food becomes a CS that will elicit nausea and aversive sensations in the future. When they are sexually receptive, female primates often give off a variety of cues, such as special ways of walking, approaches to males, and coloration of the genitals. When males approach receptive females who are showing these cues, they are more likely to experience genital stimulation than when approaching nonreceptive females. Thus, most males experience the following Pavlovian conditioning: The cues of female receptivity are paired with genital contact, a US that elicits the reflexive responses of penile erection and ejaculation (UR's); hence the cues of receptivity become CS's that can elicit sexual

PLATE 4.2. A male chacma baboon looks as a female presents to him. Her appearance provides $^+$CS's that reinforce his looking. (*Photo by G. S. Saayman.*)

responses (such as penile erection) even before the male makes physical contact with a receptive female.

Pavlovian conditioning allows reflexive responses to be elicited by CS's because these stimuli have regularly been paired with certain US's in the past. Higher order Pavlovian conditioning occurs when additional new CS's are created by pairing neutral stimuli with CS's rather than with US's. Once a certain food has become a CS associated with nausea and illness, any new locations where the food is regularly found may become second order CS's due to pairing with the food CS (even though the food is not eaten, hence the US of bad food in the stomach never appears). As Pavlovian conditioning creates new CS's, it increases the number of stimuli that an individual can respond to with biologically significant responses.

Organisms are biologically prepared to respond to some US's more easily than others, and certain stimuli can be conditioned into CS's more quickly than others.[22] These types of preparedness are usually under-

[22] Once it was thought that a stimulus had to appear within one second of a US in order to produce conditioning, and in many cases this is true; but conditioning based on a high degree of preparedness can be established with much longer time lags (Revusky and Garcia, 1970 and Seligman and Hager, 1972).

standable in terms of natural selection. A monkey may eat some small red berries and be listening to a bird call before the US of bad food in the stomach elicits regurgitation and aversive sensations. Due to biological preparedness, visual or gustatory stimuli from foods that preceded the regurgitation reflex are much more likely to become CS's for nausea than are sounds that were heard before the sickness began.[23] Natural selection favors individuals with physiological mechanisms that associate sights and tastes with illness responses, while not associating irrelevant stimuli (such as sounds) with the reflex. This does not mean, however, that no irrelevant conditioning ever occurs or that the precise nature of the conditioned stimuli can be predicted from data on selection alone. Conspecifics living in different environments can learn to respond to quite different CS's, depending on the nature of their local environments. In one environment, small red berries may elicit illness and cause squirrel monkeys to respond to these berries as a CS for nausea. However, in another environment another species of plant may bear small red berries that are nutritious and nontoxic. In this environment squirrel monkeys will learn to respond to red berries as a CS for salivation.

As conditions change in any given environment, they create new patterns of Pavlovian conditioning that change the associations between CS's and the relevant reflexes. First, if an established CS is no longer paired with the stimuli that elicit a given reflex, it gradually loses its ability to elicit the reflexive responses. This process is called extinction. Second, new stimuli that become paired with the US's or CS's of a reflex may become new CS's that can elicit the reflex. These two processes allow the continuous adjustment of conditioned reflexes as environmental conditions change. For example, sudden or sharp stimulation near the eyes elicits the eyeblink reflex. When the infant primate rides on its mother's body, its face may occasionally be brushed by foliage as mother moves through the forest. Due to this conditioning, the sight of foliage ahead may become a CS that elicits the eyeblink. After the infant grows up and gains skill at jumping through the branches, it may learn operant skills for avoiding having foliage hit its eyes. Since the sight of approaching foliage is no longer paired with blows to the eye, the eyeblink will cease to appear in response to the previous CS of approaching foliage. However, the maturing individual may be exposed to new conditioning. New stimuli—such as the sight of an aggressive male swatting toward the face—may become new CS's that elicit the eyeblink.

Thus, Pavlovian conditioning helps adjust each individual's responses to its local environment and allows changes all through life as either the environment or the individual's relation to the environment change.

---

[23] Wilcoxon et al. (1971).

Pavlovian conditioning provides a much more sensitive and rapid mechanism for modifying reflexive responses than does natural selection.

US's can have two functions: (1) as *eliciting stimuli* that elicit unconditioned reflexes, and (2) as *unconditioned reinforcers* or *unconditioned punishers* that shape operant behavior. After a neutral stimulus has become a CS due to Pavlovian conditioning, the CS can have similar functions: (1) as an *eliciting stimulus* that elicits a conditioned reflex, and (2) as a *conditioned reinforcer* or *conditioned punisher* that shapes operant behavior.

CS's as Eliciting Stimuli

If there were no mechanisms for Pavlovian conditioning, the unconditioned reflexes would provide only limited service and protection for an individual. If animals could not learn from past experience, the reflexes would only appear *after* the biologically determined US's were present. The eyeblink would appear only after a twig hit the eye or face. Penile erection would appear only after genital contact had been initiated. In some cases (though not all), this slowness to respond would be to an individual's disadvantage. The eye might be injured before the lid closed. During a brief sexual opportunity, the male might not respond fast enough to gain intromission.

Learning mechanisms that allow an individual to respond to cues that precede US's confer a selective advantage. The animal who blinks before a twig hits the eye may escape an eye injury. The male who has an erection before mounting a female may have a higher probability of successful copulation, especially if time is short. Pavlovian conditioning allows new stimuli that have preceded the US's in the past to become CS's for the relevant reflex. Because these CS's are likely to appear before the US in the future, they can elicit a form of the reflex before the US actually appears. Thus, CS's that precede US's serve as "priming signals" or "warning signals" that activate the reflexive mechanisms early, producing early or incipient versions of the response. By priming the reflexive mechanisms, CS's can also speed the occurrence of the full unconditioned response when the US does appear, and—as described below—coordinate the response into relevant operant chains. Rapid, coordinated responses are sometimes crucial to survival and reproduction. An eyeblink before being hit or a rapid sexual response need not always influence survival and reproductive success, but they are more likely to help than hinder.

Even the CS's that appear during (though not prior to) the presence of a US can function to facilitate survival and reproduction. Any CS's based on a given US that are present when the US is present add to the total stimulus input to create a stronger total eliciting effect. The extra eliciting power of the US combined with CS's helps guarantee that the response will appear in a strong, fully developed form. For example, during copulation a sexually experienced individual should have a stronger sexual response than an inexperienced one, since prior sexual contacts would have conditioned various stimuli present during coitus into CS's that help elicit stronger responses.

The US's that elicit unconditioned reflexive responses tend to be the most universal and unchanging stimuli related to the response. Touch to the genitals, objects in the esophagus, and bad food in the stomach are the most universal and unchanging correlates of sex, choking, or food poisoning. They tend to correlate with the relevant reflex in almost all environments. Natural selection favors individuals who respond to these universal, unchanging correlates as US's for unconditioned responses, since these individuals respond appropriately in whatever environment they live. Then during Pavlovian conditioning, numerous additional stimuli in each individual's unique environment become CS's that also elicit relevant reflexes. Thus, all monkeys regurgitate in response to bad food in the stomach, but one monkey becomes nauseous at the sight of small red berries whereas another becomes nauseous at the sight of green caterpillars. It is usually adaptive for primates to respond to the most unchanging and universal of biologically meaningful cues as US's, without any learning needed. And it also tends to be adaptive for them to be able to learn which particular stimuli in their own unique environments most often correlate with those US's so they can respond early and vigorously to these important stimuli.

CS's as Conditioned Reinforcers and Conditioned Punishers

Pavlovian conditioning not only increases the number of stimuli that will elicit various reflexes, it increases the number of stimuli that will serve as reinforcers and punishers. After Pavlovian conditioning in which little blue berries come to elicit salivation and little red berries come to elicit the regurgitation reflex, the blue berries can serve as conditioned reinforcers and the red ones can serve as conditioned punishers. Operants of seeking blue berries are reinforced, and operants of seeking red berries are suppressed.

During the remainder of the text, the unconditioned reinforcers—such as food for a hungry animal—will be designated as positive unconditioned stimuli, or $^{+}$US's. The unconditioned punishers—such as cuts or blows—will be designated as negative unconditioned stimuli, or $^{-}$US's. As new stimuli become CS's during Pavlovian conditioning, some will become positive conditioned stimuli ($^{+}$CS's), if they are paired with $^{+}$US's. Others will become negative conditioned stimuli ($^{-}$CS's),

PLATE 4.3. Tactile stimulation is an important unconditioned positive stimulus that reinforces grooming and makes social interaction a $^+$CS. An adult female Mayotte lemur (*Lemur fulvus mayottensis*) is shown grooming an adult male. (*Courtesy of The American Museum of Natural History and Ian Tattersall.*)

if they are paired with $^-$US's. All of these stimuli—$^+$US's, $^-$US's, $^+$CS's, and $^-$CS's—have two functions: They can serve as (1) eliciting stimuli and (2) reinforcers or punishers.

Because $^+$CS's and $^-$CS's can function as conditioned reinforcers and punishers, Pavlovian conditioning extends the number of reinforcers and punishers beyond the biologically established unconditioned reinforcers and punishers to include many new conditioned stimuli. These conditioned reinforcers and punishers can differ from individual to individual, since they depend on the past experience of each individual in its unique subset of the environment. Because Pavlovian conditioning causes each individual to respond to conditioned reinforcers and punishers that suit the unique properties of its environment, it helps adjust operant behavior to each unique environment by adjusting the conditioned reinforcers and punishers. Animals learn to seek out $^+$CS's (such as the sight of nutritious food) because these stimuli have been associated with unconditioned reinforcers in the past, and they learn to avoid contact with $^-$CS's (such as poisoned food) because these stimuli have been associated with unconditioned punishers in the past.

Since $^+$CS's and $^-$CS's are created and maintained by regular pairing with $^+$US's and $^-$US's, conditioned reinforcers and punishers usually correlate well with unconditioned reinforcers and punishers. Because the $^+$US's and $^-$US's are biologically adjusted by natural selection, both US's and the correlated CS's usually produce operant conditioning that is biologically adaptive. For example, as the young infant has repeated positive experiences with its mother—who is the source of such $^+$US's as food, warmth, and appropriate tactile stimulation—the mother becomes a $^+$CS for the infant. The $^+$CS's can both elicit reflexes (such as the emotional responses of security) and reinforce operant behavior. Once the mother becomes a $^+$CS for an infant, even the sight of mother can elicit positive emotional responses of security and help calm an infant who has been hurt or frightened.[24] The $^+$CS's also function as conditioned reinforcers that reward the infant for such adaptive operants as staying near mother, traveling with her in group processions, and approaching for interaction.

There are, however, interactions between operant and Pavlovian conditioning that can produce maladaptive operant behavior. For example, needless fears and avoidance responses often fail to extinguish, even when it would be adaptive for them to do so. That is, a $^-$CS often fails to become a neutral stimulus even when it is no longer associated with a $^-$US. This is true because the $^-$CS may motivate such strong operant avoidance responses that the individual never comes close enough to contact the $^-$CS and discover that it is no longer associated with a $^-$US. Thus, animals who avoid the $^-$CS never have a chance for extinction to take place. This can produce maladaptive operant behavior. Once the sight of an aggressive adult male has become a $^-$CS for many group members, the $^-$CS may motivate consistent avoidance of that male. Avoidance prevents or retards extinction, such that the group members might not cease to fear the male even if the male lost his health and aggressive abilities. If unnecessary fears of an old, incompetent male prevent younger animals from gaining access to scarce food or sexual opportunities that the old male might monopolize, the unnecessary $^-$CS's would clearly be causing maladaptive operant behavior. The young would miss reinforcers of food or sex and perhaps suffer decreased fitness.

THE PRIME MOVERS OF CONDITIONING

The prime movers of operant conditioning are the unconditioned reinforcers and punishers, that is $^+$US's and $^-$US's. Conditioned reinforcers and punishers can also modify operant behavior, but these conditioned stimuli all take their power from the $^+$US's or $^-$US's with which they have been paired.

---

[24] Rheingold and Eckerman (1970) and Mason et al. (1974).

US's are also the prime movers of Pavlovian conditioning.[25] A neutral stimulus becomes a CS when it is paired with a US. Later new CS's can be created through higher order conditioning when neutral stimuli are paired with already established CS's. However, in the final analysis, all CS's take their strength from pairing with US's, the prime movers.

Because US's are the prime movers of both operant and Pavlovian conditioning, it is common to find both kinds of conditioning intertwined whenever the prime movers appear. When US's follow stimuli, they cause the stimuli to become CS's. When $^+$US's or $^-$US's follow behavior, they cause the frequency of the behavior to be modified, and antecedent stimuli to become S^D's or S^Δ's. Since the origin of all US's can be traced to natural selection, US's help tie proximal and distal causes for behavior into unified theories of natural learning.

We will usually refer to the prime movers as reinforcers and punishers—or differential reinforcement—because (1) most of the overt behavior of primates in their natural habitats is operant (rather than reflexive), (2) most of the US's (though not all) are either reinforcers or punishers ($^+$US's or $^-$US's),[26] and (3) all conditioned reinforcers and punishers take their strength from $^+$US's and $^-$US's.

BEHAVIOR CHAINS

Behavior often appears in sequences called chains. The structure of chains reveals yet another way in which proximal and distal causes are interwoven in the ongoing behavior of higher organisms. Therefore, the analysis of behavior chains is valuable in constructing balanced behavioral theories.[27]

Most behavior chains terminate in the acquisition of positive reinforcers or in the escape from aversive consequences. The following are common chains in primate life. A hungry monkey inspects an abandoned squirrel's next, climbs into a tall tree, lifts some branches, unfurls curled leaves, grasps an insect, puts the food in its mouth, chews, and swallows. A male and female might consort for an hour—moving together, exchanging glances, sniffing sexual odors—before the chain ends with copulation. A monkey might see a predator approaching at a distance, look up several times each minute to check the predator's location, then jump up into a tree when the predator comes too close.

---

[25] Terrace (1971) observes that this and other considerations may warrant a single factor learning theory that no longer distinguishes between operant and Pavlovian conditioning.

[26] Not all US's are unconditioned reinforcers or unconditioned punishers. For example, changes in light intensity cause reflexive changes in pupil size but are not reinforcers or punishers except in extreme circumstances (Staats, 1963:53).

[27] See Breland and Breland (1966) and Teitelbaum (1977) for further elaboration of these ideas.

Let us deal with chains that end in positive reinforcers before dealing with those involving the escape from aversive consequences.

Chains Ending with Unconditioned Positive Reinforcers

Many behavior chains lead to the acquisition of unconditioned positive reinforcers such as food, water, sex, optimal temperature, or the tactile stimulation of grooming. As is shown in Figure 4.2, these behavior chains typically begin with several operant behaviors (such as hunting for food, seizing it, putting it into the mouth, and chewing it) and lead to consummatory responses (such as salviating and swallowing). The earliest links of the chain—hunting and seizing—generally show the greatest degree of flexibility and freedom to be modified by proximal causes. Within a given species, different individuals may learn different variations on hunting and locating food, depending on their unique histories of learning experience. At the other end of the chain, the consummatory responses are usually much more biologically prepro-grammed and stereotyped than the earlier operant behavior, though they can be modified to some degree by both operant and Pavlovian conditioning.[28] As an individual progresses through a chain from the earliest operants toward the consummatory response, learned responses (predominantly under proximal control) grade into more biologically wired-in responses (predominantly under distal control). Behavior typically involves progressively less variation and learning as the chains reach the consummatory response. Chewing shows less variation than does hunting; swallowing shows less variation than does chewing. The chain of eating responses eventually merges into a chain of digestive responses in the alimentary tract, and these show the least variability and least conditioning.

The means by which behavior chains are learned reveals how proximal and distal causes interact during the development of behavior. The stimuli that come between the end of the operant chain and the beginning of the consummatory responses are $^+$US's that serve as (1) unconditioned reinforcers for the operants that precede them and (2) eliciting stimuli for the reflexive responses that follow them. For example, food is a $^+$US for a hungry animal. Food reinforces the operants of

FIGURE 4.2. A chain of feeding responses.

hunt →	seize →	ingest →	chew →	salivate →	swallow
OPERANT	OPERANT	OPERANT	OPERANT	CONSUMMATORY RESPONSE	CONSUMMATORY RESPONSE

[28] Miller (1969) and Terrace (1971).

OPERANT _ _ _ ➤ OPERANT _ _ _ ➤ OPERANT _ _ _ ➤ OPERANT _ _ ⁺US _ _ ➤CONSUMMATORY
LINK # 4   LINK # 3   LINK # 2   LINK #1   RESPONSE

FIGURE 4.3. Operant links are learned in reverse order.

putting food in the mouth and chewing. Once the food is in the mouth, this US elicits salivation and eventually swallowing. (Due to Pavlovian conditioning, hungry animals may begin to salivate before the food enters the mouth, when they see or smell CS's that have been paired with food in the past.)

When chains are learned via differential reinforcement alone (without models), they are typically learned in reverse order. The operant link closest to the ⁺US (the unconditioned reinforcer) is learned first, then additional operants are learned one at a time in reverse order to produce links 2, 3, and 4, (see Figure 4.3). The animal is born with the capacity to produce the reflexive consummatory response once the ⁺US is present; and operant conditioning allows it to learn those operants that have been effective in the past in bringing the animal into contact with the ⁺US.

The newborn infant is biologically programmed to respond to a variety of biologically important stimuli as ⁺US's that elicit consummatory responses and function as reinforcers. Consider the process by which the newborn primate learns to find food when it is hungry. When objects touch the mouth of a neonate, they serve as US's that elicit the sucking reflex if the infant is hungry. When food enters the mouth, the neonate swallows reflexively. Any operant behavior—such as crawling to the nipple—that happens to occur before these two consummatory reflexes produces the ⁺US's that both elicit the reflexes and function as unconditioned reinforcers for the operant. Because it is followed by reinforcement, the operant of crawling to the nipple is reinforced to higher probability, and thus becomes the first link in the infant's earliest chain of learned feeding responses.[29] Operant conditioning also causes various parts of the mother's body to become S^D's for crawling to the nipples and S^Δ's for not crawling elsewhere. Thus, clinging to mother's back provides S^D's for crawling under the arm toward the nipple; clinging to her stomach provides S^D's for crawling upward to the nipple. In addition, Pavlovian conditioning causes the stimuli that occur before nursing to become ⁺CS's that elicit conditioned reflexes and function as conditioned reinforcers. Thus, the mere act of crawling toward nipple produces stimuli (from inside and outside the body) that become ⁺CS's that elicit salivation and serve as conditioned reinforcers. Figure 4.4

[29] Note that this first link, closest to the consummatory response, is in large part based on reflexive crawling responses, which helps reveal how operant chains grade into more biologically wired-in consummatory responses.

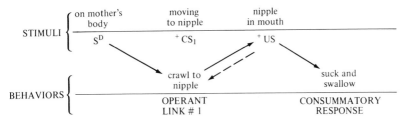

FIGURE 4.4. The S^D and CS in a one link operant chain.

shows the feeding chain at this stage of operant conditioning. The solid arrows indicate that one element in the chain leads to the next. A broken arrow indicates that a stimulus reinforces the prior operant.

After the first operant link has been learned and has become a positive conditioned stimulus (^+CS), this conditioned reinforcer can cause operant link #2 to be added to the chain. Responses that happen to precede link #1 can become operant link #2 because they are followed by the $^+CS_1$ (the conditioned reinforcers of link #1). For example, once the infant is old enough to leave its mother and explore the environment, time is spent both on and off her body. If an infant is hungry, climbing off the mother's body cannot become linked to the operant #1 of crawling to the nipple. However, if the hungry infant climbs onto its mother, it is exposed to the S^D's for crawling to the nursing position, and crawling to the nursing position is the $^+CS_1$ that reinforces the prior operant (link #2) of climbing onto mother's body. Gradually, climbing onto mother's body when hungry becomes well established as link #2 in the chain due to repeated reinforcement by $^+CS_1$; and through Pavlovian conditioning it becomes a second ^+CS ($^+CS_2$) because it is paired with the $^+CS_1$ of link #1. In addition, climbing onto mother comes under control of the $S^D{}_2$ of being near mother (while being hungry). Figure 4.5 shows the chain at this stage of development.

Once link #2 becomes a ^+CS, it can reinforce any response that commonly precedes it, and this permits the learning of operant link

FIGURE 4.5. The S^D's and CS's in a two link operant chain.

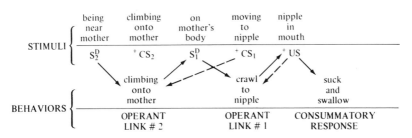

#3 in the chain. For example, when a hungry young infant is several meters away from its mother, it might generate a variety of responses, such as exploring the physical environment, vocalizing, sitting still, or running to mother. Of these various responses, running to mother is the one most likely to be followed by the reinforcer ($^+CS_2$) of climbing onto mother (link #2). The other responses do not lead to the reinforcer of link #2. Thus, differential reinforcement causes running to mother to become established as link #3 of the chain leading to nursing (Figure 4.6). Additional links may be added to the chain in this reverse order, making the chain even longer.[30]

As chains become longer, a considerable time lag can arise between early links and the unconditioned reinforcer (the ^+US). The time lag makes it appear that the individual is "working for a delayed reinforcer." However, the early links are reinforced by the ^+CS's that immediately follow them, even though the unconditioned reinforcer may not appear for many minutes. A male may consort with a receptive female for an hour or more, watching her, following slowly, and waiting for positive signs before approaching to mount. But watching, following, and looking for positive signs are all ^+CS's that reinforce the links leading up to copulation.

Several factors facilitate the learning of very long chains. Animals often have considerable genetic preparedness to learn certain types of operants and ^+CS's, and this preparedness allows long chains to be assembled relatively easily, with considerable time lags before the unconditioned reinforcer. Species with higher cortical capacity (and verbal ability in the case of humans) have an advantage in learning associations between early behavior links and delayed unconditioned reinforcers, hence they can learn to produce quite long behavior chains associated with delayed unconditioned reinforcers. A lengthy history of prior conditioning makes possible the learning of ever longer chains: As repeated conditioning adds more links, each link becomes an increasingly stronger ^+CS that can reinforce earlier links. Due to variable patterns of reinforcement, early links in long chains are sometimes followed quickly by unconditioned reinforcers; this strengthens the ^+CS's of early links and makes the chain quite resistant to extinction.[31] A consorting male may gain access to copulation within five minutes on one occasion (A), yet wait 60 minutes before copulation on another occasion (B). During the brief encounters (occasion A in Figure 4.7), the close asso-

---

[30] A more fine-grain analysis of this chain could have broken the chain into a larger number of small links. The level of analysis depends on the researcher's goals.

[31] Variable schedules of reinforcement produce strong conditioning that is resistant to extinction because the individual has learned that reinforcement can come at any time, early or late, hence continues to perform even when unconditioned reinforcers are delayed (Nevin, 1971 and Houston, 1976:160).

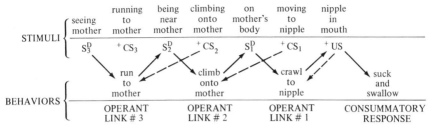

FIGURE 4.6. The S^D's and CS's in a three link operant chain.

ciation between early behavior links—such as link #4, watching receptive females—and copulating (the $^+$US) strengthens the $^+$CS's of those links, providing extra conditioned reinforcement that helps maintain behavior during longer waits (occasion B).

Not all behavior chains are learned in reverse order. Observational learning makes it possible for links to be acquired in other temporal orders. When a young male sees two adults consorting and then copulating, he may approach and watch. The young male may observe long chains of behavior, as the adult male and female exchange glances, approach, touch, sniff, groom each other, and finally the adult male mounts for intromission. The young male may imitate any of a variety of the adult's responses—without necessarily having to imitate link #1 before performing link #2 or #3.[32] For example, the young animal may approach an adult female, watch, and touch her side (links 5, 4, and 3) but not mount or thrust (links 2 and 1). If the early links (5, 4, and 3) lead to any reinforcement (novel experience, grooming, or perhaps play), they may become part of the young male's behavior repertoire, though not as the high probability responses that they will later be when the male learns the entire chain and experiences the $^+$US's of genital stimulation during copulation.

FIGURE 4.7. Five operant links (5, 4, 3, 2, and 1) may be closely or distantly associated with a $^+$US.

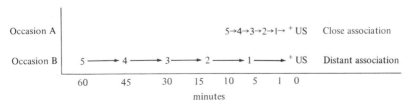

[32] de Benedictis (1973).

Chains Involving Unconditioned Punishers

Some behavior chains involve unconditioned punishers such as cuts, stings, falls, or painful blows. Chains that end in the onset of an unconditioned aversive stimulus are suppressed due to punishment, whereas chains that lead to the escape from or avoidance of an unconditioned aversive stimulus are strengthened by negative reinforcement. Experience with punishment precedes learning by negative reinforcement hence will be dealt with first.

An infant monkey may have learned a two-link chain—run toward and grab—due to the positive reinforcers of food or social play. If at a later time the infant runs toward a wasp and grabs it, the behavior chain is followed by the ⁻US of a sting. Grabbing the wasp (link #1 in Figure 4.8) is suppressed by the punishment and becomes a ⁻CS due to association with the ⁻US. Running toward wasps (link #2) will also become suppressed by the punishers that follow it. In addition, link #2 will become a ⁻CS, though weaker than the ⁻CS of link #1. The aversive stimuli tend to suppress the behavior in chains that end in unconditioned punishers (especially if the ⁻US is strong and there are no counteracting positive stimuli to reinforce the responses). The further an individual moves into an aversive chain, the stronger are the punishers; thus there is stronger response suppression as the individual nears the most powerful punisher, the ⁻US. After two stings, a monkey may still run part way toward a wasp the next time it sees one, but then show hesitancy about close approach, and no tendency to grab the wasp.

When the infant first grabbed the wasp and was stung, the aversive experience produced another effect besides punishment. The ⁻US of the sting elicited the reflex of hand withdrawal, which facilitated escape from other possible aversive consequences. This withdrawal reflex is a biologically wired-in response that functions effectively in quickly terminating contact with many types of ⁻US's. The ⁻US also caused the proximity of wasps and the sight of the hand moving toward the wasp to become ⁻CS's due to Pavlovian conditioning. In the future, when the infant sees a nearby wasp or sees its hand near a wasp, the ⁻CS's may elicit the hand-withdrawal reflex. In addition, any operants that help the individual escape the proximity of wasps or avoid stings will be negatively reinforced by the decreased salience of ⁻CS's. Thus, a

FIGURE 4.8. A chain involving an aversive stimulus.

monkey might learn the following operant chain for coping with wasps after the reflexive hand withdrawal: jump away to a safe distance, walk away while looking back from time to time, and watch closely for other wasps (Figure 4.9).

When learned via differential reinforcement alone (without models), the links of avoidance chains are usually learned in forward order, though the sequence of learning is less rigid than in positive chains. Once a monkey has been stung by wasps, wasps become $^-$CS's that can function as punishers and negative reinforcers. Any operant link that helps escape or avoid the $^-$CS will be negatively reinforced. However, the early links—such as jumping away—are most likely to be learned first since they are generated while the monkey is nearest the $^-$CS, and proximity makes the $^-$CS a more salient, potent negative reinforcer. Once the monkey has moved 4 meters away from the wasps (link #2), the $^-$CS occupies a relatively smaller portion of the monkey's perceptual field, hence has less ability to strengthen the second link in the chain. Thus, the early links are more likely than later links to be learned quickly and to be reinforced to high probability.

After a negatively reinforced chain is learned, the individual may enter the chain at any point and usually avoid the $^-$US. The sight of wasps is not only a $^-$CS, it is an S^D for all the operants of escape and avoidance. If the monkey sees wasps at 2 meters, the S^D's may evoke walking away. If it sees wasps at 0.2 meters, the S^D's may evoke jumping back, then walking away. The stronger the conditioning, the less likely the individual is to wait until directly contacting the $^-$US before responding. Eventually, distant perception of the $^-$CS will motivate the avoidance sequence.

As each primate grows up and gains experience, it may learn that various insects, predators, poisonous foods, and aggressive group members are sources of aversive stimulation. As these stimuli become $^-$CS's, the individual learns to be alert to the presence of these danger stimuli and to avoid them. If an avoidance chain begins to extinguish and fails to prevent contact with the $^-$US, renewed contact with the $^-$US will punish careless responding and recondition stronger $^-$CS's that will motivate stronger avoidance in the future.

Observational learning can allow individuals to learn avoidance responses to stimuli that they have never contacted. If they observe a model avoiding a stimulus and generating $^-$CS's that correlate with the

FIGURE 4.9. Avoidance chains are learned due to negative reinforcement.

presence of the avoided stimulus, the avoided stimulus is likely to become a ⁻CS for the observers without their having any direct aversive
contact with the stimulus themselves. If a mother squirrel monkey
shows a strong fear response to snakes and avoids them, her infant
learns by observation to avoid snakes, too.[33] Because the mother's alarm
calls, flight, and agitation have previously become ⁻CS's for the young,
they cause the snake to become a ⁻CS by higher order Pavlovian conditioning. The infant may imitate the mother's avoidance links #2 and
#3 (which are negatively reinforced by the escape from the ⁻CS's of
the snake) without ever learning escape link #1 (which would have
been learned from direct contact with a snake).

OBSERVATIONAL LEARNING

Not all behavior is learned by differential reinforcement. Primates can
acquire information about behavior from observing the behavior of others, and this information facilitates the production of imitative responses. Although observational learning occurs in prosimians, it tends
to be more common in advanced primates with larger brains;[34] and each
species doubtlessly has limits on the complexity of responses its members can acquire via imitation.[35] Because humans can learn operant
responses from differential reinforcement, observation, prompts, and
verbally encoded rules, their modes of behavior acquisition are more
complex than those of the nonhuman primates (Chapter 8).

Observational learning provides a means of acquiring new operant
behavior and discriminations that is more rapid than differential reinforcement alone.[36] In many social species, the capacity for observational
learning can greatly increase an individual's probability of survival and
reproduction. Individuals who can learn by observation do not need to
have firsthand experience with predators, poisonous foods, or other
dangerous stimuli to acquire appropriate responses: They can learn by
observing the few who have had first hand experience (i.e., whose
behavior has been shaped by differential reinforcement). Novel innovations and group traditions can be acquired by observation, allowing
all group members to learn from the discoveries of a few. For example,
a female Japanese macaque named Imo began washing her sweet potatoes in the sea before eating them, As others imitated, the practice
spread to some 90% of her group within 10 years.[37] Imo also invented
a method of separating out wheat grains that had become mixed with

---

[33] Huebner et al. (1979).
[34] Beck (1974) and Welker (1976).
[35] Feldman and Klopfer (1972); Beck (1973); and Chamove (1974).
[36] Bandura (1969) and Jouventin et al. (1977).
[37] Kawai (1965) and Itani and Nishimura (1973).

PLATE 4.4. Two adult male chimpanzees are "fishing" for termites. This behavior is passed to the young through observational learning. (*Photograph by C.E.G. Tutin.*)

sand: She took the wheat and sand mixture to the water and dropped it in. When the sand sank, the wheat was left on the surface, where it could be scooped up and eaten. As other monkeys observed and imitated this practice, the new skill was spread throughout the group. Imitation tends to be most common among familiar individuals, regardless of whether they are kin or not, which helps explain the routes of transmission by which innovations spread through groups.[38] Because each individual can learn from others, all can acquire a behavior repertoire larger than any single individual would be able to learn by itself.

Observational learning plays an important role in behavioral development. Because young primates usually grow up in groups, they can observe older animals who model behavior that is often associated with reinforcing results. The very young may be able to imitate only the simplest of modeled behavior; but as they mature and learn more com-

[38] Kawai (1965); Wechkin (1970); Menzel (1972); and Itani and Nishimura (1973).

plex skills, they can successfully imitate ever more complex behavior. An observer may not be able to perform a modeled behavior instantly, but crude early imitations serve as the behavioral raw material from which more sophisticated behavior can be shaped by differential reinforcement. For example, young chimpanzees imitate adult termite fishing only crudely at first; but repeated observational learning coupled with the differential reinforcement of successes and failures leads to the gradual learning of correct tool use.[39] Usually, the easier the task is and the more behavioral skills already existing in the observer's repertoire, the faster the observer will learn to produce an adequate imitation of the model's behavior. Difficult tasks are not learned quickly, even if observation is involved (Figure 4.10).

It is important to emphasize that imitative responses depend on reinforcement to be mastered and retained in an individual's behavior repertoire: Nonreinforcement or punishment will cause any given imitative response to become less frequent. Thus, an innovative response is likely to become a group tradition spread by imitation only if the new response produces reinforcing consequences.[40] If the environment changes such that an old tradition is no longer reinforcing, even established traditional responses extinguish and fail to be propagated by imitation.

Generalized imitation is not common.[41] Primates see more behavior modeled each day than they can possibly imitate; and most individuals learn early in life to imitate only a subset of all the behavior that they see modeled by others. What determines which behavior will be imitated? Primates learn to become discriminating imitators, and they learn to imitate models and behaviors similar to those whose imitation led to reinforcement in the past. They are less likely to imitate models and behavior that was associated with nonreinforcement or punishment in the past. Thus, as an infant imitates mother's feeding practices or traveling patterns and finds these reinforcing, the reinforcement increases the probability of imitating any traditions, tool use, or other behavior modeled by mother. The infant may even make repeated attempts to imitate responses that are beyond its present level of skill—hence that bring no reinforcers to the infant—merely because mother is such a strong S^D for imitation. However, if the infant imitates the mother's jump at a wide gap and experiences a hard fall, it will begin to discriminate between behaviors whose imitation leads to reinforcement and those whose imitation leads to punishment. Thus, reinforcement and punishment are in yet another way crucial determinants of observational learning.

[39] van Lawick-Goodall (1968, 1970).
[40] Beck (1975).
[41] Bandura (1969, 1977).

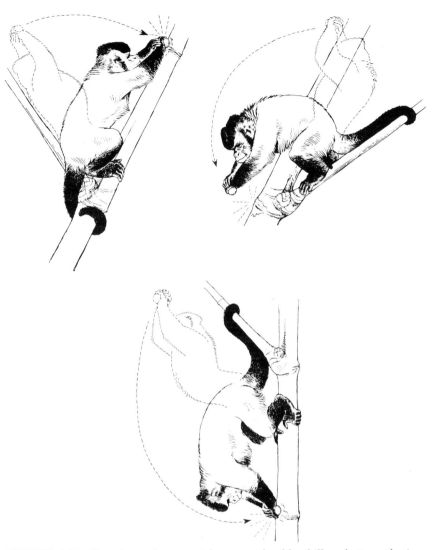

FIGURE 4.10. Opening palm nuts takes considerable skill and strength since the nuts are thick and difficult to open. Young capuchins learn from observing adults and from practicing until differential reinforcement shapes the appropriate skills. (*Courtesy of K. Izawa.*)

OTHER FORMS OF LEARNING

There are three forms of learning that are sometimes held out as exceptions to the general rule that reinforcers and punishers are the prime movers of learning. These three are insight, imprinting, and nonreinforced (or contiguity) learning.

Insight

When an animal solves a problem without any apparent differential reinforcement or observational learning, the behavior is sometimes described as insightful learning.[42] The term "insight" is thus a descriptive category rather than an explanation. The causes of insight are not yet fully understood.

Insight is more commonly found in advanced species with highly developed cortical processing ability. Köhler's (1925) experiments clearly indicate that chimpanzees can solve new problems without having to learn each particular solution from scratch via operant conditioning or from models. However, the chimpanzees in his experiments had extensive prior learning experience, hence had learned large repertoires of operant behavior for coping with many environmental situations.[43] Insightful responses may result from having a large, complex behavior repertoire that allows an individual to combine several skills to produce novel responses.[44] A new combination of old skills may result, in part, from an extension of prior skills to a new situation through the process of generalization. Toying with novel recombinations is usually quite reinforcing for primates, due to the sensory stimulation it brings.[45] Prior reinforcement for creative combinations of old skills can increase the probability of creative combinations to a significant level.[46] A large cortex and special genetic preparednesses doubtlessly facilitate the process even further. Premack and Woodruff's (1978) analysis of insight supports the view that chimpanzee insight consists of recombining and linking together in a novel way several operants that have previously been acquired through differential reinforcement or observation. New chains that are successful in producing reinforcing consequences appear to be adaptive and are easily labeled insightful. However, some newly combined chains may not lead to the rewards of successful problem solving hence not appear to be insightful, even though many of the same behavioral processes were involved in producing both the successful and unsuccessful responses.

The research on learning sets may help clarify insight, too. When primates are given several sets of related problems to solve and correct solutions are reinforced, the animals gain skill in problem solving.[47] During early learning sets, an individual may be slow in learning the solution, as differential reinforcement slowly shapes the correct behavior needed to solve the problem. After learning how to solve several related

---

[42] Maier and Maier (1973:105).
[43] See Beck (1978) for a similar critique of Köhler's work.
[44] Spence (1938) and Birch (1945).
[45] Harlow et al. (1950); Chapter 7, below.
[46] Pryor et al. (1969) and Rumbaugh (1974).
[47] Harlow (1949); Miles (1965); Rumbaugh (1970); and Essock-Vitale (1978).

sets of problems, the individual gains skills at problem solving; and the early slow solutions are replaced by more rapid solutions that look more like insight. Thus, individuals who have had considerable experience with complex environments may learn how to produce such successful solutions to new problems that one gets the impression that they are solving the problems due to abstract cognitive processes alone. However, when we consider the prior history of differential reinforcement and observational learning, it is likely that in many cases insight is only a variation on operant and observational learning.

No matter how one approaches insight, it is clear that insight is largely under the control of reinforcers and punishers as prime movers (as are operant conditioning, Pavlovian conditioning, and observational learning). Köhler's chimpanzees made their insightful responses of stacking boxes on top of each other because these responses led to the acquisition of food reinforcers—such as bananas suspended from the roof. Imo, the innovative Japanese macaque who initiated several group traditions, was also behaving under the influence of food reinforcers when she discovered methods of sweet potato washing and separating wheat from sand.[48] Reinforcement is also an important determinant of the future frequency of insightful behavior. Insightful behavior that leads to punishment or nonreinforcement is not likely to be repeated in the future, but insightful acts that lead to reinforcement are likely to become a part of the individual's active behavior repertoire.

According to Lloyd Morgan's (1894) Canon, "In no case may we interpret an action as the outcome of the exercise of a higher psychical faculty if it can be interpreted as the outcome of the exercise of one that stands lower in the psychological scale." According to this criterion, animal insight appears to be closely related to operant and observational learning, though perhaps involving special preparednesses to recombine old operants in novel ways and to have incipient responses modified by conditioned reinforcers without necessarily having to act them out first.[49]

Imprinting

Imprinting, as defined by Lorenz (1937b), Hess (1959), and other early researchers was considered to be a permanent and irreversible type of learning that could occur only during a critical period—usually during

[48] Kawai (1965) and Nishimura (1973).

[49] Human insight also benefits from symbolic mediation and the internal dialogue that people carry on as they covertly talk to themselves (Mead, 1934; Staats, 1963, 1968, 1975; Meichenbaum and Cameron, 1974; Mahoney, 1974; and Rosenthal and Zimmermann, 1978). People often produce remarkably insightful responses after considerable prior experience has allowed them to respond to large "chunks" of the present stimulus context as an S^D for adaptive responses (Larkin et al., 1980).

early development. Imprinting was seen most often in precocial birds—such as chicks and ducklings—who follow and become strongly attached to their mothers in the first days of life. It was suggested that this type of rapid, irreversible learning was very different from operant and Pavlovian conditioning. Subsequent research raised serious questions about the early characterization of imprinting.[50] It was discovered that imprinting is not permanent or irreversible. It can occur at various ages, not merely during a limited critical period. Once a chick or duckling is imprinted on one target stimulus, it can also be imprinted on others. Recent experiments by Hoffman and his colleagues have provided strong evidence that Pavlovian conditioning is "the heart of imprinting."[51]

Imprinting, as defined by Hoffman, occurs when an animal—e.g., a young chick or infant monkey—is exposed to a stimulus that serves as an unconditioned positive reinforcer. Movement, certain colors, and sounds serve as these $^+$US's for young birds; contact comfort and warmth are $^+$US's for young primates. After a young animal has several exposures to a mother or a surrogate mother who provides $^+$US's, Pavlovian conditioning causes the unique features of the mother to become $^+$CS's. Thus, mother becomes a conditioned positive reinforcer. Eventually, merely seeing mother at a distance elicits positive conditioned emotional responses, and the young animal learns to perform operants—such as following, staying near, or calling if lost—that allow it access to the stimulus. New associations can be learned at a later time, allowing the individual to become attached to more than one stimulus.[52] Thus, Pavlovian conditioning produces the positive conditioning called "affection;" and operant conditioning produces the more visible overt behavior of staying near mother.

Following Hoffman's approach, we categorize imprinting as Pavlovian conditioning and appropriate infant behavior as operants which are differentially reinforced by access to the positive stimulus of mother. Hence attachment processes described in this book will be explained in terms of Pavlovian and operant conditioning. The term imprinting will not be used, in order to minimize confusion with the concept as defined by Lorenz and other early workers.

Nonreinforced Learning (Contiguity Learning)

Contiguity theory states that stimulus patterns can be learned without reinforcement, merely because certain stimuli appear in contiguous patterns. As mentioned in Chapter 2, there are forms of learning that are

---

[50] Hinde (1963); Salzen (1966); and Salzen and Meyer (1968).
[51] Hoffman and Ratner (1973a,b) and Hoffman and DePaulo (1977).
[52] Harlow et al. (1972) and Mason and Kinney (1974).

based on differential sensory experience that may not involve differential reinforcement. Differential exposure to sensory inputs tends to produce differential development of those pathways in the central nervous system that mediate the processing of these stimuli.[53] Individuals who have experienced certain stimulus patterns develop greater cortical processing capacity for dealing with those stimuli than do conspecifics who have not had experience with those stimulus patterns. Each individual may develop different processing specialties depending on its unique past experiences, and this within-species variability in processing mechanisms is not genetically determined.

Hebb's (1949, 1972) theory of cell assembly development suggests that nerves may become functional units merely as the result of being stimulated at the same time while processing any given pattern of stimulus inputs, without the need for reinforcement. Data from animals who have had restricted sensory experience support the theory that pathways in various brain regions become better constructed the more they are stimulated and used.[54] Although reinforcement may not be needed for these constructive processes to occur, Hebb (1972:100) indicates that reinforcement may prolong the neural activity of those cell assemblies related to reinforcement and thus facilitate their development.

Contiguity learning deviates furthest from the model that equates reinforcers and punishers with the prime movers of natural learning. Contiguity learning fits more easily into balanced biosocial theory as a mode by which differential exposure to the constructive environmental inputs of sensory stimulation cause differential development of neural mechanisms.[55]

LEARNING SPECIES-SPECIFIC BEHAVIOR

Primates of the same species, but living in two different environments, often show considerable behavioral differences, and these behavioral variations have led many primatologists to study the effects of proximal causes on behavior. Data on variability in behavior provided some of the earliest evidence for the importance of learning in animals living in their natural environments.

It should be clear that proximal causes also influence behavior that has little within-species variability. Nutrition, exercise, sensory stimulation, and other constructive inputs make crucial contributions to nor-

---

[53] Hebb (1949, 1972) and Houston (1976).
[54] Riesen (1961, 1965); Levitsky and Barnes (1972); Davenport et al. (1973); Greenough (1975) and Rosenzweig (1976).
[55] Although latent learning was once thought to be a form of nonreinforced learning, it is likely that latent learning is reinforced by optimal levels of sensory stimulation obtained during exploration (see Chapter 7).

mal behavioral development, even though they may not introduce much variability into the behavior of a species. Learning also makes important contributions to many behaviors that show little within-species variability.

As Crook (1970b:154) pointed out, "Many quite stereotyped . . . behaviours are in fact a consequence of conditions of learning being more or less uniform in a population." In the past, there was a tendency for researchers to assume that stereotyped behavior represented fixed action patterns or innate responses that were genetically programmed. Demonstrating that a behavior had little variability was often considered adequate evidence for strong genetic causation. Learning theory indicates that this need not be the case. Highly malleable behavior would be expected to show little variability from environment to environment if the controlling variables—the reinforcers, punishers, and models—did not vary between the environments.[56]

The nonsocial and social environments often expose a large number of individuals of a given species to relatively constant learning experiences, thus condition similar responses. For example, many nonsocial tasks impose similar contingencies of reinforcement on all individuals. If baboons living in arid country dig holes in low sandy areas, the digging may be reinforced by access to water.[57] If they dig elsewhere they are unlikely to find water. The cues that predict when and where water will be found will be approximately the same for all animals, hence all individuals will form similar discriminations and their digging will come under the stimulus control of very similar S^D's. Because all baboons have similar anatomical structures for digging in sand, similar response patterns are likely to be reinforced. Thus, the similarity of the task and of the anatomical tools will condition similar response patterns. Chimpanzees living in different environments often show similar styles of opening foods, carrying objects, or building sleep nests because each task imposes similar contingencies of reinforcement on all individuals. Naturally, few tasks impose identical contingencies of reinforcement on all individuals, hence careful observation would reveal a certain amount of variability in even the most stereotyped of learned behavior.

The social environment often imposes similar contingencies on conspecifics, too, thus conditioning similar responses. Consider the social task of a male and female macaque in coordinating a sexual interaction.[58] From early in life, young male macaques show several sexual reflexes, among which are penile erection, pelvic thrusting, and a foot clasping

---

[56] It is possible to demonstrate experimentally the degree to which an invariant behavior is learned by systematically changing the controlling variables and observing whether the behavior changes, too.

[57] Kummer (1971) and Hamilton et al. (1978a).

[58] Hanby (1976); Testa and Mack (1977); Wolfe (1978); Goy and Wallen (1979); and Wallen et al. (1977). Also see Hopf (1979).

PLATE 4.5. A male rhesus monkey performs the species-typical mounting response. (*Courtesy of J.D. Loy.*)

response. In infants, these reflexes are not adequate to produce adultlike sexual interactions. When young male macaques first mount each other during play, there is considerable variability in postures. The variable behavior brings variable results—some of which are reinforcing and some of which are not. Mounting that approximates the adult posture is more likely to result in contact of the male and female genitalia. Because genital stimulation is a reinforcer for both partners, mutual reinforcement causes the mutually stimulating patterns to become more common than other mounting postures. Mounting in any other posture produces less reinforcement for at least one of the two partners, hence the use of the nonreinforced positions becomes less frequent. Gradually, mounting the partner's side or shoulder appear less often, and mounting that produces mutual genital stimulation becomes the predominant pattern. If the young imitate older animals, the learning process is usually hastened.[59] Because the anatomical fit between male and female ma-

[59] de Benedictis (1973).

caques allows only certain positions to produce the mutually rewarding genital stimulation, these positions are most likely to be learned as the species-typical copulatory postures. Given the similar contingencies of reinforcement, it is not surprising that there is a high degree of similarity in sexual behavior among the adults of any given species of macaques living in social groups (though variations do occur since no two animals have identical learning experience). Of course, laboratory individuals who are raised in social isolation do not have the relevant social learning experience and differential reinforcement. As a result they do not learn to produce the species-typical adult mounting behavior (Figure 4.11).[60] Depending on the anatomical location of the genitals, geometry of the body parts, cortical processing capacity, and environmental conditions, some species can learn a considerable variety of copulatory positions that produce reinforcement for both male and female.[61]

Problems to Be Faced

The fact that operant behavior sometimes shows little variability within a species creates several problems for theories of animal behavior— problems that have not yet been adequately considered. First, data that demonstrate that a behavior is invariant or stereotyped do not *prove* that the behavior is innate or under strong genetic control. Even if the stereotyped behavior is highly adaptive—as is heterosexual mounting in the previous example—the double argument of adaptiveness and stereotyped performance does not prove that the behavior is under strong genetic control. Thus two of the arguments most frequently used by sociobiologists to "demonstrate" genetic causation are not sufficient. Sociobiologists will need to be knowledgeable about learning theory and skillful in experimenting with the controlling variables that affect learned responses before they can clearly demonstrate that learning is not operating in the development of a given stereotyped behavior.

Second, balanced biosocial theories also cannot use data on behavioral invariability and adaptiveness as the only evidence for determining the weightings of distal and proximal causes involved in producing a given behavior. Attempts to establish empirically defensible weightings of distal and proximal causes will require data on all developmental factors that influence behavior to ascertain the degree to which invariable behavior can be traced to genes or to crucial invariable features of the species' environment. All environmental causes must be investigated

---

[60] Mason (1960); Rogers and Davenport (1969); and Rogers (1973).

[61] Schaller (1963); Nadler (1976); and Savage-Rumbaugh and Wilkerton (1978). Laboratory and zoo environments often create very boring conditions in which animals receive reinforcers of sensory stimulation for exploring many varied sexual practices; thus sensory reinforcers can increase the range of sexual behavior seen in a given species (e.g., Akers and Conaway, 1979).

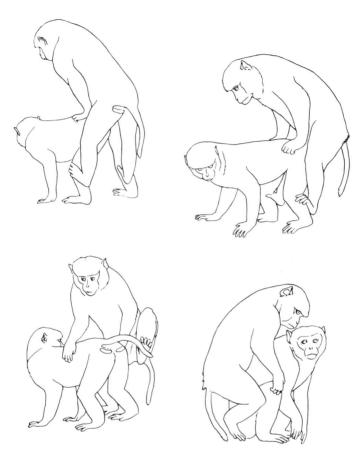

FIGURE 4.11. The top two figures show typical mounting postures of wild born rhesus monkeys. The bottom two pictures show the inadequate mounting postures of rhesus males who were deprived of relevant social learning experience during earlier years. (*Courtesy of W.A. Mason.*)

before one can rule out proximal causation and infer strong genetic causes for stereotyped behavior.

Third, these considerations add to the difficulties of comparing the behavior of different species in search of evolutionary trends in behavior.[62] In the past, observers often inferred that all differences in species-typical behavior between two species reflected genetic causes and unique evolutionary adaptations. Hence comparisons between species were presumed to reveal evolutionary trends or adaptations. When it is realized that some stereotyped behavior does not reflect strong genetic causation, it becomes clear that data on species-typical, invariant

[62] Hamilton et al. (1978a).

behavior do not warrant the inference of genetic causation and hence do not allow facile evolutionary comparisons. This problem is exacerbated by the fact that current studies often underestimate within-species variability (hence overestimate invariability). Since it takes many studies in different environments to locate and describe within-species variability in behavior, it takes extensive research on a species in numerous settings to estimate the extent of behavior variability. Thus, even behavior that was once thought to be invariable may prove to be quite variable once the behavior is studied in different environments.

BEYOND LAMARCKIAN LOGIC

Many biologists approach learning with Lamarckian views. They see learning taking place, recognize that there has been a rapid adjustment to current environmental conditions, then conclude that the animal has adjusted its behavior "by itself." This removes puzzlement, and removes interest in the processes by which learning takes place. The view that the animal adjusts itself to the environment stifles research on the means by which environmental stimuli condition and control learned behavior.

In the 1800s, there were similar problems in understanding evolution.[63] Many scientists were willing to recognize that the species changed and evolved, but the cause of change was thought to be in the organism itself, not in the environment. Lamarck argued that organisms had a built-in drive for perfection, and this type of teleological argument allowed many 19th century scientists to believe that the organism could change "by itself." Thus, few focused attention on the mechanisms by which the environment served as the agent of evolutionary change. When Darwin discovered the mechanism of selection, he greatly expanded our understanding of evolution. He observed that animal breeders were the environmental agents who caused change in domesticated species. In nature, predators, disease, conspecifics, and other environmental agents play the role of selector, determining which individuals reproduce and which do not. The organism plays an important role in evolution, but it is not the role of adjusting "by itself." For natural selection to occur, organisms must show variation, and selective agents must favor some variations over others. The individual's role is not to change itself, but to display the traits that will be selected by the environmental agents. Male baboons, for example, did not attempt to evolve long canines. They merely showed variation in canine length, and the environment favored the survival and reproduction of the individuals with long canines.

Any contemporary biologist who attributed evolutionary change to

---

[63] Mayr (1972, 1978).

the organism "itself"—without attention to ecological pressures, differential reproduction, and related mechanisms—would be soundly criticized for using Lamarckian logic. Unfortunately, many students of behavior continue to apply Lamarckian teleological logic to learned behavior. For example, primates are often described as intelligent and highly adaptable, as if these two characteristics of the animal "itself" were enough to explain how an individual adapts itself to the environment. Primates are often described as seeking adaptive solutions, learning to cope, solving ecological problems, and adjusting to their local environment. The emphasis is on the individual adjusting itself. Genetic idealism makes it easy to believe that organisms are genetically programmed to learn and adapt themselves in order to optimize fitness—the modern version of Lamarck's built-in drive for perfection.[64] When these teleological explanations are accepted as adequate, there is little motivation to look further, to analyze the mechanisms of learning, and to study how reinforcers, punishers, and models in the environment modify learned behavior.

There are enough similarities between the mechanisms of natural selection and learning (pages 26–43) to warrant a serious questioning of the Lamarckian approach to learning. Differential reinforcement is the prime mover of much of learning, much as differential reproduction is the prime mover of evolution. Variation in behavior provides the raw material from which differential reinforcement shapes new performances, much as genetic variation is the raw material for the natural selection of new evolutionary forms. The environment is the main determinant of both differential reinforcement and differential reproduction. Food, sex, water, hard blows, stings, and other reinforcers and punishers come from the environment. Food, water, conspecifics, predators, disease, and other determinants of differential survival and differential reproduction come from the environment. Thus learning theory directs our attention to the environmental distribution of reinforcers and punishers that produce differential reinforcement; and evolutionary theory directs our attention to the environmental distribution of resources and dangers that cause differential reproduction.

Although they are prime movers, differential consequences are not the only causes of learning or evolution. Learning is also influenced by models, induction, generalization, differential exposure to stimulation, and numerous other factors. Evolution is influenced by phylogenetic

---

[64] "Behavior scaling" and "multiplier effects" are genetically programmed "mechanisms" that Wilson (1975) postulated to allow the organism to adjust itself to its environment.

Words such as "adaptability," "intelligence," and "insight" are sometimes used by sociobiologists and others to indicate the existence of a self-adjusting capacity within the organism. These three terms can be used in a non-Lamarckian manner if the behavior from which adaptability, intelligence or insight is inferred is traced back to and explained in terms of a balanced weighting of proximal and distal causes.

inertia, mutations, gene flow, isolation, and numerous other factors. However, none of these secondary factors justify the reintroduction of teleological beliefs that the organism adjusts itself to its environment.

Biologists advanced their understanding of natural selection when they began to abandon Lamarckian teleological logic. In balanced bio-social theories, it is also important to deal with natural learning without using Lamarckian logic. Biologists made significant progress in analyzing the evolution of species when they began to study ecological patterns of food distribution, predator densities, and other determinants of differential reproduction. In order to make progress in the study of learning in natural environments, we need to analyze the ecological patterns of reinforcers, punishers, and models that mold the learned components of behavior.[65] Ecology becomes a key variable that unifies both our theories of natural selection and natural learning.

Learning has been well analyzed in artificial environments. The time has come to turn to more natural environments—both social and non-social—and study the major patterns of reinforcement, punishment, and modeling that operate there. Much as Darwin—already in possession of naturalistic data—utilized information on the artificial selection of domestic stocks to synthesize his theory of natural selection,[66] students of behavior can utilize the data on behavior in natural environments to extend laboratory analyses of learning to explain the ecological determinants of natural learning in natural environments. The next two chapters will further develop the model of natural learning by analyzing the microecological patterns that influence the behavioral development of the individual (Chapter 5) and the larger ecological patterns that shape social organization (Chapter 6). The study of conditioning and modeling in natural contexts is in its infancy and much remains to be done in elaborating on the basic model presented here.

CONCLUSION

In this chapter we have discussed the most important single topic neglected by sociobiology, learning. We have attempted to explain the processes of conditioning and observational learning in a way that clarifies their evolutionary importance and demonstrates how they interact with distal, biological variables. Although the old nature–nurture debate

---

[65] Although some fear that tracing the causes of behavior to the environment leads to a "passive organism" model, this is not the case. The organism is just as active as ever—it is merely that the environment makes some of the activities more frequent and others less frequent through differential selection or differential reinforcement. Exploration and play are two operant activities that are especially important in making primates active agents in discovering the properties of the environment and gaining skill in coping with the environment (Chapters 7 and 8).

[66] Darwin (1859).

tended to polarize behavioral scientists into studying either learning or evolutionary theories, it is time to go beyond either–or logic and discuss natural learning in terms that dovetail with evolution and discuss evolution in ways that interface with natural learning. By going beyond Lamarckian logic, balanced biosocial theories can treat learning in much the same way that Darwin taught us to deal with evolution. The advantages of removing teleology from learning promise to be as great as they were for removing teleology from evolution.

THE ROLE OF NATURAL LEARNING IN PRIMATE BEHAVIORAL DEVELOPMENT

Sociobiology has been criticized for being a *pre-formationist* theory because it assumes that the most important features of behavior are pre-formed by natural selection and are relatively uninfluenced by proximal factors during development.[1] Studies on behavioral development that are done from this preformationist perspective tend to see behavioral development as an automatic, preprogrammed unfolding of predetermined behavior traits. Development is usually viewed by sociobiologists as if behavior unfurled in a chronologically fixed sequence, much as a plant goes through a chronologically fixed pattern of germination, growth, flowering, fruiting, and dying. The "plant model" of behavioral development acknowledges the role of the environment in providing nutrients and a growth medium; but it places the greatest emphasis on genetically programmed developmental stages, each of which is presumed to be appropriate and functional for the relevant chronological age. Life cycle changes in behavior are traced to and explained by the operation of natural selection. For example, infant primates often play an hour or more a day, whereas adults rarely play. A preformationist theory

[1] Blute (1976); cf. Lehrman (1953).

would explain these data by showing that it is functional for infant monkeys to exercise and play so that they can grow strong and develop more adult behavior, whereas it is functional for adult monkeys to stop playing and allocate their efforts to foraging, defense, and reproduction. According to the logic of genetic idealism, each stage of behavioral development is a product of selective pressures that program adaptive age-specific behavior.

There is no question that biological maturation does determine and constrain the development of behavior to some degree. However, a heavy reliance on maturational explanations of behavior leads to a neglect of the role of proximal causes in the development of behavior. At some phylogenetic levels, this neglect of proximal causes may not be too problematic; but when dealing with advanced species the strategy can produce severely unbalanced theories of behavior.[2]

In this chapter we will draw upon data from the primates in order to demonstrate how proximal causes—especially natural learning—influence behavioral development. The emphasis will be on describing general primate patterns that clarify the basic developmental features common to most species. The study of behavioral development helps explain how biological determinants of behavior are interwoven with natural learning throughout the life cycle of the individual.

REFLEXES AS STARTERS

At birth, most primates are rather helpless and highly dependent on their mothers for protection, nurturance, warmth, transportation and, in short, survival. The newborn primate has a repertoire of inborn reflexive responses that function from birth to promote the infant's survival and attachment to its mother. These early reflexes include grasping, clinging, righting, crawling, rooting, sucking, alerting, visual orientation, vocalizations, along with several others.[3] The repertoire of early reflexes serves as the newborn's "survival kit" that helps the infant

[2] Even sociobiologists in their more cautious moments admit that nongenetic factors account for a large portion of behavior in advanced species. For example, Barash's (1977:41) Figure 3.1 indicates that some 58 to 85% of the behavior of nonhuman mammals might be traced to nongenetic causes, reaching about 87% in the case of humans. (Although Barash was not trying to put firm numbers on these weightings, the values shown in the figure clearly admit a heavy weighting of nongenetic causes.) Unfortunately, sociobiology gives no adequate theory for dealing with the nongenetic causes.

[3] Other reflexes include negative geotropism, sexual responses, head up, tail hanging (in some species), along with undifferentiated general body movements (Schusterman and Sjoberg, 1969; Rosenblum, 1971b; and Kaack et al., 1979). Reflexes often progress from an early "involuntary" stage to a later "voluntary" stage (Castell and Sackett, 1973). Some reflexes are not fully functional at birth, but become stronger during the "involuntary" period after birth. Operant conditioning is involved in shaping reflexes into "voluntary" activities.

get started in life. These inborn responses are, however, quite primitive and totally inadequate to assure survival away from the protective environment provided by the mother. Maturation of the muscles, nerves, and other behavioral mechanisms clearly establishes a precondition for the development of greater behavioral sophistication; and this maturation is dependent on genetic programming along with adequate nutrition, growth hormone, insulin release, sensory stimulation, and so forth.[4] Within the limits set by these biological constraints, each individual's learning experience accounts for the particular skills that are shaped from the early reflexes.

The clinging reflex is usually strong enough to guarantee that the newborn infant will have an adequate grip on its mother's fur to stay attached to her and not fall off even if she moves suddenly. In most species the mother does not need to support the infant at all. However, there are some species (e.g., chimpanzees and gorillas[5]) in which the newborn infant's clinging reflex is not adequate to guarantee attachment. Due to negative reinforcement the mother learns to provide extra support that prevents the infant from falling off her body or becoming distressed. When an infant slips into an insecure position, it may give reflexive distress vocalizations which come to serve as S^D's for the mother's adjusting and supporting the infant better.[6]

When the mother is stationary and the infant is not sleeping, the infant's crawling reflex may cause it to move over the mother's body to various positions. If the infant is hungry, tactile stimulation to the infant's face or lips functions as the US that elicits the rooting reflex: The infant pokes around with its mouth open, as if searching for something to put in the mouth. If something does enter the mouth, the stimulus is the US that elicits the sucking reflex. These three reflexes—crawling, rooting, and sucking—are usually quite adaptive because they help the infant find the mother's nipples and obtain milk without the need for prior learning. Of course, crawling, rooting, and sucking do not always result in nipple contact: Rooting and sucking may lead the infant to suck on the mother's tail, body hair, or ear. However, the absence of milk reinforcement—and perhaps a nudge from mother—serves to terminate and extinguish the nonnutritive sucking while orienting the infant to crawl and root further until eventually the nipples and milk reinforcers are discovered. After several exposures to this differential reinforcement, the infant begins to learn how to locate the nipples quickly and efficiently.[7] Various parts of mother's body become S^D's and S^Δ's that guide the infant to the nipple. In some species (such as

---

[4] Cheek (1971); Elias and Samonds (1974); and Rosenzweig (1976).
[5] van Lawick-Goodall (1967a:291f) and Schaller (1963:263).
[6] Mason (1968:75) and Ransom and Rowell (1972:110).
[7] Rogers (1973:190).

PLATE 5.1. Infant Japanese macaques often begin life riding in the ventral position (*right*) then switch to dorsal riding (*left*) as they gain increasing strength and skill. Dorsal riding is reinforced by the sensory stimulation of a better view of the environment. (*Photo by G. Gray Eaton of the Oregon Regional Primate Research Center.*)

the chimpanzee) it is not uncommon to see experienced mothers help their newborn infants reach the nipple.[8] However, "chimpanzees do not typically hold and carry the neonate at the breast area and primparous mothers do not reflexively place the hungry infant on the nipple" (Rogers and Davenport, 1970:367). Experienced mothers learn to help their infants because this maternal behavior is reinforced by nipple stimulation and milk release, which are $^+$US's for the mother.[9]

The infant also begins to learn where to cling to mother's body while riding or sleeping at night. During the night or other cool rest periods, the infant may learn to cling to mother's ventrum as she huddles to keep herself warm. The differential reinforcement from being warm or cold shapes these thermoregulatory responses.[10] When the mother joins group progressions during the warm daylight hours, the infant may

[8] Nicolson (1977).
[9] In zoos and cage environments, females may be deprived of the natural learning experience needed to produce adaptive maternal behavior (Arling and Harlow, 1967; and Missakian, 1969).
[10] Jeddi (1970); Harlow and Suomi (1970); and Baysinger et al. (1973).

learn to cling to other parts of the mother's body, due to differential reinforcement from clinging and riding in positions which protect it from scrapes with twigs, thorns, or branches and minimize the risks of slipping and falling.[11]

During the first days or weeks of life, the infant may spend much time riding passively and sleeping. From time to time it may crawl on the mother's body, nurse, and gaze about. However, day by day it shows increased levels of activity and prolonged periods of gazing at stimuli in the environment. Part of the increased activity results from maturational changes in the nervous and muscular systems. Part of the increased behavioral competence reflects the infant's learning of increased coordination and skill in coping with its environment. For example, baboon infants shift from ventral riding to dorsal riding as they gain strength, have less need for nipple contact, and become more curious about the environment.[12] Strength and skill allow the infant to ride on mother's back without the aversive consequences of slipping and falling; and the positive reinforcement for making the shift comes from being able to better observe the environment, hence obtain more reinforcers of novel sensory stimulation.

INBORN PERCEPTUAL CAPACITY

Newborn primates have a certain degree of genetically preprogrammed ability to perceive and respond to biologically significant stimuli from the nonsocial and social environment (provided that they have received adequate nutrition, sensory stimulation, and protection from injury, poison, or severe illness to permit the normal development of their perceptual and brain mechanisms).

The neonate has inborn mechanisms for perceiving important features of the *nonsocial* environment. Experiments have demonstrated that newly hatched birds and newborn mammals of many species can perceive depth sufficiently well to avoid "walking off the deep end" in tests with a visual cliff.[13] The inborn perceptual capacity doubtlessly conveys a selective advantage by helping newborn animals avoid falls without having to learn the hard way. Yet the inborn perceptual capacity is not adequate to prevent young animals from having some falls.[14] For example, young howler monkeys sometimes attempt to jump arboreal

---

[11] Infants raised in different environments may learn to cling and ride in different positions depending on the contingencies of reinforcement in their environments (Gartlan, 1973).

[12] Ransom and Rowell (1972:121).

[13] Gibson and Walk (1960); Walk and Gibson (1961); Rosenblum and Cross (1963); and Walk (1965).

[14] Carpenter (1934) and Glander (1975).

gaps that are too wide for their strength and skills, especially if they are behind the group and in danger of becoming separated. After a series of successes or failures at jumping gaps of different sizes, individuals learn finer discriminations than the inborn mechanisms provide about the size of gaps to be avoided. Small gaps that can be jumped easily become S^D's for jumping because jumping is reinforced by being able to stay with the group. Large gaps where an individual has had a fall become S^Δ's for not jumping, due to the prior punishment. Thus, differential reinforcement conditions discriminations about the sizes of arboreal gaps. These learned discriminations change for each individual as it matures. As a young primate gains strength and skill and can successfully negotiate wider gaps, a gap that was once an S^Δ for not jumping may become an S^D for jumping, as the individual learns to jump progressively wider gaps without aversive consequences. Also, stronger individuals learn different discriminations than weaker ones; and animals in forests with fragile branches that often break under the stress of a jump learn discriminations that differ from those of animals living in forests where the branches do not break when monkeys land on them. Besides an inborn perception of depth, infants appear to have inborn discriminations for most of the US's, certain distance cues, stimuli looming toward the eyes, and other important features of the physical environment.[15] These early discriminations are altered and elaborated on by the unique learning experiences each individual has in its own subset of the environment.

Some degree of *social* perception appears to be inborn, too. Sackett (1966, 1971) reported that infant monkeys without prior social learning experience recognize and spend more time orienting toward adult females of their own species than toward either females of other species or males of their own species. Infants raised with only 30 minutes a day exposure to pictures of monkeys responded playfully to pictures of infants (after 30 days of age) and fearfully to threat displays (after 80 days of age). Sackett (1971:106) summarized his findings as follows: "Even in primates, complex, unlearned mechanisms may underlie the development of species-normal social attachment behaviors and social communication functions." However, the data also demonstrate that "a built-in bias toward biologically appropriate behavior must be reinforced by specific experiences during infancy." For example, the early attraction to individuals of the same species breaks down once monkeys from restricted rearing begin to interact with their own species, perhaps due to aversive social exchanges or to the lack of positive reinforcement the isolate monkeys experience in these situations.[16]

[15] Schiff (1965) and Bower et al. (1971).
[16] Sackett (1971:69–70).

Although early innate social perceptual ability can facilitate the development of appropriate early social contacts, social learning experience is needed to build from the early abilities and condition the subtle and up-to-date discriminations needed for coping with the ever-changing social environment. Chamove and Harlow (1975:135) report that when rhesus macaques are raised with pigtail macaques, the rhesus quickly "learn to withdraw from the hostile lipsmack of the pigtails instead of responding by approach to what in rhesus language would be an affiliative or appeasement gesture." Thus, the lipsmack—which would be an S^D for approach in rhesus groups—becomes an S^Δ for not approaching after approach results in aversive interactions. Anderson and Mason (1974) found that rhesus monkeys raised in groups developed more sophisticated perceptual (and behavioral) skills than individuals raised in physical, but not visual, isolation. When tested in social groups at 11 months of age, "the experienced monkeys seemed to take into account more of the social information potentially available to them than did the deprived monkeys" (p. 689). The extra experience caused many subtle social cues to become S^D's and S^Δ's that controlled more complex social coordination than was seen among animals with less social conditioning. Monkeys reared in social isolation are incapable of utilizing much of the information in facial displays which feral monkeys can use.[17] Due to the lack of differential social reinforcement, these isolates have not learned to respond to the informative cues as S^D's and S^Δ's that set the occasion for appropriate operant responses.

THE INFANT'S ATTACHMENT TO MOTHER

The young infant forms a strong attachment to its mother for various reasons. Mother is a source of warmth, protection, milk, transportation, and contact comfort; and these reinforcers condition approach and attachment to the mother (page 104). Contact comfort is one of the most important $^+$US's that conditions the infant to respond to mother as a $^+$CS. Experiments with surrogate mothers indicate that the contact comfort provided by a soft terry cloth surrogate is more effective in causing an infant to attach to the artificial mother than are milk, warmth, or other stimuli. When infants are given a choice of a soft, terry cloth mother without milk or a wire mother with a milk nipple, they spend about 60–65% of their day on the soft terry cloth mother versus about 8% of the day on the milk-providing wire mother.[18] If the two surrogate mothers are located next to each other, the infant often clings to the soft

---

[17] Miller et al. (1967).
[18] Harlow (1959).

PLATE 5.2. An infant rhesus monkey maintains contact with its terry cloth surrogate mother while reaching for milk from the wire mother. (*Courtesy of H.F. Harlow.*)

mother and merely leans over to nurse from the wire mother without letting go of the soft mother (Plate 5.2).

Having access to mother in times of distress is crucial for the infant's learning increased autonomy. As the infant begins exploring the environment, it is exposed to various fear-arousing stimuli or stress-inducing stimuli. Returning to mother (or to a soft surrogate mother) and clinging to her soft, familiar, furry body provide the $^{+}$US's that counteract the fear and stress. As early as the first week of life, contact with a soft mother will suffice to reduce heart rate in infants whose heart rate was elevated by exposure to overly novel stimuli.[19] Contact also decreases plasma cortisol production (an indicator of stress). Thus, the mother

---

[19] Hill et al. (1973) and Coe et al. (1978).

serves as a source of security and arousal reduction for the infant when the infant has become overly aroused by environmental inputs, for example while exploring or playing. It is not uncommon to see infants wander off to explore the environment, encounter too many stimulating inputs, then hurry back to mother for a period of contact and security before resuming exploration.[20] After obtaining comfort and arousal reduction from mother, the infant is again ready to venture out, explore, and learn more about its world.

The arousal-reducing properties of contact comfort are probably the most important maternal qualities that reinforce the small infant's attraction and attachment to its mother.[21] The contact comfort experienced with a soft terry cloth mother is so reinforcing for infants that they will form strong attachments to stationary terry cloth mothers who do not "behave" at all.

However, infants develop more normal behavior if they are raised on soft mothers who provide both contact comfort and sensory stimulation. Mason (1968) found that infants raised on moving robot mothers made of terry cloth developed more normally than infants raised on identical but stationary terry cloth surrogates. The mechanically moving robot mothers provided more than contact comfort for the infants: Their "behavior" created stimulating inputs. For the young infant who rode on a mobile robot, the mother's movements provided gentle rocking as "she" turned corners while moving around the cage. The infant was exposed to more variation in visual input on a moving mother than if it were on a stationary mother. Later, when the infant began to leave its roaming mother and explore the cage, the mother's movements provided stimulating "games" for the infant. The randomly moving robot mother often "ran away" from the infant or "sneaked" up on it and bumped into it. These interactions created more stimulating experience than stationary mothers could and created differential reinforcement for the infant to learn to coordinate with the randomly roaming surrogate mother. The infant learned to keep an eye on mother and avoid being bumped due to the negative reinforcement of minimizing aversive consequences. Playing chase with mother was positively reinforced by increased sensory stimulation (Chapter 7). Thus, robot mothers exposed the infants to more varied experiences and conditioned more coping skills than did stationary mothers. When tested at various ages, the infants raised with moving mothers were less fearful of novelty than were the infants who were raised with stationary mothers. They explored the environment more, were more active, and were more likely to approach the experimenter (Plate 5.3). When tested at 4 to 5 years

[20] Mason (1965a, 1968) and Harlow and Harlow (1965, 1969).
[21] Mason (1965a, 1968).

PLATE 5.3. Rhesus infants raised on moving robot mothers (*left*) are more explorative and approach the experimenter more than infants raised on stationary mothers (*right*). (*Courtesy of W.A. Mason.*)

of age, the infants who had had mobile mothers in the first year of life were considerably more like normal wild-born animals than were infants raised on stationary mothers.[22]

When Mason allowed infant rhesus monkeys to be adopted by dogs, he found that the infants formed very strong attachments with the dogs.[23] It did not matter whether the infants had previously lived with their mothers, agemates, or cloth surrogates, they formed close relations with the dogs, even if they were put with the dogs as late as ten months of age (Plate 5.4).[24] The gentle, accepting female dogs provided many of the basic positive stimuli that are reinforcers for rhesus infants: contact comfort, warmth, grooming, movement, and play. Even infants that had been raised in isolation for 10 months formed close bonds with the dogs. Later, when given a choice of contacts, the infants strongly preferred being with their canine surrogates rather than with an unfamiliar monkey. Thus, it appears that infants will form close, affectionate re-

[22] Anderson et al. (1977).
[23] Mason and Kenney (1974).
[24] This indicates that attachment formation is not a "once-in-a-lifetime" event, confined to early infancy, as the early imprinting literature on birds had suggested. Also see Novak (1979).

PLATE 5.4. When placed with a gentle dog, young rhesus monkeys form strong attachments with the canine surrogate mother. (*Courtesy of W.A. Mason.*)

lations with any source of the major reinforcers to which infants respond. In the wild, mother provides the crucial reinforcers: Thus, the mother becomes a positive stimulus (a $^+$CS) due to Pavlovian conditioning, and the infant learns the operant behaviors of follow, approach, and cling, since these lead to positive consequences. If mother dies, the infant may learn similar affectional responses to another individual who mothered and protected it.

Even though nipple contact and milk are less important reinforcers than contact comfort and maternal stimulation in causing the infant to learn affection for its mother, they do influence the infant's relations with her. The infant learns to go to the mother's nipples when it is hungry, during periods of relaxation, and when distressed.[25] When infant chimpanzees begin active exploration of the environment, they show an increase in security nursing. By four years of age, most chim-

[25] van Lawick-Goodall (1967a); Clark (1977); and Nash (1978a).

panzees can feed themselves adequately and no longer need mother's milk; yet after being distressed or overaroused, they still run to mother for comfort and a reassuring suckle.[26] Contact with mother's body and nipples has a calming effect on the young, even after there is no longer any milk. Thus, the infant remains psychologically dependent on the nipple as a $^+$CS after it is no longer nutritionally dependent. When mothers wean their young from the nipple, the young often give distressful calls or have tantrums due to the loss of this reinforcer.[27]

THE EARLY SOCIAL ENVIRONMENT

In some groups, newborn or young infants attract the attention of other group members, especially the females.[28] Younger females may approach the mother and her small infant to gaze at, touch, or interact

PLATE 5.5. The adult female gelada baboon on the left shows interest in another mother's infant—lifting its tail and turning it upside down—while her own infant nurses from her. (*Courtesy of U. Mori.*)

[26] Clark (1977:246).
[27] van Lawick-Goodall (1967a); Clark (1977); Nash (1978a:751).
[28] It is not unusual to see young females giving much more attention to infants than young males do (Jay, 1965; Chamove et al., 1967; Gartland and Brain, 1968; Spencer-Booth, 1968; Baldwin, 1969; and Mori, 1979); but males are not devoid of interest in infants (Redican, 1976; Mitchell, 1977; and Suomi, 1977).

PLATE 5.6. Male Japanese macaques sometimes "adopt" younger group members, such as this 10-month-old female. (*Photo by G. Gray Eaton of the Oregon Regional Primate Research Center.*)

playfully with the infant.[29] Adult females—sometimes called "aunts"—may show similar interest and some may direct maternal behavior toward the infant. In some cases mothers tolerate these approaches and even allow the infants to be handed from female to female for inspection.[30] In other cases, mothers do not permit other animals to contact the small infant, though they may allow contact once the infant grows older and more independent. In some species—such as marmosets titi monkeys, night monkeys, Gilbraltar macaques, and Japanese macaques—adult males may also take the infant to play with, care for, or carry.[31]

The amount of social interaction that an infant has with animals other than mother influences its range of early social learning experience considerably. Those infants who have no social experience except with mother often learn fewer social skills and discriminations than same-age infants who have a broader range of social contacts.[32] In addition, infants with few contacts have less opportunity to habituate to novel, varied sensory experience than infants who regularly receive attention

[29] Lancaster (1971) and Burton (1972:33).
[30] Jay (1965).
[31] Redican (1976).
[32] Harlow and Harlow (1969); Anderson and Mason (1974, 1978); and Novak (1979).

from an "aunt" or from juvenile females who play with the infant, carry it, groom it, and so forth. Infants who learn more social skills and discriminations and who habituate to high levels of novel, varied experience are better equipped to progress rapidly to the next phases of infant development—leaving mother and exploring the broader environment. Thus, mothers who are overprotective and prevent their infants from having early social contact partially deprive their infants of the learning experiences that facilitate the infants' gaining early independence. However, maternal restrictiveness is only one of several factors that influences the infants' gaining independence. For example, once infants begin peer interaction, even infants of overprotective mothers learn social skills from their peers; and some catch up with their peers in social development within a few months.[33]

HOW THE INFANT AFFECTS ITS MOTHER

Although the mother is the larger and more skilled member of the mother–infant dyad, the infant plays an active role in establishing and shaping the development of mother–infant interactions.[34] Both the mother and the infant influence each other and shape each other's behavior (and both are influenced by social and nonsocial factors from outside the relationship).

The small infant brings reinforcers to its mother. Once the infant's reflexes lead it to the nipple and it initiates nursing, it provides nipple stimulation and causes milk release, which are reinforcers for the mother. The infant's movements on the mother's body provide sensory stimulation reinforcers and tactile stimulation reinforcers for mother. If other group members are attracted to the infant and groom or travel with mother to be near the infant, the mother may receive additional social reinforcers.[35] Because all these positive reinforcers are paired with the presence of the small infant, the infant becomes a $^+$CS for the mother—even if she has had little prior experience with infants. Since the young infant is small and gentle, it produces few aversive stimuli to condition negative associations with it. Thus even primiparous mothers learn to love their first infants, that is, to experience positive emotional responses elicited by the $^+$CS's of the infant.

In addition, the infant's responses to its mother differentially reinforce maternal protectiveness of the infant. If the mother behaves inappropriately toward her infant—perhaps holding it upside down, pressing it too tightly to her body, or dropping it—the inappropriate behavior creates $^-$US's for the infant and these cause the infant to give distress

---

[33] Baldwin (1969).
[34] Harper (1970); Rosenblum (1971b); Bell (1974); and Fragaszy and Mitchell (1974).
[35] Seyfarth (1976).

calls, squirm, and grip her hair tightly.[36] The infant's distress responses are aversive to the mother, hence they suppress the inappropriate behavior and negatively reinforce responses that avoid causing distress to the infant. There is also positive reinforcement for protective behavior. When the mother is supportive, helpful, and protective, the infant is more likely to produce those behaviors that are positive reinforcers for the mother and this increases the probability of her protective activities. (Protectiveness skills also result, in part, from earlier learning: for example, when juvenile females play with infants or whenever individuals learn to protect any positive stimulus—such as food or play objects—from loss or expropriation by others.)

Male infants are often more active and rowdy than females of the same age.[37] At first, this may cause the mother to attend to the newborn male more than the female. However, the male's higher activity level becomes aversive to the mother, and mothers often begin to reject sons earlier than daughters, motivated by the escape from aversive stimuli. Thus, male infants are often allowed to leave mother earlier and the more rewarding female infants are protected and kept near mother longer.

Because each infant has a unique genetic inheritance, unique learning experiences, and perhaps unique constructive or destructive inputs, each develops a unique behavior repertoire, or a "personality."[38] Each infant's unique behavioral characteristics can influence the further development of the mother–infant social relationship. Active, assertive infants may be punished or rejected more vigorously than quiet, rewarding infants. Infants who learn to groom mother bring more positive reinforcers to their mothers, and the extra reinforcers strengthen the mother–infant relationship. Handicapped infants who are weak and more dependent on mother evoke much greater maternal care than normal infants (for a while at least).[39]

Finally, infants are active in exploring their environment and seeking out social experience, either from the mother, the peer group, or other animals. In safe environments where there is a great deal to explore, the infant will find many reinforcers for leaving mother and interacting with others. However, in more dangerous environments or in very small groups where there are few young animals with whom an infant can interact, the infant is likely to turn its social exploration to its mother and initiate a high frequency of interactions with her.[40] Infant-initiated

[36] Mason (1968:75).
[37] Jensen et al. (1968); Sackett (1972); Rosenblum (1974a,b); but also see Young and Bramblett (1977).
[38] Nash (1978a) and Stevenson-Hinde and Zunz (1978).
[39] Berkson (1977) and Fedigan and Fedigan (1977).
[40] Jensen et al. (1967) and Nicolson (1977).

activity can influence the mother–infant interaction in many ways, depending on the type and frequency of behavior of the infant, whether the mother finds that behavior rewarding or aversive, the mother's responses to the behavior, and other factors.

EARLY INDEPENDENCE

As the infant's strength, coordination, and operant skills develop, it begins to venture off the mother's body and explore the environment. Its first departures are likely to occur while mother is resting quietly. The mother's quietude becomes an S^D for crawling after the early crawling is followed by reinforcement or punishment, depending on whether the mother is resting quietly or moving. The first departures from mother's body are variations in early movement patterns as the infant's explorative crawling responses merely carry it off mother's body. By the second week of life, the infant baboon may climb off mother and remain on the ground next to her for 10 or 15 minutes at a time.[41] The infants of arboreal species often do not leave their mothers' bodies as early as do infants of closely related terrestrial species—even when both species are living in similar cage environments.[42] This indicates that the timing of the infant's leaving mother is to some degree genetically determined. The later departure of arboreal infants from mother is adaptive since it decreases their risk of falling out of the trees during the early period when locomotor skills are still somewhat crude. There is also variability within species in the timing of the infant's leaving, depending on proximal environmental factors such as the protectiveness of the mother, the complexity of the environment, and the responses of other group members.[43]

When the infant begins to leave its mother and explore the environment, both the infant and the mother usually begin to learn increased levels of coordination with each other. When the infant is off mother, it learns to be attentive to her actions. The small infant is still quite dependent on mother for milk, transportation, warmth, and other reinforcers; and the loss of these stimuli negatively reinforces attention to signs that mother may move, possibly leaving the infant stranded. Signs that predict that mother is about to move—such as when other group members begin to move, when mother becomes restless or gets up— become S^D's that cue the infant to return to mother, to climb on and ride. Inattentiveness and unresponsiveness to the cues may be punished by isolation if the infant is left alone, physical effort if it has to catch up

---

[41] Ransom and Rowell (1972:110).

[42] Chalmers (1972); also see Sussman (1977).

[43] Jensen et al. (1967); Baldwin (1969); Chalmers and Rowell (1970); and Rosenblum (1971b).

with mother by itself, or other aversive consequences. When the infant begins exploration, the mother usually learns to protect and coordinate with her infant more than she did before.[44] Once the infant begins to climb off her body, the mother is more likely to become separated from this source of reinforcers or to have contact with an agitated, distressed infant if it gets hurt. Both contingencies of reinforcement condition maternal protectiveness and coordination to avoid the loss of positive reinforcers. As a result, many mothers learn to pick the infant up before moving off or to retrieve it if it gives distress calls.

In most cases, once infants begin to venture away from their mothers, they spend increasing amounts of time exploring out from her, and wander off to greater distances as their increasing strength and skills permit. The novel patterns of sensory stimulation that the infant finds in the environment serve as the major reinforcers that condition exploration to a high-frequency behavior (Chapter 7). The infant's explorations expose it to opportunities to learn about the environment, both social and nonsocial. Most group members are quite tolerant of small infants and allow the exploring infant to crawl onto or over them without punishment.[45] If the infant does get into trouble—perhaps falling from a tree, getting separated from the group, or becoming involved in the vigorous play of juveniles—the mother is often quick to come to its aid.[46] Thus, the infant begins life in a relatively safe, benign environment where its small repertoire of simple activities allows learning without excessive risk of danger. If the exploring infant does venture into dangerous or complex situations before physical maturation and learned skills allow it to cope successfully with these problems, a few aversive experiences will punish and temporarily suppress further exploration of these situations until more strength and skill are attained.[47]

From the early days of life, the exploring infant may put leaves, twigs, fruit, or other objects into its mouth. At first, the infant may only mouth or play with the objects, but differential reinforcement gradually causes the infant to chew and ingest those that provide the tastes that serve as unconditioned reinforcers for the species, and to avoid those that serve as unconditioned punishers.[48] Because the infant is often near its mother when she is eating, the infant may imitate the mother's choice of objects to put in its mouth. In some cases, an infant may take food from the mother, muzzle her mouth as she eats, or pick up pieces of

[44] van Lawick-Goodall (1967a); Baldwin (1969); Lindburg (1971); and Rosenblum (1971b:340).
[45] Jay (1965) and Baldwin and Baldwin (1973b).
[46] Her protectiveness is reinforced by regaining contact with the infant and by the termination of its distress responses, which are aversive to the mother.
[47] Punishment usually produces only temporary suppression of behavior (Walters and Grusec, 1977).
[48] Horr (1977) and Rhine and Westlund (1978).

food she has dropped.[49] Because these foods are paired with the $^+$CS's of mother, these foods are likely to take on heightened reinforcement value, and the infant is likely to learn food preferences similar to those of its mother. In addition, the infant may explore other sources of food. Because sensory stimulation is a reinforcer, foods with novel or conspicuous colors and shapes are more likely to attract an infant's attention and be tasted than are less colorful or conspicuous foods.[50] Because novelty is a reinforcer and young animals have not yet learned strong habitual food preferences, an explorative infant or juvenile may discover a new food source that has not traditionally been used by the group. If others imitate, the discovery may spread through the group. However, the infant is not always free to explore novel foods. Mothers and older siblings may take novel food out of an infant's hands or mouth, thus suppress the exploration of foods that are not commonly used by the group.[51] Within the first year or two of life, infants of many species have learned the basic food preferences of their group, though they may not be able to pick, open, or capture certain foods that require adult strength, speed, or skill to obtain.[52]

The rewards of novel experience obtained while exploring the environment are prime movers that gradually seduce the infant to spend increasing amounts of time away from its mother. But physical handicaps or other biological limitations can retard the process by which the infant becomes independent. Fedigan and Fedigan (1977) describe a handicapped male infant Japanese macaque with motor coordination problems that prevented him from moving through the environment efficiently. The infant was much more dependent on his mother than most infants of similar age. When he explored away from his mother, he was more likely to fall and experience punishment than other infants were, and he never attained the independence that the other infants did. For one month, a female agemate took interest in the handicapped infant and played gently with him. However, when playing with him lost its novelty and the female no longer sought him out, the handicapped infant returned to spending more of his time with his mother.

There have been cases reported in which infant monkeys have become separated from their groups and adopted by a group of another species. For example, Singh and Sen (1977–78) describe the behavior of two juvenile rhesus monkeys who were adopted by and living in a langur group for some time. Although rhesus monkeys are usually quite aggressive compared to langurs, the two rhesus monkeys living in the langur group "did not seem to grow up with all the peculiarities gen-

---

[49] van Lawick-Goodall (1973a) and Fedigan and Fedigan (1977).
[50] Mason and Harlow (1959).
[51] van Lawick-Goodall (1973a).
[52] McGrew (1977).

erally found among rhesus monkeys" (p. 137). Their behavior resembled langur behavior in several ways. They groomed with the langurs in the manner typical of langurs. Their diet was that of langurs rather than the typical rhesus diet. They responded appropriately to langur alarm calls (and the langurs responded to theirs). They played as equals with the langurs, without either species showing preferences for one species or the other as playmates. Thus, living in the langur group exposed the rhesus monkeys to differential reinforcement and models from langurs and conditioned their behavior to be relatively compatible with langur behavior.

HOW THE MOTHER AFFECTS THE INFANT

Because the mother is such an important part of the infant's social world, many features of the mother's behavior and her relations with other group members can influence the infant's development. Among these maternal characteristics are the mother's prior experience with infants, her social rank, her immediate social surroundings, her age, her personality, and her degree of protectiveness or fearfulness.

Primiparous mothers (who have given birth only once) often show less skill and more anxiety in handling their infants than do *multiparous* mothers (who have given birth more than once).[53] In a 10-year study of free-ranging rhesus groups, 45% of the infants of primiparous mothers died in the first six months of life, compared with 9% of the infants born to mothers who had had three previous infants.[54] Because they have had infants before, multiparous mothers have learned a larger repertoire of maternal behavior and discriminations than have primiparous mothers. There is, however, a considerable degree of variability in the behavior of primiparous mothers: Some are quite good mothers whereas others lack many maternal skills.[55] Some of this variability among primiparous mothers can be traced to differences in the females' prior social learning experience with infants during play, babysitting, or aunt–infant interactions.[56] When juvenile females have a chance to play with small infants, differential reinforcement from the infant's and mother's responses conditions various skills for handling infants. Inappropriate behavior is punished by the infant's distress responses and the mother's removing the infant from the juvenile. Appropriate be-

---

[53] Jay (1962); Seay (1966); Mitchell and Stevens (1968); and Mitchell and Schroers (1973).
[54] Drickamer (1974).
[55] Fedigan and Fedigan (1977:209). Some laboratory studies reveal no behavioral differences between the infants raised by primiparous and multiparous mothers (Erwin et al., 1971, 1973, 1974), indicating that in some environments females can learn to be quite skillful with their first infants.
[56] Lancaster (1971).

havior is reinforced by continued contact and play with the infant. The more social learning experience that young females have with infants, the more likely they are to learn some maternal skills from this differential reinforcement. Also, when they are following the mother, waiting to gain access to the infant, they may be learning how the mother treats her infant by observational learning.

Compared with the multiparous mother, the primiparous mother is often more restrictive and more likely to retrieve her infant when the infant is off her body.[57] In baboons, primiparous and young mothers have short, unstretched nipples; whereas the older, multiparous mothers have longer nipples.[58] The shortness of the primiparous mother's nipples makes it difficult for the first-born infant to keep contact with the nipples; hence, the primiparous mother has to assist it more. Effort from assisting the infant and soreness of the nipples are aversive stimuli that cause the young baboon mother to put her infant down on the ground and move away from it more often than the multiparous mother does. The loss of reinforcing contact and support causes the infant of the primiparous mother more frustration and distress than is experienced by the infants of multiparous mothers. Multiparous mothers and their young infants have more relaxed, harmonious, and mutually positive social exchanges. Thus, several features of a mother's prior interactions with infants influence the infant's early social learning experience and are among the factors that shape infant development.

At *weaning*, primiparous and multiparous mothers often treat their infants differently.[59] Multiparous mothers usually terminate infant care in a more direct, abrupt, and punitive manner than do primiparous mothers. The multiparous mother has had prior experience with infants, and when the infant becomes too large to carry and too boisterous to deal with easily, the experienced mother is quick to discriminate the change and ready to use force to keep the growing infant from bothering her further. During her past experiences with infants, she has learned that small dependent infants are rewarding but that large, rowdy infants are aversive; and when the S^D's of large size and boisterous behavior appear, the S^D's evoke the already well learned operants of rejecting and avoiding the infant. The primiparous mother needs time and experience (a) to learn that the once rewarding infant is now aversive and (b) to acquire the skills for avoiding aversive contacts. The primiparous mother often uses a milder, less successful method for terminating contact with the infant, and the infant is slower to learn to stop pestering its mother.

[57] Kuyk et al. (1976).
[58] Ransom (1971).
[59] Ransom and Rowell (1972).

Differences in mothering style can cause small but persistent differences in the behavior of infants raised by primiparous and multiparous mothers.[60] For example, in one study, juvenile rhesus monkeys who had primiparous mothers played less, were less aggressive, and showed more fear and stereotyped movements than juveniles raised by multiparous mothers.[61] Other differences may exist, too, depending on many biological and environmental variables.

In groups where there is a rank ordering among females, a mother's *social rank* can have a significant effect on her infant's social development.[62] High-rank mothers are often the center of attention, receiving more grooming and more social interaction than lower rank or peripheral females. Thus, their infants are more likely to receive positive social attention—grooming, care, protection, and early play—than are the infants of low-rank mothers. When near other adults, high-rank mothers are often relatively relaxed and nonfearful, whereas subordinate females are likely to be tense and anxious. Because they have learned less fear about having their infants harmed, high-rank mothers are often less restrictive of their infants than are low-rank mothers when the infants begin to wander off to explore and play. Low-rank mothers frequently limit the movements of their infants, since this action often helps avoid aversive situations. If infants do get involved in squabbles with other animals—peers or adults—high-rank mothers are likely to protect their infants. Because low-rank mothers are less likely to defend their infants, their young receive more threats and rough treatment.[63] When infants get into fights, the ranks of their mothers often determine who wins, since the high-rank mother is likely to support her infant while the low-rank mother is not.[64] Because infants of low-rank mothers are more restricted in exploration and play—and receive more punishment when they do explore or play—they often learn to avoid play and interaction with high-rank infants, even when the high-rank mothers are not nearby. They also learn to stay closer to their mothers.[65] Not surprisingly, infants often acquire social ranks similar to those of their mothers.[66] Because infants of high-rank mothers can wander out further and interact with fewer punitive consequences, they often learn to cope with their environments earlier and more effectively.[67] They also develop

---

[60] Sackett and Ruppenthal (1973:66).
[61] Mitchell et al. (1966).
[62] Dolhinow and Bishop (1970); Gouzoules (1975); Johnson et al. (1979); and Tartabini et al. (1980).
[63] Fedigan (1972b).
[64] Marsden (1968); Lindburg (1971); Eaton (1976); and Cheney (1977).
[65] Meier and Devanney (1974).
[66] Sade (1965); Marsden (1968); and Cheney (1977).
[67] Candland et al. (1978); Tartabini and Dienske (1979).

closer social relations and interact more with more individuals of high rank than do infants with low-ranking mothers.[68]

Various *environmental* factors can affect the mother's behavior and her infant's development. For example, Ransom and Rowell (1972:109) reported that the behavior repertoire of infant baboons developed earlier in forest-living groups than DeVore (1963a) had reported for savanna-living baboons. Numerous environmental features could cause such effects. A frightening or dangerous environment would be expected to provide punishers that suppress and retard the infant's leaving the mother. The complexity of the environment can have numerous effects on both mother and infant. When mother–infant pairs of pigtail macaques are raised in sensory-rich cages, both mother and infant show less interest in each other than when mother–infant pairs are raised in sensory-impoverished cages.[69] In sensory-rich environments the mother leaves her infant more and the infant orients to the environment more. In both kinds of environments, mothers learn to punish their infants when the infants pester them, and the punishment suppresses the frequency of pestering.[70] However, in the sensory-rich environment the punishment also causes the infants to leave their mother and gain independence, whereas the infants in impoverished environments stay near mother even when she punishes them because she is the only source of rewarding stimulation in the environment.

Nicolson (1977) compared the development of mother–infant social relations and infant development in chimpanzees living in the wild, in a large enclosure, and in a small cage. The complexity of the environment was a crucial determinant of infant development and mother–infant interaction. Because they had little else to do, mothers in simple environments explored and manipulated their newborn infants more than was seen in the wild. Because their environment was safe, simple, nonthreatening, and easy to explore alone, the infants living in simple environments ventured away from their mothers at an earlier age. However, once the infants explored their simple environments, they grew bored and returned frequently to try to interact with their mothers. The captive mothers found these repeated contacts aversive and rejected their bothersome infants more, causing them to whimper more than was the case in the wild. When a baboon mother and infant are caged with other baboons, the mother is often more restrictive than are mothers in the wild.[71] The caged mother learns to protect her infant from being snatched by other females or from getting into squabbles. If an

---

[68] Gouzoules (1975) and Seyfarth (1977).
[69] Jensen et al. (1967).
[70] Jensen et al. (1969).
[71] Ransom and Rowell (1972:114).

adult male is present in the caged group there is less risk of baby snatching and squabbles, hence the mothers are less restrictive than if the adult male is absent.[72] Thus the complexity of the environment and social composition of the group influence mother–infant relations and the infant's learning experiences.

In some groups there are *birth seasons*, and births occur only during a limited period of the year. The infants who are born early have different social learning experiences than infants born later.[73] Because they are the first ones to arrive, early-born infants are more likely than later-born infants to receive attention and social stimulation from juvenile females and young adult females. Compared with the later-born infants, the early-born infants have a head start in gaining weight, strength, and skill. When play groups begin to form, the small size and limited skills of the later-born put them at a disadvantage in their early peer interactions, causing them more aversive experiences. Although the younger infants gradually catch up with the first-born in size, strength, and skill, their original handicaps influence early behavioral development and may have lasting effects.

Idiosyncrasies of the mother's behavior can also influence the infant's behavior.[74] For example, some chimpanzee mothers often travel with other mothers and their offspring, which facilitates social play among the young. In contrast, other mothers are loners, and their infants have fewer chances to play with peers. Shy and anxious mothers are likely to be more withdrawn or protective of their infants than are other mothers, and these responses restrict the infant's range of learning experiences and can retard the infant's behavioral and social development to a certain degree.[75]

MOTHER–INFANT SEPARATION

The degree of mother–infant separation during and after weaning varies both between species and within species. In some cases, separation is complete; but in others, offspring may maintain social relationships with their mothers all through life. Complete separation is common in the more primitive primates. Among the advanced primates there are more examples of enduring relations between mother and offspring. Various proximal causes can influence separation within a given species. Forest-living baboons are less likely to have complete mother–infant separation than are baboons living in the harsher savanna environment.[76] The

[72] Chalmers (1972:73).
[73] Baldwin (1969) and Lancaster (1971:171f).
[74] Ransom and Rowell (1972); Clark (1977:239); and Nash (1978a).
[75] van Lawick-Goodall (1967b:166) and Baldwin (1969).
[76] Ransom and Rowell (1972:126).

severity of weaning and completeness of mother–infant separation depend on factors such as the infant's degree of helplessness, independence, and ability to bring reinforcing experiences to mother, along with the mother's age, behavioral idiosyncrasies, and number of prior offspring.

Separation is a mutual emancipation process. The infant is exploring ever-widening spheres of activity and expanding its network of social relations with individuals other than mother; and the mother is terminating the aversive components of her interactions with her large, sometimes bothersome offspring. Some infants find the process of weaning very aversive and others less so, depending on the mother's style of weaning and the alternative sources of rewarding social interactions available to the infant.[77] Multiparous mothers tend to be more abrupt and successful in terminating aversive interactions with their young. Although some mothers begin weaning the infant from the nipple before they resume the estrus cycle, the resumption of the estrus cycle usually causes an increase in weaning activities.

Various environmental factors can influence the process, too. For example, baboon mothers observed in some habitats do not begin weaning until the sixth or tenth month, whereas weaning has been observed in the baboons at Gombe Stream as early as 2.5 months. At Gombe, the mothers who began rebuffing their infants early did not have to use nearly as aversive measures as those who began later. "Perhaps because of the longer period of greater harmony and security that preceded rejection, the late-group infants showed greater persistence in their attempts to suckle than did infants that experienced earlier rejection, and they appeared to be much more disturbed by the change in behavior."[78] Some species display more punitive methods of weaning than do others. For example, pigtail macaque mothers are more rejective and punitive than bonnet macaque mothers when weaning their infants.[79] Not surprisingly, the pigtail infants learn to avoid their mothers more than bonnet infants avoid their mothers. Chimpanzee mothers usually use nonaggressive methods for blocking the infant's access to the nipple.[80] Even though the mothers use the minimum of punitive methods, the loss of contact and nipple reinforcers is sufficiently aversive to the infant chimpanzees to elicit whimpers and sometimes tantrums. Mothers often learn to placate distressed infants with positive reinforcers—by grooming them or playing with them. Maternal grooming and playing are negatively reinforced by the termination of the infant's distress behaviors and sometimes positively reinforced by the infant's turning to groom

[77] Jay (1965).
[78] Ransom and Rowell (1972:125).
[79] Rosenblum and Kaufman (1967).
[80] Clark (1977).

mother. Eventually mutual grooming replaces the earlier nursing interaction. Mutual grooming provides both partners with tactile reinforcers
and serves as a competing response that distracts the infant from its
otherwise preponent response of seeking nipple contact. In her study
of chimpanzees, Clark (1977:256f) observed that "mutual grooming, in
particular, appeared to be very reinforcing to the mother–infant relationship during the time of stress just as lactation ceased and suckling
ended."

Mother–infant separation is often not complete in baboons, chimpanzees, and certain other species. The infant may continue to sleep
with the mother and groom with her much more than with other individuals. However, weaning does orient the infant to turn increasing
attention to peers, older juveniles, and adults for social contact. The
social relations between mother and infant may not be completely se-
vered, but they undergo a series of changes as the young individual
becomes more independent. Because the early mother–infant relationship involved a frequent exchange of powerful positive reinforcers, positive interactions may continue even after weaning. Family networks
are often visible, especially in grooming relations, rest groups, coalitions, and patterns of proximity.[81]

THE JUVENILE PERIOD

As mother–infant separation progresses, the offspring is allowed less
and less access to the sheltered environment it enjoyed during infancy.
In addition, the juvenile ventures further away from mother since exploring the environment produces the reinforcers of novel experience.
As it has decreasing contact with mother for food, security, transport,
and protection, the juvenile is increasingly exposed to contingencies of
reinforcement that condition increased skill and self-sufficiency. There
are reinforcers for learning how to find and open food without mother's
assistance, how to locate water holes, how to cope with hostile group
members, and so forth. Failure to learn leads to hunger, thirst, painful
swats, and other aversive consequences. This differential reinforcement
conditions the independence skills that help the individual locate the
reinforcers and avoid the punishers typically found in its unique subset
of the environment.

Mother–infant separation can be stressful for the offspring, since the
infant loses access to the multiple reinforcers it once received from
mother, and it may have to interact with a social or nonsocial environment that is hostile and aversive. However, many young primates can

---

[81] Yamada (1963); Koford (1963); Sade (1965, 1967); Kawamura (1965); Hopf (1978); and
Nash (1978b).

turn to peers for rewarding social interactions that ease the transition at weaning. The peer group provides many kinds of social contact— grooming partners, travel companions, and play partners—as the young primate becomes increasingly independent from mother. The peer group serves as a stepping stone for the young primate to develop an ever-broader range of social contacts in the group and become integrated in the group's larger social network.[82] Social play with peers provides the young primate with a chance to practice and learn many social skills needed for adult social interactions.[83] The role of exploration and play in primate socialization will be dealt with in greater detail in Chapter 7.

Although young infants may have learned simple food preferences from watching mother's feeding habits, infants generally lack the skill to imitate or innovate such complex group traditions as tool-use or complex food preparations. In contrast, the older infants and juveniles are sufficiently skillful to imitate complex traditions and sometimes to innovate new patterns themselves. Tests on Japanese macaques reveal that their ability to learn solutions to problems related to traditions improve during the first 6 or 7 years of life.[84] Infant chimpanzees begin to build nests during the last year of suckling, though they come to mother's nest to spend the night.[85] After weaning, the young chimpanzees begin to sleep in their own nests and learn improved nest building skills. Although adult chimpanzees are proficient in crumbling leaves to serve as a sponge to remove water from tree holes, it takes years of imitation and differential reinforcement for young chimpanzees to learn these skills.[86] Chimpanzees eat both termites and driver ants. Termite "fishing" is mastered by 5 to 6 years of age (a year or so after weaning), but ant dipping is not mastered until later, since it requires more skill. Driver ants can deliver painful bites that suppress playful imitation of adult ant dipping techniques and retard learning until advanced skills are learned. "Ant dipping is the only Gombe chimpanzee tool-use behavior which involves pain, and it is the only one in which proficiency is not achieved until adolescence."[87]

The Japanese have reported considerable variation in group traditions of Japanese macaques.[88] Observations on the macaques at Gibralter indicate that a group's repertoire of traditions can change significantly over time.[89] At least some of the variation and change in traditions may

[82] Jay (1965) and Baldwin (1969).
[83] Poirier (1972a); Poirier and Smith (1974); and Novak (1979).
[84] Tsumori (1967).
[85] Clark (1977).
[86] van Lawick-Goodall (1968) and McGrew (1977).
[87] McGrew (1977:284).
[88] Frisch (1968); Yamada (1971); and Itani and Nishimura (1973).
[89] Burton (1972:56).

be related to "economics" imposed by the local environment.[90] For example, baboons living in desert areas do more object manipulation than conspecifics living in a swamp. In contrast, the swamp-living baboons do more social manipulation. Differences in environmental resources impose different contingencies of reinforcement.

MATURING INTO ADULTHOOD

As primates mature into adulthood, they usually become less innovative and more conservative.[91] They become the repositories of the "tried and true" while the young continue to explore new alternatives.

Maturing into adulthood is different for males and females. Sex differences in body weight, size, physical strength, hormones, and structures of the central nervous system often exist prior to adulthood and become even more pronounced as maturity is attained.[92] These physical differences between the sexes in turn cause males and females to have different learning experiences before adulthood and especially after becoming adult.

Juvenile and adolescent females usually withdraw from peer play earlier than males.[93] Differences in size and weight explain some of the variance in sex differences in behavior.[94] Because males are generally larger and stronger than females, the females are more likely than males to be hurt during rough play, hence they learn to avoid rowdy play groups and seek out quieter activities. In addition, the effects of prenatal hormones may bias the central nervous system in ways that cause females to seek lower levels of sensory stimulation than males do, hence causing females to find the higher activity levels of males to be aversive.[95] As they withdraw from rowdy play subadult females sometimes become the most isolated, unintegrated members of their groups.[96] They often turn to object play,[97] thus obtain the reinforcers of novel stimulation without the risk of aversive stimulation from rowdy males. The most rewarding form of social interaction available to the young females is likely to be contact with infants and adult females. If a juvenile female approaches a mother with infant, she may get to play with the infant. Since the infant is smaller and weaker, the play is usually gentle and the juvenile female is not likely to be hurt. Thus, juvenile female's interactions with infants are more reinforcing than peer play with males.

---

[90] Hamilton et al. (1978a).
[91] Rowell (1972); Itani and Nishimura (1973); and Baldwin and Baldwin (1978a).
[92] Baldwin and Baldwin (1977a:372f); Robinson and Bridson (1978).
[93] Jay (1965); Baldwin (1969); Wolfheim (1977b); Caine and Mitchell (1979); and Mori (1979).
[94] Nadler and Braggio (1974); Baldwin and Baldwin (1977a:373); and Kaack et al. (1979).
[95] Goy and Phoenix (1972); Goy and Resko (1972); Sackett (1972); and Rosenblum (1974a).
[96] Altmann (1968); Burton (1972); and Clarke (1978).
[97] Nadler and Braggio (1974); and Wolfheim (1977b).

In addition, the juvenile female learns how to handle infants.[98] As the young female plays with an infant, both mother and infant provide differential reinforcement for the juvenile's skills of handling small infants without alarming them. The contingencies of reinforcement are as follows: If the juvenile is rough and alarms the infant, mother is likely to threaten the juvenile and perhaps take the infant away, which ends the rewarding interaction. If the juvenile plays with the infant without upsetting it, she has prolonged access to the rewarding interaction. In addition to this differential reinforcement, juveniles who approach mothers with infants can observe the mothers' modeling of maternal skills, and learn maternal responses via observational learning, too.

As juvenile females begin to associate more with adult females, the rewards of interacting with the older females are contingent upon their learning adultlike behavior.[99] The differential reinforcement provided by the adult females causes younger females to learn to act more like adults. When the juvenile females are too active, the adult females avoid them or punish them, but when the juvenile females behave more like adults, the adults allow interaction, hence reinforce more adult behavior (Figure 5.1).

When sexual maturity is reached, hormonal changes initiate estrus cycling, which in turn leads to sexual interactions with adult males, then pregnancy, and eventually birth. When the first infant is born, the new mother is usually not as skillful as experienced mothers are, but the first infant imposes patterns of differential reinforcement that condition additional maternal skills (pages 127–128). After rearing one or two offspring, an adult female usually learns a rather large repertoire of maternal skills. Because there can be variation in the learning experiences that different individuals have, each female acquires enough different behavior to have a "personality" and "maternal style" of her own.

Maturing males usually have a longer passage to adulthood than do females. In some species there is a special subadult phase—lasting one or more years—through which males pass before attaining sociosexual maturity. Spermatogenesis and adult hormone production normally begin during the subadult stage, but social maturity is not achieved until full adulthood.[100] Males usually continue to play well into the subadult period, long after the females have withdrawn from the play groups. Subadult males are typically quite active and find high levels lf sensory input to be very reinforcing. The males' play is often rough, and at times aggressive. Rapid chases and mock fights expose the subadult males to differential reinforcement that conditions rapid running, chasing, dodg-

[98] Lancaster (1971).
[99] Baldwin and Baldwin (1978a:370f); and Cheney (1978).
[100] Ploog et al. (1967); Hanby (1976); and Hopf (1979).

FIGURE 5.1. *Top:* An adolescent female chimpanzee quietly looks at a baby on its mother's body. Apparently the adolescent bothered the mother, causing the mother to hit her. *Middle:* The adolescent retreats to a distance of 4 meters and screams. *Bottom:* About a minute later, the adolescent returns and yelps while the mother gives her a kiss of consolation. After that, the mother tolerated the adolescent's attention to her baby. (*Drawing by Frans de Waal, from de Waal and van Roosmalen, 1979.*)

ing, and lunging.[101] These are skills that can make a life or death difference in coping with predators or fights among adult males. During vigorous play, a false step or poorly timed jump is punished by a hard fall; skillful moves are reinforced by the sensory stimulation resulting from continued play. The skills that the young males learn during play will help some of them acquire high rank, central social positions, and reproductive success, once they reach adulthood.

Subadult males are generally quite independent of their mothers and wander freely throughout the group. They are usually attracted to sources of novelty and excitement, hence investigate any strange, new events in the environment. Thus, they may appear to function as watchguards, often among the first to arrive on the scene when a predator or strange group is sighted.[102] They are frequent participants in intergroup encounters, one of the more active and stimulating events in primate daily life.

Subadult males often become peripheral members of their natal group, and in most cases they venture away from their groups and join other groups.[103] Sometimes subadult males leave their natal group during intergroup encounters in which the male finds a sexually receptive female in the strange group and leaves in her company, apparently responding to the reinforcers of novelty and sex. In Japanese monkeys, a maturing male may find it easier to stay in his natal group and enter the group's central male hierarchy if his mother has high rank and travels with the central adult males.[104] When male Japanese monkeys do try to enter new groups, their entry depends in large part on whether or not the adult females in the group get along well with the new male. A large number of other variables influence a male's success in attaining an integrated position in a group: the number of adult males in the group, coalitions among them, past reinforcement for aggression to new males, friendship networks among the adult males and females, the personality of the young male and its compatibility with those of other group members, and so forth. Due to considerable variability in the social contingencies of reinforcement, there can be considerable variation in interactions between subadult males and new groups.

ADULTHOOD

During early adulthood both females and males learn many of the skills needed to cope with sexual interactions, infant care, the adult social network of the group, and the environment. As these skills are mas-

---

[101] Symons (1978).

[102] Dunbar and Nathon (1972) and Hausfater (1972).

[103] Rowell (1969); Boelkins and Wilson (1972); Drickamer and Vessey (1973); Cheney (1978); and Enomoto (1978).

[104] Yamada (1971) and Norikoshi and Koyama (1975).

tered, the adult's behavior patterns usually change less rapidly than before. There are several reasons for this. Once the adult's physical growth and muscular development have stabilized in early adulthood, there is less change in the physiological mechanisms of behavior. With the cessation of physical development, the individual no longer experiences the changing contingencies of reinforcement that resulted from changes in size and strength; thus, a major cause for changes in learned behavior disappears. Once reproductive maturity is reached, the animals' social roles in their group usually become stabilized; and stable social relations produce stable contingencies of reinforcement, which in turn produce more stable behavior patterns. After a few years of adulthood, most individuals have acquired enough skills to cope with their environments, and they settle into a routine manner of dealing with everyday life. As explained in Chapter 7, the reinforcers for exploration and play have usually disappeared by adulthood; hence two activities that introduce variability into the life of the immature animals decline in adulthood.

On the other hand, there are some factors that induce change into adult behavior. The female reproductive cycle and cycles of rearing infants introduce cyclic changes into the female's life and into the lives of animals with whom she interacts. In groups with yearly birth seasons, many of the social relations within the group are influenced by alternations between mating seasons and birth seasons.[105] Many changes in adult behavior result from unique experiences that influence an individual's health, social interactions, or learning. If an individual is injured in a fight or a fall, the injury can cause changes in the individual's feeding routine, dominance relations, ability to keep up with the group, and so forth. The death or defeat of a high-ranking animal can influence the social relations of other group members, sometimes leading to considerable reorganization of a group's social networks.[106] As a group grows in size, it may split into two fragments, creating new social networks which in turn alter each individual's social learning experience.[107] If behavioral innovations appear in the group, the adults may acquire new traditions from imitating the young. Some primates live long enough to be influenced by the physical decline of old age.[108]

Thus, learning and behavioral change do not cease in adulthood; but behavior change occurs less frequently. Because the changes in an adult's behavior often result from unique experiences and are not synchronized by maturational changes (as is more often the case in immature individuals), adult behavioral changes are often idiosyncratic,

---

[105] Lancaster and Lee (1965) and Baldwin (1968, 1971).
[106] Sugiyama (1967) and Chalmers (1972).
[107] Furuya (1968, 1969); Koyama (1970); and Aldrich-Blake and Chivers (1973).
[108] Davis (1978).

hence not easily predictable without specific information about the environment.

CONCLUSION

From this brief overview of the development of behavior in primates, it should be clear that natural learning plays an important role in determining the behavior of individuals at each phase of development. There is a continuous interplay between natural learning and biological factors throughout development. The neonate's reflexes provide the raw material from which later operants are shaped by differential reinforcement. Physical maturation puts constraints on the rate of learning, since operants that go beyond an individual's physical capabilities at any phase of maturation are likely to be punished by falls, threats, swats, or other aversive consequences. Maturational changes in body size, weight, and strength influence the mother–infant social relation and the onset of weaning. Hormonally induced sex differences in weight, size, strength, and central nervous system structures cause young males and females to interact and play differently, and this contributes to the differences between male and female behavior. The onset of sexual maturity places males and females under quite different contingencies of reinforcement, as females learn to be mothers and males learn their positions in the group structure. Thus, maturation sets a general timetable for physical changes that thrust the developing individual into changing sets of relationships with its social and nonsocial environment; and the changing environmental contingencies condition behavior changes that continue steadily until maturational processes slow during adulthood.

THE ROLE OF NATURAL LEARNING IN PRIMATE SOCIAL ORGANIZATION

Primate societies are composed of behaving individuals. Since natural learning plays an important role in shaping the behavior of the individual, it is only to be expected that it also influences the social organization of primate groups. The goal of this chapter is to explore various methods for integrating theories of natural learning with models of social organization. These models should explain the role of natural learning in social organization in ways that allow other proximal and distal causes besides learning to be introduced later, to produce a balanced biosocial theory.

We will begin with an early model proposed by Carpenter in 1952, then add embellishments suggested by more recent research and theory. Because reinforcers and punishers are the prime movers of operant and Pavlovian conditioning, it is reasonable to analyze the influence of learning on social organization in terms of patterns of reinforcement and punishment in the social and nonsocial environment. The model based on reinforcers and punishers can be expanded by adding information on species-typical features of learning, models, and other proximal variables, such as nutrition, injury, and disease.

GROUP STRUCTURE AND ENVIRONMENTAL PATTERNS OF REINFORCEMENT

Carpenter (1952) provided a starting point for analyzing the effects of reinforcement patterns on primate social organization. His theory is based on a balanced, multifactor model of primate behavior. Carpenter proposed to explain the structure of primate societies in terms of genetics, maturation and growth, social interaction, and learning. This view allows both distal and proximal determinants of behavior to be interwoven. Carpenter postulated the existence of centripetal and centrifugal forces that operate on all members of primate societies (Figure 6.1). *Centripetal forces* pull each individual primate (P_i) into the group (G); and *centrifugal forces* repel the individual from the group toward the outside environment (ENV). Centripetal forces produce a cohesive group; and centrifugal ones lead to low group cohesion, dispersion, or fragmentation. Genetic and maturational factors can contribute to both centripetal and centrifugal forces to the degree that they partially determine characteristics that attract individuals or repel them. As Carpenter pointed out, genetics and maturation explain a large component of species-typical patterns of "locomotion, grasping, vocalizations and some aspects of perception" along with "the basic or primary needs . . . like temperature demands, intake needs, preponent motor responses like sucking, clinging or grasping, and sexual activities, as well as preponent avoidance responses." Given this biologically established raw material, individuals learn social discriminations and responses through "reciprocal interaction," in which each individual's behavior conditions the behavior of the other. For example, genetic and maturational factors almost always guarantee that a mother and her young infant will learn mutual approach and coordination patterns, since each provides stimuli that fulfill "primary needs" of the other, i.e., each produces unconditioned reinforcers for the other. The unique behavior repertoire and discriminations that each individual learns during its socialization have a significant influence on the kinds of reinforcers and punishers each individual will exchange with its partner during reciprocal interaction.

FIGURE 6.1. According to Carpenter (1952), each individual primate (P_i) is influenced by centripetal forces that pull it toward its group (G) and centrifugal forces that pull it toward the environment (ENV) outside the group.

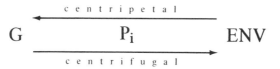

Carpenter described several positive reinforcers—food, warmth, play, and sex—that condition approach (centripetal forces) among animals of different maturational levels. In addition, aversive stimuli outside the group can reinforce centripetal tendencies. Carpenter stated that competition within the group for positive reinforcers—along with subsequent conflicts and aggression—creates aversive circumstances that condition some animals to avoid others, and perhaps to leave the group. Thus, aversive social experiences, along with reinforcers from outside the group, are the cause of the centrifugal forces that can result in decreased cohesion, dispersal, or group fragmentation. The sociometric patterns established by various individuals' selective avoidance or approach to each other account for much of the social organization and spatial distribution of the group.

FOUR BASIC CONDITIONING PATTERNS

Figure 6.2 elaborates on Carpenter's model by emphasizing that it is positive and negative stimuli—$^+$US's, $^+$CS's, $^-$US's, and $^-$CS's—from inside and outside the group that are the prime movers that condition centripetal and centrifugal movement. Centripetal tendencies can be established by either positive reinforcement from the group or negative reinforcement (caused by punishers) from outside the group (arrows 1 and 2 in Figure 6.2). Centrifugal tendencies can be established by either positive reinforcement from outside the group or negative reinforcement (caused by punishers) from the group (arrows 3 and 4 in Figure 6.2). Since reinforcers and punishers are the prime movers of conditioning, these four patterns should represent fundamentally different contingencies of reinforcement that shape each individual's behavior.

With a slight modification in the model, it is possible to consider an individual's interactions vis à vis each other member of its group, rather than vis à vis the group as a whole. Thus, the "G" in Figure 6.2 could be replaced by single individuals, allowing one to evaluate whether a given individual would approach some group members and avoid oth-

FIGURE 6.2. Carpenter's model can be elaborated upon by locating the four sources of reinforcers and punishers (from the group, G, and from the environment, ENV) that condition centripetal and centrifugal activities in any given individual primate (P_i). Positive stimuli ($+$) are $^+$US's and $^+$CS's. Negative stimuli ($-$) are $^-$US's and $^-$CS's. The numbers correspond to the four patterns of conditioning discussed in the text.

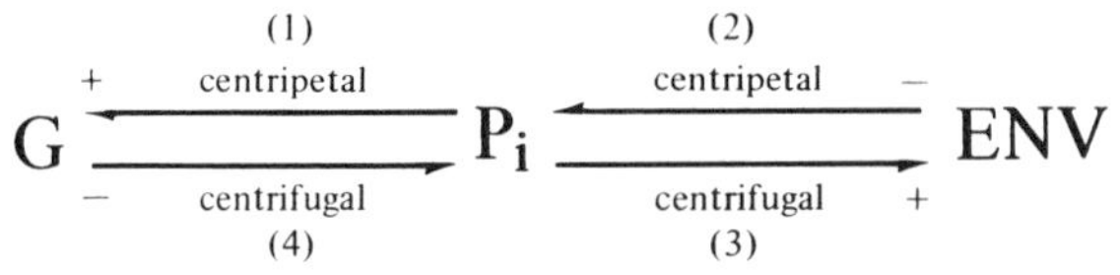

ers. For example, an infant would be expected to show strong centripetal movement toward mother, protective aunts, and same-age playmates due to the positive reinforcers it obtains from them. Yet it could learn centrifugal movements from rowdy juveniles or hostile adult males (due to aversive interactions). By tracing an individual's history of centripetal and centrifugal conditioning vis à vis each groupmate, it should be possible to explain much of the individual's social interaction patterns.

Since the stimuli that serve as unconditioned reinforcers and punishers ($^+$US's and $^-$US's) are largely determined by natural selection (pages 78–81), a species' genetic inheritance has a considerable effect on patterns of social organization and cohesion shown by the species, even though mediated by conditioning. Other stimuli can become conditioned reinforcers and punishers ($^+$CS's and $^-$CS's) if they are regularly paired with the biologically established $^+$US's and $^-$US's. Because they are created by stimulus pairing, conditioned reinforcers and punishers usually correlate well with unconditioned reinforcers and punishers. The main difference is that conditioned reinforcers and punishers allow animals to find relevant activities to be reinforcing or punishing during the intervals between contacts with $^+$US's and $^-$US's.

Certain reinforcers and punishers are more likely than others to be located within the group (e.g., milk for the nursing infant, the sensory stimulation of play, genital stimulation, bites from an aggressive male); and others, more likely to be found outside the context of social interaction (e.g., solid food, water, insect stings, attacks by a predator). A mapping of these reinforcers and punishers into either the group context or the environment outside the group locates the prime movers of the following four patterns (as numbered in Figure 6.2).

Positive Centripetal Conditioning (1)

There are both mutual and unilateral forms of positive centripetal conditioning. When group members engage in *mutual* exchanges of positive reinforcers, the positive stimuli condition social cohesion and reinforce the social skills involved in producing those exchanges. Mutually rewarding interactions produce the "friendly" relations that are one of the most important elements that hold primate groups together.[1] Mother–infant exchanges appear to be among the most frequent of these highly reinforcing, mutually positive exchanges.[2] Playing, grooming, consorting, copulating, and cuddling together for warmth are other common mutually reinforcing activities.

---

[1] Jolly (1966); Sugiyama (1968, 1976); Rowell (1969); Fedigan (1972a); Wolfheim (1977a); and Lancaster (1979).
[2] Horwich and Wurman (1978).

PLATE 6.1. The mother-infant relationship is one of the major positive mutual attractions that produces group cohesion. Here a mother langur and her offspring embrace in greeting. (*Courtesy of J.R. Oppenheimer.*)

First, in virtually all primate species, the mother–infant relationship offers prolonged mutually reinforcing exchanges, even if no other social relationship does. The infant receives from the mother such positive reinforcers as contact comfort, warmth, nutrition, fluids, and optimal levels of sensory stimulation. Through Pavlovian conditioning the mere sight or odor of mother becomes a $^+$CS which functions as a conditioned reinforcer for approach and interaction, even when unconditioned reinforcers are absent (such as after weaning). The mother receives the positive reinforcers of nipple stimulation, milk release, mild sensory stimulation from the infant, and at times, social attention from other group members who are attracted to the infant. Because of the typical patterns of female socialization,[3] these reinforcers cause most females to respond to small infants as $^+$CS's that function as conditioned reinforcers for approach and interaction. (Naturally, as the infant becomes larger, heavier, and rowdier, it may begin to produce aversive stimuli that countercondition the early positive associations.)

Second, heterosexual interaction can be a source of mutually reinforcing social exchange (if competition for sexual reinforcers does not introduce disruptive aversive contingencies[4]). Rhesus males find the genital odors of receptive females to be reinforcing; and males will bar-press for access to females if these odor cues are present.[5] Male squirrel monkeys and howlers often approach adult females to smell their sexual odors.[6] Depending on the species and the setting, either sex may approach the other for copulation; and consort relationships can last for hours or days, in which the animals exchange various reinforcers—such as genital stimulation, tactile stimulation via grooming, warmth, and conditioned reinforcers. In groups that have mating seasons and peripheral males, it is common to see the peripheral males attempt to enter groups during the mating season, then drift out to more peripheral positions after mating season.[7] Thus, changes in the availability of sexual reinforcers produce seasonal changes in positive centripetal conditioning.[8]

Third, even though social grooming does not appear to be equally common or important in all primates, it does provide a mutually rewarding mode of interaction in many. Grooming behavior appears to be shaped by a variety of reinforcers[9] because (a) the mild scratching and massaging of the skin are rewarding to the recipient, (b) the interaction produces mild levels of overall sensory stimulation for both groomer and groomee, (c) grooming establishes friendly contact which may facilitate other rewarding social interactions—such as sexual interaction, "aunt"-to-infant contact, or proximity to and friendship with a larger animal who provides safety or protective support; and (d) these positive reinforcers help relax overaroused individuals by counterconditioning, hence they ease social tensions and decrease the probability of aggression.

[3] Baldwin and Baldwin (1977a:372f).
[4] Richard (1974) and Drickamer (1975, 1976).
[5] Michael and Keverne (1968).
[6] Baldwin (1970); Glander (1975); and Strayer and Harris (1979).
[7] Nishida (1966); Baldwin (1968); Lindburg (1969); Boelkins and Wilson (1972); Rowell and Dixson (1975); and Drickamer (1975, 1976).
[8] The fact that sexual reinforcers are merely a fraction of all the reinforcers exchanged in primate groups lends support to the conclusions of Lancaster and Lee (1965), Wilson and Vessey (1968), Rowell (1972), and others who have shown the inadequacies of Zuckerman's (1932) hypothesis that sex is the central attraction holding primate societies together.
[9] Baldwin (1969:57); Mitchell and Tokunaga (1976); Seyfarth (1977); and McKenna (1978).

PLATE 6.2. Social grooming—as shown here in chimpanzees—is an important source of tactile reinforcers that helps unify social groupings. (*Photograph by C.E.G. Tutin.*)

A fourth important type of mutually positive attraction is based on behavioral similarity. Several studies have suggested that—aside from heterosexual relations and the highly reinforcing mother–infant interaction—immature animals and adult females often prefer interactions with familiar animals of similar age and sex.[10] This mutual preference occurs because interaction with similar individuals is mutually reinforcing. It is helpful to examine the interaction of similar individuals from the viewpoint of exchange theory.[11] Individuals with similarities in optimal activity level, behavior repertoires, and preferences for reinforcers are most likely to be able to coordinate positive activities while

[10] Altmann (1968); Sugiyama (1968); Sackett (1971); Baldwin (1971); Simonds (1974a); Rowell and Dixon (1975); Wolfheim (1977a); Symons (1978); Hopf (1978); and Davis (1978). Patterns of male preferences are more complex, since the reinforcers based on behavioral similarity are sometimes intermixed with punishers resulting from competition and aggression (Eisenberg et al., 1972).

[11] Thibaut and Kelley (1959:52f) and Homans (1974:65).

not incurring the interference costs (i.e., punishers) that often arise when two individuals' behavior styles are significantly different. For example, play groups tend to attract animals of similar age and size.[12] When two juvenile males play together, their similar size, strength, behavioral sophistication, and preference for rowdy play allows them to exchange high levels of positive reinforcement. However, when an infant and a juvenile play, there is a mismatch between the two players due to the infant's smaller size, relative weakness, less sophisticated behavior repertoire, and preference for gentler play. The smaller player is likely to become hurt or overaroused, and the juvenile to become understimulated or "bored." Neither will find as much reinforcement together as in play with agemates. As a consequence, in groups that have enough members for immature animals to locate several other individuals of similar age, it is not uncommon to observe infants and juveniles playing and moving in separate groups.

For similar reasons, adult females often seek each other's company. Although adult females have highly reinforcing interactions with small nursing infants, their stimulation preferences and behavior repertoires are often very different from those of juveniles and adult males, and most similar to those of other adult females. Due to behavioral similarity, there are reinforcers for forming all-female (plus infant) groupings. Adult females frequently exchange low intensity stimuli—for example, when grooming or huddling together—which are reinforcing because of the tactile stimulation, body contact, warmth, and security they provide.[13] In many species these mutually reinforcing exchanges draw the adult females together to form a stable core of the group.[14] Infants are, of course, strongly attached to the adult female core; and older offspring (especially females) are often sufficiently attached to produce an extended family grouping or a social organization based on matrilineal kinship.[15] The reinforcers of grooming, contact security, and play can, of course, operate across kin lines and help unify nonkin within a group.[16] Adult males sometimes form subgroups within a larger group, as do subadult males.[17] However, the fact that adult males can be the most aggressive group members in some species introduces aversive

[12] Baldwin (1969; 1971); Symons (1978); and Rhine and Hendy-Neely (1978).

[13] Koyama (1973); Mitchell and Tokunaga (1976); and Hopf (1978).

[14] Sade (1965, 1972); Eisenberg and Kuehn (1966); Vandenberg (1967); Neville (1968a); Rowell (1969, 1972); Poirier (1969); Baldwin (1971); Eisenberg et al. (1972); Simonds (1974a); and Drickamer (1976).

[15] Yamada (1963); Sade (1965, 1972); Koyama (1967); Struhsaker (1967a); Marler and Gordon (1968); Rosenblum (1971a); van Lawick-Goodall (1973b); Massey (1977); and Nash (1978b).

[16] Yamada (1963).

[17] van Lawick-Goodall (1967b); Altmann (1968); Baldwin (1968); Sugiyama (1969); and Simonds (1974a).

PLATE 6.3. A group of three spider monkeys is resting in physical contact. The reinforcers obtained from physical contact play an important role in producing social unity. (*Photo by C.M. Hladik made during fellowship at the Smithsonian Tropical Research Institute.*)

exchanges and centrifugal conditioning (discussed below) that can hinder the formation of all-male groupings in those species.[18]

Mutually reinforcing social exchanges should produce the strongest and most cohesive positive relationships. Some mutual positive relationships are relatively brief—such as sexual consort pairs—because the period of reinforcement is circumscribed. However, when reinforcers

---

[18] Eisenberg et al. (1972).

are available for a prolonged period, mutually reinforcing exchanges may be long lived, such as in some mother–offspring relations, play groups, grooming partnerships, or all-female groupings. As individuals share mutually reinforcing interactions, they become familiar and positive for each other; this in turn helps animals be more tolerant and less aggressive with each other.[19]

A *unilateral* transfer of positive reinforcers may cause one animal to approach another even though the approach is not reciprocated. A young chimpanzee may be curious to see what an older one is doing as the older "fishes" at a termite mound.[20] Novel sensory input (and perhaps some food reinforcers if the young one successfully imitates the behavior) reward the young animal for approaching the older animal; whereas the older animal may receive negligible amounts of reinforcers and punishers from the younger and may neither approach nor avoid it.

When one individual discovers food, water, or an interesting object, the individual's positive emotional responses to it may serve as ^+CS's that reinforce the attention and approach of other nearby animals. The unilateral flow of reinforcers from the discoverer to the observer increases the probability that clumped sources of environmental reinforcers will reward animals for coming together. Once they have discovered a cluster of reinforcers, the animals are likely to remain together due to environmental reinforcers. This sometimes happens when large, clustered food sources or centralized shelter areas (e.g., sleeping cliffs) reinforce proximity.[21] Because they are experiencing positive reinforcers while in social proximity, the animals may learn to respond to each other as increasingly positive stimuli (^+CS's), which in turn reinforce proximity even when the animals are not near clusters of environmental reinforcers.[22]

In competitive interactions centered on scarce resources, one animal may obtain reinforcers at the cost of reinforcers lost for the second. For example, a larger, high-rank animal may regularly receive reinforcers for approaching and taking food from a low-rank groupmate; however the low-rank individual experiences aversive consequences that produce centrifugal conditioning to avoid the food stealer (page 161) or that condition aggressive responses if aggression prevents food from being stolen (page 165).

[19] Burton, J. (1977).
[20] van Lawick-Goodall (1968).
[21] Haddow (1952); Kummer (1968, 1971); Hayashi (1969); Aldrich-Blake et al. (1971); Denham (1971); Southwick (1972); and Suzuki (1979).
[22] Baldwin and Baldwin (1973a).

Negative Centripetal Conditioning (2)

Primates—especially the young, and sometimes females of all ages—may escape or avoid aversive stimuli by staying close to the group. The strange, perhaps hostile world outside the group can contain punishers that negatively reinforce attachments to the group. Protection from predators is probably one of the most important functions of group living in primates[23]; thus the negative reinforcement of escaping aversive experiences would be expected to be a crucial component of centripetal conditioning.

Individuals who have learned to fear being alone, or to fear being away from close social contact, would be expected to have an especially strong motivation to maintain proximity to the group. In laboratory experiments infant monkeys run to their mothers or surrogate mothers more frequently and stay near them longer when a frightening object is put in the test environment than they do in baseline conditions.[24] In the wild, infants run to their mothers—and other group members often close ranks—in times of group alarm caused by a predator, heavy rain, high wind, humans, and so forth.[25] Of the 11 factors that Altmann and Altmann (1970:111) observed that cause yellow baboons to close ranks, seven involved threat from outside the group.

Although aversive stimuli in the nonsocial environment often condition avoidance of these stimuli, that avoidance would not necessarily lead an individual to seek out contact with its group if the group did not provide escape from the aversive stimuli. However, aversive experiences that an individual encounters when alone in the environment outside the group are often followed by safety and fear-reducing social interactions after it returns to the group. The successful termination of aversive stimulation provides negative reinforcement for centripetal responses. For example, infants who have been frightened while off their mothers' bodies learn to return to mother, because contact comfort facilitates fear reduction, hence provides negative reinforcement for returning. When the frightened infant clings to its mother, her warm, soft body provides arousal reduction.[26] Thus, the mother becomes a $^+$CS for comfort and an S^D for approach when the infant encounters too many aversive stimuli in the nonsocial environment. Through generalization, other group members may cue approach responses when the infant has been overaroused or frightened. After the infant has approached various group members, differential reinforcement will determine which individuals the infant will approach in future cases of

---

[23] Rowell (1979).

[24] Harlow (1959); and Harlow and Harlow (1969).

[25] Even in fish (Breder, 1959), birds (Tinbergen, 1951), and various mammals (Eisenberg and Lockhart, 1972), group members often close ranks in the presence of external danger.

[26] Mason (1968).

distress. The infant may learn to discriminate between a friendly "aunt" who will allow it to cling to her warm, soft body when distressed, and an unfriendly adult female who threatens the infant when it comes near. As primates grow up, they learn to seek out peers, kin, or special friends for proximity or contact when frightened. Proximity or contact with a familiar, friendly individual facilitates anxiety reduction, and hence enhances negative centripetal conditioning.

In some groups, the larger, stronger animals may chase predators away from the group. When this is the case, the protected individuals find that staying close to the group is associated with the termination of fear stimuli and hence negatively reinforced.

Negative centripetal conditioning from the nonsocial environment can be enhanced by "fear socialization" from social sources. Fear socialization is most likely to occur during infancy, as older group members cause the infant to fear environmental stimuli that it had not previously feared. For example, when an infant squirrel monkey fearlessly explores objects or places that are $^-$CS's to its mother and elicit her fear, the mother may respond by running up to the infant for a fear-inducing retrieval, consisting of loud vocalizations, sudden movements, and rapid flight, which clearly makes the infant anxious.[27] Immediately after a mother sweeps up her infant in a fear-inducing retrieval, she may flee from the source of environmental danger and withdraw to safety and quiet. Thus, for the infant, the environmental stimulus is paired with aversive events, and social contact is paired with arousal reduction. The infant learns to fear the environmental stimuli and to find subsequent social interaction the means of escaping that fear.[28] This conditioning process causes the infant to fear many of the same stimuli that its mother fears. Fear socialization can be adaptive in passing on a mother's fears to her young. Capuchin monkeys who fear humans appear to pass on their fears to their young (much as a group tradition) via fear socialization, in which a mother's alarm calls and flight are paired with the sight of an environmental fear stimulus.[29] Washburn and Hamburg (1965:619f) reported the development of a fear tradition in a group of baboons, as the fear responses of a few animals were communicated to others who had not experienced the original fear-inducing situation. They concluded: "It is highly adaptive for animals to learn what to fear without having to experience events directly themselves."

Laboratory studies suggest that the effects of negative centripetal conditioning and fear socialization might be more long-lasting than those of positive centripetal conditioning.[30] When an individual learns to fear

[27] Baldwin (1969).
[28] Mowrer (1960).
[29] Baldwin and Baldwin (1977b).
[30] Miller (1948) and Sidman (1966).

a given stimulus, the fear often motivates avoidance of the stimulus. Avoidance of a stimulus makes it unlikely that the fear could extinguish, even if the stimulus ceased to be aversive or the individual learned skills for coping successfully with the stimulus. Thus, both fears and the avoidance behavior that they motivate can be very persistent, even when there is actually nothing to fear. Positive associations, on the other hand, extinguish quickly when the individual approaches a once positive stimulus and finds that it is no longer positive. For this reason, negative, centripetal conditioning experiences can have more impact and long-lasting effect on behavior than equally intense positive conditioning experiences. Once a primate has a few frightening experiences after becoming separated from its group, it may learn to avoid becoming separated, hence show a strong, persistent attraction to its group even in situations where being alone might not be dangerous. Certain forms of centrifugal conditioning can reverse this effect (page 159).

Because most primates are in fact safer from predators and more likely to experience positive reinforcers when they are in social contact rather than alone in the environment outside the group, there is both negative and positive reinforcement for centripetal responses. In general, if being with the group provides positive exchanges, security, and safety from danger, the whole group will take on positive value that promotes cohesion among the members. This general cohesion is, of course, coupled with the specific attractions and repulsions that individuals show to each other due to specific positive and aversive experiences with each groupmate.

Positive Centrifugal Conditioning (3)

The environment outside the group contains many positive reinforcers that can condition centrifugal movement away from the group. Reinforcement for moving away from the group can change an individual's sociometric relation to the group and increase the likelihood of its becoming peripheral or changing groups. One might argue that centrifugal conditioning is a "desocialization" process, since it moves the individual away from social contact with its group. However, this term is misleading since centrifugal conditioning is an important part of the normal social learning experience of many individuals. As we shall show, social learning may be involved as an antecedent factor that facilitates centrifugal conditioning; and social functions may be fulfilled when centrifugal movement leads to the investigation of widely scattered food sources, mobbing of strangers, "group protector" behavior, or intergroup transfer.

The nonsocial environment provides a diversity of positive reinforcers, located where there are food sources, water holes, exposed branches for sunning or drying on cool mornings or after a rain, novel places and objects to be explored, and so forth. Environmental reinforcers (on the occasions when they are present and environmental fear stimuli are absent or relatively less salient) can attract an individual away from social contact. An entire group can become fragmented when there is an abundance of widely scattered reinforcers to reinforce dispersal. Instead of reinforcing aggregation (as scarce, clumped reinforcers do), widely scattered food or shelter provides reinforcement for the animals to split up and spread out.[31] If several individuals in a group experience centrifugal conditioning, this decreases the social cohesion within the group and produces a more diffuse social structure. Those individuals who have numerous positive experiences away from their group would be expected to find distance or separation from their group less aversive and more rewarding than other group members without such positive centrifugal conditioning.

Social learning can facilitate the acquisition of skills that subsequently promote centrifugal conditioning. First, the more proficient an animal is at manipulation, dexterity, flight, and other independence skills, the less likely it is to be hurt or frightened while exploring or venturing away from the group. Since many independence skills are learned by imitation or operant conditioning during social interaction, social learning experience can condition the independence skills that eventually allow some animals not to fear leaving the group when extragroup reinforcers attract them.

Second, peer play often functions to countercondition those fears of the environment that the young infant acquired during exploration or through fear socialization from mother or other caretakers.[32] The counterconditioning of environmental fears occurs because the positive reinforcers of play often draw players into risky or strange situations that a cautious, lone, or nonplaying youngster would avoid; then, if there are no negative consequences, the absence of aversive experience and the presence of positive play reinforcers (of optimal sensory stimulation) countercondition early fears of the environment. Thus, social experience helps reduce fears of the environment that might have retarded exploration away from the group and increases the likelihood that positive centrifugal conditioning can occur.

Third, there is reason to believe that maturing males can cope with the extragroup environment more successfully than females: The males

---

[31] Thorington (1967, 1968) and Aldrich-Blake et al. (1971).
[32] Baldwin (1969) and Dolhinow (1971).

of many species are stronger, larger, equipped with longer canine teeth, and more habituated to highly novel inputs than are females of the same age.[33] All through the males' lives, the extra body size, muscles, "weapons," and preference for high stimulation give them an advantage in learning independence skills. For example, during play, a male would have the advantage over a smaller, lighter female of his age: Because of his greater strength, weight, and high stimulus preference, it is likely that he would experience more positive reinforcers and fewer aversive consequences in play than she. She would be more likely to be hurt, to withdraw from play, and to seek the security of her mother's side or quiet activities than he. Staying in play, the male would be more likely to habituate to even higher levels of rowdy activity, novelty, and surprising events than the female. All of these factors cause the male to learn a larger behavior repertoire for coping successfully with the dangers and surprises of the extragroup environment and for finding positive reinforcers there. As a consequence, subadult and adult males are more likely than females to move to the group vanguard and periphery in group progressions, or even to break off as isolated individuals or subgroups.[34] When confronted with a predator, strange individual, or strange group, adult males tend to be more fearless, "more self-assured and bolder than their smaller conspecifics" (Harding, 1977:352). Consequently, if the extragroup stimulus is not excessively frightening the adult males are the most likely to approach and investigate the stimulus. If the extragroup stimulus is either strange or threatening, it may elicit the males' aggression.[35] Thus, males would be more likely than females to function in the "group protector" role. This analysis is compatible with Rowell's (1974a) data that species with larger, more dimorphic males show a stronger tendency for the males to act as group protectors. However, if the fear stimulus is sufficiently aversive, even large dimorphic adult males can be motivated to flee. Under these circumstances, the entire group may take flight, sometimes with the adult males at the head of the column and the mothers, carrying heavy infants, at the end closest to the fear stimulus.[36] At the other extreme, there are reports of primates taking aggressive action against leopards and lions, "thus raising the possibility that some troops may learn by experience to become more assertive than others in response to predators" (Saayman, 1971:48). The contingencies that produce this type of response are discussed below (page 165).

---

[33] Baldwin and Baldwin (1977a:372–375).

[34] Carpenter (1934); Schaller (1963); Hall and DeVore (1965); Baldwin (1968, 1971); Rowell (1969, 1972); Weber and Vogel (1970); Eisenberg et al. (1972); van Lawick-Goodall (1973b); Rhine (1975); and Mori (1979).

[35] Stoltz and Saayman (1970); Konrad and Melzack (1975); Marler (1976).

[36] Rowell (1966a:362).

Negative Centrifugal Conditioning (4)

Centrifugal movement is negatively reinforced when there are aversive stimuli associated with group life. All primates probably experience some aversive interaction with certain group members; thus all learn, via negative reinforcement, some tendency to avoid aversive interactions with these individuals. The more negative social reinforcement an animal experiences, the more likely it is to space itself away from the source of aversive stimuli (other factors being equal).[37]

Negative centrifugal conditioning begins in infancy. The infant learns to separate itself from its mother in part because of the increased punishment she gives the maturing infant when it ceases being as positive for her as the small infant is.[38] As infants grow up and explore social relations with other group members, they may find that interaction with or mere proximity to certain animals is associated with aversive consequences, hence learn to avoid these individuals.[39] Body size, weight, muscular development, and canine development appear to be among the most important variables that influence patterns of negative centrifugal conditioning. Large, strong, healthy individuals have a clear advantage in interactions where aversive or painful stimuli may be exchanged, hence are more likely to give than receive the punishers that cause negative centrifugal conditioning. (The fact that larger animals have the potential to harm smaller ones does not, of course, mean that they will necessarily learn the aggressive behavior. A large juvenile in a group that has few juveniles is likely to learn to play gently with smaller playmates because (a) hurting the smaller individuals causes them to avoid playing with the larger animal, hence punishes the juvenile's rowdy play with a loss of play reinforcers, whereas (b) playing gently with small animals leads to prolonged play and more reinforcement.)

Aggressive adult males can cause adult females to avoid them, and thus decrease their chances of successful copulation.[40] In laboratory studies on adult sexual interactions, females bar-press least for access to those males who have been most aggressive to them in the past, indicating that prior aversive interactions created $^-$CS's and avoidance.[41]

A major example of negative centrifugal conditioning involves the peripheralization of subadult or young adult males by larger adult males.

---

[37] The apparently anomalous case of infants' clinging more to their mothers when the mothers are punitive (Rosenblum, 1971b) can be explained as follows: Since punishment is arousal inducing, it exacerbates the infant's need for arousal reduction; and the only source of arousal reduction for the infant is contact comfort from the mother. Hence, it seeks out contact from the individual who caused the overarousal in the first place.

[38] Jensen et al. (1969, 1973).

[39] van Lawick-Goodall (1973b).

[40] Baldwin (1968) and Bernstein (1976b).

[41] Michael et al. (1978).

The subadult and young adult males of many primate species are chased, harassed, and fought by the group's adult males. These aversive interactions produce negative centrifugal conditioning which—in conjunction with the positive centrifugal conditioning discussed above—often causes the young males to become peripheral or to leave the group completely.[42] The expulsion of subadult and adult males can be a complex process showing significant within-species variability. Since high-ranking mothers often protect their infants from threats and aversive interactions with other group members,[43] it is understandable that these protected males are least likely to experience the aversive conditioning that is in part responsible for males' leaving their natal group; and as a consequence these protected males are less likely to leave.[44] In siamangs and gibbons, both subadult males and subadult females are treated hostilely at 4 to 6 years of age, which negatively reinforces both sexes' leaving the natal group and maintains the stability of group size and structure.[45]

In squirrel monkeys, the adult females constitute the group core, and frequently form coalitions to drive the adult males away from the core areas.[46] During mating season, the adult males show a strong attraction to adult females (apparently due to sexual reinforcers), and they continue to reapproach the females after being chased away. However, when not in mating season (with few sexual reinforcers to attract the males to the female core), the adult males often are repelled to a peripheral position.

There can be significant variability in the "personalities" of the leader males and females in a group: Some groups have relaxed, friendly leaders, while others have aggressive leaders, depending on a variety of social learning experiences, including group traditions.[47] The more hostile and aggressive the group leaders are, the stronger is the centrifugal conditioning that causes other individuals to scatter and perhaps leave the group. In a very spacious and nonthreatening environment with scattered food sources, tyrannical leaders might find themselves being left alone or assiduously avoided, thus either losing members of their group or having few chances to display their aggressive behavior. However, in a hostile, dangerous environment, individuals would seek security in togetherness with others; thus centrifugal conditioning caused by tyrannical leaders would be, to some degree, counteracted by cen-

---

[42] Nishida (1966); Hall (1967); Baldwin (1969); Yamada (1971); Aldrich-Blake and Chivers (1973); Drickamer and Vessey (1973); and Mori (1979).

[43] Marsden (1968); Fedigan (1972b); and Eaton (1976).

[44] Norikoshi and Koyama (1975).

[45] Chivers (1971); Fox (1972); and Aldrich-Blake and Chivers (1973).

[46] DuMond (1968) and Baldwin (1968, 1971). Also see Wolfheim (1977a) and Packer and Pusey (1979).

[47] Yamada (1971).

tripetal conditioning from the hostile environment. As a consequence, tyrannical leaders could be more aggressive in hostile environments than in nonhostile ones, since the victims of their aggression would be less likely to flee from the group. Therefore, a hostile environment should both cause increased group cohesion and make possible (though not necessarily cause) the rise of aggressive styles of leadership. Comparative data on primates in hostile and nonhostile environments support this hypothesis. Data on baboons living in open savanna or forest environments and rhesus monkeys living in urban or forest environments indicate that in the more dangerous environments, groups are less likely to fragment and males do sometimes display more aggressive, tyrannical behavior.[48]

Provisioning and clumped food resources serve as a second factor that can cause individuals to crowd together in spite of the centrifugal conditioning of intragroup hostilities. For example, Japanese monkeys who are not provisioned maintain large individual distances and have relatively few social interactions due to avoidance responses; however, when provisioned, the monkeys are attracted into much closer proximity, in spite of the increased aggression that results from crowding.[49]

The behavior of each member of a group is shaped by many types of reinforcers and punishers from inside and outside the group. Any single pattern of centripetal or centrifugal movement will result from complex vector sums of all the four types of conditioning discussed above. Thus, an individual may approach a tyrannical male if other reinforcers outweigh the avoidance responses motivated by the $^-$CS's of the male. For example, small chimpanzees will approach large adult males, whom they normally avoid, if the males have meat that might be shared.[50] Small baboons often run to dominant males when being chased by other animals, because being next to the adult male provides protection from attacks by the chasers.[51] The vector sums for the actions of all individuals determine how strongly the group members will be attracted or repelled. According to Carpenter's (1952 [1964:383]) formulation, "the centripetal and centrifugal processes interact and result in varying degrees of group cohesiveness and dynamic stability. It is proposed that the vector sums of the centripetal and centrifugal forces equal the degree of group cohesiveness." Cohesiveness is most likely to be high in small, friendly groups living in somewhat threatening environments. The loss of cohesion and group fission are likely to occur when groups become too large for animals to share friendly interactions, when intragroup hostilities

---

[48] Hall and DeVore (1965); Rowell (1966a); Singh (1968, 1969); and Southwick (1972).
[49] Mori (1977).
[50] van Lawick-Goodall (1968).
[51] Kummer (1967).

arise, when scattered resources reinforce group fragmentation, or when external threats decrease.[52]

THE CONTINGENCIES OF REINFORCEMENT

The model developed above has analyzed the *location* of reinforcers and punishers, not the *contingencies* of reinforcement and punishment. In many cases, information on the location of reinforcers and punishers is adequate to explain the centripetal and or centrifugal movement of an individual. However, this is not always the case. Although most natural contingencies of reinforcement and punishment condition movement toward positive reinforcers and movement away from punishers, certain contingencies can produce different effects. There are enough cases in which the location of reinforcers and punishers fails to explain behavior, that special attention must be paid to the contingent relationships between behavior and consequences.

Most natural contingencies of reinforcement do not provide positive reinforcers until the individual has approached the reinforcers; thus approach becomes a common response to positive reinforcers. A monkey usually must approach food before it can eat. However, there are cases in which positive reinforcement is contingent upon not approaching, or even contingent upon moving away; and these contingencies usually condition responses other than approach. When stalking prey, a predator learns to be attentive to any sign that the prey is becoming aware of its presence; and these signs of wariness from the prey become S^D's for the predator's freezing temporarily and not approaching. A young monkey who has not had much experience hunting insects or lizards may run directly toward prey and fail to catch it; but differential reinforcement is likely to shape a more stealthy approach, with pauses interspersed whenever the prey looks around, since crucially timed pauses increase the overall chances of catching the prey. The contingencies of reinforcement imposed by detour situations condition movement away from the reinforcer as a prerequisite for finally contacting the reinforcer. Again, it may take time and experience before an individual learns to move away from its group in order to get around an impassable arboreal gap and recontact the group via an indirect route. Even ducklings that have been imprinted on a certain stimulus (making it a ^+CS) will learn *not* to approach or follow the stimulus if following causes the ^+CS to disappear and not following causes the ^+CS to reappear.[53]

Most natural contingencies of punishment condition avoidance of the

---

[52] Koyama (1970) and Chepko-Sade and Oliver (1979).
[53] Hoffman et al. (1969).

punishing stimulus because avoidance usually minimizes the individual's contact with the aversive stimulus. However, there are important exceptions in which approaching or staying near the source of punishers allows the individual to avoid punishment. In these cases individuals may learn not to avoid the source of punishers. When a female hamadryas baboon wanders too far away from the adult male who controls her social unit, the male approaches the female and bites her neck.[54] After several conditioning experiences, the female learns not to stray too far from the male: She learns to avoid—not the male, but rather—being bitten. Other subordinate individuals may also be placed in situations where staying near and placating a dominant individual (e.g., by grooming[55]) helps minimize punishment. A second way of minimizing punishment is to attack the source of the aversive stimuli. Not all attacks are successful, and some may precipitate stronger punishment than if there had been no attack. Therefore not all individuals will learn to attack sources of punishers. Most advanced species have a reflexive attack response that can be elicited by painful stimuli, and animals who cannot avoid painful stimuli will often attack and bite any conspicuous stimulus in response to the aversive stimulation.[56] Thus a young male might attack and bite another male if cornered and trapped by him. However, the future frequency of the attack and bite response depends on the consequences that follow the response.[57] If attacking is followed by punishers (even if these are the same aversive stimuli that elicited the first reflexive attack), the frequency of future attacks will be suppressed. On the other hand, if approach and attack are followed by reinforcers (such as the termination of aversive stimuli) the approach and attack responses are reinforced to higher probability. In order to predict whether a given individual will attack in any particular situation, it would be important to know the individual's past history of learning related to aggressive responses. Aggression would be most likely in individuals who have frequently seen models of aggression and gained access to positive reinforcers or escaped victimization when they themselves were aggressive. (This in turn will be influenced by the animal's age, sex, size, weight, social support, impressiveness of displays, and so forth.[58])

There are other possible contingencies involving models and schedule effects—along with rules and prompts, in the case of humans—that can condition movement away from positive reinforcers or movement toward aversive stimuli. When any of these contingencies operate, indi-

---

[54] Kummer (1968).
[55] McKenna (1978).
[56] Azrin et al. (1964, 1965).
[57] Azrin (1970).
[58] Riss and Goodall (1977).

viduals may show patterns of centripetal or centrifugal movement that could not be predicted from data on the location of reinforcers and punishers alone. Thus it is important to supplement data on the location of reinforcers and punishers with information on any controlling variables that might produce exceptions to the predictions based solely on locational data.

THE EXTRAGROUP ENVIRONMENT

Figure 6.3 elaborates on Figure 6.2 by including strange individuals or strange groups as stimuli existing outside the group boundary. Primate groups often repel strange individuals, or at least tend to be slow in accepting them into the group structure. Since group members recognize each other as familiar stimuli with somewhat predictable behavior to which each other member can adjust, a strange animal is, in comparison, quite novel and unpredictable. Marler (1976) presents data indicating that strangeness is the single strongest factor that causes animals to avoid or aggress against individuals who do not belong to their group; whereas familiarity is a primary bond that holds group members together. Strangers do, however, often persist in trying to join a group. Because subadult and adult males are the animals who most often leave their natal group, they are the ones most likely to seek entrance into new groups.[59] Since entries are much more common in mating season than in other seasons, it is reasonable to assume that the sight and odors of estrus-cycling adult females are among the more important positive reinforcers for the males' approaches.[60] Entry into a group is usually not an all-or-none event decided by one crucial interaction. It may be weeks or months before group members habituate to the proximity of

FIGURE 6.3. Carpenter's model is further expanded by adding the reinforcers and punishers associated with a strange primate (P) and strange group (G).

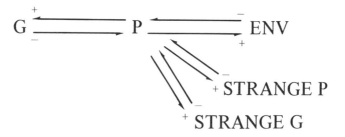

[59] Lindburg (1969); Rowell (1969); Yamada (1971); and Packer (1975).
[60] Baldwin (1970) and Rowell and Dixson (1975).

PLATE 6.4. An adult male gelada baboon directs paternal care to an infant as a means of gaining acceptance into a new group. (*Courtesy of U. Mori.*)

an entering individual and even longer before they interact with the individual as they would with a more familiar group member.[61]

A strange group presents an even more aversive stimulus complex than does a single strange individual. The two most reinforcing modes for coping with aversive stimuli are (1) to avoid or withdraw and (2) to threaten or chase away. Avoidance is the most common response in primates.[62] A given individual's and a group's response to a strange group will be determined by genetic predispositions for avoidance or attack, past reinforcement and punishment associated with both avoidance and attack, and the nature of the present stimuli (within the home group and from the strange group). Aggression is most likely to be reinforced in larger, stronger individuals with the health, skills, and genetic propensity for aggressive behavior. As group size increases there is an increased likelihood that several assertive individuals will be present, which makes it easier for large groups to displace smaller ones.[63] Under certain circumstances, peripheral males are more likely to engage

[61] Nishida (1966); Lindburg (1969); Boelkins and Wilson (1972); and Glander (1975).
[62] Marler (1968).
[63] Drickamer (1975).

in intergroup contacts (either hostile or friendly) than are the group's central males.[64]

Certain environmental conditions—such as scarce food or high population density—can increase the reinforcers for aggression (rather than avoidance). As a result, groups that spaced by mutual avoidance under some conditions would show aggressive territorial responses in others.[65] In general, territoriality and aggressive confrontations appear to be less common than mutual avoidance in primates.[66] In gorillas, for example, daily patterns of group movement are more influenced by the avoidance of strange groups than by food distribution or other factors.[67] Since each strange group elicits fear in the other group, it is easy for groups to mutually avoid each other or at least to maintain safe distances from each other (unless high population density makes it difficult to avoid other groups). Group members may show a guarded interest in a distant, strange group—due to its novelty and safe distance—but show fear of close approach because approach makes the strange stimuli so salient that they elicit fear.[68]

When strange groups are attracted simultaneously to a source of environmental reinforcers (e.g., a waterhole, a sleep area, a flowering or fruiting tree), many possible patterns can emerge: (1) conflict over scarce resources (resulting in either territoriality or dominance–subordination); (2) signs of anxiety or approach–withdrawal conflict as the environmental reinforcers draw the groups into closer proximity than they can tolerate without anxiety; (3) alternation back and forth in using the resource; and (4) habituation or desensitization to each other after enough time in proximity (if they share the positive reinforcers without conflict). It would be necessary to have data on the multiple determinants of learning and the species' biological predispositions in order to predict which patterns would be most likely to appear in any given context. The format of intergroup encounters depends on the age–sex composition and size of the groups, the size and resources of their home ranges, and their past history of interaction.[69]

Two groups of different species can be drawn together if (1) they share similar preferences for food, shelter, or other resources (i.e., respond to similar stimuli as reinforcers), and (2) clumped resources reinforce their utilizing the same space.[70] Once two species are drawn together at a clumped resource, interaction and attraction across species boundaries is possible if their behavior repertoires are sufficiently similar

[64] Hausfater (1972).
[65] Yoshiba (1968); Chivers (1969); Richard (1974); and Hamilton et al. (1976).
[66] Marler (1968).
[67] Fossey (1974).
[68] Baldwin and Baldwin (1978a:241).
[69] Hamilton et al. (1975).
[70] Haddow (1952).

that individuals can interact with a mutual exchange of reinforcers and without aversive components. From field observations and a review of the literature, Rose (1977) found that play and grooming (which are mutually reinforcing activities) are the most common forms of interaction between primate species and that they appear most frequently where the animals are provisioned (thus drawn together by clumped food reinforcers). In addition, play between species is most likely to be prolonged (an indicator that it is mutually reinforcing) if the animals are of similar ages and sizes and if their activity patterns are performed in a similar manner. This again indicates the importance of behavioral similarity in producing mutually reinforcing interactions (page 152).

MAPS OF REINFORCERS AND PUNISHERS

In some cases it might be desirable to create maps of all the reinforcers and punishers that group members obtain from the environment and from each other.[71] Figure 6.4 is a hypothetical map of the reinforcers and punishers that one group member might receive from the nonsocial environment. Each individual would have a somewhat different mapping, due to its own unique history of conditioning experiences. A temporal sequence of such maps would facilitate an ecological analysis of behavior by focusing on the spatial and temporal distribution of resources and dangers. Areas with valuable resources would become $^{+}CS's$, thus positive conditioned reinforcers (indicated by + signs in the figure) due to pairing with positive reinforcement. Sleep trees, waterholes, sources of abundant food, safe trails, efficient routes, open play areas, sunning spots, and other areas where reinforcing activities occurred would become conditioned reinforcers for the animals, hence attract them and become focal areas for their activities. Familiar arboreal and terrestrial routes leading to positive locations would also become positive.

Within the home range, certain areas would become $^{-}CS's$, thus conditioned punishers (indicated by − signs in the figure) due to pairing with aversive incidents. Such negative locations might include a thicket where predators had occasionally been encountered (A in Figure 6.4), a wide arboreal crossing where several animals have had painful falls

---

[71] The mappings discussed here are not to be confused with "cognitive maps." The maps of reinforcers and punishers are intended to serve as a device for locating the prime movers of individuals' behavior in the real world, not in the animals' heads. At any point in time, the animals will tend to respond to only a portion of the salient reinforcers and punishers, rather than picturing the totality of their environments. This does not deny the fact that primates have good memories of their environment (cf. Altmann and Altmann, 1970:198); it merely states that those memory responses are evoked by currently salient S^{D}'s, and that only portions of those memories (not entire maps) are evoked at any given time.

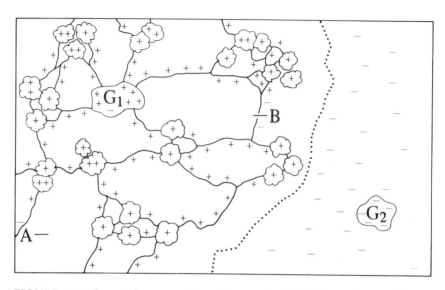

FIGURE 6.4. The reinforcers and punishers an individual associates with various parts of the environment are represented as a mapping of positive and negative stimuli. The home range of G_1 is mostly positive to the animals in that group, especially areas with favorite travel routes, fruiting trees, and sleep trees. Areas outside the home range boundary (*dotted line*) and a strange group (G_2) are negative. The mapping of positive and negative stimuli will differ from individual to individual.

(B in Figure 6.4), a tree containing wasp nests, and so forth. For example, Altmann and Altmann (1970:80) report that baboons stopped using a once popular sleeping grove after two group members were killed there by a leopard. However, they also point out (p. 175) that some dangerous areas are not avoided because they also contain essential resources (positive reinforcers) that attract the animals. For most primates, strange groups and the area outside their home range or territory are negative stimuli that negatively reinforce avoidance. Adult males are more likely than other group members to find the environment outside their group and home range positive, though adult females in some species (e.g., colobus, chimpanzees, and gorillas[72]) also leave their natal group, entering new areas and joining new groups.

Thus, the existence of numerous environmental reinforcers and punishers causes the landscape to become a complex and often changing patchwork of positive and negative stimuli that attract or repel each individual according to its unique history of conditioning. Because group members have somewhat different positive and negative associations

---

[72] Nishida and Kawanaka (1972); Teleki et al. (1976); Harcourt et al. (1976); and Marsh (1979). But also see Sugiyama and Koman (1979).

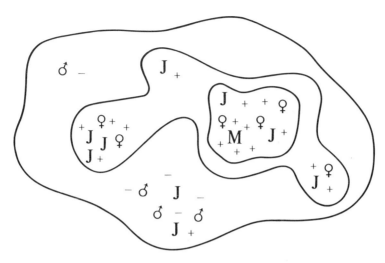

FIGURE 6.5. The reinforcers and punishers an individual associates with its groupmates are represented as a mapping of positive and negative stimuli embedded in the group structure. In this example, an infant finds its mother (M) and her close associates most positive, other females and juveniles (Js) positive, and the group males negative. Each individual would have a different mapping of positive and negative associations.

with the various stimuli in the extragroup environment, there are often differences in the approach, avoidance, and utilization responses that each individual shows to various parts of the environment. Responses also change over time. After discussing the variability in group movement patterns in baboons, Harding (1977:352) concludes: "In short, baboons change their dispersion patterns in response to past experiences in different parts of their range." As the availability and nutritive value of various foods change over the yearly cycle, the number of hours spent foraging to obtain adequate food reinforcers varies.[73] As individuals mature and gain coping skills, a given environmental stimulus may take on different positive or negative reinforcement values. A certain wide arboreal crossing may be a $^+$CS for the adults who can jump it easily, but a $^-$CS for the younger animals, who sometimes fall while trying to cross. However, as the young animals mature and gain skills at jumping, the wide gaps cease to be negative (and eventually become positive if they are superior to alternative routes).

The intragroup environment can also be analyzed as a map of positive and negative stimuli (Figure 6.5). Each individual in the group will have its own unique set of positive and negative associations for its fellow group members, resulting from past experiences with each member and

[73] Davidge (1978).

from generalization. If an individual has positive interactions with one group member, the sight and proximity of that animal become positive reinforcers;[74] whereas negative interactions condition fear associations.[75] An individual may learn to respond to some cues from a given groupmate as $^+$CS's and to other cues as $^-$CS's, thus learning to approach when that individual shows playful responses ($^+$CS's) but to avoid when it gives threats ($^-$CS's). A complex history of social learning can clearly condition complex patterns of social responses as each individual learns to seek out rewarding interactions and avoid punitive ones.

The reinforcement model is quite compatible with Kummer's (1967) theory of tripartite relations, though the number of individuals need not be held to three. Kummer found tripartite relations to occur when one animal (A) attacked a second (B), who ran to a third (C) for protection. Animal B responds to A as a $^-$CS. If B's running to C is negatively reinforced by escaping aversive consequences, animal C becomes a $^+$CS for B. For example, a large juvenile (A) may chase an infant (B), who runs to mother (C) for protection. More than three animals may be involved. For example, when she is not sexually receptive, a female talapoin or squirrel monkey learns to avoid rowdy adult males and seek the protection of proximity to several other females, because a male is reluctant to approach a cluster of several adult females.[76] When enough females band together, they can "gang up" on the male to chase him away. Thus, the centrifugal conditioning that makes nonreceptive females usually avoid adult males in these species need not produce group fragmentation: The success of female coalitions provides a counteracting source of centripetal conditioning to unite the females. As a consequence, females form the group core and unisexual subgroups of adults are common in both talapoins and squirrel monkeys.[77]

As an individual matures, has ever-changing experiences with other group members, and discriminates when others will respond in positive or negative ways, relevant features of its social map change. These intragroup maps correspond closely to sociograms used to reveal the positive and negative relations between group members. Since the structure of positive interactions need not be the converse of the structure of negative interactions, separate sociograms for positive and negative relations often reveal more about group structure than do single sociograms.[78]

---

[74] Mason et al. (1974).
[75] Murphy et al. (1955).
[76] Baldwin and Baldwin (1972); Wolfheim (1977b).
[77] Thorington (1968); Balwin (1971); Fairbanks (1974); Rowell and Dixson (1975); and Wolfheim (1977a).
[78] Virgo and Waterhouse (1969).

Because different patterns of reinforcement operate in different situations in an individual's daily life, social relations vary as the situation varies. Situational (or context) cues become S^D's for different types of interaction. A group rest period may be an S^D for an infant to approach peers to play, whereas signs of group movement may be S^D's for approaching mother to ride. Thus, the complete web of social relationships cannot be described by one map or sociogram that reflects all situations.[79] Different sociograms are needed to reveal the complexity that results from the different contingencies of reinforcement operating in different situations. Situational sociograms provide valuable information by showing how positive and negative interactions are contingent on current environmental conditions and ongoing behaviors.[80]

THE SOCIAL STRUCTURE OF ATTENTION

Chance's (1967, 1976) theory of social attention can be made to dovetail nicely with the reinforcement model. Chance describes four basic types of social attention structures that result from combining either *centric* or *acentric* attention modes based on either *hedonic* or *agonistic* types of interactions. Centric attention focuses toward the center of a group or social subunit, and acentric focuses away from the center. Centric and acentric attention correspond to the centripetal and centrifugal directions in Carpenter's model. Hedonic and agonistic types of exchanges correspond to some degree with interactions shaped by reinforcers and punishers.

Centric–Hedonic. Attention is focused toward the group or a specific individual due to the positive reinforcement that results from coordination and interaction. For example, a mother and her newly independent infant often exchange glances during group progressions because this centric–hedonic attention allows them to coordinate their movements, thus facilitating rewarding interactions. Likewise, two players or a consorting male and female often focus attention on each other because centric attention increases the probability of coordinating a rewarding interaction. Positive cues (^+CS's) from a partner often function to reinforce centric–hedonic attention. In laboratory experiments, socially reared juvenile female rhesus monkeys (with relevant social learning experience) bar-press more frequently to see pictures of affectionate facial expressions (^+CS's) than pictures of threats or fear grimaces (^-CS's).[81] Because novelty is usually a positive reinforcer, primates tend

[79] Hanby (1975).
[80] Kummer (1968); Koyama (1973); and Baxter and Fedigan (1979).
[81] Redican et al. (1971).

to direct extra attention to conspecifics who present some novel stimulus features.[82]

Acentric–Hedonic. Friendly individuals may look away from each other, merely because (1) they are so familiar with each other's behavior that they can coordinate with tactile or auditory cues or with a minimum of glances, and (2) other stimuli in the group or the environment provide stronger reinforcement for their visual attention. This is especially true in times of group rest or low activity, when there are few situations requiring spatial adjustments and coordination via visual attention. Since visual attention to a friend is not needed (i.e., not reinforced) when both animals are quiet and inactive, the animals may gaze at the environment, focus their vigilance on other group members, or close their eyes. As a consequence, close friendship patterns are often better measured by contact, grooming, huddling together, and the exchange of other reinforcing interactions than by visual attention alone.[83]

Centric–Agonistic. Animals will look toward a source of aversive stimuli if such looking is negatively reinforced, i.e., if the visual information they obtain helps them avoid punishment or avoid uncertainty about future events.[84] Primates learn to keep an eye on any individual that might hit or bite them, since visual attention gives them access to the S^D's that cue them to escape from or avoid aversive stimuli. This is compatible with Rowell's (1966b) view that the behavioral manifestations of hierarchies result in large part from the cautious behavior of subordinate individuals (though this behavior is conditioned by the ^-US's and ^-CS's from the dominant individuals).[85] Threat displays by aggressive individuals increase the salience of the ^-CS's that motivate attentiveness, hence increase the probability of centric–agonistic attention.

Acentric–Agonistic. When a possible source of aversive stimuli poses no threat or danger, individuals are likely to look away: Since there is no real danger, there is no negative reinforcement for attending; and the ^-CS's motivate looking away to avoid aversive stimulation.[86] Thus, animals do not look at the threat displays of a male who never follows his threats with aversive stimuli: There is no negative reinforcement for

---

[82] Deni and Drake (1977).

[83] Pitcairn (1976) and Anderson and Chamove (1979).

[84] Steiner (1970); Nevin (1971a,b); Haude et al. (1976).

[85] Because many stimulus features of an aggressive animal become ^-CS's to others, the aggressive animal need only yawn, stand up, or walk by to provide the ^-CS's that motivate centric–agonistic attention. Thus subordinate individuals may show frequent signs of attention and moving away even though the aggressive individual may seldom attend to or overtly threaten them.

[86] Redican et al. (1971).

watching. In laboratory tests rhesus monkeys avoid looking at aversive stimuli presented on color slides:[87] Looking is punished by seeing aversive stimuli and never reinforced by facilitating escape from some other aversive events. (Naturally, if the novelty or new information content of the slides is very high, novelty will reinforce looking at aversive slides until they cease to be novel.[88])

Although Chance's model of social attention reveals part of the social structure of groups, attention is only one of the behaviors shaped by the prime movers of social behavior—i.e., by the reinforcers and punishers—and it need not correlate with other important social activities that are shaped by other contingencies of reinforcement. Hence, we view the social structure of attention as only a subset of all the behavior molded by the structure of reinforcers and punishers; and we advocate studying the broader issues involving the entire mapping of reinforcers and punishers and their contingent relation to behavior rather than believing that social attention alone will reveal social structure.

THE TOTAL MAP

By superimposing appropriately scaled social maps of reinforcers and punishers onto the environmental maps of positive and negative consequences, it is possible to integrate both the ecological and social reinforcers and punishers that jointly condition the learned components of primate behavior and social organization. For example, a small-scale version of Figure 6.5 could be located in the correct position on Figure 6.4. Since food is one of the most important reinforcers affecting primate social organization, we will briefly examine some of the data demonstrating the value of total consequence mapping for understanding the effects of ecological reinforcers and punishers on social organization and behavior.

Home Range Size. Several studies have shown that groups living in areas with abundant food tend to have smaller home ranges than conspecific groups with less abundant food.[89] Clearly, if food supplies are exhausted in a small area, the ecological distribution of food provides reinforcers for animals' traveling further and expanding their range to locate more food; thus scarce, poor quality food resources condition wider ranging. Wide ranging would not be expected in areas where preferred foods were abundant. Because prolonged effortful behavior is aversive, traveling unnecessarily large distances is punished and sup-

---

[87] Kremer et al. (1978).
[88] Humphrey and Keeble (1974).
[89] Gartlan and Brain (1968); Suzuki (1969, 1979); Durham (1971); Poirier (1972b); and Hamilton et al. (1976).

pressed (unless other overriding reinforcers maintain the effortful actions). Thus, when animals live in an area with abundant food, the extra effort of wide ranging would suppress the unnecessary group movements. Naturally, agile species or species with a high threshold for finding effort aversive would have their excess ranging behavior less strongly suppressed than species (such as howler monkeys) in which extra effort appears to suppress behavior easily.[90] These considerations alone explain a large portion of the variance which Milton and May (1976) reported in comparing the sizes of home ranges of 36 primate species.

Locus of Activity. The location of food affects behavior. Sugiyama's (1976) study on Himalayan langurs demonstrates that even species that are biologically adapted for one niche (e.g., arboreal feeding, in the case of langurs) will learn to feed elsewhere (on the ground in this case) if the food reinforcers are located such that there are more reinforcers for leaving the biologically natural niche. In addition, seasonal changes in food supply can reinforce seasonal changes in arboreal or terrestrial feeding in langurs.[91] Similarly, much of the seasonal variation in chimpanzee use of space and social organization in the savanna woodland is a result of seasonal changes in the distribution of food supplies.[92]

Social Spacing and Organization. Food distribution and scarcity can influence social spacing and organization.[93] Squirrel monkey groups in forests with highly scattered food sources often break into small foraging parties.[94] However, when food is scarce and clumped at a small number of fruiting plants, squirrel monkeys maintain closer individual distances and their groups are less likely to fragment into small foraging parties.[95] In this latter case, the animals receive food reinforcers when they cluster together around a fruiting plant, hence togetherness (rather than fragmenting) is reinforced, and proximity becomes a $^+$CS that reinforces close spacing even when the animals are not foraging. Similar effects of scattered food have been observed in baboons[96] and vervets.[97] Provisioning can reinforce animals' crowding into unusually close quarters.

Menzel's (1973, 1974) data on social organization and the use of space in chimpanzees reflect the influence of food as a reinforcer that attracts individuals to certain environmental loci and effort as a punisher that

[90] Milton (1977) and Baldwin and Baldwin (1978b).
[91] Oppenheimer (1977).
[92] Suzuki (1969, 1979).
[93] Denham (1971).
[94] Thorington (1967, 1968).
[95] Baldwin and Baldwin (1972, 1973a).
[96] Compare Hall and DeVore (1965); Rowell (1966a); and Aldrich-Blake et al. (1971).
[97] Gartlan (1973).

suppresses movement to more distant areas. A cost–benefit analysis (of effort punishers and food reinforcers)—in conjunction with data on modeling effects—predicts the chimpanzees' patterns of social organization as well as Menzel's more cognitive interpretation.

Aggression. When clumped food is scarce and animals crowd together, some may learn aggressive responses for obtaining more free space or more food.[98] Larger, stronger animals would be more likely than small, weak animals to learn aggressive responses, since there would be few group members who could punish and suppress these responses which lead to free space or food reinforcers. Once certain individuals learn aggressive responses, the aversive threats, bites, and blows they deliver to others condition alertness, avoidance, and submissive activities via negative reinforcement. This type of behavior lends itself to being described in terms of dominance relations. Scarce, clumped food is, of course, only one of the ecological factors that can condition dominance behavior (page 161f).

Although dominance was once considered a reasonable single measure of group structure, numerous studies[99] reveal the inadequacy of the concept of a unitary hierarchy for explaining primate social organization, and the need for multiple measures of group structure. Dominance is frequently situational: One animal may dominate another only in certain S^D contexts, for example, when competing for food or when certain coalition members are present. Since dominance is based on aversive control—one animal threatens, fights, chases, or supplants another—excessive attention to dominance can distract one from studying friendly relations based on the exchange of positive reinforcers.

Food and Fear. Food can be located in areas that otherwise are ⁻CS's that elicit fear. For example, baboons and the predators of baboons are often attracted to the same geographic area by the reinforcers of food, water, or shade.[100] Past experience with predators conditions close spacing, since individuals are safest when close to others. This negative centripetal conditioning adds to the positive centripetal conditioning from the food, water, or shade to account for much of the closest spacing observed in the baboons. Vervets show similar responses to food and fear.[101]

When one realizes that more reinforcers and punishers than food, effort, and fear of predators are constantly operating (from within the

---

[98] Southwick (1972); Wrangham (1974); and Mori (1977).

[99] Gartlan (1968); Bernstein (1970, 1976b); Stoltz and Saayman (1970); Castell and Heinrich (1971); Rowell (1972, 1974b); and Richard (1974).

[100] Altmann and Altmann (1970).

[101] Fairbanks and Bird (1978).

group and from the environment) to shape and control behavior, it becomes clear that many factors will need to be taken into consideration in explaining the behavior and social organization of primate groups. However, the task of analyzing the ecological distribution of reinforcers, punishers, and models that influence natural learning will not be any more complex than the analysis of the numerous ecological pressures that influence natural selection. In fact, the study of natural learning may prove to be easier than the study of the distal causes of primate behavior: It is easier to obtain empirical measures of learning than of natural selection. Learning is a rapid process, and learned responses can be traced to recent controlling variables. Evolution is a slow process, and evolutionary products must be traced to controlling variables that are often lost in the distant past.

CONCLUSION

The thesis of the present chapter is that much of primate group structure and social organization can be analyzed in terms of the reinforcers and punishers that are the prime movers of natural learning. Various methods are presented that integrate the effects of natural learning on individuals into a larger social and ecological model.

When studying the effects of natural learning on social organization, a researcher can choose among any of a variety of methods for describing the effects of environemtnal and social variables. It is unlikely that one would use all the possible methods at one time. Depending on the research topic, some will be of greater utility than others, and at present it would be difficult to create a single overall dynamic model that integrates all the controlling variables of natural learning into one manageable system. However, an awareness of the multiple considerations at a theoretical level can be useful in guiding the researcher toward the selection of models that describe the crucial controlling variables operating in any given situation.

AN EXAMPLE
OF BALANCED BIOSOCIAL THEORY

In Part II, we dealt with issues that have been neglected by sociobiology in order to demonstrate the importance of major variables that are not woven into the sociobiological model. Because sociobiology is an unbalanced theory that favors nature over nurture, the neglected topics discussed in Part II involve nurture more than nature. Hence, the discussion does not fulfill the criteria of balanced biosocial theory.

In the present section we attempt to present an example of balanced theory. At this time, it is probably premature to attempt an all-encompasing balanced biosocial theory that analyzes all types of behavior at all phyletic levels. For the purposes of this book, we have opted to present one didactic example that demonstrates how nature and nurture can be interwoven in a balanced manner. The contents of the example are in some senses less important than the structure of the example, i.e., the means by which nature and nurture are interwoven.

In Chapter 7, we demonstrate what we perceive to be the design features of a balanced biosocial theory. We use exploration and play in primates as our example because these behaviors have been the target of our own past research. This choice of examples does not imply that other behaviors are less well suited to balanced biosocial analyses. In Chapter 8, continuing with the example of exploration and play, we demonstrate how theories of animal behavior can be extended to deal with human behavior without losing proper balance. This is an important task for anyone interested in using animal data in the study of human behavior. It is also crucial to any program that seeks to create a unified theory of behavior in which animal studies and human studies are united.

EXPLORATION
AND PLAY IN PRIMATES

In this chapter we present a general theory that explains the broad patterns of exploration and play seen in most primate species. This generalized theory focuses on the controlling variables that operate in all primate species—and in many other advanced species—and it allows for changes in the weightings of these causal factors in different species. The generalized theory presented here can be adjusted to fit any given species by using data on the unique adaptations and behavioral specializations of that species in order to "tune" the theory. We provide an example of this tuning in Chapter 8, where we demonstrate how the general theory of primate exploration and play can be adjusted to explain exploration and play in humans.

In order to construct a balanced biosocial theory, one must integrate data on all the variables discussed in Chapter 2: evolutionary causes, physiological mechanisms, and proximal environmental causes. The data on all the variables must be presented in a way that facilitates their integration into the larger balanced model. At present, no complex primate behavior has been adequately studied at all analytic levels; hence it is important to identify the areas in which further research is necessary.

The present analysis of exploration and play

in primates begins with considerations of natural selection, adaptiveness, and physiological mechanisms of behavior. Then it proceeds to
explain the development of behavior from birth to adulthood, inter-
twining natural learning with various biological factors.

EXPLORATION AND PLAY

Exploration and play are closely related activities. Creativity is sometimes involved in exploration and play, and will be dealt with when it
is relevant to the discussion. Hutt (1966) suggested a useful definition
that helps to distinguish between exploration and play. Exploration is
usually a cautious or tentative behavior, in which an individual con-
centrates attention on a target stimulus (either an object, body part or
individual) and acquires information about it. The goal of exploration
is "getting to know the properties" of the target stimulus, and the
methods of exploration are influenced by the properties of the target.
Once an individual has learned the properties of the target, there may
be a transition to play, in which the player uses or interacts with the
target to produce activity and stimulating experience. Creativity is often
closely related to exploration and play. Creative behavior consists of
those activities that produce novel results; and, as we shall see, novelty
plays a key role in reinforcing exploration, play, and creativity.

The following example may clarify the relationship between exploration, play, and creativity. A young monkey may explore among some
palm fronds, tentatively touching them, mouthing them, and learning
how to handle them. Attention is directed to the fronds during this
period, as the monkey learns the properties of the fronds and learns
skills for handling them. Later, two monkeys may use a palm frond
during chasing play, as one runs away from the second and the second
attempts to take the frond from the first while they jump through the
branches. Creative use of the frond may appear whenever novel elements are introduced into the play interaction. The first monkey may
release the frond just before having it taken by the second, then jump
down to retrieve it, and dash off well ahead of the second player.

Both exploration and play are sometimes described as *stimulus-seeking
behavior*.[1] During exploration, an individual looks at, tastes, feels, lifts,
or otherwise manipulates the target, taking in the stimulus properties
of the target through one or more sense modalities. During play, the
individual does things to or with the target, thereby generating noise,

---

[1] Ellis (1973:83–110). Stimulus-seeking behavior is a broader category than exploration,
play, and creativity. Pastimes and self-stimulation (e.g., rocking or head banging) are
other modes of stimulus seeking. Also, a certain amount of stimulus seeking occurs in
pursuing other reinforcers, as when an animal hunts for food (Baldwin and Baldwin,
1977a, 1978a).

movement, visual patterns, or other types of stimulus input. Thus, exploration is the stimulus-seeking behavior that is done before the individual has learned the properties of the target stimulus. Play is the stimulus-seeking behavior that is done after the individual has learned the properties of the target and learned how to use the target to generate even more stimulation. Exploration usually grades slowly into play as the properties of the target are learned. Because creative behavior produces novel effects, it also produces stimulation and qualifies as a stimulus-seeking behavior.

In most primate groups, exploration and play are relatively common activities, especially among the young, but considerable variability in the frequency of these behaviors has been reported.[2] Although primate creativity has not been studied as much as have exploration and play, it occurs often enough and is sufficiently important to warrant attention. To understand the causes and origins of these three stimulus-seeking behaviors (exploration, play, and creativity), it is important to analyze and integrate data on natural selection, relevant physiological mechanisms, and behavioral development.

NATURAL SELECTION

The first question to be asked when constructing balanced biosocial theories comes from the evolutionary perspective. What are the distal causes for exploration and play? Evolutionary logic directs our attention to issues of adaptation. Are there ways in which stimulus-seeking behavior functions to enhance an individual's chances of survival and reproduction? The answer is "yes." At least 30 adaptive functions of exploration and play have been presented in the scientific literature (see Table 7.1), and at least to some degree, all appear to apply to primates.

Multiple Factors

Without going into great detail on each of the 30 points, we will briefly describe how exploration and play fulfill the 30 adaptive functions in primates.[3]

Physical Benefits (Item 1 in Table 7.1). Exploration, and especially play, involve physical exercise. Exercise is quite important for young primates when their muscles and bones are developing. Vigorous play tends to be most frequent during the early years of physical development. It is easy to see that individuals who exercise vigorously during play early

---

[2] Loy (1970) and Baldwin and Baldwin (1977a: 386f).
[3] See Table 7.1 for references related to each adaptive function.

184

TABLE 7.1. Listing of the Common Functions that Have Been Attributed to Exploration and Play[a]

PHYSICAL DEVELOPMENT

1. Providing physical exercise	Brownlee (1954), Dobzhansky (1962), Ewer (1968), Fagen (1976).

PSYCHOLOGICAL BENEFITS

2. Providing sensory input that stimulates development of the nervous system.	Riesen (1961, 1965), Levitsky and Barnes (1972), Volkmar and Greenough (1972), Cummins et al. (1977), Floeter and Greenough (1979).
3. Keeping the nervous system at optimal arousal for effective performance.	Yerkes and Doddson (1908), Hebb (1955), Fiske and Maddi (1961), Ellis (1973).
4. Developing perceptual skills and latent learning.	Welker (1961), Glickman and Sroges (1966).
5. Developing motor skills and coordination.	Southwick et al. (1965), Dolhinow and Bishop (1970), Poirier (1970), Simonds (1974b), Symons (1978).
6. Increasing behavioral flexibility.	Miller (1973).

COPING WITH THE NONSOCIAL ENVIRONMENT

7. Sampling and discovering diversified information about the environment.	Washburn and Hamburg (1965), Loizos (1967).
8. Discovering how the environment responds to attack, shaking, biting, pulling, etc.	Lorenz (1956).
9. Providing familiarity with objects that may facilitate tool use.	Birch (1945), Schiller (1957), Eibl-Eibesfeldt (1967), Lethmate (1977).
10. Facilitating adaptive innovation and learning in new environments.	Tsumori (1967), Fedigan (1972b).
11. Developing predator defenses.	Lancaster (1971), Symons (1978).
12. Counterconditioning early fears of the environment.	Baldwin (1969), Dolhinow (1971).
13. Overcoming early anxiety and helplessness by developing mastery and competence.	White (1961), Dolhinow and Bishop (1970).

SOCIAL ADJUSTMENT

14. Facilitating initiation and integration into the group structure.	Southwick et al. (1965), Rosenblum and Lowe (1971), Poirier and Smith (1974).
15. Developing social bonds.	Carpenter (1934), Jay (1965), Southwick et al. (1965), Suomi and Harlow (1971), Poirier (1972a).
16. Facilitating normal personality development.	Harlow and Harlow (1969), Poirier (1972a).
17. Learning what species the individual belongs to.	Loizos (1967), Poirier (1972a).
18. Learning communication skills.	Mason (1965a), Dolhinow (1971), Jolly (1972), Poirier and Smith (1974), Poirier et al. (1978).
19. Developing social perception.	Fedigan (1972b).
20. Learning group traditions.	Itani (1958), Tsumori (1967), Baldwin (1969).

(continued)

21. Learning and practicing adult behavior.	Pycraft (1912), Hansen (1962), Washburn and Hamburg (1965), Loizos (1967), Ewer (1968), Dolhinow and Bishop (1970), Suomi and Harlow (1971).
22. Developing sex roles.	Harlow and Harlow (1965), Baldwin (1969).
23. Developing reproductive skills.	Eibl-Eibesfeldt (1967), Dolhinow and Bishop (1970), Poirier (1972a), Hanby (1976), Hopf (1979).
24. Learning dominant and subordinate roles.	Jay (1965), Poirier (1972a).
25. Establishing dominance relations.	Carpenter (1934), Harlow and Harlow (1965), Hall (1965), Dolhinow and Bishop (1970).
26. Learning controlled aggression.	Dolhinow and Bishop (1970), Suomi and Harlow (1971).
27. Working out aggression.	Dolhinow (1971).
28. Learning limitations of self-assertiveness.	Poirier (1972a).
29. Learning maternal skills during play-mothering.	Lancaster (1971).
30. Play-mothering increases the chances that abandoned infants will be adopted.	Lancaster (1971).

[a] Although several categories overlap each other, they have been kept separate to retain the views of the authors.

in life might have a better chance of surviving to adulthood and reproducing their own kind than individuals who had not benefitted from the exercise of play. With better physical development, they would have a better chance of escaping predators, catching or opening food, competing with conspecifics over scarce resources, mating, and rearing offspring. Thus, natural selection would be expected to favor the transmission of the genes that predispose an individual to explore and play. (The nature of those genes and the nature of the physiological mechanisms of behavior that they control are not easily inferred from functional analyses, but some of this information will be specified in later segments of the construction of the balanced biosocial theory.)

Psychological Benefits (Items 2–6). Stimulus-seeking behavior exposes an individual to a variety of experiences that promote adaptive psychological development. For example, exploration and play expose an individual to sources of sensory stimulation. This sensory stimulation, in turn, activates and "exercises" the central nervous system, much as physical activity exercises the musculature. Sensory stimulation promotes nerve growth, dendrite branching, and synaptic development—all of which help realize the genetic potential for the central nervous system's mechanisms of behavior, and thereby favor the survival and reproduction of the individual. An individual with relatively full development of the central nervous system should be able to learn, process inputs, and respond to its environment much more rapidly and effectively than an individual with less complete development of the central processing mechanisms. As will be explained in detail below (pages 194–195), the brain operates most efficiently when provided with intermediate levels of sensory input, and stimulus-seeking behavior provides this sensory input. Therefore, exploration and play help maintain the levels of brain activity that promote efficient central processing and behavioral output; and this has obvious advantages for survival. In addition, stimulus-seeking behavior exposes the individual to learning experiences that enhance perception and discriminative ability, foster latent learning, and advance the development of motor skills and coordination. Exploration, play, and creativity also enhance behavioral flexibility by partially freeing the individual from tight stimulus–response patterns. To the degree that all these forms of psychological development confer survival advantages, they favor the transmission of the genes that predispose an individual to explore and play.

Coping with the Nonsocial Environment (Items 7–13). Several of the functions attributed to stimulus-seeking behavior stress the value of exploration and play in preparing the individual to cope with the nonsocial environment. As the young primate explores by climbing through vines and lianas, it will discover that some supports carry its weight whereas others do not. As it jumps on a wasp nest during a play chase, it will discover still other properties of its environment. During both exploration and play, the animal's behavior will be modified by the consequences of its actions: It will learn to discriminate the differences between strong and weak vines and identify wasp nests; and its behavior will come under increasingly precise S^D control. Thus, stimulus-seeking behavior exposes the individual to learning experiences that may help it cope more effectively with its environment in the future. Since exploration and play sometimes contain creative activities, the individual may even learn a creative new way of coping with the environment— perhaps innovating a new way of manipulating objects or discovering a new tool.

During exploration and play, individuals also learn skills that increase the chances of coping effectively with predators and dangerous situations. The individual who has explored many of the arboreal pathways through the canopy will have more options and be able to flee more rapidly when confronted with a predator than will an individual who has explored less. Because play often involves play chases that condition skills of rapid motion through the environment, play also conditions skills that may help an individual escape from a predator or cope with an accident (such as landing on a weak branch that breaks under the

PLATE 7.1. Two young spider monkeys gain skill at brachiating while playing in the lianas. (*Photo by C. M. Hladik made during fellowship at the Smithsonian Tropical Research Institute.*)

animal's weight). Play fighting is another common form of play. Play fights train skills of sparring, dodging, pouncing, feinting, and fleeing, all of which can help an individual cope with predators.

Finally, as stimulus-seeking behavior exposes an individual to the environment and trains coping skills via positive reinforcement, early fears of the environment that were conditioned during infancy are likely to disappear (due to extinction and positive counterconditioning). Although it is adaptive for the youngest infants to fear venturing too far from the safety of mother's side, it is adaptive for the older infants and juveniles to overcome these fears, venture out further, and gain greater independence. By venturing further from mother's side—and eventually leaving her—the maturing individual can expand its arena of activities and gain increasing skills and information that may facilitate survival and reproduction.

Coping with the Social Environment (Items 14–30). Stimulus-seeking behavior leads a young primate into interaction with its social environment, allowing it to gain skill, information, and discriminations about conspecifics. Exploration and play take the infant away from mother

PLATE 7.2. Play chases condition skills that help animals deal with predators. A juvenile rhesus monkey leaps at an infant during a play chase. (*Courtesy of D. Symons.*)

and increase contact with other group members in ways that have been shown to increase integration with the group at large and hasten the development of social bonds. The social experience appears to facilitate normal "personality" development and a knowledge about the species to which the individual belongs. This social integration and behavioral normalcy help the individual establish a safe, secure position in its group. Since most primates depend on membership in a group for protection and could not survive alone very long, being an integrated member has important adaptive consequences.

Exploration and play often serve as a context in which young primates learn communication skills and develop the social perception that allows them to respond to various social signals. During social exploration and play, individuals are likely to imitate and practice the group traditions that are modeled by other group members, thus stimulus-seeking behavior facilitates the acquisition of traditions. Basic aspects of sexual behavior and reproductive roles are initially learned during social exploration and play, and this learning can clearly affect an individual's reproductive success and the transmission of the genes that predispose

PLATE 7.3. Two hanuman langurs engage in a play copulation. (*Courtesy of J.R. Oppenheimer.*)

the individual to explore and play. During play fights and play chases, primates learn, practice, and hone skills for fighting, defense, and controlling aggression that may help them cope with intragroup conflicts. Play fights also help establish dominance relations among individuals in groups with dominance hierarchies. Since stable dominance relationships are one means of facilitating smooth group social interactions, learning one's place (rather than having to fight over each new social situation) smooths social relations and minimizes the risk of serious fights. Finally, stimulus-seeking behavior often brings young females (and to a lesser degree, young males) into contact with infants, where the young females are likely to learn a modicum of mothering skills before having their own first infants. This social learning experience increases the chances that they will handle their own first infants correctly, which is adaptive in increasing the females' reproductive success. Interaction with infants also increases the chances that these females might adopt an infant that had lost its mother, which increases the female's inclusive fitness if the adopted infant is related.

Which Function?

It seems unlikely that all the 30 functions in Table 7.1 were equally crucial in the evolution of the genetic information that predisposes primates to explore and play. Some of the functions are doubtless of less importance than others, thus they may have played only a minor role in favoring the transmission of the genes that provided distal control for stimulus-seeking behavior.[4]

It would be desirable to assign a weighting to each of the 30 functions in order to explain which causes were most influential in molding the evolution of the genes for mechanisms of exploration and play. Such an analysis might help explain some of the motor patterns seen during stimulus-seeking behavior. For example, if exploration and play in one species were primarily the result of adaptive selection based on benefits from coping with predators, the behavioral mechanisms for producing exploration and play might be organized for shaping skills at chasing and fighting. But if the mechanisms mediating exploration and play in a second species were primarily the result of selection based on the benefits of acquiring group traditions, it is likely that chasing and fighting would be somewhat counterproductive whereas imitative and manipulative activities would be more adaptive. Thus, an analysis of adap-

---

[4] Some have argued that *a* behavior must have *a* function, and hence have tried to reduce lists of functions for any given behavior to *the* single most likely function. We agree with McFarland's (1976:55) rebuttal to this argument: "However, to identify *a* function with any particular characteristic of an animal is an oversimplification, since any modern form must be the outcome of competition between various selective pressures."

tiveness would lead us to expect a preparedness for play chasing and play fighting in one species and a preparedness for explorative imitation and manipulative play in the second; and these evolutionary preparednesses would help explain why stimulus-seeking behavior involves different motor patterns in different species.

If there were little variability in primate exploration and play, it might be possible to establish a simple ranking or weighting of functions. However, there is significant variability in exploration and play among species, and often considerable variation within species when comparing exploration and play in different environments.[5] In one environment, a species' stimulus-seeking behavior may produce numerous adaptive payoffs in terms of escape from predators; yet, in a second environment, stimulus-seeking behavior by the same species might function primarily to foster the innovation and transmission of group traditions. In a third environment, both adaptive functions might play an important role. When we add the fact that exploration and play are clearly adaptive in facilitating exercise, nerve growth, independence from mother, and social integration (among other benefits), it becomes clear that in each species many different weightings of the 30 functions are likely to have occurred during the evolution of the genes that provide distal control for exploration and play. In addition, the significant amount of within-species variability in primates leads us to expect considerable variability in the importance of the 30 functions in any given species in different parts of its range. As evolutionary pressures changed in the various parts of a species' range, certain functions might have gained a higher weighting of importance while others took on less importance. Given the millions of years of evolution in which stimulus-seeking behavior influenced survival and reproduction rates, it might be very difficult to assign a single summary weighting that accurately reflected all the changes in the relative importance of the 30 functions that had operated in producing the current mechanisms for exploration and play.

It must be stressed that exploration and play need not always be adaptive.[6] Too much exploration or play may pass the point of diminishing returns, where energy expenditures are not compensated by adequate beneficial returns. Since stimulus-seeking behavior often exposes primates to danger, there are costs that counterbalance the benefits. One study of mice showed that the most explorative mice were those most likely to be eaten by owls.[7] Infant and juvenile monkeys have high mortality rates, which result, in part, from the dangers they expose

[5] Baldwin and Baldwin (1977a:386f).
[6] Baldwin and Baldwin (1977a:382f).
[7] Glickman and Morrison (1969).

themselves to during exploration and play.[8] Given these dysfunctional features of stimulus-seeking behavior, one would expect the evolution of mechanisms that curtail exploration and play, set limits, and terminate the behavior in certain counterproductive circumstances. Some of these will be discussed below (pages 212–214).

PHYSIOLOGICAL MECHANISMS OF EXPLORATION AND PLAY

Natural selection does not directly cause a *behavior* to evolve.[9] It changes the frequencies of genes that encode information for various mechanisms of behavior that mediate the behavior in question. Thus, exploration and play did not evolve. Rather, genes evolved for various physiological mechanisms that mediate the production of exploration and play.

This logically leads to the next question needed to create balanced biosocial theories: What are the physiological mechanisms that mediate exploration and play? Although not all the mechanisms are known, this section summarizes current information about the physiological mechanisms that mediate stimulus-seeking behavior. The role of some of these mechanisms is less well understood than that of others. Nevertheless, enough is known to explain at least part of the physiological mechanisms. The mechanisms are important because they are the locus in which evolutionary causes and current environmental influences are interwoven to produce behavior (page 19f).

The Genes

The first physiological mechanisms involved in producing exploration and play are the genes themselves. If individuals who explore and play reproduce more successfully than individuals who do not, the genes that encode information that predisposes individuals to explore and play will be transmitted to the next generation in greater numbers. At present, there is no information about the nature of these genes; but these genes are theoretically important because it is the genes—not the behavior of exploration and play—that evolve. Even though it is sometimes said that behavior evolves—for example, "Play evolved in many advanced species"—this simple wording can lead to extreme evolutionary positions in which selection appears to explain all. Although it is clumsier to say "The genes evolved that encode information con-

---

[8] Berger (1972) and Teleki (1973).
[9] This distinction is of least importance when dealing with behavior that shows little within-species variability; but it is crucial with any behavior that is highly influenced by learning or other proximal causes.

trolling the physiological mechanisms that mediate play," this wording helps one to think in terms of multiple factor mediational models and helps direct attention away from extreme genetic theories.

A Healthy Body

During fetal and postnatal development in primates, the genes are interfaced with countless constructive (and some destructive) environmental inputs to produce the physiological mechanisms that mediate the entire repertoire of behavior. In most individuals the environmental inputs will be sufficiently constructive to insure adequate development of the physiological mechansisms needed for exploration and play. The development of an intact, well-formed, healthy body is a basic prerequisite for the production of exploration and play. Although minor handicaps may not disrupt stimulus-seeking behavior noticeably, major handicaps can suppress or disrupt the behavior significantly.[10] Adequate development of the sensory receptors and musculature is especially crucial for perceiving the inputs and producing the behavior outputs of exploration and play. Likewise, the central nervous system must also be well developed to mediate the numerous complex behavior patterns seen in exploration and play—and behavior in general.

The Reticular Formation

But what special physiological mechanisms are needed to produce exploration and play—as opposed to producing behavior in general? The reticular formation in the brainstem appears to be a key biological mechanism for mediating exploration and play.[11] The reticular formation is a diffuse neural network in the lower brain (see Figure 7.1) that mediates several important bodily processes, one of which is to monitor the overall activity level in the central nervous system. Located near the top of the spinal cord, between the brain and the body, the reticular formation is "at the crossroads for incoming and outgoing messages" (Lindsley, 1961:175). It is in a good position for measuring the total amount of sensory input coming into the brain from the body, and the total stim-

---

[10] Berkson (1970, 1977) and Fedigan and Fedigan (1977).

[11] Lindsley (1951, 1961), Jasper (1958), and Samuels (1959) were among the first to develop the reticular formation theory. More recent data have tended to support the theory (Glickman et al., 1964; Segundo et al., 1967; Peterson et al., 1976; Siegel and McGinty, 1977; and Bross et al., 1980). Even if the actual mechanisms differ somewhat from those described here, it does not detract from our point that physiological mediating mechanisms, influenced by constructive and destructive environmental inputs, must be considered in order to produce a balanced biosocial theory of exploration and play (or any other behavior).

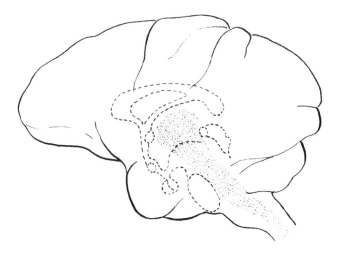

FIGURE 7.1. The general location of the reticular formation (*shaded area*) in the brainstem. (*Courtesy of R.F. Thompson.*)

ulus output going out from the brain to the body. The reticular formation also receives collateral fibers (or remote input channels) from the cerebral cortex that indicate the amount of activity in the cortex. Thus, the reticular formation is a structure that is well suited for making measurements of the overall activity levels in the entire central nervous system.

Why would it be important to measure the overall activity level in the nervous system? The central nervous system functions best when it is neither overloaded nor underloaded.[12] *Intermediate levels of activity* allow the central nervous system to process data most efficiently for producing the well-integrated behavior needed for survival. *Stimulus overload* tends to produce disruptions in central processing. Too much activity in the cerebral cortex disrupts memory, recall, and behavior output, causing performance to be disorganized and inefficient. At the other extreme, *stimulus underload* produces lethargy, drowsiness, inattentiveness, and sometimes sleep, all of which interfere with efficient learning, recall, and behavioral output. Although several hours of sleep per day are beneficial, it is clearly adaptive for individuals not to sleep too much and not to spend their waking hours in a drowsy state, behaving in an inefficient manner.

Efficient learning, recall, and behavior performance occur when the brain activity is at intermediate levels, and the brain is neither overloaded nor underloaded (see Figure 7.2).[13] It appears that the central

[12] Yerkes and Dodson (1908); Hebb (1955, 1972); and Ellis (1973).
[13] The optimal zone of central nervous activity can be different for different species, for males and females of a given species, or for a given individual depending on fatigue,

(continued)

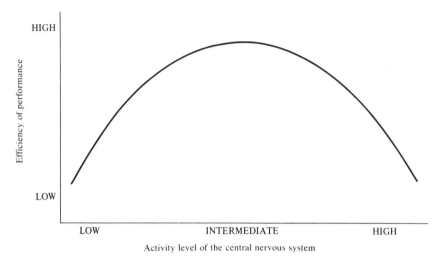

FIGURE 7.2. Understimulation leads to drowsiness, lethargy, or sleepiness, which produce inefficient performance. Overstimulation overloads the central nervous system, disrupting and interfering with performance. Intermediate levels of brain activation are most compatible with efficient performance. The shape of the curve differs somewhat for different behaviors (*Hebb, 1972:200*).

nervous system processes information most efficiently when there is enough stimulus input to activate all relevant cortical subsystems without exceeding the overload limits where there is too much input to be processed efficiently. As a result, natural selection would favor the evolution of mechanisms for maintaining optimal, intermediate brain activity. If one individual had some physiological mechanism that allowed it to maintain an optimal, intermediate level of central nervous activation more hours a day than a second conspecific could, we would expect the first individual to have a higher chance of survival, because its central nervous system would be operating at peak performance levels more hours per day. The first individual would be more alert, more efficient at learning, and more effective at producing behavioral output. Therefore, it is reasonable to assume that any individuals with genetic information for mechanisms that kept their central nervous system in the optimal, intermediate activation zone would have a better chance of surviving and reproducing their own kind.

(continued from previous page)
disease, current activities, and so forth. Herbivores usually have lower stimulus input needs than omnivores and predators (Glickman and Sroges, 1966). Males sometimes have higher optimal zones than females, depending on species characteristics and prior learning experience (Rosenblum, 1974a,b; Baldwin and Baldwin, 1977a). Fatigue, disease, and boring tasks temporarily suppress the optimal zone; whereas fight and flight raise it.

The reticular formation appears to be part of the mechanism that helps regulate the level of activity in the central nervous system by measuring whether the central nervous system is underloaded, optimally loaded, or overloaded. The reticular formation thus appears to function as part of a brain homeostat—somewhat like a thermostat—that determines whether conditions are below, inside, or above the zone of best behavioral performance. Although the reticular formation is an adequate measuring device, it takes more than a mere measurement to maintain optimal levels of brain activity. The theory must specify mechanisms by which the measurements from the reticular formation can keep the brain at optimal activation levels.

The close association of the reticular formation with the hypothalamus and hippocampus may allow the reticular formation to regulate the reinforcement and punishment centers in those areas.[14] Since reinforcers and punishers are the prime movers of operant and Pavlovian conditioning, the reticular formation would be able to regulate these primary determinants of behavior. There is ample evidence that primates—including humans—respond to understimulation and overstimulation as punishers and respond to optimal stimulation as a reinforcer.[15] Deviations from the optimal, intermediate zone produce increasingly aversive consequences, whereas approach to the optimal zone is increasingly reinforcing. Understimulation causes the condition humans call "boredom," and overstimulation causes an individual to become nervous, tense, and "wound up." Optimal levels of stimulation produce positive affect, interest, and sometimes joy or enthusiasm. Presumably, these effects are mediated by the reticular formation and its connections with the reinforcement and punishment centers.[16]

Thus, if an individual were engaging in activities that produced underactivation of the central nervous system (A in Figure 7.3), the reticular formation would measure the low activity levels and trigger the punishment centers. This would in effect punish whatever behavior was responsible for producing understimulation. If a juvenile monkey (who was well rested and well fed) were to sit passively for 30 minutes, its passive behavior would produce understimulation and hence be punished. In addition, the aversive stimulation would motivate the juvenile to avoid the punished activity. If the individual happened to approach and join a play group, the rapid social interactions of play would barrage the senses with inputs and begin to boost the general activity level of the central nervous system. Because there is considerable inertia in the brain's multiple neural systems, five or ten seconds of play might not

---

[14] Glickman (1960); Stumpf (1965); and Ito (1966).
[15] Butler (1958, 1965); Rheingold et al. (1962); Bower (1966); Leuba and Friedlander (1968); and Campbell (1972).
[16] More research is needed to describe the mechanisms with greater accuracy.

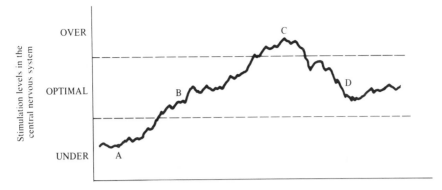

FIGURE 7.3. When an individual experiences understimulation (A), the aversive consequences motivate stimulus-seeking behavior, such as exploration and play. Activities that produce increased sensory input are reinforced, as the sensory stimulation levels rise into the optimal zone (B). Too much stimulation can create aversive overstimulation (C), which motivates the individual to stop stimulus-seeking activities until stimulation levels in the brain again decline into the optimal zone (D), at which time stimulus seeking is again reinforcing.

be enough to raise the central nervous activity level into the optimal zone. However, a prolonged bout of play might produce enough stimulating sensory input to elevate the central nervous activity into the optimal zone (*B* in Figure 7.3).[17] As the reticular formation measures increasing levels of central nervous activity approaching the optimal zone, it ceases triggering the punishment centers and increasingly activates the reinforcement centers of the brain. This, in turn, reinforces play behavior. After repeated experience, young primates learn to escape boredom (aversive understimulation) by seeking out play or other sources of sensory stimulation.

If a bout of play becomes too rowdy and the excessively high levels of sensory input overload the central nervous system (*C* in Figure 7.3), the reticular formation would measure the overload and activate the punishment centers. This in turn punishes the individual for staying in the overstimulating rowdy play and motivates the individual to withdraw (for the time being at least) from the overly arousing social interaction. In fact, it is common to see young primates—including human children—avoid boredom by exploring or playing, then stop, and perhaps withdraw, if they become overstimulated.[18] After a brief recovery

[17] Note that the idea of an optimal *zone* of brain activity does not imply that one unique level maximizes performance thus maximizes genetic fitness. The optimal zone contains a wide range of stimulation levels that suffice to keep the brain functioning well at a variety of tasks with different activation prerequisites. Ideal, maximal functioning is not implied.
[18] Schaller (1963); Ainsworth (1964); Jay (1965); Hall and DeVore (1965); Baldwin (1969); Rheingold and Eckerman (1970); and Ainsworth et al. (1978).

period in which their central nervous activity drops down below the zone of overstimulation (D in Figure 7.3), they can again find play optimally stimulating and receive reinforcers for returning to play.

Other Factors

There are other biological mechanisms that produce significant effects on the forms of stimulus-seeking behavior seen in primates of different species—and even of the same species: Among these are cortex size and complexity, structure of the perceptual system, subtlety of the motor output mechanisms, and body build. The advanced primates tend to have more complex and well-developed cerebral cortices than primitive primates, and they show greater behavioral diversity and creativity.[19] Since the advanced primates usually show more complex patterns of exploration and play than primitive primates, there is reason to believe that cortex size and complexity are two of the many factors that influence stimulus-seeking behavior.[20] For example, Menzel (1969) compared the responses of rhesus monkeys and chimpanzees when exploring various objects in a 0.9 acre compound. The chimpanzees explored and manipulated a much greater variety of objects than did the rhesus monkeys. The chimpanzees also showed much more behavioral flexibility and skill than the rhesus monkeys in investigating their environment. Thus, the stimulus-seeking behavior of the chimpanzees is much more complex, allowing the chimpanzees "to use and exploit their world in a far more detailed fashion than do macaques" (p. 79). Apparently the chimpanzees' greater cortical processing capacity allowed them to find more novel sensory-stimulation reinforcers to maintain prolonged attention to the objects.

A species' perceptual and motor capabilities also influence its patterns of exploration and play. These perceptual and motor specializations of the central nervous system can, in turn, often be explained in terms of adaptations to species-typical ecological niches. For example, orang-utans appear to have perceptual systems that are biased to focus a great deal of attention on foreground cues. Whereas chimpanzees and gorillas will attend to distance cues if confronted with problems whose structure reinforces attention to distance cues, orang-utans fail to look beyond the foreground stimuli. Although most primates cannot see the forest for

[19] Parker (1973, 1974, 1978).

[20] There is no simple correlation between phyletic level and types of exploration and play. In their natural environments, some prosimians are quite playful and some apes play very little (Jolly, 1966; MacKinnon, 1971; and Horr, 1972). Clearly, many variables besides phyletic level and cortex structure alone must be considered. A species' typical habitat and specializations are among the good predictors of exploration (Glickman and Sroges, 1966).

the trees, the orang-utans seem to be "unable to see the trees for the leaves" (Rumbaugh et al., 1973:188). This tendency to attend to the immediate foreground may reflect the orang-utan's specialization for arboreal life, in which the most relevant cues tend to be nearby.[21] In studies on play in captivity, orang-utans show more interest in contact and close range play—including mouth contact—than do chimpanzees.[22]

There are also species differences in the subtlety and complexity of motor output. Some primates, such as capuchin monkeys, show a great deal of manual dexterity; whereas howler monkeys, which are not too distantly related, show little. The capuchins are omnivores, who must be skillful at manipulating many kinds of fruits, nuts, insects, and other food sources; whereas the howlers are herbivores who do not need complex manipulative capacities to obtain the leaves, fruits, and flowers on which they feed. Compared with the howlers, the capuchins are manipulative wizards; and they show much more complex patterns of motor output during exploration and play than howlers do. In general, species that are specialized as omnivores, opportunists, or predators are more explorative and playful than herbivores.[23]

There are various reflexes or fixed action patterns that primates sometimes display while engaging in exploration and play.[24] These relatively invariant behavior patterns reflect the operation of biologically preprogrammed neural mechanisms. The orienting reflex is a reflex that is obviously related to stimulus-seeking behavior, serving to orient an individual to any novel or unexpected stimulus. Many species have a "play face" signal and certain vocalizations that are given during play (and certain other situations).[25] These relatively fixed patterns often become complexly interwoven into the behavior chains produced during exploration and play, as learned and reflexive behaviors interact (pages 90–95). The species-typical behavior patterns help make the stimulus-seeking behavior of each species somewhat different and distinctive.

An animal's size, weight, limb length, and other structural features also influence exploration and play to a noticeable degree.[26] The long-limbed, heavy-bodied howlers, gorillas, and male orang-utans have play patterns that appear to be in "slow motion" compared with the play of smaller, lighter, more agile primates. Within each species, there are variations in body weight, limb length, and body size that relate to age and sexual dimorphism, and these physical differences also influence exploration and play. The older, heavier individuals are often slower

---

[21] Rumbaugh (1974).

[22] Maple (personal communication) and Maple and Zucker (1978).

[23] Morris (1964) and Glickman and Sroges (1966).

[24] Primates show fewer fixed action patterns and more learned behavior in play than do less advanced species (Morris, 1964).

[25] van Hooff (1967, 1972); Redican (1975); and Leresche (1976).

[26] Vilensky (1979).

in their movements and the punishers of effortfulness suppress prolonged bouts of active play; whereas the smaller, more agile subadults
move around much more rapidly and energetically.[27] Maturation also
influences muscle strength, and strength alone influences many of the
actions and consequences seen in stimulus-seeking behavior.

Although there are no consistent sex differences in exploration,[28] there
are often sex differences in play and some of these can be traced to the
influences of testosterone.[29] Testosterone affects both the central and
peripheral mechanisms of behavior. Prenatal exposure to testosterone
appears to bias the central nervous system in ways that make males
somewhat more active or make them have slightly higher optimal zones
for sensory stimulation.[30] Beginning early in life, males prefer slightly
higher levels of activity than do females, i.e., find higher levels of activity
to be reinforcing. In most primate species, males are larger and stronger
than females, even during the years before sexual maturity.[31] Because
they are larger and stronger, the males are less likely to be hurt during
active exploration and play, hence are less likely to withdraw from these
activities due to punishment effects.[32] Sexual maturity induces further
differences, as females become mothers and males experience heightened testosterone production, that leads to even further increased size
and strength in the more dimorphic species.

BEHAVIORAL DEVELOPMENT

The physiological mechanisms discussed in the previous section are not
capable of producing fully developed exploration and play in newborn
infants. Maturation and learning are needed to bring all the biological
components into action and interweave their contributions into an integrated whole. A crucial question for balanced biosocial theories is:
How do the mechanisms of maturation and learning interact with an

---

[27] Simonds (1965) and Symons (1978).

[28] Glickman and Sroges (1966).

[29] Testosterone is, of course, only part of the cause of sex differences in exploration and
play. The physiological differences between males and females are interfaced with numerous environmental variables (especially social ones) to produce the final behavioral
differences visible in the natural environment (Baldwin and Baldwin, 1977a:373f). This
distinction is important, since it helps clarify that sex differences in behavior are not solely
the result of biological mechanisms.

[30] Goy and Phoenix (1972); Goy and Resko (1972); and Sackett (1972). Males continue
to have much higher testosterone levels during the first several months after birth, which
may also produce physiological differences between the two sexes (Robinson and Bridson,
1978).

[31] Dawes (1968); Long and Cooper (1968); and Kaplan (1974).

[32] When rhesus females are treated with testosterone between 6.5 and 14.5 months of
age, they gain weight, become 28% heavier than male agemates, and dominate the males.
At this time, the intimidated males cease playing (Joslyn, 1973).

individual's local environmental conditions to produce that individual's unique behavior patterns?

Beginning with the earliest behavior patterns shown at birth, let us trace the development of exploration and play from early forms through peak development before adulthood, and then to the decline typical in adulthood. As with much of primate behavior, stimulus-seeking behavior begins with reflexive patterns, then operant exploration and play appear due to natural learning. Creativity may appear at various points during development, though it is more common in play than during exploration. The developmental analysis of stimulus-seeking behavior is still in its early forms, thus many of the details of the ontogeny of exploration and play remain to be studied and analyzed. The following broad outlines will suffice, however, to demonstrate the balanced biosocial approach to analyzing behavior.

Reflexive Exploration

Primates are born with a repertoire of reflexive responses. Some of these reflexes serve to initiate contact with mother, initiate nursing, and produce adaptive riding postures. Several of the reflexes produce the infant's earliest exploration, and serve as the foundation for learning more complex patterns of exploration and, eventually, play. The reflexes that function to attach the infant to mother and move the infant to the nipple also function to initiate exploration. When the neonate wakens from sleep, it may engage in reflexive crawling that eventually leads it to the nipple. However, the crawling reflex is also causing it to explore the mother's body and thus to learn the nature of her contours, where there is enough hair to cling, where it is safe to ride when mother is moving, etc. As the infant reflexively mouths things and sucks on them, it is doing reflexive exploration, and it begins to learn the different properties of the nipple, a mouthful of mother's hair, or a twig in the mouth. Even when the infant is not actively moving around on the mother's body, its fingers and toes sometimes flex and relax, producing a form of early tactile exploration of the mother's body and hair. Reflexive mechanisms cause the infant to gaze around and attend to conspicuous stimuli. Sudden sounds or visual stimuli may cause a startle response and elicit orientation reflexes.[33] Young primates also produce a relatively large amount of nonspecific, undifferentiated body movements, and these provide a wealth of behavioral variations from which numerous stimulus-seeking behaviors can be shaped by differential reinforcement.

---

[33] Although the gazing and orienting reflexes are apparently purer cases of stimulus-seeking behavior than are the other reflexes, this does not mean that they play a more important role in initiating early exploration.

Learned Exploration

Because several of the early reflexes propel the infant into contact with its mother and the environment, they expose the infant to sensory stimulation, which in turn is the main reinforcer that will shape operant patterns of stimulus-seeking behavior. When reflexes produce behavior that leads to optimal levels of stimulus input (hence optimal activation of the nervous system), the reflexive exploration is reinforced. When other variations in reflexive exploration lead to too little or too much sensory stimulation—hence to too little or too much activity in the nervous system—these patterns of exploration are punished by the aversive consequences of stimulus underload or stimulus overload. Thus the reinforcers and punishers of optimal and nonoptimal sensory stimulation gradually begin to modify reflexive exploration into operant exploration.

Other reinforcers and punishers beside sensory stimulation also affect the learning of exploration.[34] Exploration that leads to taking a piece of food from mother's hand is reinforced by both novel stimuli and food. Exploration that leads the infant to slip off mother may be punished by a painful fall. While sensory stimulation reinforces stimulus-seeking behavior in general, the various other reinforcers and punishers cause the infant to learn the properties of its environment and condition operant responses to environmental cues. During early exploration the infant learns where the nipple is and learns to crawl rapidly to it; and it learns that crawling out onto mother's leg is associated with falls if mother moves.

Because the reinforcers and punishers of sensory stimulation play a key role in shaping the development of all stimulus-seeking behavior, it is important to discriminate between various components of sensory stimulation.[35] The *rate* of stimulus input clearly affects the activity of the central nervous system. A stimulus that moves or flickers frequently produces more total stimulus input than one that has lower rates of change. The *intensity* of a stimulus correlates directly with its impact on the central nervous system. Loud, strong, harsh stimuli produce more total sensory input than quiet, soft, mild stimuli. *Novel* stimuli produce more central activation than old, familiar stimuli. Seeing a novel sight causes more cerebral processing than does seeing a familiar one, in part because the process of habituation causes organisms to respond less and less to stimuli as they are repeatedly encountered. Habituation is the process by which a stimulus "loses its novelty" after an individual has

---

[34] In fact, various types of exploration and play correlate with the proportion of sensory reinforcers and other reinforcers involved (Baldwin and Baldwin, 1978a).
[35] Fiske and Maddi (1961); Wilcoxon et al. (1969); and Campbell (1972).

had repeated experience with it.[36] Thus it loses its ability to provide sensory stimulation reinforcers for attention, exploration, and play. The first time a young monkey sees a squirrel, the sight is novel and it creates stimulating input that reinforces further attention to the squirrel. After seeing squirrels on many different occasions, the novelty declines, there is less sensory stimulation reinforcement for further watching, and the monkey's attention is likely to be turned to other, more stimulating targets. The *complexity* and *unpredictability* of a stimulus are somewhat related to novelty. Complex stimuli are more likely to contain novel stimulus combinations than simple stimuli. Unexpected stimuli produce surprise effects, which are novel deviations from the familiar, expected patterns. Again, repeated exposure and habituation reduce the sensory stimulation available from complex, once unpredictable stimuli.

Recovery effects operate in the opposite direction from habituation.[37] After an individual has explored or played with a stimulus (and become somewhat familiar with it), a period of separation from the stimulus will allow the stimulus to regain a portion of its original novelty or surprise. With renewed novelty, a stimulus can again provide positive sensory stimulation reinforcers, hence maintain a period of renewed exploration or play, until habituation again robs the stimulus of its novelty and its reinforcing properties. Thus, after a period of separation from a given stimulus, there is often a rebound of exploration or play, then a return to lower levels of interaction.[38] If a monkey had not seen a squirrel for several months, the first contact with a squirrel after this recovery period would provide the monkey with enough novel stimulation to again reinforce attention (until habituation once more removed the novelty effects).

Developmental Patterns

The rate, intensity, novelty, complexity, and unexpectedness of stimuli—in conjunction with habituation and recovery effects—help explain the developmental patterns seen in exploration and play. For the newborn infant, the whole world is novel and full of surprise. Everywhere it turns, the infant finds novel, complex, and unexpected input.[39] As long as these inputs provide optimal levels of sensory stimulation, any

---

[36] Both the hippocampus and reticular formation may be involved in the system that mediates habituation (Roberts et al., 1962 and Peterson et al., 1976).

[37] Welker (1961).

[38] Oakley and Reynolds (1976) and Baldwin and Baldwin (1976).

[39] The sensory stimulation that reinforces exploration and play can come through any of the five external senses or the internal sensations of muscle movement, vestibular stimulation, and so forth.

explorative responses that expose the infant to the inputs will be reinforced by the optimal stimulation. Thus, there is usually reinforcement for crawling around on mother's body, feeling her hair, and reaching out to touch leaves near her. If any of the components of sensory stimulation become so high that they lead to overstimulation, the infant's exploration is punished by the overstimulation. Thus, in times of overstimulation, exploration is suppressed by punishment; and clinging to mother's soft, warm, familiar body is reinforced by escape from aversive overstimulation.

Habituation plays a key role in explaining the subsequent development of exploration and play. During stimulus-seeking behavior—or any other experience with a target stimulus—habituation effects are at work, destroying the novelty of the target stimulus during each repeated experience with it. Although the neonate finds novel stimulation in running its hands through mother's hair, the novelty eventually "wears off" and tactile exploration of mother's hair ceases to function as stimulating input. As habituation destroys the novelty of the stimuli to be found on mother's body, it modifies the contingencies of reinforcement associated with the infant's stimulus-seeking behavior: If the infant continues to explore on the mother's body, the lack of novelty will produce the aversive effects of understimulation; but if the infant ventures a few centimeters off her body, the novel experiences of being off her body, feeling new things, and trying its legs on new substrates will provide reinforcing new stimulus inputs. Those responses that lead the infant to have increased contact with new parts of the environment are reinforced, whereas responses that cause contact with old, familiar stimuli are extinguished. These patterns of reinforcement and extinction are so universal, that virtually all infants learn to begin exploring off mother's body as contact becomes familiar.

Naturally, there are other influential variables, such as maturation, maternal protectiveness, reinforcers and punishers from the environment, species preparedness for leaving mother, and other species predispositions. If an infant begins to explore off the mother's body before it is strong enough, falls and hard knocks will punish and suppress this type of exploration until enough maturation is attained for successful departures. Protective mothers may punish or physically restrain their infants' early departures, and thus retard the process.[40] Hunger, thirst, cold, sickness, wounds, and other environmentally induced deprivation states or aversive experiences can suppress exploration and play. A frightening or overstimulating environment can expose the infant to aversive inputs that punish and suppress early exploration.[41] The pres-

[40] Baldwin (1969) and Johnson et al. (1979).
[41] Rosenblum (1971b).

ence of gentle, accepting "aunts," on the other hand, can serve to shelter the infant from some of these punishers. There are also species differences in behavioral precocity and readiness to leave mother that affect the process.[42]

Because habituation converts novel stimuli into familiar ones, stimuli that produced optimal stimulation levels one week may cease to be optimally stimulating a week or two later (unless the input rate and intensity of the stimuli are high enough to compensate for the decreased novelty). As a consequence, stimulus-seeking behavior often involves a search for novel stimuli (or familiar stimuli with moderately high input rates or intensity.) Thus, during youth at least, exploration and play become a dynamic process of seeking out new experiences. When the infant first ventures a few centimeters away from mother, it discovers ample novelty to reward early venturing forth. However, as the novelty of exploring the environment within one meter of mother wears off, the infant must venture even further away to find new experience. It will learn to move more quickly, climb more nimbly, and jump further, since these activities help it locate new and more stimulating experience as habituation robs old activities of their novelty. Explorative behavior that leads to novel experience will be more strongly reinforced than exploration that leads to the old, familiar stimuli.

Thus, habituation is the main reason why primates expand their domain of experience. If habituation did not destroy the novelty of stimuli with repeated experience, maturing individuals would always find their neonatal environment and activities novel, hence would miss a major motivation for giving them up and would be retarded in leaving behind their infantile ways. Without habituation, feeling mother's hair and crawling on her body would always remain novel and reinforcing. The reinforcers from exploring mother's body would tend to hold the individual in an infantile stage of psychosocial development, or at least produce competing responses that retarded the exploration of broader horizons. However, because habituation does destroy novelty, there are reinforcers for the infant's venturing further afield, where new experience awaits. The reinforcers of novel experience cause the individual to be active in expanding its own horizons, thus in exercising, learning, and realizing a greater portion of its own genetic potential.

Social Exploration

Most primates live in groups. Thus, the infant is likely to encounter other group members when it ventures away from its mother in periods of group rest or quiet. Young infants often explore these other animals

[42] Chalmers (1972) and Sussman (1977).

much the same as they would explore the physical environment.[43] An infant may crawl over an adult male's body, put a female's tail in its mouth, or touch the hand of a juvenile who is reaching out to initiate play. Some of this early social exploration is reinforced by optimal levels of sensory stimulation, much the same as nonsocial exploration is. However, some social exploration produces too much sensory stimulation or other punitive consequences. When an infant explores interaction with a group of playing juveniles, the juveniles' rowdy, high intensity behavior can easily overstimulate the infant, who has not yet habituated to such high levels of stimulus input. Once overstimulated, the infant may give distress calls as a reflexive response to the aversive overstimulation. It may also hurry back to mother, since in the past, returning to mother for the low intensity stimulation of contact comfort has led to the reinforcing consequences of escaping the aversive overstimulation. Thus, the small infant begins to learn discriminations: Social exploration of quiet, resting individuals is reinforced, whereas exploration of rowdy, juvenile players is punished. Quiet individuals become S^D's for exploration and rowdy juveniles become S^Δ's for not exploring.

As the infant learns to discriminate the differences between quiet individuals and rowdy juveniles, it directs more of its early social exploration toward individuals in the quieter, safer parts of the group. Since other infants are likely to be in these quiet parts of the group, the exploring infant is likely to come across other infants with similar strength and skills. Because behavioral similarities often facilitate compatible and reinforcing social interaction (page 152), an infant's social exploration of agemates is likely to be rewarding. Early social exploration of peers is often tentative, consisting of touching, holding, and gentle pulling or pushing. Because the recipient of the acts is likely to respond by moving, pushing back, or gently wrestling, early social exploration usually produces abundant sensory stimulation (usually more than exploring the physical environment does); but social exploration of agemates is less likely to produce aversive consequences than does exploration of rowdy juveniles. Because peer exploration tends to be mutually reinforcing, infants learn to approach each other and acquire skills at interacting. If an infant encounters too much novelty, surprise, stimulus intensity, or total sensory input, it will become overstimulated and withdraw temporarily; and it is common to see such pauses in early social exploration and play. However, each time the infant returns to explore peer interactions further, there is less novelty (due to habituation) and less likelihood of aversive overstimulation. With less likelihood of overstimulation, the early tentative bouts of social exploration change into longer bouts with fewer aversive interruptions. As the youngsters be-

---

[43] Harlow and Harlow (1965:312) and Baldwin and Baldwin (1978b).

come more accustomed to each other, they spend increasing amounts of time exploring the properties of peer interaction and these interactions soon become more active, merging into social play.

Social Play

Although infants and juveniles do not stop exploration of the physical environment when they begin social play, social play provides much more novelty, stimulus complexity, and unpredictability than the physical environment can; hence play has the potential to provide more sensory stimulation than can exploration of the nonsocial environment. Because there are so many possible ways that young primates can play together (more ways than there are to interact with inanimate objects that do not respond), it takes a great deal of time before they can explore them all and have habituation destroy their reinforcing properties. In some circumstances social play can provide enough diverse forms of sensory stimulation to reinforce hours of play a day.[44]

The development of social play is influenced by maturation, increasing experience, skill, strength, and by the interplay between novelty and habituation. Early peer play tends to be gentle, as the young players push, pull, wrestle, or gently paw at each other. Since all these activities are quite novel for the young animal, who is experiencing them for the first time, there is ample sensory stimulation to provide reinforcement. Social play can even be overstimulating for the younger players, causing them to pause or temporarily retreat to mother. But as the days pass and the players habituate to their early patterns of social play, there is less chance of overstimulation. As the habituation process continues, the novelty of early social play declines even further, and eventually early play patterns lose their ability to provide optimal levels of stimulation. The early play patterns become boring, incapable of producing reinforcers. However, all during play new response patterns are likely to appear through induction (page 37f). These new variations bring novelty reinforcers, hence these play patterns are reinforced as the old, early patterns decrease in frequency. For example, as young howler monkeys gently paw and swat at each other in early play, there is variation in their responses: The variations range from very gentle pawing to relatively strong swats. Very gentle pawing is unlikely to produce novel experience for the players, who have already explored the gentlest forms of social play. However, the stronger variations create new tactile experiences and new social situations for the players. The novelty positively reinforces the stronger swats and negatively reinforces agile

---

[44] However, deprivation, aversive stimuli, and competing responses can suppress play to very low levels (Loy, 1970 and Baldwin and Baldwin, 1976, 1977a).

PLATE 7.4. Wrestling provides generous quantities of sensory stimulation: movement, surprise, and tactile stimulation. Two juvenile hanuman langurs wrestle near a river's edge. (*Courtesy of J.R. Oppenheimer.*)

movements that help evade receiving a hard swat in a sensitive area. Due to differential reinforcement, the players show gradual changes in their play patterns as old, boring games are replaced by new play patterns that provide more sensory stimulation.[45] It was the variations in early play that served as the raw material from which new play patterns were shaped by differential reinforcement.

A primate's repertoire of play patterns changes when new variations arise, due to induction, and are reinforced, due to novelty. Because players are growing stronger and more skillful each day, their games can also involve greater strength and skill. This further expands the

[45] Some early forms of play—such as wrestling and chasing—persist in the play of older primates, due to several types of reinforcement. First, there are many unexpected movements that can be made during wrestling and chasing, thus there is always some element of surprise even after months or years of wrestling or chasing play. Second, as animals gain strength and skill, they often learn new forms of wrestling and chasing that bring novelty reinforcers. Third, active play produces the reinforcers of stimulus intensity and high input rates, even when novelty is low. Fourth, wrestling also produces the reinforcers of tactile stimulation. Fifth, after older juveniles no longer find novelty in *any* kind of play, they sometimes engage in wrestling play merely because it is more stimulating than doing nothing.

possibilities for novel variations that were not available when the players were younger, weaker, and less skillful. As infants mature into juveniles, play patterns gradually become rowdier and more active, including more running, chasing, and jumping. These changes allow play to produce increasing stimulus intensity, novelty, and total stimulus input rates that reinforce each step of new developments in social play patterns.[46]

Creativity

Creativity consists of producing a new behavior that has not appeared before. Because novelty is a source of reinforcement in most situations (unless the total sensory input produces overstimulation), acts of creativity are usually followed by sensory stimulation reinforcers. Sensory stimulation is the natural reinforcer for creativity, since novel stimulation appears naturally after creative acts, even if other reinforcers do not. A creative behavior may be repeated until the novelty wears off; or it may persist even after habituation has destroyed the novelty if the creative response leads to other sources of reinforcement, such as food, warmth, sex, or rewarding social interaction.[47]

Novel behavior can arise from several sources. First, natural variations in old behavior patterns sometimes produce a novel behavior: In the example above, a few strong swats appeared as natural variations in early, gentle play and introduced new patterns into the play interaction. Day to day or moment to moment variations in an individual's level of hunger, muscle tension, posture, fatigue, sickness, hormone titer, and physical maturation can augment the natural variability in behavior. Second, there are always variations in each individual's field of stimulus input; hence the S^D's that control behavior vary in ways that can cause an individual to emit behavior chains containing novel recombinations of old responses. If the present S^D's tend to evoke competing responses or mutually facilitating responses, the interaction of the old responses may lead to novel behavioral output. Third, having a large behavior repertoire increases the probability that creative recombinations of old responses can occur.[48] Fourth, behavior that has been learned on var-

---

[46] As the players become progressively stronger they can cause pain and overstimulation for play partners; and these aversive events set limits on the vigor of play interactions. Play forms that are too aversive are usually infrequent because of the punishment they induce. Too much aggression and dominance behavior can suppress play; but when neurosurgery on the aggressive animal reduces aggression, there is a reappearance of play (Kawai, 1966).

[47] Naturally, creative acts that lead to punishment—such as a painful fall—may be suppressed if the punishment outweighs the total level of reinforcement. The punishers of effort suppress more active forms of creativity in less healthy and strong individuals.

[48] Rumbaugh et al. (1972).

PLATE 7.5. Two rhesus monkeys are leaping during play. Young animals have to gain considerable strength, skill, and coordination before they can engage in this type of play. (*Courtesy of D. Symons.*)

iable schedules of reinforcement is more variable than behavior learned on fixed schedules, hence more likely to produce creative effects.[49] Fifth, imitation is often a source of creative responses. When an observer sees a model do a behavior, the observer will seldom obtain enough information to allow the imitative response to be a perfect copy of the modeled behavior. Sixth, the observer usually differs from the model in body size, strength, behavior repertoire style, or skill; and this increases the probability that the observer's imitative response will be different from the model's response. Thus, imitation usually introduces variations into behavior and is a source of creativity. Seventh, imitative creativity is increased when the observer sees multiple models who display several possible variations on a given behavior.[50] When an observer imitates these multiple models, the observer is likely to combine bits of information from each model to produce a unique combined effect that differs from the response that would have been emitted after observing only one model. Eighth, operant skills for producing novel recombinations of old responses can be conditioned to higher frequencies if creativity is reinforced.[51]

All these sources of creative new responses add novelty to exploration, play, or any other activity, hence produce more sensory stimulation than noncreative, repetitious behavior does. Except when a primate is overstimulated by the total sensory input, creativity is reinforced by the novel stimulation that it brings, though other reinforcers and punishers also influence the future frequency of creative behavior. Few species have a genetic potential or live in an environment that causes creativity to become a very frequent part of daily life. However, creative responses need not be frequent, spectacular, or highly visible to have an important effect on behavioral development. In most primates, small, creative variations are much more common than large behavioral variations. Nevertheless, a series of small innovations can have a large cumulative effect that facilitates the adaptive shaping of new operant skills (pages 35–38).[52] Exploration, play, and creativity play an important role in natural learning, because they generate behavioral novelties which are the raw material from which new operants can be shaped. The behavioral novelties play the same role in natural learning as mutations play in natural selection: Both provide the variability that allows differential reinforcement or differential reproduction to mold new forms.

[49] Boren et al. (1978).

[50] Bandura et al. (1963).

[51] Pryor et al. (1969); Goetz and Salmonson (1972); and Goetz and Baer (1973).

[52] The prescientific analysis of the creation of the species portrayed creation as a rapid six day process. Now we realize that the species were created by many slow cumulative changes. New operant behavior is also created by many slow gradual changes in most circumstances, except when modeling or other forms of social learning allow one individual to learn from the behavior of others.

The End of Exploration and Play

In most primate species, individuals usually stop playing by late adolescence or early adulthood.[53] There is usually a decline in exploration
and creativity, too, though these activities may not decline as rapidly
as play since they require less effort. Are the declines in stimulus-seeking
behavior biologically preprogrammed? Is it inevitable that exploration,
play, and creativity must decline by early adulthood?

From the evolutionary perspective it has been argued that it is adaptive
for primates to stop exploring and playing by adulthood. Because stimulus-seeking behavior exposes the individual to potential risks, a
cost–benefit analysis suggests that it is adaptive for individuals to stop
exploring and playing once they have received the adaptive benefits
that these activities provide for the young, developing individual (Table
7.1). Rowell (1972) argues that an infant or juvenile is much more easily
replaced than an adult, hence it is functional for the young to take the
risks of exploration and play and for the adults to follow more conservative, low-risk behavior patterns. Whereas the young are playful
and innovative, the adults are conservative creatures of habit whose
behavior repertoires are repositories for the tried and true behavior that
has stood the test of time. The decline in exploration and play helps
stabilize the repository of personal and traditional skills.

From the proximal perspective, the decline in exploration and play
can be traced to several behavioral mechanisms. First, the process of
habituation is a biologically established feature of learning that is of
primary importance. For the young primate, exploration and play produce novel and stimulating consequences, which in turn serve to reinforce stimulus-seeking behavior. The habituation process produces
adaptive results for the young animal, because it forces the young individual to venture further afield to discover new sources of novel stimuli, and this is functional in broadening the experiences of the young.
But what happens when a juvenile has broadened its realm of activity
as far as possible in its environment? It has explored the nonaversive
parts of the group's home range, explored the range of social interactions
available in its group, and developed as many types of play activities
as is possible given its species' behavioral limitations and current environmental conditions. After the juvenile has explored all the accessible
sources of novelty in the environment and habituation has taken its toll,
there are declining amounts of sensory stimulation to maintain exploration and play. Naturally, the exhaustion of novelty is a gradual process; but as it occurs, exploration and play cease to be followed by novelty
reinforcers. Due to nonreinforcement (and the punishment of effort),
stimulus-seeking activities begin to become less frequent.

[53] Glickman and Sroges (1966).

Second, limitations of skill and strength accelerate the decline in exploration and play. Individuals with a large repertoire of skillful responses for manipulating the social and nonsocial environment, locating complex new experiences, and creating new response patterns will be able to locate and generate more novelty in a given environment than less skillful individuals. Because the skillful individual can gain access to more sources of sensory stimulation hence obtain more sensory reinforcement, this individual will receive more reinforcers that can maintain exploration and play later into life. Strength also helps animals explore into more different kinds of situations and participate in a broader variety of play activities. Thus, strength makes it possible to locate more novelty reinforcers, hence to have exploration and play maintained later into life. For similar reasons, health and vigor increase an individual's chances of locating novelty and having a later decline in stimulus-seeking behavior. However, age does eventually lead to a decline in reaction time, memory, attention, and other behavioral capacities involved in exploration and play.[54]

Third, there are several punishers that can suppress the frequency of exploration and play. The more punishers that are associated with exploration and play—and the earlier in life that they appear—the sooner exploration and play will be suppressed by punishment. Effortful behavior is a punisher. As long as vigorous chasing is novel, young primates will generate the effortful behavior, but when the novelty wears off, the punishers of effort suppress the behavior. Not surprisingly, high-effort play patterns are usually among the first to drop out of an individual's behavior repertoire as adulthood approaches.[55] Although a young monkey may hop and jump around an older juvenile, directing play at it, the older juvenile is likely to sit and play with the younger animal by making a few skillful low-effort swats at it, without getting up to chase it.

Exploration and play that lead to aversive experiences are likely to be suppressed by the punishment and replaced by caution[56]—unless the sensory stimulation reinforcers are strong enough to counteract the punishment.[57] Thus, when young primates explore near a wasp nest or an unfriendly coati, they may experience aversive consequences that suppress further exploration of these stimuli. Since punishers often have more long-lasting effects on behavior than positive reinforcers (page 157f) the numerous punishers experienced during exploration and play

---

[54] Davis (1978).
[55] Simonds (1965) and Symons (1978).
[56] Burton (1972).
[57] Bernstein (1976a) found that juvenile and subadult males living in the relative deprivation of captivity responded to an electric shock grid as a very exciting plaything. The stimulating challenge of playing with the grid outweighed the punishment of shock.

eventually condition caution or suppress the exploration of many stimuli. Low-status individuals tend to receive more social punishers during
active play than do high-status animals. Because female primates tend
to be smaller and weaker than same-age males, they usually receive
more social punishers than males. Not surprisingly, these punished
individuals usually engage in less exploration and play—or are more
guarded and cautious in their exploration and play—than are other
agemates.[58]

Fourth, reinforcement for competing responses can cause a decline
in exploration and play; and maturing primates experience several
changes in reinforcement patterns that often produce these competing
responses. For example, as a young primate ceases obtaining milk from
mother's nipples, it must spend increasing amounts of time searching
for food. Food reinforcers increase foraging behavior, which is a competing response that can interfere with and suppress exploration and
play.[59] Both maturation and increased social skill allow the developing
individual to obtain increasing access to sexual reinforcers. Increased
attention to sexual interaction is a competing response that takes time
away from exploration and play. Sexual maturity further increases the
amount of nonplayful behavior that is reinforced by sexual reinforcers.
Once a female has given birth, the reinforcers of nursing and interacting
with a small infant increase attention to infant care, and this competing
response further suppresses exploration and play in females. Likewise,
other adult responses serve as competing responses that contribute to
the decline in stimulus-seeking behavior.

The present theory predicts that a decline in play is not inevitable in
all circumstances. Individuals should be able to remain explorative and
playful relatively late into life if they are healthy, have a large behavior
repertoire of skills, live in an environment with multiple sources of
sensory stimulation, and have few competing responses or punishers
for stimulus-seeking behavior. This has important humanistic implications for people who wish to retain explorative and playful behavior
well into adulthood (page 239f).

CONCLUSION

According to this balanced biosocial theory, both the rise and decline
of exploration and play are the result of multiple factors—both distal
and proximal—rather than the result of genetically programmed changes
that automatically regulate the frequency of exploration and play to
produce the optimal adaptive outcomes and optimal genetic transmis-

[58] Baldwin (1969); Fedigan (1972b); and Symons (1978).
[59] Baldwin and Baldwin (1978b).

sion. In order to produce a balanced biosocial theory of exploration and play—or any other behavior—it is necessary to analyze natural selection, the physiological mechanisms that mediate the behavior, and the influence of proximal causes. Data on each of these causes must be approached in ways that facilitate their integration with data from the other levels of analysis.

EXTENDING THEORIES
OF ANIMAL BEHAVIOR TO HUMANS

The general primate theory presented in the last chapter explains the basic findings on exploration and play in most primates. In order to increase the accuracy of the theory when dealing with any given species, it is necessary to have special data on the species—on its evolutionary history, ecological specializations, and unique biological mechanisms of behavior, including special behavioral capacities, predispositions, and limits. Data on current environmental conditions are also needed. The more data that are available, the more sensitively one can "tune" the general primate theory to suit the particular species.

In this chapter, we will demonstrate how the general primate theory of exploration and play can be adjusted to explain stimulus-seeking behavior in humans. Each aspect of the general theory from Chapter 7 must be examined to determine the degree to which the data on humans resemble or differ from the general primate theory. This involves the investigation of evolutionary considerations, biological mechanisms of behavior, and special features of human learning. Attention to each part of the multifactor model is needed to adjust the entire model to suit human behavior.

USING ANIMAL DATA WISELY

It is particularly important that we demonstrate how balanced biosocial theories based on animal data can be adjusted to relate to human behavior.[1] Incorrect use of animal data for explaining human behavior can be quite misleading, if not even dangerous. For millenia, people have been observing animal behavior and trying to use their observations to better understand human behavior. Obviously many of these efforts have led to the zoomorphic interpretations of human behavior that are as objectionable as anthropomorphic explanations of animal behavior. Analogies between animal behavior and human behavior abound in folklore and science. Argument by analogy from one species to another has been severely criticized[2] because it does not consider whether the behavior in question has been produced by different behavior mechanisms that operate in very different ways. Animal theories often carry a heavy weighting of distal causes; thus they are likely to be unbalanced if applied directly to human behavior, since human behavior is much more influenced by proximal causes than is the behavior of other species. If these and other problems are to be avoided, it becomes important to know how animal data *should* be used. How should they be transformed, translated, qualified, and supplemented if they are to improve our understanding of human behavior?

Some might say that we could solve these problems by merely neglecting the animal data or forbidding the use of such data in theories of human behavior. In actuality, it is very unlikely that future theories of human behavior will rely less on animal data than do present theories. The growing interest in and research on animal behavior guarantees that the animal data will become more abundant. If there are well reasoned and empirically tested guidelines for extrapolating from animal studies to human behavior, animal research can be of great use to the science of human behavior.

There are, in fact, several advantages for using animal data to help understand human behavior. Animal behavior is usually simpler than human behavior, hence it allows us to see simple patterns, overviews, and generalizations that are often difficult to see in the complexity of human behavior. As Premack (1971:186) suggested, animal research can serve as a "drawing board" for sketching out and analyzing simplified models of behaviors that are often exceedingly complex in humans. For example, primate play is much simpler than human play, hence, it

---

[1] For simplicity of wording, we refer to the nonhuman animals as animals and the nonhuman primates as primates. Contrasts that arise when discussing animals and humans or primates and humans are not intended to imply that humans are not animals or primates.

[2] Lehrman (1953); Boulding (1967); Montague (1968); Allen et al. (1976); von Cranach (1976); and Ruse (1978).

allows us to see generalizations and locate underlying causal mechanisms. Theories of animal behavior can then serve as simplified hypotheses around which to construct adjusted theories that incorporate the unique features of human behavior. Because there has been an enormous amount of research done on animals—including many experiments that could never be done on humans, due to their long life spans or due to ethical reasons—we have a wealth of animal data on topics that cannot easily be studied in humans. If we use these data wisely, we stand to learn more than if we disregard them.

Since animal behavior is different from and usually simpler than human behavior, extrapolations from animal theories to human behavior should automatically involve two steps, in which (1) differences are taken into account and (2) special human behavioral complexities are added to the theories. In balanced biosocial theories, these two steps must be taken at each level of analysis from evolution to physiological mechanisms and behavior development. This strategy allows a balanced animal theory to be adjusted for humans and rebalanced at each level of analysis. In the following sections we will demonstrate how the balanced biosocial theory of exploration and play in primates (from Chapter 7) can be adjusted at all levels to deal with stimulus-seeking behavior in humans. One could conduct a similar analysis of any behavior for which a multiple factor, balanced model was available, though one would expect to need to make fewer adjustments when extrapolating to humans from primates rather than from more distantly related species. This method of extrapolation from animal behavior to human behavior parallels von Cranach's (1976:359) method of breaking comparisons down into separate "levels of comparison," or Masters' (1976) "levels of analysis." By comparing animal and human data at each level separately, it is possible to minimize the problems that arise when using large global concepts that are difficult to operationalize.[3]

EVOLUTIONARY CONSIDERATIONS

There are several strategies that can be used to evaluate similarities and differences between primates and humans in the evolution of exploration and play. One strategy consists of constructing an "evolutionary series" from primitive to advanced species, locating patterns of evolutionary change, and extrapolating the trend to approximate the human condition. Extrapolating from primates to humans would be expected to be more fruitful than extrapolating from other species.[4] Mazur and Robertson (1972) analyzed a biological series consisting of tree shrews,

---

[3] For a more extensive discussion of the methods and limitations of drawing inferences about human behavior from animal data, see von Cranach (1976) and Fairbanks (1977).
[4] von Cranach (1976:377).

lemurs, tarsiers, squirrel monkeys, baboons, macaques, and chimpanzees. Moving up the evolutionary series, there is a consistent increase
in the number of years of pre-adult socialization—with lemurs, having
2 or 3 years and chimpanzees, about 12 years—hence an increased
number of years for play. In the more primitive species, play is stylized
and object manipulation is absent. Advancing up the biological series,
there are decreases in stylized elements and increases in object manipulation. Candland et al. (1978) came to similar conclusions in their more
specialized analysis of object play in primates. There is a significant
increase in object-oriented exploration and play when one traces these
behaviors from primitive to advanced primates. Also, there is an increase
in the complexity of interactions with objects, and objects become incorporated in play as a means of enriching play (i.e., making it more
stimulating and rewarding). These evolutionary trends appear to extend
to humans, since humans show the longest subadult dependency period
in which exploration and play can occur without the competing demands
of "making a living" with adult behavior. Humans are clearly outstand-
ing at object manipulation, having specialized hand structure and behavioral capacities for tool-use that facilitate the process. Human social
play is also enormously complex and often involves objects—balls,
cards, tokens, counters, vehicles, and so forth—that complicate and
enrich the social interaction. These objects increase the sensory stimulation obtained from stimulus complexity, unexpected combinations of
outcomes, and the complex cortical processing needed to play many
kinds of games.

   Although evolutionary trends doubtless exist, they predict only a
limited amount of behavior at each phyletic level.[5] While a few broad
trends can be located with general evolutionary comparisons, closer
examination of data on several species at any phylogenetic level reveals
that there are many exceptions to most of the trends. In addition to
considerable variability in behavior within each phylogenetic level, there
are behavioral variations within species that make it difficult to typify
a given species as having "one" characteristic type of stimulus-seeking
behavior. Data on monkeys and apes indicate that primates of a given
species may play several hours per day in one environment, yet play
very little in another environment.[6] Because there is considerable behavioral variation between and within species at each phylogenetic level,
extrapolations from a general evolutionary series must be somewhat
tentative.

   A second strategy for evaluating the similarities and differences in
exploration and play in different species involves analyzing the rela-

   [5] Glickman and Sroges (1966); Denham (1971); Eisenberg et al. (1972); and Clutton-Brock
(1974).
   [6] Baldwin and Baldwin (1977a:386f).

tionship between a species' stimulus-seeking behavior and its ecological adaptations.[7] Nocturnal primates do not appear to be very playful—perhaps because rowdy play in the trees at night increases the risk of dangerous falls. Thus, the dangers of nocturnal play tip the cost–benefit ratio of exploration and play to favor the survival of less playful individuals. Also, when compared with terrestrial species, the infants of arboreal species leave mother later in life for their first explorations of the physical environment.[8] Because this difference is visible when related species are housed in similar cages, it appears to be a genetically established difference resulting from the dangers of early arboreal exploration. When exploring a novel stimulus, arboreal species are inclined to be observers whereas terrestrial species tend to manipulate the stimulus. Species that are specialized for eating leaves tend to play less than closely related species that are omnivores or opportunists. Because it takes less skill, ingenuity, and knowledge about the environment to find and ingest leaves than it does to locate and capture animal food or to survive on the complex diet typical of opportunistic species, there are fewer adaptive advantages for herbivores to evolve mechanisms that favor high frequencies of stimulus-seeking behavior.

Since humans evolved as opportunistic omnivores with hunting and gathering abilities, suited to terrestrial life on the savannas, it is reasonable to assume that evolutionary processes favored those biological mechanisms that facilitate exploration and play. As tool-use became more important in human adaptation, there were increased evolutionary advantages for object play as a means of training manipulative skills and producing knowledge about objects that could potentially be used as tools. The human specialization for group cooperation increased each individual's dependency on the group and need for social integration; and social play doubtless became more important for facilitating integration in the group. Because social interaction is vastly more complex than interaction with the nonsocial environment, a key human adaptation involved adjusting to handle the complexities of social life. Because exploration and play are reinforced by stimulus novelty and complexity, they usually cause individuals to investigate complex situations and learn how to cope with them.[9]

A third strategy for extending evolutionary analyses to humans involves comparing the 30 functions of exploration and play in primates (Table 7.1) with the particular functions that influence humans. Some of the 30 primate functions would be expected to overlap with human functions, but new functions unique to humans could be added to the list. Although one could compare each of the 30 items on the list, we will only comment briefly on the four broad categories. It seems likely

----

[7] Morris (1964); Glickman and Sroges (1966); Aldis (1975).
[8] Chalmers (1972) and Sussman (1977).
[9] Compare with Humphrey (1976).

that throughout most human evolution *exercise* was as important an adaptive consequence of exploration and play in humans as in other primates. The same can be said for the *psychological* functions: nerve development, optimal levels of central activity, perceptual and motor development, and increasing behavioral flexibility. The *environmental* functions probably became more important during human evolution. Since humans specialized as an opportunistic terrestrial species with a large home range—hence, with a great deal to be learned about their physical environments—exploration and play could become increasingly valuable in helping individuals learn information about the physical environment. The prolonged years of immaturity and playfulness in humans allow the learning function to be extended. The previously presented data on increased object play during primate and human evolution also support theories of environmental learning. Greater manual dexterity, increased perceptual and discriminative ability, along with more advanced cortical processing, all, no doubt helped hominids locate more sensory stimulation in objects in their environment, hence facilitating exploration of and play with objects. Although some primates make and use rudimentary tools, it is clear that tool-use became especially important during human evolution. Thus, the functional benefits of exploration and play related to tools—their invention, manufacture, and use— would have had an increasing impact on the evolution of the biological mechanisms related to exploration and play with objects.

The *social* functions of exploration and play for humans are at least as important as in the other primates, and several of them are clearly more complex and more important. Since human society is so much more complex than that of the nonhuman primates, both exploration and play allow the developing individual to discover a very broad range of social experiences. The long dependency period of human young provides many years for exploration and play to facilitate this social learning. Most of the social functions in Table 7.1 appear to apply to humans: Human exploration and play facilitate the learning of group structure, traditions, social roles, social bonds, controlled aggression, status relationships, and so forth. As children imitate adult behavior during exploration and play, they gain practice at adult roles, which are much more complex in humans than in other species. Mead (1934) emphasized the importance of the multiple roles the child takes during play: Role-play allows the child to learn to respond to "self" as to "others," thus gaining an understanding of "self as object"; and these experiences greatly facilitate personality development and the acquisition of social skills.[10] Because human communication systems are vastly more

[10] At one moment, the child is playing the role of mother, telling the children how to act, and the next moment, playing the children in response to the mother's statements. By repeatedly shifting roles, the child learns to play various social roles and understand the meanings attached to each role (Mead, 1934 and Denzin, 1975).

complicated than those used by other primates, the function of exploration and play for learning communication skills was probably much
more important during human evolution than in the evolution of other
primates.[11] Since children often engage in hours of language play each
day—often talking to themselves, dolls, real playmates, or imaginary
playmates—it appears that language is an especially stimulating and
rewarding thing with which to play.[12] Because verbal behavior requires
little effort, language play is less likely to be suppressed by the punishers
of effortfulness than is physical play, and it is common to see adults
engaging in verbal play long after rowdy physical play has declined due
to the punishers of effort.

A few special features of human exploration and play require additions to be made to the list of functions from the primate literature.
Humans can play at either "play" or "games." Games are distinguished
from free play by the presence of rules.[13] Although young children
prefer unstructured free play to games, social learning increases their
verbal skills and ability to follow, modify, and invent rules; this in turn
allows children to find games more rewarding as they grow older and
gain experience. Games train players to interact within structural and
sometimes legalistic constraints, to negotiate new rules, and to cope
with exceptions.[14] For a species whose societies are often built upon
and permeated with rules and norms, games function to train the rule-
use skills that facilitate adult social interaction, especially in more bureaucratic, legalized settings. A study by Lever (1976) indicates that in
our society boys engage in more rule-governed play than do girls. Lever
speculates that "boys' games may help prepare their players for successful performance in a wide range of work settings in modern society"
(p. 484). The lower level of rule structure in girls' games may handicap
them in learning the skills of rule manipulation needed to deal effectively
with the complexities of bureaucratic institutions.[15]

Anthropological studies have demonstrated relationships between the
complexity of societies and types of games played in those societies.[16]
Games of strategy are most likely to appear in societies with complex
political integration, high social straticification, relatively advanced and
specialized technologies, large settlements, more jurisdictional levels
beyond the local community, and high gods. Games of strategy appear
to function in socializing the young for playing a variety of roles—

[11] Bruner (1972).
[12] Singer (1973).
[13] Denzin (1975).
[14] Vacha (1976).
[15] Sex differences do not appear in all environments (Hamer and Missakian, 1978). Also
see Sutton-Smith and Rosenberg (1961).
[16] Roberts et al. (1959; 1963) and Roberts and Sutton-Smith (1962).

commanding, obeying, and disobeying—according to the changing demands of complex social situations.

Anthropologists have pointed out that aggressive societies tend to have combative forms of play and games.[17] Studies on aggressive sports also indicate that aggressive games can contribute to the training of higher levels of aggressiveness.[18] To the degree that aggression has helped some societies to survive in times of war, conquest, invasion, or cultural conflict, aggressive games and sports can function to train these skills. But aggression is not the only route to survival. Intelligence, strategy, and commitment to one's group can also help a culture to survive; and exploration and play can help train these, too.

Humor is a form of verbal play that is a common feature of human behavior.[19] Humor is largely based on the production and perception of surprising and unexpected verbal combinations; hence humor fits within the domain of stimulus-seeking behavior that is reinforced by novel sensory stimulation. Humor has many social functions,[20] the most important of which are easing social tensions, solidifying social ties within a group, marking off the targets of humor as "outgroup" members, and fostering hostility toward the outgroup.

One of the most remarkable human specializations is the large cerebral cortex that appeared so rapidly during the past two million years of human evolution, clearly paralleling the human specialization for cognition and abstract processing. Platt (1961) speculates that human evolution thrust early hominids into environments that were much more complex and constantly changing than those of other primates. Presumably, the brain became increasingly structured to deal with high levels of novelty and to search for "crucial regularities in the flux of strangeness" (p. 412). According to Platt's theory, humans should tolerate—and even thrive on—higher levels of novel input than do other species. This should be functional in helping humans cope with their more complex environments. Platt uses this theory to explain why people respond positively to combinations of surprise and pattern in art, music, and poetry. Humphrey (1976) argues that intelligence may have arisen during evolution primarily because it helps humans cope with the complexity of their social environment. If this is true, intellectual curiosity and playfulness may have functioned in the evolutionary past more to develop cognitive skills for coping with highly complex social environments than to develop cognitive skills for coping with the physical environment. Even if Humphrey's view of the evolution of intelli-

---

[17] Sipes (1973).
[18] Coakley (1978).
[19] McGhee (1979).
[20] Martineau (1972).

gence is true, it does not negate the current importance of intellectual exploration and play in dealing with the physical environment.

PHYSIOLOGICAL MECHANISMS

In order to adjust theories of animal behavior to deal with the behavior of humans, it is important to evaluate the similarities and differences in the physiological mechanisms that mediate the behavior at the relevant phylogenetic levels. The mechanisms that mediate exploration and play in humans show both similarities to and differences from the physiological mechanisms of other primates. The similarities appear in homologous physiological structures, and the differences reflect unique human specializations. Homologous structures—such as the reticular formation, reinforcement centers, and cortex—generally allow the safest inferences about similarities in behavior from one species to another.[21] Differences must be studied to reveal unique features of humans that do not fit general primate models of behavior.

The special physiological mechanisms involved in human exploration and play have not been well analyzed. Since the structure and function of many subcortical areas of humans resemble those of other advanced primates, it is reasonable to believe that the reticular formation, reinforcement centers, and punishment centers of the human brain operate much the same as the homologous structures in other primates.[22] Thus, one would expect humans to respond to understimulation and overstimulation as punishers, but to optimal, intermediate levels of stimulation as a reinforcer. A relevant study by Brackbill (1971) found that an anencephalic infant with an intact cerebellum and brainstem responded to increased stimulus input in much the same way as normal infants, with increased heart rate and mean respiratory rates. "Thus, it appears that the change in arousal level . . . is not an adjunct of some cognitive, cortically mediated function but is instead the product of a primitive, subcortical mechanism" (p. 25). Behavioral data (page 228f) strongly support the view that *some* central mechanism—whether the reticular formation or not—functions to monitor the overall levels of activity in the human nervous system and activate reinforcement or punishment centers, depending on whether the stimulation levels are optimal or nonoptimal. Zuckerman (1978) provides a good summary of the current data relating stimulus-seeking behavior to neurophysiological, biochemical, and genetic variables.

The peripheral behavioral mechanisms of humans show both simi-

---

[21] Analogy is a weak method of arguing that the behavior of one species is similar to that of another. Homology—reflecting similar form, function, and evolutionary history—is a much more reliable method (von Cranach, 1976).

[22] Bross et al. (1980).

larities and differences when compared with those of the nonhuman primates. The physical structure and body size of each species impose constraints on movement that produce the unique forms of exploration and play of that species. The same is true of the peripheral sensory and motor systems. These factors must be taken into account in adjusting the general primate model to humans. Hormones play an important role in regulating physical development and are in part responsible for sex differences in human exploration and play.[23]

Many reflexes shown by humans are homologous with those shown by other primates. The human infant's earliest exploration results from orienting and gazing reflexes, rooting and sucking reflexes, clasping and general undifferentiated body movements[24] that clearly resemble the reflexes of nonhuman primates. In addition, the human infant has special reflexes that are not found (or are not well developed) in other primates. The infant's babbling response appears to function to produce early language exploration. The infant's smile and gaze reflexes—which are elicited when novel stimuli appear—may help reinforce parental attention to the infant.[25] In addition, the unconditioned reinforcers and punishers to which humans respond are similar to those known for other primates, though variations in taste and light preferences do exist. Finally, many of the mechanisms that mediate operant and Pavlovian conditioning, observational learning, habituation, and other features of learned behavior are similar and homologous in humans and other primates. There are, of course, human specializations in learning (page 232f), but the most basic features of human and primate conditioning are quite similar.

The size and complexity of the human cortex permit much more complex exploration and play than is seen in other species because advanced cortical development allows more subtle perceptual capacity, complex cognitive processing, and refined motor output. The presence of Broca's area, Wernicke's area, the angular gyrus, and other language processing centers in the human brain adds to the processing capacity for producing and understanding language.[26] Language adds a special component to the human behavior repertoire that allows us to locate, create, and enjoy symbolic stimulation. Jokes, puns, and other verbal play can prove to be highly stimulating, even in the absence of other types of sensory input (as when an audience listens passively while a commedian produces novel, unexpected verbal output). Even serious conversation (without elements of verbal play) can provide enough sensory stimu-

[23] Wilmore (1975, 1977) and Mathews and Fox (1976).
[24] Brazelton (1961).
[25] Ambrose (1959); Robson (1967); van Hooff (1972); Fraiberg (1974); and Stern (1974, 1977).
[26] Lancaster (1968), Geschwind (1974, 1979); and Zurif and Blumstein (1978).

lation that people do not drop into the boredom or understimulation zone.[27] Fantasy, daydreams, and conversations with oneself are all self-generated forms of sensory stimulation, many of which rely heavily on verbal mediation.[28]

At present, too little is known about the neurophysiology of human cortical processing to add many specific predictions to a balanced biosocial theory of exploration and play in humans. Since the human cortex is predominantly an organ of cogitation and learning, there is support for the evolutionary and behavioral data that human exploration and play involve more complex mediation and learning. Future research in neurophysiology should help in adjusting general primate theories to explain special human behavioral capacities. A balanced biosocial theory welcomes additions at all levels of analysis, and physiological data can be especially valuable because the physiological mechanisms of behavior provide the biological substrate through which distal and proximal causes are interwoven to produce behavior (page 19f).

BEHAVIORAL DEVELOPMENT

Many of the behavioral mechanisms that make human behavior different from the behavior of other primates are best understood, at present, as they appear in behavioral development—rather than in terms of physiological mechanisms. Thus, the factors that influence development can yield valuable information for adjusting primate theories to fit human behavior.

Deprivation from sensory stimulation and nutrition produce effects quite similar to those seen in other primates. Human children who are raised in environments that deprive them of sensory stimulation are significantly slower to begin exploration and play than children raised in environments without deprivation. For example, Kagan and Klein (1973) observed Guatamalan Indian children in an isolated rural village. The children were confined inside small, dark, windowless huts and not even allowed to explore much of this environment for the first 10 to 12 months of life.

> The infant is usually close to the mother, either on her lap or enclosed on her back in a colored cloth, sitting on a mat, or sleeping in a hammock. The mother rarely allows the infant to crawl on the dirt floor of the hut and feels that the outside sun, air, and dust are harmful.

---

[27] Meaningfulness becomes an especially important form of sensory stimulation in humans, in addition to novelty, complexity, intensity, and rate of input (Fiske and Maddi, 1961). Meaningful stimuli can trigger long sequences of cortical processing, hence create considerable central nervous activity, for example when a serious conversation leads to hours of subsequent thought (Baldwin and Baldwin, 1981).

[28] Patterson's (1978a,b) gorilla, Koko, converses with herself using sign language.

The infant is rarely spoken to or played with, and the only available objects for play, besides his own clothing or his mother's body, are oranges, ears of corn and pieces of wood or clay. These infants are distinguished from American infants of the same age by their extreme motoric passivity, fearfulness, minimal smiling, and, above all, extraordinary quietness. A few with pale cheeks and vacant stares had the quality of tiny ghosts and resembled the description of the institutionalized infants that Spitz called marasmic. Many would not orient to a taped source of speech, not smile or babble to vocal overtures, and hesitated over a minute before reaching for an attractive toy. (Pp. 949–950.)

When the children begin to leave the hut at about 15 months of age, they are slow to explore the larger environment. The effects of early deprivation are visible for several years. At three years, the children are still passive, timid, and quiet. The early deprivation does not, however, appear to produce permanent or irreversible damage, and after years of more stimulating experience the children eventually attain normal functioning. By 11 years of age, the children catch up with American children in most measures of cognitive and intellectual functioning.[29]

Malnutrition and starvation can also suppress exploration and play by producing conditions of fatigue, apathy and physical decline.[30] Food deprivation also increases the effectiveness of food in reinforcing food-getting behavior, which in turn is a competing response that suppresses exploration and play.

In the absence of deprivation, aversive stimulation, or excessive competing responses, the early development of human exploration and play follows the same general patterns seen in most primates. The infant's reflexes initiate early contacts with the environment and expose the infant to many kinds of stimuli. Gradually the reinforcement or punishment of optimal or nonoptimal levels of sensory stimulation begin to condition the early reflexes and nonspecific body movements into operant stimulus-seeking behavior. For example, early untargeted gazes become shaped into directed gazing, or operant visual exploration, due to differential reinforcement. If an object suspended above the crib provides more novel, complex sensory input than many other parts of the environment, the infant's gaze is shaped to focus on the novel object.[31] After the object loses its novelty (due to habituation), the infant gradually ceases looking at it and turns its attention to other stimuli. If the object is removed for a week, the recovery process causes the child to find renewed novelty in the object when next exposed to it, and the increased novelty will reinforce increased attention for a while.

---

[29] Davis (1940, 1947), Dennis and Najarian (1957), Curtiss (1977), and others also present data showing that early deprivation need not cause permanent damage.
[30] Winick (1979).
[31] Brazelton et al. (1974).

Overstimulation results in aversive consequences and elicits the re-flexes of fretting, crying, or screaming.[32] The aversive consequences serve to punish the exploration of overly stimulating targets, and the vocalizations usually bring a caretaker who can provide familiar, low level sensory inputs that calm the infant. Prolonged understimulation is also aversive; and the child learns to explore and play in part because these operants are most likely to lead to increased stimulus input, thus, an escape from boredom. As the child grows older and has more ex-posure to models, rules, and prompts, the child learns increasingly complex patterns of stimulus-seeking behavior. Optimal levels of sen-sory stimulation serve as the natural reinforcer that shapes exploration and play; but other reinforcers and punishers also influence the devel-opment of exploration and play.

Sensory Stimulation as Reinforcement or Punishment

Numerous studies have demonstrated that humans respond to optimal and nonoptimal levels of sensory input as reinforcers and punishers throughout life, much as other primates do. Thus, the basic reinforce-ment mechanisms that shape stimulus-seeking behavior appear to be the same in humans as in other primates.

Data from research on human infants show that sensory stimulation can serve as a reinforcer from the first weeks of life and that exploration and play are among those behaviors reinforced by sensory input. Infants as young as 2 weeks old learn operant head turning responses if the responses are followed by a "peek-a-boo" from an adult.[33] The "peek-a-boo" provides enough novel and multimodal sensory stimulation to reinforce early infant behavior. Older infants learn in a similar manner when a "peek-a-boo" or other forms of sensory stimulation are used as reinforcers. Observations on a 10-week old infant revealed that the infant selectively hit at a swinging toy when the toy was stationary, but not when it was moving.[34] Because hitting occurred most frequently when it was instrumental in escaping conditions of low sensory input by producing moving visual inputs, it appears that the response was con-trolled by sensory stimulation reinforcers. Infants begin targeted visual exploration of the environment after several weeks of life.[35] There is a gradual decline in the early reflex-like response of randomly wandering gaze, and an increase in visual exploration, in which the infant focuses

---

[32] Korner (1974). In adults overstimulation can induce panic, disorientation, hysteria, and complete behavioral disorganization (Bindra, 1959:243f and Hebb, 1972:199).
[33] Bower (1966).
[34] Watson (1966).
[35] Berlyne (1958).

its gaze on a selected stimulus. When tested with cards containing different stimulus patterns, infants who were 3–19 months old focused most attention on the cards with the greatest internal contours and stimulus complexity. Rheingold et al. (1962) studied 6-month-old infants in a special seat equipped with a metal sphere within easy reach. The infants learned to manipulate the sphere when it activated a motion picture display of moving, colored geometric forms on a screen in front of them. When this sensory input was given "free" (i.e., not contingent upon the infants' manipulating the sphere), the explorative touching responses became less frequent. Thus, the lights did not elicit reflexive manipulation, but rather they functioned as reinforcers and manipulation appeared only when it was instrumental in producing sensory stimulation. Leuba and Friedlander (1968) studied 20 children, 7–11 months of age, to see which knob they would explore when presented with two knobs that were associated with different types of sensory stimulation. After an initial period of handling both knobs, the infants learned to focus more of their activities on the knob that tiggered a door chime and lights than on the one that produced little sensory stimulation.

Even in adults, sensory stimulation continues to reinforce attention and other behavior. The coming and going of fads reflects the effects of novelty reinforcers and their removal due to habituation. When people interact with strangers, they spend more time looking at the other person than when they interact with friends.[36] Novel partners provide more sensory reinforcers for visual exploration.

Sensory stimulation is a positive reinforcer only at intermediate levels. When people are presented with sequences of tones of intermediate volume but varying levels of pattern complexity, the patterns with least variability and least unpredictability are ranked as unpleasant.[37] With increasing pattern complexity, the subjects rank the tones progressively more pleasant, up to a point. As the pattern complexity and unpredictability rise beyond that point, there is a decline in pleasantness, eventually reaching aversiveness.[38] There is also an interaction of stimulus complexity and past learning: People with musical backgrounds find higher levels of tone complexity to be optimal, whereas other subjects prefer lower levels of complexity. As people have increasing experience with music (or any other form of stimulation), habituation allows them to tolerate and enjoy higher levels of complexity and var-

[36] Rutter and Stephenson (1979).
[37] Vitz (1966).
[38] Computer music that is midway between random and highly ordered is generally judged to be more pleasant than either extreme (Gardner, 1978). Stimulus variation and alternation are crucial elements that make any type of music more interesting (Platt, 1961 and Patterson, 1974).

iability. Scholtz and Ellis (1975) studied 4- and 5-year olds in an environment that could be arranged to provide high or low levels of background sensory stimulation. They found that when the environmental sensory stimulation was high, the children selected toys that provided sensory stimulation of low complexity and low unpredictability; but when the environmental input was low, the children selected more complex and stimulating targets of play. Thus there is an inverse relation between the amount of sensory input the environment brings to people without their having to create it and the amount of sensory stimulation people learn to create for themselves.[39] When background conditions provide ample sensory input, people usually select activities that do not add much more stimulation (and hence avoid overarousal); but when the background conditions are underarousing, people turn to more stimulating activities to avoid aversive understimulation and obtain optimal levels of sensory stimulation. Einstein once observed: "I lived in solitude in the country and noticed how the monotony of a quiet life stimulates the creative mind."[40] Even noncreative thinking can be a pleasant alternative to understimulation, as Einstein observed: "When I have no special problem to occupy my mind, I love to reconstruct proofs of mathmatical and physical theorems that have long been known to me. There is no *goal* in this, merely an opportunity to indulge in the pleasant occupation of thinking."[41] People who work at boring jobs are likely to learn pastimes and social diversions to help escape aversive understimulation.[42] Being able to chat, gossip, and "fool around" helps break the monotony. When country music star Dolly Parton was asked why she dresses so outrageously—with gaudy outfits, blonde teased wigs, and excessive make-up—she answered: "It's fun for me. Why not? Life's boring enough, it makes you try to spice it up."[43] Saul Steinberg—a world famous cartoonist and contemporary artist—once said:

> The life of the creative man is led, directed and controlled by boredom. Avoiding boredom is one of our most important purposes. It is also one of the most difficult, because the amusement always has to be newer and on a higher level. So we are on a kind of spiral. The higher you go, the narrower the circle.[44]

Thus, optimal levels of sensory input—especially novel input—provide the natural reinforcers for exploration, play, and creativity in humans, much as in the other primates.

[39] Similar effects have been observed in children's fantasies (Freyberg, 1973) and the exploration of laboratory animals (Glickman, 1958).
[40] *Science News*, 31 March, 1979; p. 213.
[41] *Time*, 19 February, 1979; p. 75.
[42] Roy (1959–60) and Schrank (1978).
[43] *Playboy*, October, 1978; p. 82.
[44] *Time*, 17 April, 1978; p. 92.

Other Reinforcers and Punishers for Exploration and Play

Although an optimal level of stimulus input is the natural reinforcer for stimulus-seeking behavior, all the other reinforcers and punishers can influence stimulus-seeking behavior, too. Although all of the unconditioned reinforcers and punishers (Table 5.1) function much as they do in other species, several of the conditioned reinforcers and punishers— such as verbal praise, money, fame, criticism, disparagement, and mockery—are unique to humans. We will examine only a few of the more important reinforcers and punishers.

Effortful behavior is aversive, and it clearly influences human exploration and play. Young children find a great deal of novelty in simple physical activities; thus running, jumping, and other vigorous activities are often so novel and stimulating that the sensory reinforcers outweigh the punishers of effort and maintain hours of high-level activity per day. As habituation removes the novelty from running, chasing, and jumping, there is a decline in sensory reinforcement without a concomitant decline in the punishers of effort. As a result, high-activity behavior often becomes less frequent after the childhood period (unless social, symbolic, or other reinforcers are present to maintain the person's participation in athletics, sports, or exercise programs after the novelty is gone).

Falls, accidents, burns, stings, and other painful stimuli also function to suppress the types of exploration and play that lead to these aversive consequences. Hence, children learn to avoid playing with bees, wasps, hot machinery, and so forth (or at least they learn very cautious forms of exploration and play, shaped by negative reinforcement). Because young children find simple physical activities more novel than do older individuals, novelty reinforcement often maintains physical exploration and play that involves pain longer in children than in older individuals. A child may try rollerskating and fall down dozens of times without losing interest in the activity. The sensory reinforcement is greater than the punishment. Because adults have already experienced many different kinds of motion activities, they are less likely to find rollerskating as novel or rewarding as children do, and a few painful falls may suffice to suppress their skating quite effectively.

Social attention is a powerful positive reinforcer for children and most adults. Children who receive social attention whenever they build creative structures while playing with building blocks learn to produce increasing numbers of creative structures.[45] Conversely, children who receive attention for noncreative block-building learn to produce less creative structures. Because many teachers do not have time to pay attention to each child in the classroom, they usually cannot give social

[45] Goetz and Baer (1973).

reinforcement for most of their students' novel, inventive, or creative behavior. In fact, teachers often find novel, innovative behavior in the classroom to be distracting to themselves and to the students. Although teachers like high-IQ students more than average students, they do not like highly creative students more.[46] Even though exploration, play, and creativity can be reinforced by social liking and approval, parents and teachers often give more social reinforcers for academic conformity than for diversity and creativity.[47]

Exploration and play are often reinforced by the social consequences of being popular, liked, well known, or famous. Playful and creative people of all ages not only produce novel sensory stimulation for themselves, they often create positive sensory experience for others and thus they are often liked because they bring positive reinforcers to others. Since being liked or popular are generally reinforcing, playful people often receive social reinforcers contingent upon their production of exploration and play. Success, fame, money, and Nobel Prizes are other social reinforcers that can increase the probability of exploration, play, and creativity.

Social Learning

Although reinforcers and punishers are the prime movers of operant and Pavlovian conditioning, there are three facilitators of conditiong that have considerable influence on human behavior: models, rules, and prompts.[48] Although real life models play an important role in non-human primate learning, symbolic models, rules, and prompts are predominantly human modes of learning. Therefore, when adjusting the general primate theory of exploration and play to apply to humans, it is important to expand the general theory to incorporate data on symbolic models, rules, and prompts. The study of social learning is, in fact, one of the most important topics for those who wish to adapt models of animal behavior to fit human behavior. This emphasis does not detract from the importance of reinforcers and punishers as the prime movers of learning. All facilitators—models, rules, prompts—have only temporary influences on behavior if there is no reinforcement for performing the behavior indicated by the relevant model, rule, or prompt. Thus even the facilitators of learning are dependent on reinforcement for their impact on behavior.

[46] Getzels and Jackson (1963).
[47] Of course, not all stimulus-seeking behavior is socially desirable (Farley, 1973). For example, juvenile delinquency is in part the result of stimulus seeking—or "thrill seeking"—and is certainly less desirable than stimulus seeking through music, art, humor, sports, etc.
[48] Baldwin and Baldwin (1981).

Although there are numerous similarities between the exploration and play of humans and that of other primates, the use of symbolic models, rules, and prompts introduces some unique features to human exploration and play.

Models. Observational learning in nonhuman primates usually involves learning from real models. In humans, observational learning involves real and symbolic models.[49] Real models are physically present for the observer to see and hear. The behavior of symbolic models is presented by spoken or written descriptions, pictures, movies, or TV. Although nonhuman primates *can* learn from symbolic models (e.g., from photographs or TV pictures), this mode of learning is not a part of their natural learning.

A comparison of modeling effects in humans and other primates helps explain some of the similarities and differences in exploration and play between these two groups. Nonhuman primates can learn new forms of exploration and play by watching and imitating the behavior of real models. Imitation helps spread innovations or traditions through the group. Because imitation rarely produces perfect copies of the modeled behavior, imitation is also a source of innovation. The presence of multiple models for imitation increases the likelihood of creative innovations even further, since the imitator may piece together bits of information from each model to produce a very novel effect. Whenever imitation produces novel forms of exploration, play, or traditions, the reinforcers of novel sensory input help maintain the new responses—at least until habituation removes the novelty or punishers suppress the responses.

Throughout much of early human evolution, people lived in small groups not much larger than many primate groups, hence the number of real models in a group was similar. However, even in these small groups, people were able to create a large number of symbolic models by describing the behavior of ancestors, people in neighboring groups, and even people seen in dreams, fantasies, or hallucinations. The presence of symbolic models makes human behavior different from the behavior of other animals in several ways. First, by increasing the number of models, symbolic modeling gives each group member a much increased chance of learning a large variety of different responses. A young person who heard that a courageous ancestor once climbed the highest mountain on the island might engage in fantasy play centered on this theme or might engage in explorative climbing, even though there were no real models for climbing. Second, since symbolic models increase an individual's exposure to multiple models, there is an increased probability of creative recombinations based on information

[49] Bandura (1969, 1977).

obtained from numerous models. The child who is playing warrior may produce very original, creative senarios based on stories told by father, two uncles, a neighbor, and observations of real life fights. Third, since models who are described symbolically may live in a different environment—with perhaps different climate, different social organization, different culture, and so forth—the symbolic model may behave in ways that differ considerably from the behavior of any of the real models in an individual's immediate environment. These alien symbolic models provide information that can increase the breadth and variability of an individual's behavior repertoire considerably. When a traveler visits a group and tells of the "strange" games played in a distant land, it would not be surprising to see at least some of the young children imitating the games—based on the information given and on the skills in their own behavior repertoires. This does not guarantee a good copy of the distant practices, but the creative imitation is likely to add variety to the behavior repertoire of the imitators.

As humans began to live in larger groups and societies, the number of real and symbolic models to which an individual could be exposed rose above the number experienced in small human groups. A modern city dweller may see millions of different people during the course of several years. Not all models need to be seen well, closely, or for extended periods to influence the observer's behavior. Catching a glimpse of someone walking down the street with a wreath of colorful flowers in her hair may set the occasion for a playful or creative imitative response based on information from the model's response and the imitator's past experience. The growth of symbolic technologies has greatly increased people's exposure to multiple symbolic models—even if they do not live in large cities. Through the mass media, most people have seen a large number of models who are exploring the arts, sciences, sports, alternative life styles, and many other areas of life. They have seen models playing many different kinds of games and engaging in many forms of free play. These multiple models bring great quantities of modeled information to all observers, and this helps broaden and enrich everyone's potential for exploration, play, and creativity. Although observers do not imitate everything that they learn, they will tend to imitate the subset that is most often associated with reinforcement.

Children raised in culturally impoverished environments and exposed to few models for complex play do not learn varied forms of play or broad repertoires of creative responses.[50] When these children are exposed to models who demonstrate complex, creative play, the children learn to produce more original, playful responses.

---

[50] Feitelson and Ross (1973); Griffing (1974); and Lovinger (1974).

Rules. Rules are symbolically encoded directives that explain when, where, how, or why to do a certain behavior. Verbal cues about "when" and "where" specify the correct S^D context for the behavior. Verbal information about "how" and "why" specify the structure of the behavior and the reinforcers or punishers that can be expected for various types of performances. Complete rules contain information on all three elements (S^D's, behavior, and consequences). "If you bring the cards after dinner, we will play bridge and have some fun." Incomplete or sketchy rules may describe only certain portions of the three elements. "Everybody follow me!" If people have had enough relevant learning experience, incomplete rules are often adequate for evoking the desired behavior or guiding the acquistion of that behavior. People usually hear or read countless rules each day, but they follow only a small portion of them. People usually follow the rules when there are S^D's in the rules, the source of the rules, or the context that have been associated with reinforcement for rule use in the past.[51]

Since nonhuman primates do not use rules and humans do, we would expect human exploration and play to contain rule-governed features that were not present in the stimulus-seeking behavior of other species. One such difference is that human exploration and play often contain rules such as "Do this" or "Do that." These instructions can help people coordinate previously learned behavior or learn new responses from each other. Since coordination helps decrease the punishers (or "interference costs"[52]) that arise from uncoordinated interactions, rule use can help make play less aversive, and this should help reduce the factors that suppress exploration and play. Instructions can also speed the learning process by which a listener learns a new play pattern from a rule giver. If an older girl can teach a younger girl how to bounce a ball back and forth, both gain increased access to sensory stimulation reinforcers. The older girl benefits by gaining a new partner with whom to play; and the younger girl benefits by learning a novel game and gaining a new playmate. Thus, rule giving and rule using are both reinforced by the positive consequences of sensory stimulation and social reinforcers.

Games are special forms of play that are constrained and guided by rules.[53] The rules often increase the amount of sensory stimulation available in play by making play more complex and complicated. In addition, rules impose the stimulating challenge of playing within the limits specified by the rules.[54] For example, playing hopscotch according to the rules requires more alertness, skill, and planning than does simply

---

[51] Staats (1968); Karen (1974); and Ferster et al. (1975).
[52] Thibaut and Kelley (1959:51f).
[53] Denzin (1975).
[54] Redl (1959) and Eifermann (1971).

jumping around without the challenges imposed by the rules. Playing bridge according to the rules requires more cognitive skills, strategy, planning, and alertness to detail than are needed to simply flip through or casually play with 52 cards without rules. The activities of planning, attending to detail, and weighing alternative strategies all increase the sensory stimulation of game play. Very young children do not need rules to find sensory stimulation in early free play, nor are they skillful at following rules. However, as they cease to find ample sensory stimulation in free play and gain skills at rule use, they can begin to enjoy the increased stimulus complexity and challenge that can be obtained from rule-governed games.

There is more to games than merely following rules or playing within the constraints of a fixed set of regulations. Rules are seldom so precise and all-encompassing that they can specify all permissible behavior "once and for all." There is often room to play with the rules or to negotiate the acceptability of outcomes that fall near the boundary lines of acceptable or unacceptable play. These negotiations in and of themselves produce sensory stimulation and are rewarding parts of many games.[55] Children and adults often spice up games by arguing about whether a ball was foul or fair, challenging the umpire, and bickering over the acceptability of pinch hitters or bunting.[56] All the argumentation becomes part of the game, a stimulating side game that provides its own challenges. As people grow older and exhaust the easily available sensory stimulation of simple games, they often turn to increasingly complex games with more complicated rules and structures, or to simple games that require sophisticated skills and strategies. Whereas children may be challenged by a simple crossword puzzle with 10 words, adults may spend hours on puzzles containing over a hundred rare or unusual words. Bridge replaces Old Maid. Chess supercedes checkers. As players explore the more advanced levels of play, they may turn to books on technique and strategy and obtain a new level of sensory stimulation related to the game.

Rules also facilitate creativity.[57] Most cultures provide their members with symbolically encoded guidelines for producing arts, crafts, amusements, and other sources of stimulation. Rules play a valuable role in fostering intellectual exploration, scientific investigation, and artistic creativity because rules allow people to learn more from others than any single individual can learn alone, without rules. Because a culture provides *multiple* rules, each individual has access to a superabundance of

[55] Lever (1976).
[56] Vacha (1976).
[57] Maltzman (1960).

information from which he or she can piece together unique, novel performances. Hence, rules can expand a person's behavior repertoire and foster behavioral variation.[58] Also, because rules are rarely 100% inclusive, they leave room for variable implementation. Finally, each individual has different behavioral skills that interact with the rules to produce unique performances.

Prompts. Prompts are physical, mechanical, or verbal assists that help a person produce a new behavior.[59] If the behavior is then reinforced, the frequency of the behavior will increase such that prompts are eventually not needed. A parent may hold the child's arms in the correct position while teaching the skills of shooting a bow and arrow, thus helping the child learn the correct postures and motor patterns. These prompts facilitate the child's exploration and play with the bow and arrow. As the child begins to gain skills, the parent can fade the prompts. Although humans have often used prompts to teach animals a variety of responses,[60] animals are less likely to prompt each other's behavior. Thus prompting is primarily a human form of social teaching.

Prompts can be used to help others learn a wide variety of skills—including skills of exploration, play, and creativity.[61] Being prompted in the skills needed to play tennis, swim, play music, or dance allows a person to learn the skills with less effort and wasted time, hence less aversiveness, than if no prompts were used. This reduction in punishment facilitates the exploration, play, and creativity that utilize the prompted skills. Much the same as with models and rules, prompts can increase creativity. When the dance instructor is prompting the student to hold the arms higher and straighter, there is no assurance that the prompts teach the student to produce precisely the behavior the teacher would have performed. The inability of the teacher to prompt all types of muscle movements and each student's having a unique behavior repertoire with which to reproduce the prompted behavior both help generate creative variability in behavior as it is taught by prompts. Thus, all forms of social learning introduce variability—hence novelty—into behavior. The novelty helps produce sensory stimulation reinforcers, and the variability may serve as the raw material for future innovations.

---

[58] Naturally, strict patterns of reinforcement for adherence to very precise rules can produce high levels of conformity and low levels of creativity, but rules are often not precise or not coupled with strict contingencies of reinforcement.

[59] Moore and Goldiamond (1964); Bandura (1969); Kanfer and Phillips (1970); and Reese (1972).

[60] Fouts (1973).

[61] Buell et al. (1968).

A Complex Cultural Environment

Modern humans benefit enormously from culture. The entire cultural accumulation of unwritten traditions and recorded information makes it possible for most people to learn a large, complex repertoire of behavior. As von Cranach (1976:383) points out, one of the most important differences between animals and humans is the environment in which they live. To a large degree, the human environment is culture, a complex, multifaceted, deeply layered accumulation of human creations that surround people throughout life and influence most of their behavior.[62] The complexity of the environment makes it relatively easy for modern people to generate complex behavior and thus locate many types of sensory stimulation that early humans and other species cannot obtain. Exploration of the cultural environment—via travel, reading, TV, films and so forth—can bring much stimulating experience into a person's life. Many of the games and common forms of free play seen in Western culture have been passed down through the generations (with changes occurring over time due to imperfect imitation, innovations, influences from other cultures, and so forth).[63] Culture gives people the skills and media through which to play with ideas, games, music and other art forms, thus locate sensory stimulation reinforcers. Naturally, not all people benefit equally from culture. Poverty, hunger, the necessity of working at monotonous jobs many hours a week, compulsory pregnancy and childcare, or other factors can trap people in behavior patterns that interfere with exploration and play.[64] Nevertheless, culture makes it possible for many to learn large, complex repertoires of stimulus-seeking behavior that facilitate the discovery of a broad range of novel, complex, stimulating inputs.

Because culture allows people to learn very large repertoires of stimulus-seeking behavior and to enjoy contact with complex stimulus environments, most humans can locate large quantities of sensory stimulation. Thus culture provides a sensory-rich environment that reinforces exploration and play later into adulthood in humans than in other species. Most primates have ceased playing by adulthood, but humans often remain playful well into adulthood, if not throughout their lives. Exploration and play that involve language are especially likely to persist all through life, since thinking, talking, reading, and writing are less effortful than are more physical behaviors. However, not all people generate exploration, play, and creativity at equal levels or equally late

---

[62] Alland (1972) and Williams (1972).

[63] Opie and Opie (1959); Sutton-Smith and Rosenberg (1961); and Avedon and Sutton-Smith (1971).

[64] Children from poor neighborhoods show less spontenaity in play and less sociodrama play than do children from "good" neighborhoods (Gesell and Lord, 1927; Smilansky, 1968).

into adulthood. Many cease to be explorative and playful at an early age, hence miss many of the varied experiences that can make life more zestful and rewarding.

Humanistic Implications

It should be clear that people need not become less explorative and playful during adulthood. The loss of exploration and play is not biologically programmed in the genes. Several humanistic implications for fostering exploration and play—and preventing their decline—are easily derived from the present theory.[65]

Exploration and play are most likely to yield sensory reinforcers in *sensory rich environments*. An abundance of novel stimuli and varied activities available in the environment make it easy for stimulus-seeking behavior to produce sensory reinforcers. Unfortunately, poverty often forces people to live in stark environments with little variety in daily activity. Many adults allow themselves to slip into monotonous routines that limit them to overly familiar sensory environments and deprive them of the varied experience needed to reinforce exploration and play. By making stimulating environments available to more people, it should be possible to enhance exploration and play. The many facets of culture—including "popular" culture—can enrich many people's lives.

Among the most crucial determinants of exploration and play are the size and complexity of a person's repertoire of *stimulus-seeking skills*, and the person's ability to add to those skills as needed. As one set of skills ceases to bring novel or stimulating experience into a person's life, it is necessary to add new skills that open doors to new experience. The skill factor becomes increasingly important with increasing age and experience. Because everything is novel for the young child, the child does not need a great deal of skill to locate novel experience. Crawling around the house or pulling the contents out of drawers and shelves all produce generous quantities of sensory input and sensory reinforcers. Simple forms of play—such as running around the yard, chasing the puppy, or playing with simple toys—are clearly rewarding for small children. However, the sensory stimulation that can be easily located with few skills is eventually exhausted; and gradually skill becomes an increasingly important determinant of the subsequent development of exploration and play.[66] Families that provide multiple models, numerous rules, and appropriate prompts for stimulus-seeking skills—and social reinforcers for acquisition of these skills—make it easy for their children to learn the skills for successfully locating new sources of sen-

---

[65] Also see Ellis (1973:119f) and Baldwin and Baldwin (1978a:249f).
[66] Csikzentmihalyi and Bennett (1971).

sory stimulation and sensory reinforcers.[67] Families with few models, rules, prompts, or reinforcers for stimulus-seeking skills are likely to produce children with relatively few skills for exploration and play.[68] As children begin to leave home, the models, rules, prompts, and reinforcers at school, in the peer group, and in the community as a whole shape their further learning of stimulus-seeking skills. At all subsequent phases of life, a person can acquire or fail to acquire the physical, cognitive, and social skills that are crucial if exploration and play are to be successful in turning up new sources of stimulating experience.[69]

Because everyone has room to learn more skill at exploration and play, everyone can benefit from gaining the knowledge that allows them to learn more stimulus-seeking skills. People can learn the skills of exploration and play from observing good models, seeking good advice (rules) from explorative and playful individuals, seeking prompts from skillful people, and improving the ratio of reinforcers to punishers for learning the skills of exploration and play. Multiple models, multiple rules, and varied prompts help increase the variability and creativity in a person's repertoire of exploration and play skills, hence, increase the likelihood of locating stimulating experience. A person can increase the contingent reinforcement for attaining these skills by asking friends to comment approvingly when progress is being made, by setting aside speical rewards for gaining the crucial stimulus-seeking skills, or by practicing self-reinforcement[70] (for example, thinking or saying, "Nice job, I drew the eyes and nose much better this time").

It is one thing to have stimulus-seeking skills and another to perform them. Exploration and play must be followed by frequent *reinforcement* to be active components in a person's behavior repertoire. A variety of reinforcers and punishers can influence the frequency of exploration and play. Sensory stimulation is the natural reinforcer for stimulus-seeking behavior. If a person lives in an adequately stimulating environment and has an adequate level of skills to locate sensory stimulation,

---

[67] Bandura (1977:104).

[68] Griffing (1974) and Lovinger (1974).

[69] It should be noted that the mass media provide cheap (low effort) sensory stimulation that rewards passive forms of stimulus-seeking behavior, and hence does not shape many skills. The person who explores music or sports by actively playing them reaps sensory stimulation reinforcers contingent upon increasing skills, but not so the person who explores music or sports via mass media or mechanical reproduction. As our populace spends increasing hours in front of TV, going to high-sensory stimulation movies, or consuming mass entertainment, their skills for creating their own sensory stimulation may go undeveloped. As we let the machines and entertainment industry do the work of generating sensory stimulation for us, we may become dependent on them and less creative ourselves. It might be desirable to avoid overdependence on passive modes of stimulus seeking if one wants to come under the contingencies for learning the active forms.

[70] Bandura (1977).

the sensory reinforcers will automatically strengthen exploration and play. Social reinforcers such as attention, friendship, praise, or reciprocated play can strengthen a person's exploration and play above and beyond the level that would result from sensory stimulation reinforcement alone. Likewise, social punishment such as hostile criticism, derision, disparagement, mockery, or loss of friends can suppress the frequency of exploration and play. Unfortunately, after people reach adulthood in many cultures, they often receive social punishment for exploration and play, since these behaviors are often considered to be childish, immature, or otherwise not acceptable for adults. Exploration and play are also affected by patterns of self-reinforcement and self-punishment, which in turn can be traced to prior social learning.[71] Nonsocial punishers can also suppress adult play, for example when play results in an accident or broken bone. As mentioned in Chapter 4 (page 157f), punishers can have more long-lasting effects on behavior than reinforcers do; hence the cumulative effects of many punishers over two or three decades—due to falls, hard knocks, criticisms, and so forth—can eventually outweigh the effects of reinforcers.

Clearly, any effort to increase the ratio of reinforcers to punishers can help promote exploration and play. Parents, teachers, and friends can all appreciate their role in providing social reinforcers for the exploration and play of others. Individuals can help themselves. A person can ask friends to help reinforce exploration and play by making supportive comments each time they see the person do an explorative or playful act, and to abstain from negative comments about these behaviors. Seeking out positive models who enjoy exploration and play also helps, since their signs of enjoyment serve as sources of vicarious reinforcement for the observer[72] and they are likely to give social approval rather than criticism. By seeking out environments with high densities of sensory stimulation, a person can also expect higher rates of sensory reinforcement for stimulus-seeking behavior.

Leisure time and *competing responses* can have opposite effects on exploration and play. Having leisure time is a prerequisite for exploration and play. If leisure time is not filled, the boredom that ensues will usually motivate exploration and play (if a person has the skills and prior reinforcement to make stimulus seeking a high probability response to boredom). On the other hand, competing responses and the lack of leisure time interfere with and prevent exploration and play. Some adults become so heavily burdened with responsibilities, monotonous jobs, or the task of satisfying their basic daily needs that they

---

[71] Wallace (1977).
[72] Bandura (1977).

have little time left for exploration and play. Obviously, people who wish to facilitate explorative and playful behavior might attempt to design more leisure and fewer competing responses into their lives.

Good health and *physical fitness* are often helpful in producing and enjoying exploration and play, especially in those areas where stimulus-seeking behavior requires activity, strength, dexterity, endurance, and so forth. The active, energetic, healthy person who is not overweight is likely to find a long hike or tennis match more rewarding than someone less healthy or fit. One of the main constraints that limits exploration and play in older age is the loss of health and physical fitness. The afflictions of affluence—overweight, heart problems, emphysema—often rob people of their health and vigor long before old age, and this hastens the decline of active exploration and play. Maintaining good health and physical fitness allows one to pursue active modes of stimulus seeking to an older age with the minimum of punishment due to effortfulness.

CONCLUSION

In Chapter 7 we showed how a balanced theory of primate behavior could be constructed to interweave data on evolution and function, physiological mechanisms, and the development of behavior. The present chapter demonstrates how such a theory of primate behavior can be modified to deal with human behavior. First, each variable in the animal theory must be analyzed and adjusted to suit the relevant data on human evolution, physiology, and behavioral development. Second, unique human specialities must be added to the basic animal theory. Since balanced biosocial theories interweave data on evolution, physiology, and environmental determinants of behavior, the two steps must be repeated at each level of the balanced theory. Since proximal influences on behavior play an especially important role in human behavior, special attention must be given to the complexities of the human environment and the special modes of social learning through which the proximal environment affects behavior.

WHAT NEXT?

A great deal remains to be done. There is a need for balanced biosocial theories covering all types of behavior at all phylogenetic levels. There is room for considerable progress in developing theories of natural learning. Because the social sciences have not traditionally been built on a biosocial base, much remains to be done in producing balanced biosocial theories of human behavior and society. The goals of balanced biosocial theory are within our reach. The time has come to move beyond unbalanced theories.

PART

THE NEW HORIZONS

During the past 120 years, the Darwinian Revolution has completely changed the way humans think about living things and the way they behave. Since Darwin's day, an increasing number of biological phenomena have been analyzed and brought into the Darwinian framework, until today the modern theory of evolution stands "as the organizing principle of biology."[1]

Having seen the great power of the theory of natural selection, biologists are understandably enthusiastic about extending the theory to cover new phenomena. In their eagerness to apply "the theory of natural selection in its simplest and most austere form"[2] to all aspects of animal behavior and social organization, the sociobiologists overemphasized the evolutionary causes of behavior and virtually forgot all else. They forced the theory onto data that did not conform to the basic assumption that proximal causes can be disregarded. A series of successful discoveries in the social insects and other primitive species reinforced their belief that their extreme emphasis on distal causes—or "ultimate causes" as they would say was warranted. Since much

[1] Mayr (1978:47).
[2] Williams (1966:270).

of mammalian behavior appears to be adaptive, it too could be interpreted as fitting the theory.

However, extreme positions in the nature–nurture controversy are untenable, and the sociobiologists' overemphasis on genetic causes produces unbalanced theories of behavior, especially for the more advanced species. A central thesis of this book is that we can go beyond the limitations of sociobiology and construct more balanced biosocial theories. The program described in this book suggests one possible route to balanced theories, without pretending to be the ultimate step. If it can help make visible the new horizons, it will have served its purpose.

TOWARD A THEORY OF NATURAL LEARNING

A balanced biosocial theory will need to analyze selection, genetic causes, physiological mechanisms, constructive and destructive determinants of development, and learning. One of the weakest areas in modern behavior theories is the understanding of learning in the natural environment. Most biological theories pay careful attention to the biological determinants of naturally occurring behavior, but they are deficient in their coverage of natural learning. On the other hand, most learning theories have been developed in highly controlled laboratory environments, and many field observers do not find it easy to generalize findings from the artificial environment to the natural environment. Thus the role of learning in natural environments is often overlooked or neglected in favor of studying topics that fall within well-established research paradigms—such as natural selection, adaptation, physiological mechanisms, and maturation. In our effort to develop balanced biosocial theories, we need to strengthen our theories of natural learning—and do it in ways that allow the theories of natural learning to dovetail with other biological variables to produce balanced syntheses.

The task of developing a theory of natural learning is somewhat similar to the task Darwin faced in producing his theory of natural selection.[3] Three phases in the development of the theory of natural selection parallel current attempts at creating a theory of natural learning.[4] First, during his voyage on the *Beagle* (1831–1836), Darwin made naturalistic observations that convinced him of the importance of variability and change in living things, and convinced him of the need to search for a mechanism that would explain the origin of that variability and change. Second, after returning from the voyage, Darwin began to study the

---

[3] The task is only *somewhat* similar because Darwin was trying to analyze selection, and the similarities between selection and learning are limited (pages 26–43). Hence, one would not expect the task of developing a science of natural learning to parallel completely Darwin's work.

[4] Darwin (1859, 1860, 1876, 1888).

means by which breeders created variation and change in domesticated plants and animals. In so doing he followed the model of his friend Sir Charles Lyell. "After my return to England it appeared to me that by following the example of Lyell in Geology, and by collecting all facts which bore in any way on the variation of animals and plants under domestication and nature, some light might perhaps be thrown on the whole subject."[5] Beginning in July, 1837, Darwin "collected facts on a wholesale scale, more especially with respect to domesticated production, by printed enquiries, by conversation with skilful (sic) breeders and gardeners, and by extensive reading." In the following months Darwin gained considerable knowledge about artificial selection and even conducted breeding experiments of his own. "I soon perceived that selection was the keystone of man's success in making useful races of animals and plants. But how selection could be applied to organisms living in a state of nature remained for some time a mystery to me." Third, Darwin had to discover the link that would allow him to apply his information about artificial selection to naturalistic data. The problem was to explain how selection could occur in nature without the presence of human breeders or conscious plan. Darwin's reading of Malthus provided the key: the high fertility of the species causes overproduction of young; this creates competition and causes the death of many. "It at once struck me that under these circumstances favourable variations would tend to be preserved, and unfavourable ones to be destroyed." Predators, disease, intraspecific competition, and other environmental agents replaced the human breeder in selecting which variations would or would not survive and reproduce. Once he could see the link between artificial selection and the natural environment, Darwin was well on his way to understanding natural selection.

The task of developing a theory of natural learning roughly parallels these three phases of Darwin's work. First, naturalistic observation on primates and other advanced species has revealed considerable variability in behavior and the presence of rapid behavior change. The extent of variability and rapidity of change could not be explained by the slow modification of genes through natural selection; hence various observers began to look for behavior mechanisms that would explain the naturalistic data.[6]

Second, studies of learning in artificial environments have provided valuable information on the controlling variables of learned behavior. In the highly simplified laboratory environment, environmental variables can be systematically manipulated, which makes it possible to identify the controlling variables of learning more easily than one can in complex natural environments. Learning in artificial and oversimplified

---

[5] All quotes in this paragraph are from Darwin's autobiography (1876 [1958:119–120]).
[6] Imanishi (1957); Yamada (1971); Paterson (1973); van Lawick-Goodall (1973a); Beck (1974, 1975); McGrew (1977); and others.

environments will, of course, be somewhat different from natural learning, but laboratory data on learning may be most useful in preparing for the third step, the development of theories of natural learning. Darwin also faced the problem that selection in an artificial environment might be so different from processes in nature that generalizations from artifical selection would not be warranted. However, his studies of selection in domesticated stock turned out to be invaluable. In *The Origin of Species* he wrote: "Nor have I been disappointed; in this and in all other perplexing cases I have invariably found that our knowledge, imperfect though it be, of variation under domestication, afforded the best and safest clue. I may venture to express my conviction of the high value of such studies, although they have been very commonly neglected by naturalists."[7] Even though many biologists and naturalists are skeptical of laboratory research on learning, these studies may provide the best guidelines available for the development of theories of natural learning.

    Third, there is the question: What agency shapes and molds learned behavior in natural environments, where there is no human intervention? The answer to this question will be obvious to many. The environment conditions behavior, whether it is a natural environment or an artificial environment. Reinforcers, punishers, and models located in the environment modify animal behavior, and these controlling variables are augmented by rules and prompts in the case of humans. The task of creating a theory of natural learning involves mapping the controlling variables in the natural environment and studying their effects on behavior. Given the fact that natural environments are considerably more complex than laboratory learning environments, it is only to be expected that learning theories will have to be modified and elaborated in order to do justice to the complexities of natural learning. In addition, general theories of natural learning will have to be adjusted for each species to incorporate data on the species' preparednesses, limitations, and other specializations, along with the influences of constructive and destructive environmental inputs.

    It may not seem obvious to everyone that environmental variables control learning, much as ecological variables are the agents of natural selection. In the section on Lamarckian logic in Chapter 4 (pages 110–112), we noted that many behavioral researchers believe that learning involves the organism adapting itself to the environment "by itself," much as Lamarck postulated in his theory of evolution. Darwin placed the causes of biological evolution in the environment: predators, disease, conspecifics, and other environmental agents of natural selection determine which individuals will reproduce more and which will repro-

---

[7] Darwin (1859 [1915:4]).

duce less. The mechanism of differential reproduction replaced the teleological urges toward perfection that Lamarck had postulated. It is now time to remove the teleological urges for self-adaptation that some read into learning and place the causes of learning in the environment—recognizing the power of differential reinforcement in shaping behavior much as evolutionary theory recognizes the power of differential reproduction.

Darwin's major contribution to the evolutionary theories of the 1800s was in explicating the mechanism of natural selection.[8] Before Darwin, many had believed that evolution occurred through gradual and continuous change; but few saw the mechanisms by which variations were modified by differential survival and differential reproduction. The evidence presented in the prior chapters supports the hypothesis that differential reinforcement is the single most important mechanism by which variations in learned behavior are modified by the environment. Differential reinforcement causes some operants to become more frequent and others to become less frequent. Most of Pavlovian conditioning is based on pairing stimuli with $^+$US's, $^-$US's, $^+$CS's or $^-$CS's—i.e., reinforcers or punishers.[9] Differential exposure to reinforcers and punishers causes some stimuli to become $^+$CS's and others to become $^-$CS's—both of which can elicit conditioned reflexes and serve as conditioned reinforcers and punishers.

Differential reproduction and differential reinforcement are not, of course, the only determinants of change. Although differential reproduction is the single most important factor in natural selection, there are secondary variables—phylogenetic inertia, gene flow, genetic drift, kinship, and others—that must be considered in order to understand the nuances of evolutionary change. Likewise, there are secondary variables that must be considered in theories of natural learning: such as genetic predispositions, reflexes, mechanisms of the central nervous system, and environmental distributions of models, prompts, and rules.

In order to produce balanced biosocial theories, we need both a theory of natural learning and the theory of natural selection. In order to be most useful, a theory of natural learning must dovetail with biological variables in ways that facilitate the construction of balanced biosocial theories. Learning theories that neglect or reject biological factors impede the development of balanced biosocial theories as much as do theories that neglect or reject proximal causes in favor of distal causes. For those who seek balanced biosocial theories of the behavior of any species where learning plays an important role, it is crucial to devote

---

[8] Mayr (1978).

[9] The exceptions are the cases in which the unconditioned stimulus is neither a $^+$US or a $^-$US, hence it serves to elicit reflexive responses though it cannot serve as a reinforcer or punisher (page 90).

effort to filling the gaps in our knowldge about natural learning in ways that are compatible with biological variables. There have already been several attempts to produce theories of natural learning;[10] however, a great deal remains to be done. As Darwin said in the introduction to *The Origin of Species:* "No one ought to feel surprise at much remaining as yet unexplained in regard to the origin of species and varieties, if he make due allowance for our profound ignorance in regard to the mutual relations of many beings which live around us."

TOWARD A COMPREHENSIVE THEORY OF BEHAVIOR

It is possible that balanced biosocial theories could be developed into a comprehensive theory of behavior that integrates data from all phylogenetic levels. There have already been balanced studies on many species, and it may be possible to fuse the many contributions together into an all-encompassing theory.

There is reason to believe that research on advanced species will hasten the development of balanced theories more than research on primitive species will. Data on the behavior of primitive species often appear to fit pure evolutionary models so closely that the researcher may fail to look beyond evolutionary causes. In contrast, the behavior of advanced species reflects major contributions from both proximal and distal causes, and the inadequacies of pure evolutionary models are readily visible. The inadequacies of purely proximal theories are readily visible, too. Not only do the data from advanced species encourage the search for proximal and distal causes, the advanced species provide a wealth of data on both proximal and distal variables. There are enough advanced species living in a broad range of ecological niches to provide data on phylogenetic adaptations to a variety of environmental conditions. In addition, all the proximal causes play a significant role in molding the behavior of advanced species; hence all of them can be studied as they interact in the total balanced system. The importance of learning in advanced species—especially in the primates—may provide a major impetus for advancing the development of a theory of natural learning.

However, it should be amply clear that balanced biosocial theories are desirable at all phylogenetic levels. There is no species in which behavior can be completely explained by nature alone or by nurture alone. Thus, the goal of constructing balanced theories has implications for work on all species, not just primates. There may be a temptation to justify purely genetic theories for the behavior of primitive species or pure-learning theories for human behavior, since these extreme theories may serve

---

[10] Hebb (1949, 1972); Breland and Breland (1966); Hinde (1970); Teitelbaum (1977); and Fantino and Logan (1979).

as adequate first approximations for explaining the phylogenetic extremes. However, it should be clear that even these pure-nature or pure-nurture theories could be improved if they were constructed to dovetail with data on all relevant proximal and distal causes.

Many researchers have already succeeded in constructing balanced theories on species at various phylogenetic levels, but there is room for considerable advance. As more research is directed to producing balanced theories and more balanced work appears on a larger number of diverse species, it is likely that overarching patterns and empirical generalizations will emerge that could not be predicted from the data presently available. There will doubtless be many surprises and serendipitous findings as the discipline advances. Thus, at present, it is difficult to foresee the outlines of a comprehensive balanced perspective.

Balanced biosocial theory is potentially a broad, all-encompassing theory. Because its main goal is to interweave proximal and distal causes of behavior at all phylogenetic levels in an empirically defensible manner, it can potentially serve as a unifying principle around which to consolidate work from the various behavioral disciplines. The present structure of the university system tends to separate behavioral researchers into isolated fields, each with its own traditions, favorite theories, distinctive methods, and specialized jargon. This fragmentation has doubtless retarded the development of unified theories, and perhaps will continue to do so.

A unifying theory holds the promise of coordinating the contributions of various disciplines. Sociobiology offered a unifying system, which was one of the appealing features of the theory (page 15). However, it presumed that the unity would center around population biology, socioecology, genetics, and evolutionary theory. Balanced biosocial theories will not center so exclusively on evolutionary considerations, since they recognize the importance of other contributing factors. They will allow a more flexible program of interweaving contributions from many disciplines and encourage a more cooperative spirit than does a theory that is dominated by biology. The major change that balanced biosocial theories will bring to the current practice of behavioral research in the various disciplines will be to emphasize the need for cooperation in interweaving contributions from each field into unified explanations. Researchers in each field can continue to study the issues best suited to their speciality; but they need to be sensitive to the design features of the larger balanced system into which their contributions must fit.

HUMAN BEINGS

It is understandable that people in all behavioral disciplines would have special interests in applying their science to humans. Yet, there has been little unanimity on how best to deal with human behavior. Most scientists realize the pragmatic value of animal studies for adding to our understanding of human behavior (page 217). Yet most shy away from simplistic analogies based on animal data.

Balanced biosocial theories have built-in safeguards that help minimize abuses when generalizing from animal data to human beings. Attention to every level of the theory—evolutionary concerns, physiological mechanisms, constructive and destructive inputs, and natural learning—precludes simplistic analogies. When adjusting a balanced theory of animal behavior to fit human behavior, each level of the balanced animal theory must be analyzed in light of two crucial questions (page 218): (1) What are the similarities and differences between humans and animals at this level? (2) Are there any uniquely human variables that must be added at this level? This analysis is more easily carried out at some levels than others, due to the absence of crucial data on certain topics. However, having to admit limitations in the data helps guard against unwarranted generalizations. Even though our knowledge is limited, the guidelines of a balanced theory will help integrate disparate bits of information into a unified whole. We should be able to construct better theories by unifying our fragmentary knowledge in a balanced format than by limiting ourselves to the information contained in even the most valid of the fragments.

Society

Neither sociobiology nor the balanced biosocial theories presented above have adequately dealt with human macro-societal phenomena: government, politics, economic systems, communication networks, ethical systems, and other social institutions. These macro-structures are several levels above the fundamental variables stressed in sociobiology: selfish genes, differential reproduction, coefficients of relationship, physiological mechanisms of behavior, and so forth. Sociobiology has presumed that the macro-societal structures could all be reduced to genetic explanations, at which time sociology and the other social sciences would be subsumed into evolutionary theory as "the last branches of biology . . . to be included in the Modern Synthesis."[11] A balanced biosocial view is less interested in reducing macro-societal events than in dovetailing them into a unified multilevel theory, in which the contributions from each level are recognized for their own worth. In these closing pages we will briefly sketch the outlines of a balanced theory of human behavior and society.[12] (By removing the distinctively human elements,

[11] Wilson (1975:4).
[12] Buckley (1967), Bertalanffy (1968), Staats (1975), Kuhn (1975) and others have already developed multilayered, hierarchical, systems models of behavior and society.

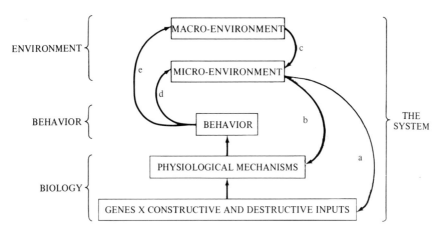

FIGURE 9.1. The multilevel system of biology, behavior, and environment.

this model could be scaled down and made more relevant to primate societies.)

Chapter 2 began with the idea that the behavior of the individual is produced by physiological mechanisms which, in turn, are the product of the interaction of genes and environment (page 19f). The environment consists of micro- and macro-elements. The entire system is shown in Figure 9.1 The micro-environment consists of the social and nonsocial stimuli that impinge directly on the person. These stimuli include both (a) the constructive and destructive inputs that allow the genetic blueprint to be actualized as physiological mechanisms, and (b) the S^D's, US's, CS's, models, rules, and prompts that impinge on the physiological mechanisms to control behavior output (a and b in Figure 9.1). The macro-environment consists of larger societal structures and those aspects of the physical environment that induce structure into the micro-environment (c in Figure 9.1). For example, capitalism and communism induce distinctive structures into peoples' micro-environments (arrow c), and these in turn affect behavior (arrows a and b). Thus, both the macro- and micro-environment have their effects on behavior. In turn, behavior has its effects on the environment. After a person's behavior has been influenced by the environment at time 1, the person's behavior will change the macro- and micro-environments at time 2. People's actions influence the objects and people in their immediate micro-environments (d in Figure 9.1); and in a small way they alter the larger societal structure and the larger physical environment (e). Thus there are reciprocal effects between the environment and the biological individual, as each shapes and molds the other in a continuous exchange that produces a dynamic integrated system.

This approach avoids the static qualities that have been typical of many of the structural–functional theories in sociology. Let us consider the dynamics of the model at two levels: the behavior of the individual and the evolution of societal practices.

The Changing Individual

In the world of the individual, there is a constant interplay between the environment and behavior. The environment modifies behavior—within the constraints imposed by genetic and other biological variables—and then behavior creates changes in the micro- and macro-environments.[13] Constructive inputs from the environment are, of course, needed to allow the development of the physiological mechanisms of behavior, and are thus a precondition for behavior. Reinforcers and punishers are the prime movers from the environment that adjust behavior, though not always producing adaptive results.[14] Those behaviors that affect the environment in ways that produce reinforcing results are likely to be retained and become more probable in a person's behavior repertoire;[15] those behaviors that affect the environment in ways that produce nonreinforcement or punishment are likely to become less probable. Models, rules, and prompts from the environment also have an impact on behavior, though they too depend on reinforcement and punishment to cause lasting effects on behavior. As the child learns a repertoire of operant behavior, he or she begins to affect the micro-environment by changing objects and influencing the behavior of others. As the years go by, the child has an increasing impact on the macro-environment, as he or she consumes more natural resources and participates ever more in the larger society outside the home. Some people—such as politicians, judges, labor leaders, corporation heads—gain entry into crucial junctures in the macro-societal networks where their behavior can have considerable impact on the macro-societal structures that affect themselves and others.

This approach to the behavior of the individual legitimizes a large number of research topics.[16] A fully elaborated model would attend to the distal causes that establish the human behavioral potential and the limits on human behavior. It would introduce physiological data whenever possible, to tie proximal and distal causes together as they interact

---

[13] Burgess and Bushell (1969).

[14] Weiner (1965, 1969) has demonstrated how easily certain contingencies of reinforcement can produce maladaptive behavior in humans. It is possible that much psychopathology and deviant behavior result from this type of maladaptive learning.

[15] Numerous examples of natural learning in humans are presented elsewhere (Baldwin and Baldwin, 1981).

[16] Mazur and Robertson (1972); van den Berghe (1975); Reynolds (1976); Barchas (1976); and Barchas and Barchas (in preparation).

in producing and modifying the mechanisms of behavior. It would consider the impact of constructive and destructive environmental inputs on the physiological mechanisms. It would trace the development of the individual throughout the life cycle, with special attention to the reciprocal interactions between the individual and his or her environment. It would explore the effects of all the reinforcers and punishers on all human behavior, along with the effects of all those behaviors on the micro- and macro-environments. It would view both the macro- and micro-environments as being in constant flux and see these dynamic environments interacting with the physical development and changing skills of the person to produce ever-changing behavior patterns, then study the effects of these behaviors as they modify the macro- and micro-environments even further.

Social Evolution

This type of dynamic model of behavior makes it easy to understand the all-pervasive nature of behavioral flux. But what creates the broader patterns of social change and social evolution? Numerous authors have seen similarities between biological evolution and social change. Societies—both their macrostructures and micro-interaction patterns—change over time, much as if undergoing some type of evolutionary process. Bronowski (1977:157) points out the main reasons why social science, during 200 years of attention to social change, has failed to produce a viable theory of social evolution.

> One plain reason is that no one has been able to lay bare the mechanism which turns one network of social relations, one set of values, one culture, into another. The machinery of competition, which worked so well in biology, and which was a favorite of the nineteenth-century sociologists, has done nothing to explain the evolution of cultures. It remains today as shallow and as false a predictor as it was in Malthus and in the eighteenth-century rationalists from whom he took it.
>
> Underneath this there is a deeper and basic reason. We do not know the mechanism for social evolution because we have not been able to pin down the units with which it works—which it shuffles and regroups, and whose mutations make the raw material for new cultures. In physics, the evolution of the elements works by building up more and more complex nuclei from two units, the protons and the neutrons. In biology, evolution has for its new units those stable mutants which Charles Darwin called "sports," and within which Gregor Mendel later found the genes. But no analysis has yet isolated an acceptable unit of social structure.[17]

---

[17] Reprinted with permission from *The New York Review of Books*. Copyright © 1965 Nyrev, Inc. Harris (1975), Blurton Jones (1976:447), and others have contrasted biological and social evolution and not been able to specify the mechanism of social change.

If the present analysis is correct, the basic units of social structure are human behaviors, and the prime movers of social change are reinforcers and punishers.[18] The "mutations" are novel behaviors that appear due to induction, play, and creativity.

A culture at any one point in time consists of a large set of behavioral practices—along with human-made objects, such as art, books, technology—which provide the models and rules that pass cultural information to those who are learning the culture. Differential reinforcement affects both the possessors of the culture and the new learners. Old cultural practices that have ceased to produce reinforcers are likely to become less frequent due to extinction or punishment. Old practices that still yield reinforcing results are maintained by the positive consequences. New practices appear as chance variations in behavior—the behavioral "mutation." Some of these innovations will lead to reinforcing consequences, and others will lead to nonreinforcement or punishment. The reinforcers or punishers can come from either the social or nonsocial environments. Depending on the location of the consequences on a continuum from strong reinforcers to strong punishers, the innovation will be adopted or suppressed. When reinforcing new social practices appear at one point in the social system, they are likely to spread out through social networks along any communication channels that allow others to learn the new practice from models of or rules about the practice.[19] At any given juncture in the social system, the new practice will be accepted, and hence passed on, only if it produces reinforcing consequences. Thus a new practice in tropical medicine might pass through the network of doctors in tropical countries but not spread through the rest of the medical profession.

Naturally, the complexity of human society and its interactions with the nonsocial environment introduces thousands of complicating extra variables into the system, and these can influence the speed and direction of social evolution. For example, the spread of rewarding innovations can be retarded or accelerated by numerous factors.[20] As the size of a social system increases, it takes longer for innovations to spread to all parts of the system (other factors holding constant). Conservative practices, strong traditions, and a fear of novelty can slow the diffusion of innovations. Geographic isolation or limited connection with the communication channels in a society can create pockets where old practices remain unchanged since new practices have few routes of entry. Conversely, the diffusion of rewarding new practices is often relatively rapid

[18] Homans (1964, 1974), Kunkel (1969, 1975), Staats (1975), Langton (1979), and others have defended subsets of the position presented here. Also see Ruyle (1973), Richerson and Boyd (1978), and Durham (1979).

[19] Burgess (1969).

[20] Zaltman et al. (1973a,b); Kunkel (1975); and Zaltman and Duncan (1977).

in small social groups with multiple and redundant communication networks, especially if there is a social tradition for rewarding (or at least not punishing) people who experiment with novel practices. Since novelty itself is a reinforcer under most circumstances, many people often imitate and spread nonaversive innovations even if there are no social reinforcers for experimentation.

The history of the automobile provides a commonplace example of these multiple processes. The earliest automotive innovations were merely variations on horse-drawn vehicles; and early change occurred rapidly as inventors explored various ways of constructing motorized vehicles. Eventually the more rewarding methods replaced the less rewarding methods and many early companies went out of business. As cars became more abundant, increasing numbers of people began to abandon horse-drawn vehicles in favor of the car, since it was the more convenient (less aversive) and more efficient (more rewarding) mode of transportation. Remote and isolated parts of the country were among the last to gain access to the automobile. Certain sectors of society resisted the innovation, and even today the Amish refuse to give up horse-drawn vehicles and related technology, thereby keeping alive practices that have "died" elsewhere in the culture. At the other extreme, there are auto enthusiasts who devote a great deal of time and effort to monitoring the communication channels that convey information about the latest auto news and innovations, their behavior being maintained by the novelty and social reinforcers they receive from the "car culture." Needless to say, the impressive spread of the car throughout much of the world has had its impact on the micro- and macro-social environments. The automobile plays a central role in the micro-environment of almost every American. It has changed the structure of the society, allowed the growth of sprawling suburbs, brought pollution, and hastened the exploitation of the world's nonrenewable resources. It has made us increasingly dependent on foreign oil imports and multinational corporations, thus creating changes in our entire international social networks. Now that some of the aversive side effects of the automobile are manifesting themselves, the contingencies of reinforcement have changed somewhat, and smaller, more efficient cars are beginning to replace the larger, inefficient ones. Limited access to fuel, high prices, and other possible future contingencies will change the picture even more.

Innovations may spread through parts of a society as either fads or valuable practices. Fads are based in large part on novelty reinforcers, and once the novelty dies (due to habituation) the fad is likely to die due to nonreinforcement. Innovations that are genuinely effective in producing stable sources of reinforcers or avoiding punishers are likely to be retained longer than mere fads, since "they really work." Effective means of dealing with the physical environment will be retained, even in the absence of social reinforcers. Effective social practices—such as politeness, etiquette, sales techniques, advertising methods—will be retained due to social reinforcers.

When an established practice ceases to produce reinforcers, it should begin to disappear, due to extinction. A variety of social factors can influence the speed of the process. Criticism or ridicule for engaging in an outmoded practice provides social punishers that help suppress the frequency of the practice. However, there appear to be many factors that operate to keep old traditions "alive," even after they cease to have any utility. Social reinforcers and sensory stimulation reinforcers are particularly effective in maintaining practices that might otherwise be extinguished. For example, even though the Civil War was over more than a century ago, Civil War buffs carry on some of the Civil War culture due to social and sensory stimulation reinforcement. When they gather for mock battles, the participants exchange generous levels of social attention for each other's new costumes, guns, tidbits of period knowledge, and so forth. The more authentic a person's replication of Civil War costumes or objects, the more social reinforcers he or she is likely to receive. In addition, there are sensory stimulation reinforcers: Recreating Civil War battles is a big game where adults can have fun playing out complex war scenarios—without the danger of being injured or killed! The social and sensory stimulation reinforcers are not limited to the battle days, either. During the months of preparation before a battle, a person's hand-crafting of a new gun is reinforced by fantasies of the next big battle, reading about the history of the weapon, talking with admiring friends about one's handiwork, and so forth. For some people, conservative socialization about the Old South and the glory of the Confederacy may help contribute reinforcers for maintaining Confederate culture.

Contemporary culture represents an accumulation of practices, books, art, and other artifacts that have been amassing for centuries. Many of the oldest elements have been lost or modified substantially since their original innovation; but a large number of recent elements remain available in the cultural environment, where they can influence behavior and be passed on to the next generation. This tremendous accumulation of previous practices, objects, and information allows moderns to learn more than any single person could learn alone, without cultural inputs. Thus, all of us stand on the shoulders of giants—or at least on a thickly layered pile of cultural accretions—benefitting from elements that once did and still may bring reinforcing results. In one sense, the older cultural elements are like stored mutations in a gene pool, available for our use (or enrichment) and likely to be spread if they bring reinforcement. Some may have considerable practical utility (e.g., Amish horse-powered agricultural technology[21]) and others may be retained only because they are entertaining (i.e., bring sensory stimulation reinforcers). One of the reasons why human culture has become so vast and complex is that many old practices retain utility for us to this day. People today still use agricultural techniques invented thousands of years ago—because these practices still produce reinforcing results. Social and sensory stimulation reinforcers operate, too. People travel to Greece to see the ruins, museums, and countryside not because of the utility, but because glimpses into the art, literature, myths, and history of a past culture provide sensory stimulation and discussion about the trip leads to social reinforcers.

Due to innovations, culture is a steadily growing accretion of practices, objects, symbolic information and other human products. Culture continues to grow year by year, being stored in a patchy, redundant, and variable manner all over the planet. Culture is stored in the behavior of the living and in human-made objects, which can be lost, damaged, or broken. Thus, the method of storage is imperfect (much as the storage of genetic information is imperfect); and this only increases the number of behavioral "mutations" in the culture. The storage systems often fail, too. Fragile objects and nonreinforced behavior are most likely to be lost; hence part of the cultural heritage is always disappearing. Only a few pot shards may remain from a prehistoric culture, revived by the work of a team of archaeologists. Many temples, manuscripts, and statues may remain from a more recent culture, and be well known to many. Fragments of the Civil War culture may be much more vividly maintained in the behavior repertoire of and objects collected by aficionados. But the past tends to become lost.

Although there is a tendency for cultural behavior to be adaptive, in the sense that it brings reinforcers,[22] it should be clear that nonreinforcing and even punitive practices can be passed on culturally. Individuals may retain practices that have little utility. Certain contingencies of reinforcement condition maladaptive behavior, in which a person generates self-punishing behavior.[23] In addition, people often engage in cultural practices that may be reinforcing for them but aversive for others. People with little social power are most often the victims of aversive cultural practices, since they do not have the power to modify

---

[21] Johnson et al. (1977).

[22] The word adaptive can be used in somewhat overlapping, but different senses. In the evolutionary vocabulary, adaptive means that a behavior advances an individual's inclusive fitness. In the vocabulary of learning theory, adaptive means that a behavior brings reinforcing results. Although the two terms may overlap considerably in many species and many aspects of human behavior, advanced learning and complex culture have allowed the two types of adaptiveness to be decoupled, to a large degree, in many areas of life.

[23] Weiner (1965, 1969); Bandura (1971); and Mahoney (1974, 1975).

the system or the behavior of those who are creating the aversive situation. Thus, the present theory contains no assumption that cultural evolution always produces adaptive practices. Whereas Darwin was very impressed by the adaptiveness of biological evolution, most observers of society are impressed that cultural evolution does not lead automatically to purely adaptive results (though it is frequently more adaptive than maladaptive).

This view of cultural evolution is clearly not a version of social Darwinism.[24] There is no reason to espouse a laissez-faire position and believe that desirable cultures will appear automatically through natural processes of differential reinforcement (or as a result of differential reproduction!). Most scholars agree that some mixture of reason, open debate, honest politics, and scientific research can produce a more adaptive and humanistic course of social evolution than would a laissez-faire policy.[25] The social sciences emerged in the Enlightenment, in large part, as an attempt to scientifically understand society and to help improve it.[26] Perhaps the discovery of the mechanism of social change will provide the social sciences with an organizing principle that will better allow them to analyze and guide the evolution of societies.

CONCLUSION

The ultimate goal of balanced biosocial theories is to integrate data on natural selection and natural learning with data on physiological mechanisms and constructive–destructive environmental inputs. At present it is difficult to judge how rapidly balanced theories might develop or how well they could succeed in fulfilling the goals set forth in this book. Even if the goal of ending nature–nurture polarities is eventually attained, new problems will arise with which future theories will have to contend; hence it is inevitable that future theories will turn to issues beyond those envisaged in this brief outline of balanced theories.

However, given the present level of theoretical development in the behavioral sciences, the construction of balanced theories might well be one of the most reasonable and important goals that we can set for

---

[24] Compare this model with Hofstadter (1944) or Klopfer (1977).

[25] As George Herbert Mead (1936) observed a half century ago, both biological and social evolution are unguided "trial and error" methods of change. They allow adjustment to take place, but trial and error is inefficient, painful, and slow. "That is where science comes in to aid society in getting a method of progress. The scientific method is, after all, only the evolutionary process grown self-conscious" (pp. 364, 366). In our present terms, a scientific theory can allow us to understand social evolution, evaluate which practices are likely to lead to positive or negative consequences (over both the short and long term), and adjust the social network wherever possible to facilitate the spread of the more rewarding practices.

[26] Cassirer (1951); Cobban (1960); and Szacki (1979).

ourselves. Balanced theories are within our reach. We should not settle for less.

In addition, there are clear pragmatic reasons for advocating balanced biosocial theories of human behavior and society. We cannot afford to use unbalanced theories to guide our actions. Balanced biosocial theories of human behavior are potentially very useful in helping people improve the quality of their behavior and avoid the causes of unhappiness. Balanced biosocial theories of society might well be helpful in speeding the process of cultural change toward humanistic goals and more ecologically compatible practices. Unbalanced theories are likely to mislead us in our attempts to understand human behavior and society, hence create more problems than solutions. Given the complex problems that humans face in the coming decades, it is crucial that we avoid unbalanced and misleading theories of behavior. Thus, the decision to go beyond unbalanced theories is one of the more important decisions we must make.

REFERENCES

Adamson, J. (1960). *Born Free*. New York: Bantam Books.

Ainsworth, M.D. (1964). Patterns of attachment behavior shown by the infant in interaction with his mother. *Merrill-Palmer Q.* 10:51–88.

Ainsworth, M.D., Blehar, M.C., Waters, E., and Wall, S. (1978). *Patterns of Attachment: A Psychological Study of the Strange Situation*. Hillsdale, N.J.: Lawrence Erlbaum.

Akers, J.S. and Conaway, C.H. (1979). Female homosexual behavior in *Macaca mulata. Arch. Sex. Behav.* 8:63–80.

Aldis, O. (1975). *Play Fighting*. New York: Academic Press.

Aldrich-Blake, F.P.G. and Chivers, D.J. (1973). On the genesis of a siamang group. *Amer. J. Phys. Anthrop.* 38:631–636.

Aldrich-Blake, F.P.G., Bunn, T.K., Dunbar, R.I.M., and Headley, P.M. (1971). Observations on baboons, *Papio anubis*, in an arid region in Ethiopia. *Folia Primat.* 15:1–35.

Alland, A., Jr. (1972). *The Human Imperative*. New York: Columbia Univ. Press.

Allen, E., et al. (1976). Sociobiology—another biological determinism. *BioScience* 26(3):182–186.

Altmann, S.A. (1967). Preface. In S.A. Altmann (ed.), *Social Communication among Primates*, pp. ix–xii. Chicago: Univ. Chicago Press.

Altmann, S.A. (1968). Sociobiology of rhesus monkeys III: The basic communication network. *Behaviour* 32:17–32.

Altmann, S.A. (1979). Baboon progressions: Order or chaos? Study of one dimensional group geometry. *Anim. Behav.* 27:46–80.

Altmann, S.A. and Altmann, J. (1970). *Baboon Ecology: African Field Research*. Chicago: Univ. Chicago Press.

Ambrose, J.A. (1959). Temporal course of smiling. In B.M. Foss (ed.), *Determinants of Infant Behaviour*, pp. 179–201. London: Methuen.

Anastasi, A. (1958). Heredity, environment, and the question "How?" *Psychol. Rev.* 65:197–208.

Anderson, C.O., Kenney, A.M., and Mason, W.A. (1977). Effects of maternal mobility, partner, and endocrine state on social responsiveness of adolescent rhesus monkeys. *Dev. Psychobiol.* 10:421–434.

Anderson, C.O. and Mason, W.A. (1974). Early experience and complexity of social organization in groups of young rhesus monkeys (*Macaca mulata*). *J. Comp. Physiol. Psychol.* 87:681–690.

Anderson, C.O. and Mason, W.A. (1978). Competitive social strategies in groups of deprived and experienced rhesus monkeys. *Dev. Psychobiol.* 11:289–299.

Anderson, J.R. and Chamove, A.S. (1979). Contact and separation in adult monkeys. *S.-Afr. Tydskr. Sielk.* 9:49–53.

Ardrey, R. (1961). *African Genesis.* New York: Atheneum.

Ardrey, R. (1966). *The Territorial Imperative.* New York: Atheneum.

Arling, G.L. and Harlow, H.F. (1967). Effects of social deprivation on maternal behavior of rhesus monkeys. *J. Comp. Physiol. Psychol.* 64:371–377.

Avedon, E.M. and Sutton-Smith, B. (1971). *The Study of Games.* New York: Wiley.

Ayala, F.J. (1978). The mechanisms of evolution. *Sci. Am.* 239(3):56–69.

Azrin, N.H. (1970). Punishment of elicited aggression. *J. Exp. Anal. Behav.* 14:7–10.

Azrin, N.H., Hutchinson, R.R., and Sallery, R.D. (1964). Pain-aggression toward inanimate objects. *J. Exp. Anal. Behav.* 7:223–228.

Azrin, N.H., Hake, D.F., and Hutchinson, R.R. (1965). Elicitation of aggression by a physical blow. *J. Exp. Anal. Behav.* 8:55–57.

Baldwin, J.D. (1968). The social behavior of adult male squirrel monkeys (*Saimiri sciureus*) in a seminatural environment. *Folia Primat.* 9:281–314.

Baldwin, J.D. (1969). The ontogeny of social behaviour of squirrel monkeys (*Saimiri sciureus*) in a seminatural environment. *Folia Primat.* 11:35–79.

Baldwin, J.D. (1970). Reproductive synchronization in squirrel monkeys (*Saimiri*). *Primates* 11:317–326.

Baldwin, J.D. (1971). The social organization of a semifree-ranging troop of squirrel monkeys (*Saimiri sciureus*). *Folia Primat.* 14:23–50.

Baldwin, J.D. and Baldwin, J.I. (1971). Squirrel monkeys (*Saimiri*) in natural habitats in Panama, Colombia, Brazil and Peru. *Primates* 12:45–61.

Baldwin, J.D. and Baldwin, J.I. (1972). The ecology and behavior of squirrel monkeys (*Saimiri oerstedi*) in a natural forest in western Panama. *Folia Primat.* 18:161–184.

Baldwin, J.D. and Baldwin, J.I. (1973a). The role of play in social organization: Comparative observations on squirrel monkeys (*Saimiri*). *Primates* 14:369–381.

Baldwin, J.D. and Baldwin, J.I. (1973b). Interactions between adult female and infant howling monkeys (*Alouata palliata*). *Folia Primat.* 20:27–71.

Baldwin, J.D. and Baldwin, J.I. (1974). Exploration and social play in squirrel monkeys (*Saimiri*). *Am. Zool.* 14:303–314.

Baldwin, J.D. and Baldwin, J.I. (1976). Effects of food ecology on social play: A laboratory simulation. *Z. Tierpsychol.* 40:1–14.

Baldwin, J.D. and Baldwin, J.I. (1977a). The role of learning phenomena in the ontogeny of exploration and play. In S. Chevalier-Skolnikoff and F.E. Poirier (eds.), *Primate Bio-Social Development*, pp. 343–406. New York: Garland.

Baldwin, J.D. and Baldwin, J.I. (1977b). Observation of *Cebus capucinus* in southwestern Panama. *Primates* 18:939–943.

Baldwin, J.D. and Baldwin, J.I. (1978a). Reinforcement theories of exploration, play, creativity and psychosocial growth. In E.O. Smith (ed.), *Social Play in Primates*, pp. 231–257. New York: Academic Press.

Baldwin, J.D. and Baldwin, J.I. (1978b). Exploration and play in howler monkeys (*Alouatta palliata*). *Primates* 19:411–422.

Baldwin, J.D. and Baldwin, J.I. (1979). The phylogenetic and ontogenetic variables that shape behavior and social organization. In I.S. Bernstein and E.O. Smith (eds.), *Primate Ecology and Human Origins: Ecological Influences on Social Organization*, pp. 89–116. New York: Garland.

Baldwin, J.D. and Baldwin, J.I. (1981). *Behavior Principles in Everyday Life*. Englewood Cliffs, N.J.: Prentice-Hall.

Bandura, A. (1969). *Principles of Behavior Modification*. New York: Holt, Rinehart and Winston.

Bandura, A. (1971). Vicarious and self-reinforcement processes. In R. Glaser (ed.), *The Nature of Reinforcement*, pp. 228–278. New York: Academic Press.

Bandura, A. (1973). *Aggression: A Social Learning Analysis*, Englewood Cliffs, N.J.: Prentice-Hall.

Bandura, A. (1977). *Social Learning Theory*. Englewood Cliffs, N.J.: Prentice-Hall.

Bandura, A., Ross, D., and Ross, S.A. (1963). A comparative test of the status envy, social power, and secondary reinforcement theories of identificatory learning. *J. Abnorm. Soc. Psychol.* 67:527–534.

Bandura, A. and Walters, R.H. (1963). *Social Learning and Personality Development*. New York: Holt, Rinehart and Winston.

Barash, D.P. (1977). *Sociobiology and Behavior*. New York: Elsevier.

Barchas, P.R. (1976). Physiological sociology: Interface of sociological and biological processes. *Ann. Rev. Sociol.* 2:299–333.

Barchas, P.R. and Barchas, J. (in preparation). *Socio-Physiology*.

Barrett, J.E. and Glowa, J.R. (1977). Reinforcement and punishment of behavior by the same consequent event. *Psychol. Rep.* 40:1015–1021.

Barrett, J.E. and Spealman, R.D. (1978). Behavior simultaneously maintained by both presentation and termination of noxious stimuli. *J. Exp. Anal. Behav.* 29:375–383.

Bateson, P.P.G. and Hinde, R.A. (1976). Conclusion—on asking the right questions. In P.P.G. Bateson and R.A. Hinde (eds.), *Growing Points in Ethology*, pp. 533–536. Cambridge: Cambridge Univ. Press.

Bateson, P.P.G. and Jaeckel, J.B. (1976). Chicks' preferences for familiar and novel conspicuous objects after different periods of exposure. *Anim. Behav.* 24:386–390.

Baxter, M.J. and Fedigan, L.M. (1979). Grooming and consort partner selection in a troop of Japanese monkeys (*Macaca fuscata*). *Arch. Sex. Behav.* 8:445–458.

Baysinger, C.M., Plubell, P.E., and Harlow, H.F. (1973). A variable-temperature surrogate mother for studying attachment in infant monkeys. *Behav. Res. Methods Instrum.* 5:269–272.

Beach, F.A. (1955). The descent of instinct. *Psychol. Rev.* 62:401–410.

Beck, B.B. (1973). Observation learning of tool use by captive Guinea baboons (*Papio papio*). *Am. J. Phys. Anthrop.* 38:579–582.

Beck, B.B. (1974). Baboons, chimpanzees, and tools. *J. Hum. Evol.* 3:509–516.

Beck, B.B. (1975). Primate tool behavior. In R.H. Tuttle (ed.), *Socioecology and Psychology of Primates*, pp. 413–447. The Hague: Mouton.

Beck, B.B. (1978). Ontogeny of tool use by nonhuman animals. In G.M. Burghardt and M. Bekoff (eds.), *The Development of Behavior*, pp. 405–419. New York: Garland.

Bell, R.Q. (1974). Contributions of human infants to caregiving and social interaction. In M. Lewis and L.A. Rosenblum (eds.), *The Effect of the Infant on its Caregiver*, pp. 1–19. New York: Wiley.

Berger, M.E. (1972). Population structure of olive baboons (*Papio anubis* (J.P. Fischer)) in the Laikipia district of Kenya. *E. Afr. Wildl. J.* 10:159–164.

Berkson, G. (1970). Defective infants in a feral monkey group. *Folia. Primat.* 12:284–289.

Berkson, G. (1974). Social responses of animals to infants with defects. In M. Lewis and L.A. Rosenblum (eds.), *The Effect of the Infant on its Caregiver*, pp. 233–249. New York: Wiley.

Berkson, G. (1977). The social ecology of defects in primates. In S. Chevalier-Skolnikoff and F.E. Poirier (eds.), *Primate Bio-Social Development*, pp. 189–204. New York: Garland.

Berlyne, D.E. (1958). The influence of albedo and complexity of stimuli on visual fixation in the human infant. *Br. J. Psychol.* 49:315–318.

Bernstein, I.S. (1970). Primate status hierarchies. In L.A. Rosenblum (ed.), *Primate Behavior*, pp. 71–109. New York: Academic Press.

Bernstein, I.S. (1976a). Taboo or toy? In J.S. Bruner, A. Jolly, and K. Sylva (eds.), *Play, Its Role in Development and Evolution*, pp. 194–198. New York: Basic Books.

Bernstein, I.S. (1976b). Dominance, aggression and reproduction in primate societies. *J. Theor. Biol.* 60:459–472.

Bernstein, I.S. and Smith, E.O. (1979). *Primate Ecology and Human Origins: Ecological Influences on Social Organization.* New York: Garland.

Bertalanffy, L. von (1968). *General System Theory.* New York: Braziller.

Bindra, D. (1959). *Motivation: A Systematic Reinterpretation.* New York: Ronald Press.

Birch, H.G. (1945). The relation of previous experience to insightful problem-solving. *J. Comp. Psychol.* 38:367–383.

Birnbrauer, J.S. (1976). Mental retardation. In H. Leitenberg (ed.), *Handbook of Behavior Modification and Behavior Therapy*, pp. 361–404. Englewood Cliffs, N.J.: Prentice-Hall.

Blurton Jones, N.G. (1976). Growing points in human ethology: Another link between ethology and the social sciences. In P.P.G. Bateson and R.A. Hinde (eds.), *Growing Points in Ethology*, pp. 427–450. Cambridge: Cambridge Univ. Press.

Blute, M. (1976). Book review of Wilson's *Sociobiology. Contemp. Sociol.* 5:727–731.

Boelkins, R.C. and Wilson, A.P. (1972). Intergroup social dynamics of the Cayo Santiago rhesus (*Macaca mulatta*) with special reference to changes in group membership by males. *Primates* 13:125–140.

Boren, J.J., Moerschbaecher, J.M., and Whyte, A.A. (1978). Variability of response location on fixed-ratio and fixed-interval schedules of reinforcement. *J. Exp. Anal. Behav.* 30:63–67.

Boulding, K.E. (1967). Am I a man or a mouse—or both? *War/Peace Rep.* 7(3):14–17.

Bower, T.G.R. (1966). The visual world of infants. *Sci. Am.* 215(6):80–92.

Bower, T.G.R., Broughton, J.M., and Moore, M.K. (1971). Infant responses to approaching objects. *Percept. Psychophys.* 9:193–196.

Brackbill, Y. (1971). Cumulative effects of continuous stimulation on arousal level in infants. *Child Dev.* 42:17–76.

Brazelton, T.B. (1961). Psychophysiologic reactions in the neonate: II. Effect of maternal medication on the neonate and his behavior. *J. Pediat.* 58:513–518.

Brazelton, T.B., Koslowski, B., and Main, M. (1974). The origins of reciprocity: The early mother-infant interaction. In M. Lewis and L.A. Rosenblum (eds.), *The Effect of the Infant on its Caregiver*, pp. 49–76. New York: Wiley.

Breder, C.M. (1959). Studies on social groupings in fishes. *Bull. Am. Mus. Nat. Hist.* 117:395–481, pls. 70–80.

Breland, K. and Breland, M. (1966). *Animal Behavior.* New York: Macmillan.

Bronowski, J. (1977). *A Sense of the Future.* Cambridge, Mass.: MIT Press.

Bross, M., Harper, D., and Sicz, G. (1980). Visual effects of auditory deprivation: Common intermodal and intramodal factors. *Science* 207:667–668.

Brownlee, A. (1954). Play in domestic cattle in Britain: An analysis of its nature. *Br. Vet. J.* 110:48–68.

Bruner, J.S. (1972). Nature and uses of immaturity. *Am. Psychol.* 27:687–708.

Buckley, W. (1967). *Sociology and Modern Systems Theory.* Englewood Cliffs, N.J.: Prentice-Hall.

Buell, J., Stoddard, P., Harris, F., and Baer, D. (1968). Collateral social development accompanying reinforcement of outdoor play in a preschool child. *J. Appl. Behav. Anal.* 1:167–173.

Burgess, R.L. (1969). Communication networks: An experimental re-evaluation. In R.L. Burgess and D. Bushell (eds.), *Behavioral Sociology*, pp. 127–142. New York: Columbia Univ. Press.

Burgess, R.L. and Bushell, D. (1969). A behavioral view of some sociological concepts. In R.L. Burgess and D. Bushell (eds.), *Behavioral Sociology.* New York: Columbia Univ. Press.

Burian, R.M. (1978). A methodological critique of sociobiology. In A.L. Caplan (ed.), *The Sociobiology Debate*, pp. 376–395. New York: Harper and Row.

Burton, F.D. (1972). The integration of biology and behaviour in the socialization of *Macaca sylvanus* of Gibraltar. In F.E. Poirier (ed.), *Primate Socialization*, pp. 29–62. New York: Random House.

Burton, F.D. (1977). Ethology and the development of sex and gender identity in non-human primates. *Acta Biotheor.* 26:1–18.

Burton, J.J. (1977). Absence of spontaneous cooperative behavior in a troop of *Macaca fuscata* confronted with baited stones. *Primates* 18:359–366.

Busch, J.A. (1979). Sociobiology and general systems theory: A critique of the new synthesis. *Behav. Sci.* 24:60–71.

Butler, R.A. (1958). The differential effect of visual and auditory incentives on the performance of monkeys. *Am. J. Psychol.* 71:591–593.

Butler, R.A. (1965). Investigative behavior. In A.M. Schrier, H.F. Harlow, and F. Stollnitz (eds.). *Behavior of Nonhuman Primates*, Vol. 2, pp. 463–493. New York: Academic Press.

Byrd, L.D. (1972). Responding in the squirrel monkey under second-order schedules of shock delivery. *J. Exp. Anal. Behav.* 18:155–167.

Caine, N. and Mitchell, G. (1979). A review of play in the genus *Macaca*: Social correlates. *Primates* 20:535–546.

Campbell, H.J. (1972). Peripheral self-stimulation as a reward in fish, reptile and mammal. *Physiol. Behav.* 8:637–640.

Candland, D.K., French, J.A., and Johnson, C.N. (1978). Object-play: Test of a categorized model by the genesis of object-play in *Macaca fuscata*. In E.O. Smith (ed.), *Social Play in Primates*, pp. 259–296. New York: Academic Press.

Carpenter, C.R. (1934). A field study of the behavior and social relations of howling monkeys. *Comp. Psychol. Monogr.* 10:1–168.

Carpenter, C.R. (1952). Social behavior of nonhuman primates. *Structure et Physiologie des Sociétés Animales*, Paris: Colloques Internationaux du Centre National de la Recherche Scientifique, 34:227–246.

Cassirer, E. (1951). *The Philosophy of the Enlightenment*. Princeton: Princeton Univ. Press.

Castell, R. and Heinrich, B. (1971). Rank order in a captive female squirrel monkey colony. *Folia Primat.* 14:182–189.

Castell, R. and Sackett, G. (1973). Motor behaviors of neonatal rhesus monkeys: Measurement techniques and early development. *Dev. Psychobiol.* 6:191–202.

Catania, A.C. (1971). The nature of learning. In J.A. Nevin and G.S. Reynolds (eds.), *The Study of Behavior*, pp. 30–68. Glenview, Ill.: Scott, Foresman.

Chalmers, N.R. (1972). Comparative aspects of early infant development in some captive cercopithecines. In F.E. Poirier (ed.), *Primate Socialization*, pp. 63–82. New York: Random House.

Chalmers, N.R. and Rowell, T.E. (1970). Behavior and female reproductive cycles in a captive group of mangabeys. *Folia Primat.* 14:1–14.

Chamove, A.S. (1974). Failure to find rhesus observational learning. *J. Behav. Sci.* 2:39–41.

Chamove, A.S. and Harlow, H.F. (1975). Cross-species affinity in three macaques. *J. Behav. Sci.* 2:131–136.

Chamove, A.S., Harlow, H.F. and Mitchell, G. (1967). Sex differences in the infant-directed behavior of preadolescent rhesus monkeys. *Child Dev.* 38:329–335.

Chance, M.R.A. (1967). Attention structure as the basis of primate rank orders. *Man*, 2:503–518.

Chance, M.R.A. (1976). Social attention: Society and Mentality. In M.R.A. Chance and R.R. Larsen (eds.), *The Social Structure of Attention*, pp. 315–333. New York: Wiley.

Cheek, D.B. (1971). Hormonal and nutritional factors influencing muscle cell growth. *J. Dent. Res.* 50:1385–1391.

Cheney, D.L. (1977). The acquisition of rank and the development of reciprocal alliances among free-ranging immature baboons. *Behav. Ecol. Sociobiol.* 2:303–318.

Cheney, D.L. (1978). Interactions of immature male and female baboons with adult females. *Anim. Behav.* 26:389–408.

Cheng, K., Shoffner, R.N., Phillips, R.E., and Shapiro, L.J. (1979). Early imprinting in wild and game-farm mallards (*Anas platyrhynchos*): Genotype and arousal. *J. Comp. Physiol. Psychol.* 93:929–938.

Chepko-Sade, B.D. and Oliver, T.J. (1979). Coefficient of genetic relationship and the probability of intragenealogical fission in *Macaca mulatta*. *Behav. Ecol. Sociobiol.* 5:263–278.

Chivers, D.J. (1969). On the daily behaviour and spacing of howling monkey groups. *Folia Primat.* 10:48–102.

Chivers, D.J. (1971). Spatial relations within the siamang group. *Proc. 3rd Int. Congr. Primat.*, Vol. 3, pp. 14–21. Basel: Karger.

Clark, C.B. (1977). A preliminary report on weaning among chimpanzees of the Gombe National Park, Tanzania. In S. Chevalier-Skolnikoff and F.E. Poirier (eds.), *Primate Bio-Social Development*, pp. 235–260. New York: Garland.

Clarke, B. (1975). The causes of biological diversity. *Sci. Am.* 233(2):50–60.

Clarke, M.R. (1978). Social interactions of juvenile female bonnet monkeys, *Macaca radiata*. *Primates* 19:517–524.

Clutton-Brock, T.H. (1974). Primate social organization and ecology. *Nature* 250:539–542.

Clutton-Brock, T.H. and Harvey, P.H. (1976). Evolutionary rules and primate societies. In P.P.G. Bateson and R.A. Hinde (eds.), *Growing Points in Ethology*, pp. 195–237. Cambridge: Cambridge Univ. Press.

Coakley, J.J. (1978). *Sport in Society: Issues and Controversies.* St. Louis: Mosby.

Cobban, A. (1960). *In Search of Humanity: The Role of the Enlightenment in Modern History.* New York: Braziller.

Coe, C.L., Mendoza, S.P., Smotherman, W.P., and Levine, S. (1978). Mother-infant attachment in the squirrel monkey: Adrenal response to separation. *Behav. Biol.* 22:256–263.

Cohen, S.N. and Shapiro, J.A. (1980). Transposable genetic elements. *Sci. Am.* 242(2):40–49.

Crook, J.H. (1970a). Social organization and the environment: Aspects of contemporary social ethology. *Anim. Behav.* 18:197–209.

Crook, J.H. (1970b). The socio-ecology of primates. In J.H. Crook (ed.), *Social Behaviour in Birds and Mammals*, pp. 103–166. New York: Academic Press.

Csikzentmihalyi, M. and Bennett, S. (1971). An exploratory model of play. *Am. Anthrop.* 73:45–58.

Cummins, R.A., Livesey, P.J., Evans, J.G.M., and Walsh, R.N. (1977). A developmental theory of environmental enrichment. *Science* 197:692–694.

Curtiss, S. (1977). *Genie: A Psycholinguistic Study of a Modern Day "Wild Child."* New York: Academic Press.

Daly, M. and Wilson, M. (1978). *Sex, Evolution and Behavior.* North Scituate, Mass.: Duxbury Press.

Darwin, C. (1859). *The Origin of Species* (1915 edition). New York: D. Appelton and Co.

Darwin, C. (1860). *The Voyage of the Beagle* (Leonard Engel, ed., 1962). Garden City, N.Y.: Doubleday.

Darwin, C. (1876). *Autobiography of Charles Darwin* (Nora Balow, ed., 1958). London: Collins.

Darwin, C. (1888). *The Life and Letters of Charles Darwin* (Francis Darwin, ed.). New York: D. Appleton and Co.

Davenport, R.K., Rogers, C.M. and Rumbaugh, D.M. (1973). Long-term cognitive deficits in chimpanzees associated with early impoverished rearing. *Dev. Psychol.* 9:343–347.

Davidge, C. (1978). Activity patterns of chacma baboons (*Papio ursinus*) at Cape Point. *Zool. Afr.* 13:143–155.

Davis, K. (1940). Extreme social isolation of a child. *Am. J. Sociol.* 45:554–565.

Davis, K. (1947). Final note on a case of extreme isolation. *Am. J. Sociol.* 52:432–437.

Davis, R.T. (1978). Old monkey behavior. *Exp. Geront.* 13:237–250.

Dawes, G.S. (1968). *Foetal and Neonatal Physiology*. Chicago: Year Book Medical Publishers.

Dawkins, R. (1976). *The Selfish Gene*. New York: Oxford Univ. Press.

de Benedictis, T. (1973). The behavior of young primates during adult copulation: Observations of a *Macaca irus* colony. *Am. Anthrop.* 75:1469–1484.

Denham, W. (1971). Energy relations and some basic properties of primate social organization. *Am. Anthrop.* 73:77–95.

Deni, R. and Drake, D.I. (1977). Conspecific images as elements of compound stimuli controlling operant responding in female rhesus monkeys. *Percept. Mot. Skills* 45:1015–1020.

Dennis, W. and Najarian, P. (1957). How reversible are the effects? *Psychol. Monogr. Gen. App.* 71(7): whole number 436.

Denzin, N.K. (1975). Play, games and interaction: The contexts of childhood socialization. *Sociol. Q.* 16:458–478.

DeVore, I. (1963a). Mother-infant relations in free-ranging baboons. In H.L. Rheingold (ed.), *Maternal Behavior in Mammals*, pp. 305–335. New York: Wiley.

DeVore, I. (1963b). A comparison of the ecology and behavior of monkeys and apes. In S.L. Washburn (ed.), *Classification and Human Evolution*, pp. 301–319. Chicago: Aldine; Viking Fund Publications in Anthropology no. 31.

DeVore, I. and Hall, K.R.L. (1965). Baboon ecology. In I. DeVore (ed.), *Primate Behavior: Field Studies of Monkeys and Apes*, pp. 20–52. New York: Holt, Rinehart and Winston.

de Waal, B.M. and van Roosmalen, A. (1979). Reconciliation and consolation among chimpanzees. *Behav. Ecol. Sociobiol.* 5:55–66.

Dobzhansky, T. (1962). *Mankind Evolving*. New Haven, Conn.: Yale Univ. Press.

Dobzhansky, T. (1967). Book review of *On Aggression* and *The Territorial Imperative*. *Anim. Beh.* 15:392–396.

Dobzhansky, T., Ayala, F.J., Stebbins, G.L., and Valentine, J.W. (1977). *Evolution*. San Francisco: Freeman.

Dolhinow, P. (1971). At play in the fields. *Nat. Hist.*, 80:66–71.

Dolhinow, P. and Bishop, N. (1970): The development of motor skills and social relationships among primates through play. In J.P. Hill (ed.), *Minnesota Sym-*

posia on Child Psychology, Vol. IV, pp. 141–198. Minneapolis: Univ. Minnesota Press.

Douglas, J.H. (1973). Genetics: A science that is coming of age. *Sci. News* 104:332–334.

Drickamer, L.C. (1974). A ten-year summary of reproductive data for free-ranging *Macaca mulatta*. *Folia Primat.* 21:61–80.

Drickamer, L.C. (1975). Patterns of space utilization and group interactions among free-ranging *Macaca mulatta*. *Primates* 16:23–33.

Drickamer, L.C. (1976). Quantitative observations of grooming behavior in free-ranging *Macaca mulatta*. *Primates* 17:323–335.

Drickamer, L.C. and Vessey, S.H. (1973). Group changing in free-ranging male rhesus monkeys. *Primates* 14:359–368.

Dua-Sharma, S. and Smutz, E.R. (1977). Taste acceptability in squirrel monkeys (*Saimiri sciureus*). *Chem. Senses Flavor* 2:341–352.

DuMond, F.V. (1968). The squirrel monkey in a seminatural environment. In L.A. Rosenblum and R.W. Cooper (eds.), *The Squirrel Monkey*, pp. 87–145. New York: Academic Press.

Dunbar, R.I.M. and Nathan, M.F. (1972). Social organization of the Guinea baboon, *Papio papio*. *Folia Primat.* 17:321–334.

Dunham, P. (1977). The nature of reinforcing stimuli. In W.K. Honig and J.E.R. Staddon (eds.), *Handbook of Operant Behavior*, pp. 98–124. Englewood Cliffs, N.J.: Prentice-Hall.

Durham, N.M. (1971). Effects of altitude differences on group organization of wild black spider monkeys (*Ateles paniscus*). *Proc. 3rd Int. Cong. Primat.*, Vol. 3, pp. 32–40. Basel: Karger.

Durham, W.H. (1979). Toward a coevolutionary theory of human biology and culture. In N.A. Chagnon and W. Irons (eds.), *Evolutionary Biology and Human Social Behavior*, pp. 39–59. North Scituate, Mass.: Duxbury Press.

Eaton, G. (1976). The social order of Japanese macaques. *Sci. Am.* 235(4):96–106.

Eibl-Eibesfeldt, I. (1967). Concepts of ethology and their significance in the study of human behavior. In H.W. Stevenson, E.H. Hess, and H.L. Rheingold (eds.), *Early Behavior*, pp. 127–146. New York: Wiley.

Eibl-Eibesfeldt, I. (1975). *Ethology: The Biology of Behavior*, 2nd ed. New York: Holt, Rinehart and Winston.

Eifermann, R.R. (1971). Social play in childhood. In R.E. Herron and B. Sutton-Smith (eds.), *Child's Play*, pp. 270–297. New York: Wiley.

Eisenberg, J.F. and Kuehn, R.E. (1966). The behavior of *Ateles geoffroyi* and related species. *Smithson. Misc. Coll.* 151(8):1–63.

Eisenberg, J.F. and Lockhart, M. (1972). An ecological reconnaissance of Wilpattu National Park, Ceylon. *Smithson. Contrib. Zool.* #101.

Eisenberg, J.F., Muckenhirn, N., and Rudran, R. (1972). The relation between ecology and social structure in primates. *Science* 176:863–874.

Elias, M.F. and Samonds, K.W. (1974). Exploratory behavior and activity of infant monkeys during nutritional and rearing restriction. *Am. J. Clin. Nutr.* 27:458–463.

Ellis, M.J. (1973). *Why People Play*. Englewood Cliffs, N.J.: Prentice–Hall.

Emlen, S.T. and Oring, L.W. (1977). Ecology, sexual selection, and the evolution of mating systems. *Science* 197:215–223.

Enomoto, T. (1978). On social preference in sexual behavior of Japanese monkeys (*Macaca fuscata*). *J. Hum. Evol.* 7:283–293.

Erwin, J., Brandt, E., and Mitchell, G. (1973). Attachment formation and separation in heterosexually naive preadult rhesus monkeys (*Macaca mulatta*). *Dev. Psychobiol.* 6:531–538.

Erwin, J., Maple, T., Willott, J., and Mitchell, G. (1974). Persistent peer attachments of rhesus monkeys: Responses to reunion after two years of separation. *Psychol. Rep.* 34:1179–1183.

Erwin, J., Mobaldi, J., and Mitchell, G. (1971). Separation of rhesus monkey juveniles of the same sex. *J. Abnorm. Psychol.* 78:134–139.

Essock-Vitale, S.M. (1978). Comparison of ape and monkey modes of problem solution. *J. Comp. Physiol. Psychol.* 92:942–957.

Ewer, R.F. (1968). *Ethology of Mammals*. New York: Plenum.

Fagen, R.M. (1974). Selective and evolutionary aspects of animal play. *Am. Nat.* 108:850–858.

Fagen, R.M. (1976). Exercise, play, and physical training in animals. In P.P.G. Bateson (ed.), *Perspectives in Ethology*, Vol. 2, pp. 189–219. New York: Plenum.

Fairbanks, L. (1974). An analysis of subgroup structure and process in a captive squirrel monkey (*Saimiri sciureus*) colony. *Folia Primat.* 21:209–224.

Fairbanks, L. (1977). Animal and human behavior: Guidelines for generalization across species. In M.T. McGuire and L.A. Fairbanks (eds.), *Ethological Psychiatry: Psychopathology in the Context of Evolutionary Biology*, pp. 87–110. New York: Grune and Stratton.

Fairbanks, L. and Bird, J. (1978). Ecological correlations in interindividual distance in the St. Kitts vervet (*Cercopithecus aethiops sabaeus*). *Primates* 19:605–614.

Fantino, E. and Logan, C.A. (1979). *The Experimental Analysis of Behavior: A Biological Perspective*. San Francisco: W.H. Freeman.

Farley, F.H. (1973). Implications for a theory of delinquency. In T.I. Myers (Chm.), The sensation seeking motive. Symposium presented at the 81st meeting of the American Psychological Association, Montreal, (August, 1973).

Fedigan, L.M. (1972a). Roles and activities of male geladas (*Theropithecus gelada*). *Behaviour* 41:82–90.

Fedigan, L.M. (1972b). Social and solitary play in a colony of vervet monkeys (*Cercopithecus aethiops*). *Primates* 13:347–364.

Fedigan, L.M. and Fedigan, L. (1977). The social development of a handicapped infant in a free-living troop of Japanese monkeys. In S. Chevalier-Skolnikoff and F.E. Poirier (eds.), *Primate Bio-Social Development*, pp. 205–222. New York: Garland.

Feitelson, D. and Ross, G.S. (1973). The neglected factor—play. *Hum. Dev.* 16:202–223.

Feldman, D.W. and Klopfer, P.H. (1972). A study of observational learning in lemurs. *Z. Tierpsychol.* 30:297–304.

Ferster, C.B., Culbertson, S., and Boren, M.C.P. (1975). *Behavior Principles* (2nd ed.). Englewood Cliffs, N.J.: Prentice-Hall.

Fiske, D.W. and Maddi, S.R. (1961). *Functions of Varied Experience*. Homewood, Ill.: Dorsey.

Floeter, M.K. and Greenough, W.T. (1979). Cerebellar plasticity: Modification of purkinje cell structure by differential rearing in monkeys. *Science* 206:227–229.

Fossey, D. (1974). Observations on the home range of one group of mountain gorillas (*Gorilla gorilla beringei*). *Anim. Behav.* 22:568–581.

Fouts, R.S. (1973). Acquisition and testing of gestural signs in four young chimpanzees. *Science* 180:978–980.

Fox, G.J. (1972). Some comparisons between siamang and gibbon behaviour. *Folia Primat.* 18:122–139.

Fragaszy, D.M. and Mitchell, G. (1974). Infant socialization in primates. *J. Hum. Evol.* 3:563–574.

Fraiberg, S. (1974). Blind infants and their mothers: An examination of the sign system. In M. Lewis and L.A. Rosenblum (eds.), *The Effect of the Infant on its Caregiver*, pp. 215–232. New York: Wiley.

Freyberg, J.T. (1973). Increasing the imaginative play of urban disadvantaged kindergarten children through systematic training. In J.L. Singer (ed.), *The Child's World of Make-Believe*, pp. 129–154. New York: Academic Press.

Frisch, J.E. (1968). Individual behavior and intertroop variability in Japanese macaques. In P.C. Jay (ed.), *Primates: Studies in Adaptation and Variability*, pp. 243–252. New York: Holt, Rinehart and Winston.

Furuya, Y. (1968). On the fission of troops of Japanese monkeys: I. Five fissions and social changes between 1955 and 1966 in the Gagyusan troop. *Primates* 9:323–350.

Furuya, Y. (1969). On the fission of troops of Japanese monkeys: II. General view of troop fission of Japanese monkeys. *Primates* 10:47–69.

Gardner, M. (1978). White and brown music, fractal curves and one-over-f fluctuations. *Sci. Am.* 238(4):16–32.

Gartlan, J.S. (1968). Structure and function in primate society. *Folia Primat.* 8:89–120.

Gartlan, J.S. (1973). Influences of phylogeny and ecology on variations in the group organization of primates. *Fourth Int. Congr. Primat.* Vol. 1, pp. 88–101. Basel: Karger.

Gartlan, J.S. and Brain, C.K. (1968). Ecology and social variability in *Cercopithecus aethiops* and *C. mitis*. In P.C. Jay (ed.), *Primates: Studies in Adaptation and Variability*, pp. 253–292. New York: Holt, Rinehart and Winston.

Geschwind, N. (1974). *Selected Papers on Language and the Brain*. D. Reidel Publishing.

Geschwind, N. (1979). Specializations of the human brain. *Sci. Am.* 241(3):180–199.

Gesell, A. and Lord, E.E. (1927). A psychological comparison of nursery school children from homes of low and high economic statuses. *J. Genet. Psychol.* 34:339–356.

Getzels, J.W. and Jackson, P.W. (1963). The highly intelligent and the highly creative adolescent: A summary of some research findings. In R.G. Kuhlen and G.G. Thompson (eds.), *Psychological Studies of Human Development* (2nd ed.), pp. 370–381. New York: Appleton-Century-Crofts.

Ghiselin, M.T. (1973). Darwin and evolutionary psychology. *Science* 179:964–968.

Gibson, E.J. and Walk, R.D. (1960). The visual cliff. *Sci. Am.* 202(4):64–71.

Glander, K.E. (1975). Habitat and resource utilization: An ecological view of social organization in mantled howling monkeys. Doct. diss., Univ. Chicago.

Glickman, S.E. (1958). Effect of peripheral blindness on exploratory behavior in the hooded rat. *Can. J. Psychol.* 12:45–51.

Glickman, S.E. (1960). Reinforcing properties of arousal. *J. Comp. Physiol. Psychol.* 53:68–71.

Glickman, S.E. and Morrison, B.J. (1969). Some behavioral and neural correlates of predation susceptibility in mice. *Comm. Behav. Biol.* 4:261–267.

Glickman, S.E. and Schiff, B.B. (1967). A biological theory of reinforcement. *Psychol. Rev.* 74:81–109.

Glickman, S.E. and Sroges, R.W. (1966). Curiosity in zoo animals. *Behaviour* 26:151–188.

Glickman, S.E., Sroges, R.W., and Hunt, J. (1964). Brain lesions and locomotor exploration in the albino rat. *J. Comp. Physiol. Psychol.* 58:93–100.

Goetz, E.M. and Baer, D.M. (1973). Social control of form diversity and the emergence of new forms in children's blockbuilding. *J. Appl. Behav. Anal.* 6:209–217.

Goetz, E.M. and Salmonson, M.M. (1972). The effect of general and descriptive reinforcement on "creativity" in easel painting. In G. Semb (ed.), *Behavior Analysis and Education*, pp. 53–61. Lawrence, Kansas: Univ. Kansas Press.

Gould, S.J. (1976). Biological potential vs. biological determinism. *Nat. Hist.* 85(5):12–22.

Gouzoules, H. (1975). Maternal rank and early social interactions of infant stumptail macaques, *Macaca arctoides. Primates* 16:405–418.

Goy, R.W. and Phoenix, C.H. (1972). The effects of testosterone propionate administered before birth on the development of behavior in genetic female rhesus monkeys. In C. Sawyer and R. Gorski (eds.), *Steroid Hormones and Brain Function*, pp. 193–200. Berkeley: Univ. California Press.

Goy, R.W. and Resko, J.A. (1972). Gonadal hormones and behavior of normal and pseudohermaphroditic nonhuman female primates. In E.B. Astwood (ed.), *Recent Progress in Hormone Research*, Vol. 28, pp. 707–733. New York: Academic Press.

Goy, R.W. and Wallen, K. (1979). Experiential variables influencing play, foot-clasp mounting and adult sexual competence in male rhesus monkeys. *Psychoneuroendocrinology* 4:1–12.

Greenough, W.T. (1975). Experiential modification of the developing brain, *Am. Sci.* 63:37–46.

Grice, G.R. (1948a). An experimental test of the expectation theory of learning. *J. Comp. Physiol. Psychol.* 41:137–143.

Grice, G.R. (1948b). The relation of secondary reinforcement to delayed reward in visual discrimination learning. *J. Exp. Psychol.* 38:1–16.

Griffing, P. (1974). Sociodramatic play among young black children. *Theory Pract.* 13:257–265.

Haddow, A.J. (1952). Field studies of the African redtail monkey: The composition, size and behaviour of bands. *Proc. Zool. Soc. Lond.* 122:297–394.

Hall, K.R.L. (1965). Behaviour and ecology of wild patas monkeys, *Erythrocebus patas* in Uganda. *J. Zool. Soc. Lond.* 148:15–87.

Hall, K.R.L. (1967). Social interactions of the adult male and adult females of a patas monkey group. In S. Altmann, (ed.), *Social Communication among Primates*, pp. 261–280. Chicago: Univ. Chicago Press.

Hall, K.R.L. and DeVore, I. (1965). Baboon social behavior. In I. DeVore (ed.), *Primate Behavior: Field Studies of Monkeys and Apes*, pp. 53–110. New York: Holt, Rinehart and Winston.

Hamer, K.H. and Missakian, E. (1978). A longitudinal study of social play in Synanon/peer-reared children. In E.O. Smith (ed.), *Social Play in Primates*, pp. 297–319. New York: Academic Press.

Hamilton, W.D. (1964). The genetical evolution of social behaviour. I and II. *J. Theor. Biol.* 7:1–16 and 17–52.

Hamilton, W.D. (1970). Selfish and spiteful behaviour in an evolutionary model. *Nature* 228:1218–1220.

Hamilton, W.D. (1971a). Geometry for the selfish herd. *J. Theor. Biol.* 31:295–311.

Hamilton, W.D. (1971b). Selection of selfish and altruistic behaviour in some extreme models. In J.F. Eisenberg and W.S. Dillon (eds.), *Man and Beast: Comparative Social Behavior*, pp. 55–91. Washington, D.C.: Smithsonian Institution Press.

Hamilton, W.J. III, Buskirk, R.E., and Buskirk, W.H. (1975). Chacma baboon tactics during intertroop encounters. *J. Mammal.* 56:857–870.

Hamilton, W.J. III, Buskirk, R.E., and Buskirk, W.H. (1976). Defense of space and resources by chacma (*Papio ursinus*) baboon troops in an African desert and swamp. *Ecology* 57:1264–1272.

Hamilton, W.J. III, Buskirk, R.E., and Buskirk, W.H. (1978a). Environmental determinants of object manipulation by chacma baboons (*Papio ursinus*) in two southern African environments. *J. Hum. Evol.* 7:205–216.

Hamilton, W.J. III, Buskirk, R.E., and Buskirk, W.H. (1978b). Omnivory and utilization of food resources by chacma baboons, *Papio ursinus*. *Am. Nat.* 112:911–924.

Hanby, J.P. (1975). The social nexus: Problems and solutions in the portrayal of primate social structures. *Symp. 5th Congr. Int'l Primat. Soc.*, pp. 25–42. Tokyo: Science Press.

Hanby, J.P. (1976). Sociosexual development in primates. In P.P.G. Bateson and P.H. Klopfer (eds.), *Perspectives in Ethology*, Vol. 2, pp. 1–67. New York: Plenum Press.

Hansen, E.W. (1962). *The Development of Maternal and Infant Behavior in the Rhesus Monkey*. Doct. diss., Univ. of Wisconsin.

Harcourt, A.H., Stewart, K.J., and Fossey, D. (1976). Male emigration and female transfer in wild mountain gorilla. *Nature* 263:226–227.

Harding, R.S.O. (1976). Ranging patterns of a troop of baboons (*Papio anubis*) in Kenya. *Folia Primat.* 25:143–185.

Harding, R.S.O. (1977). Patterns of movement in open country baboons. *Am. J. Phys. Anthrop.* 47:349–354.

Harlow, H.F. (1949). The formation of learning sets. *Psychol. Rev.* 56:51–65.

Harlow, H.F. (1959). Love in infant monkeys. *Sci. Am.* 200(6):68–74.

Harlow, H.F., Gluck, J.P., and Suomi, S.J. (1972). Generalization of behavioral data between nonhuman and human animals. *Am. Psychol.* 27:709–716.

Harlow, H.F. and Harlow, M.K. (1965). The affectional system. In A.M. Schrier, H.F. Harlow and F. Stollnitz (eds.), *Behavior of Nonhuman Primates*, Vol. II, pp. 287–334. New York: Academic Press.

Harlow, H.F. and Harlow, M.K. (1969). Effects of various mother-infant relationships on rhesus monkey behaviors. In B.M. Foss (ed.), *Determinants of Infant Behavior* Vol. 4, pp. 15–36. London: Methuen.

Harlow, H.F., Harlow, M.K., and Meyer, D.R. (1950). Learning motivated by a manipulation drive. *J. Exp. Psychol.* 40:228–234.

Harlow, H.F. and Suomi, S.J. (1970). Nature of love—simplified. *Am. Psychol.* 25:161–168.

Harlow, H.F. and Suomi, S.J. (1971). Social recovery by isolation-reared monkeys. *Proc. Natl. Acad. Sci.* 68:1534–1538.

Harper, L.V. (1970). Ontogenetic and phylogenetic functions of the parent-offspring relationship in mammals. *Adv. Study Behav.* 3:75–117.

Harris, M. (1975). *Culture, People, Nature* (2nd ed.). New York: Thomas Y. Crowele.

Haude, R.H., Graber, J.G., and Farres, A.G. (1976). Visual observing by rhesus monekys: Some relationships with social dominance rank. *Anim. Learn. Behav.* 4:163–166.

Hausfater, G. (1972). Intergroup behavior of free-ranging rhesus monkeys (*Macaca mulatta*). *Folia Primat.* 18:78–107.

Hayashi, K. (1969). Utilization of ledges by Japanese monkeys in Hakusan National Park. *Primates* 10:189–191.

Hebb, D.O. (1949). *The Organization of Behavior.* New York: Wiley.

Hebb, D.O. (1953). Heredity and environment in mammalian behavior. *Br. J. Anim. Behav.* 1:43–47.

Hebb, D.O. (1955). Drives and the CNS (conceptual nervous system). *Psychol. Rev.* 62:243–254.

Hebb, D.O. (1958). *A Textbook of Psychology.* Philadelphia: W.B. Saunders.

Hebb, D.O. (1972). *Textbook of Psychology* (3rd ed.). Philadelphia: W.B. Saunders.

Heinroth, O. (1910). Beiträge zur Biologie, insbesondere Psychologie und Ethologie der Anatiden. *Verh. V. Int. Ornith. Kongr.,* Berlin. pp. 589–702.

Hess, E.H. (1959). Imprinting. *Science* 130:133–141.

Hill, S.D., McCormack, S.A., and Mason, W.A. (1973). Effects of artificial mothers and visual experience on adrenal responsiveness of infant monkeys. *Dev. Psychobiol.* 6:421–429.

Hinde, R.A. (1963). The nature of imprinting. In B.M. Foss (ed.), *Determinants of Infant Behaviour*, Vol. 2, pp. 227–230. London: Methuen.

Hinde, R.A. (1970). *Animal Behaviour: A Synthesis of Ethology and Comparative Psychology.* New York: McGraw-Hill.

Hinde, R.A. (1974). *Biological Bases of Human Social Behaviour.* New York: McGraw-Hill.

Hinde, R.A. and Stevenson-Hinde, J. (1973). *Constraints on Learning: Limitations and Predispositions*. New York: Academic Press.

Hinde, R.A. and Stevenson-Hinde, J. (1976). Towards understanding relationships: Dynamic stability. In P.P.G. Bateson and R.A. Hinde (eds.), *Growing Points in Ethology*, pp. 451–479. Cambridge: Cambridge Univ. Press.

Hoffman, H.S. and DePaulo, P. (1977). Behavioral control by an imprinting stimulus. *Am. Sci.* 65:58–66.

Hoffman, H.S. and Ratner, A.M. (1973a). Effects of stimulus and environmental familiarity on visual imprinting in newly hatched ducklings. *J. Comp. Physiol. Psychol.* 85:11–19.

Hoffman, H.S. and Ratner, A.M. (1973b). A reinforcement model of imprinting: Implications for socialization in monkeys and men. *Psychol. Rev.* 80:527–544.

~Hoffman, H.S., Stratton, J.W., and Newby, V. (1969). Punishment by response-contingent withdrawal of an imprinted stimulus. *Science* 163:702–704.

Hofstadter, R. (1944). *Social Darwinism in American Thought*. Boston: Beacon.

Homans, G.C. (1964). Bringing men back in. *Am. Soc. Rev.* 29(5):809–818.

Homans, G.C. (1974). *Social Behavior: Its Elementary Forms*. New York: Harcourt Brace Jovanovich.

Honig, W.K. and Staddon, J.E.R. (1977). *Handbook of Operant Behavior*. Englewood Cliffs, N.J.: Prentice-Hall.

Hopf, S. (1978). Huddling subgroups in captive squirrel monkeys and their changes in relation to ontogeny. *Biol. Behav.* 3:147–162.

Hopf, S. (1979). Development of sexual behaviour in captive squirrel monkeys (*Saimiri*). *Biol. Behav.* 4:373–382.

Horr, D.A. (1972). The Borneo orang-utan. *Borneo Res. Bull.* 4:46–50.

Horr, D.A. (1977). Orang-utan maturation: Growing up in a female world. In S. Chevalier-Skolnikoff and F.E. Poirier (eds.), *Primate Bio-Social Development*, pp. 289–321. New York: Garland.

Horwich, R.A. and Wurman, C. (1978). Socio-maternal behaviors in response to an infant birth in *Colobus guereza. Primates* 19:693–713.

Houston, J.P. (1976). *Fundamentals of Learning*. New York: Academic Press.

Huebner, D.K., Lentz, J.L., Wooley, M.J., and King, J.E. (1979). Responses to snakes by surrogate- and mother-reared squirrel monkeys. *Bull. Psychon. Soc.* 14:33–36.

Humphrey, N.K. (1976). The social function of intellect. In P.P.G. Bateson and R.A. Hinde (eds.), *Growing Points in Ethology*, pp. 303–317. Cambridge: Cambridge Univ. Press.

Humphrey, N.K. and Keeble, G.R. (1974). The reaction of monkeys to "fearsome" pictures. *Nature* 251:500–502.

Hutt, C. (1966). Exploration and play in children. *Symp. Zool. Soc. Lond.* 18:61–81.

Huxley, J.S. (1963). Lorenzian ethology. *Z. Tierpsychol.* 20:402–409.

Imanishi, K. (1957). Learned behavior of Japanese monkeys. *Jpn. J. Ethnol.* 21:185–189.

Itani, J. (1958). On the acquisition and propagation of a new food habit in the troop of Japanese monkeys at Takasakiyama. *Primates* 1:84–98.

Itani, J. and Nishimura, A. (1973). The study of infrahuman culture in Japan: A review. *Symp. 4th Int. Congr. Primat.*, Vol. 1, pp. 26–50. Basel: Karger.

Ito, M. (1966). Hippocampal electrical correlates of self-stimulation in the rat. *Electroencephalogr. Clin. Neurophysiol.* 21:261–268.

Izawa, K. and Mizuno, A. (1977). Palm-fruit cracking behavior of wild black-capped capuchin (*Cebus apella*). *Primates* 18:773–792.

James, W. (1890). *The Principles of Psychology*, Vol. II. New York: Holt.

Jasper, H.H. (1958). Reticular-cortical systems and theories of the integrative action of the brain. In H.F. Harlow and C.N. Woolsey (eds.), *Biological and Biochemical Bases of Behavior*, pp. 37–61. Madison: Univ. Wisconsin Press.

Jay, P.C. (1962). Aspects of maternal behavior among langurs. *Ann. N.Y. Acad. Sci.* 102:468–476.

Jay, P.C. (1965). The common langur of North India. In I. DeVore (ed.), *Primate Behavior: Field Studies of Monkeys and Apes*, pp. 197–249. New York: Holt, Rinehart and Winston.

Jay, P.C. (1968). *Primates: Studies in Adaptation and Variability*. New York: Holt, Rinehart and Winston.

Jeddi, E. (1970). Confort du contact et thermoregulation comportementale. *Physiol. Behav.* 5:1487–1493.

Jensen, G.D., Bobbitt, R.A., and Gordon, B.N. (1967). The development of mutual independence in mother-infant pigtailed monkeys, *Macaca nemestrina*. In S.A. Altmann (ed.), *Social Communication among Primates*, pp. 43–53. Chicago: Univ. Chicago Press.

Jensen, G.D., Bobbitt, R.A., and Gordon, B.N. (1968). Sex differences in the development of independence of infant monkeys. *Behaviour* 30:1–14.

Jensen, G.D., Bobbitt, R.A., and Gordon, B.N. (1969). Patterns and sequences of hitting behavior in mother and infant monkeys (*Macaca nemestrina*). *J. Psychiatr. Res.* 7:55–61.

Jensen, G.D., Bobbitt, R.A., and Gordon, B.N. (1973). Mothers' and infants' roles in the development of independence of *Macaca nemestrina*. *Primates* 14:79–88.

Johnson, C.K., Gilbert, M.D., and Herdt, G.H. (1979). Implications for adult roles from differential styles of mother-infant bonding: An ethological study. *J. Nervous Ment. Disease* 167:29–37.

Johnson, W.A., Stoltzfus, V., and Craumer, P. (1977). Energy conservation in Amish agriculture. *Science* 198:373–378.

Jolly, A. (1966). Lemur social behavior and primate intelligence. *Science* 153:501–506.

Jolly, A. (1972). *The Evolution of Primate Behavior*. New York: Macmillan.

Joslyn, W.D. (1973). Androgen-induced social dominance in infant female rhesus monkeys. *J. Child Psychol. Psychiatr.* 14:137–145.

Jouventin, P., Pasteur, C., and Cambefort, J.P. (1977). Observational learning of baboons and avoidance of mimics: Exploratory tests. *Evolution* 31:214–218.

Kaack, B., Walker, L., and Brizzee, K.R. (1979). The growth and development of the squirrel monkey (*Saimiri sciureus*). *Growth* 43:116–135.

Kagan, J. and Klein, R.E. (1973). Cross-cultural perspectives on early development. *Am. Psychol.* 28:947–961.

Kanfer, F.H. and Phillips, J.S. (1970). *Learning Foundations of Behavior Therapy.* New York: Wiley.

Kaplan, A. (1964). *The Conduct of Inquiry.* San Francisco: Chandler.

Kaplan, J. (1974). Growth and behavior of surrogate-reared squirrel monkeys. *Dev. Psychobiol.* 7:7–13.

Kaplan, J. and Schusterman, R.J. (1972). Social preferences of mother and infant squirrel monkeys following different rearing experiences. *Dev. Psychobiol.* 5:53–59.

Karen, R.L. (1974). *An Introduction to Behavior Theory and its Applications.* New York: Harper and Row.

Kavanau, J.L. and Peters, C.R. (1979). Illuminance preferences of nocturnal primates. *Primates* 20:245–258.

Kawai, M. (1965). Newly acquired pre-cultural behavior of the natural troop of Japanese monkeys on Koshima Islet. *Primates* 6:1–30.

Kawai, I. (1966). Changes in social behavior following bilateral removal of the posterior parts of the superior temporal gyri in Japanese monkeys. *Primates* 7:1–20.

Kawamura, S. (1954). A new type of action expressed in feeding behavior of Japanese monkey in its wild habitat. *Org. Evol.,* 2(1):10–13. (In Japanese; cited in S. Kawamura, 1963 [q.v.].)

Kawamura, S. (1963). The process of sub-culture propagation among Japanese macaques. In C.H. Southwick (ed.), *Primate Social Behavior,* pp. 82–90. New York: van Nostrand.

Kawamura, S. (1965). Matriarchal social ranks in the Minoo-B troop: A study of the rank system of Japanese monkeys. In K. Imanishi and S.A. Altmann (eds.), *Japanese Monkeys: A Collection of Translations,* pp. 105–112. Edmonton, Alberta: Privately published.

Kelleher, R.T. (1958). Fixed-ratio schedules of conditioned reinforcement with chimpanzees. *J. Exp. Anal. Behav.* 1:281–289.

Kelleher, R.T. and Morse, W.H. (1968). Schedules using noxious stimuli. III. Responding maintained with response-produced electric shocks. *J. Exp. Anal. Behav.* 11:819–838.

Kimura, M. (1968). Evolutionary rate at the molecular level. *Nature* 217:624–626.

Kimura, M. (1979). The neutral theory of molecular evolution. *Sci. Am.* 241(5):98–126.

King, J.L. and Jukes, T.H. (1969). Non-Darwinian evolution. *Science* 164:788–798.

Klopfer, P.H. (1973). Does behavior evolve? *Ann. N.Y. Acad. Sci.* 223:113–119.

Klopfer, P.H. (1977). Social Darwinism lives! (Should it?) *Yale J. Biol. Med.* 50:77–84.

Koford, C.B. (1963). Rank of mothers and sons in bands of rhesus monkeys. *Science* 141:356–357.

Köhler, W. (1925). *The Mentality of Apes.* New York: Harcourt Brace.

Konrad, K. and Melzack, R. (1975). Novelty-enhancement effects associated with early sensory-social isolation. In A.H. Riesen (ed.), *The Developmental Neuropsychology of Sensory Deprivation,* pp. 253–276. New York: Academic Press.

Korner, A. (1974). The effect of the infant's state, level of arousal, sex and ontogenetic stage on the caregiver. In M. Lewis and L.A. Rosenblum (eds.), *The Effect of the Infant on its Caregiver*, pp. 105–121. New York: Wiley.

Koyama, N. (1967). On dominance rank and kinship of a wild Japanese monkey troop in Arashiyama. *Primates* 8:189–216.

Koyama, N. (1970). Changes in dominance rank and division of a wild Japanese monkey troop in Arashiyama. *Primates* 11:335–390.

Koyama, N. (1973). Dominance, grooming, and clasped-sleeping relationships among bonnet monkeys in India. *Primates* 14:225–244.

Kremer, M.E., Napierala, J.S., and Haude, R.H. (1978). Suppression of visual observing by rhesus monkeys produced by conditioned aversive visual stimuli. *Percept. Mot. Skills* 46:467–475.

Kuhn, A. (1975). *Unified Social Science: A System-Based Introduction*. Homewood, Ill.: Dorsey.

Kummer, H. (1967). Tripartite relations in Hamadryas baboons. In S.A. Altmann (ed.), *Social Communication among Primates*, pp. 63–71. Chicago: Univ. Chicago Press.

Kummer, H. (1968). *Social Organization of Hamadryas Baboons: A Field Study*. Chicago: Univ. Chicago Press.

Kummer, H. (1971). *Primate Societies*. Chicago: Aldine-Atherton.

Kunkel, J.H. (1969). Some behavioral aspects of social change and economic development. In R.L. Burgess and D. Bushell (eds.), *Behavioral Sociology*, pp. 321–365. New York: Columbia Univ. Press.

Kunkel, J.H. (1975). *Behavior, Social Problems, and Change: A Social Learning Approach*. Englewood Cliffs, N.J.: Prentice-Hall.

Kuyk, K., Dazey, J., and Erwin, J. (1976). Primiparous and multiparous pigtail monkey mothers (*Macaca nemestrina*): Restraint and retrieval of female infants. *J. Biol. Psychol.* 18:16–19.

Lancaster, J.B. (1968). Primate communication systems and the emergence of human language. In P.C. Jay (ed.), *Primates: Studies in Adaptation and Variability*, pp. 439–457. New York: Holt, Rinehart and Winston.

Lancaster, J.B. (1971). Play-mothering: The relations between juvenile females and young infants among free-ranging vervet monkeys (*Cercopithecus aethiops*). *Folia Primat.* 15:161–182.

Lancaster, J.B. (1979). Sex and gender in evolutionary perspective. In H.A. Katchadourian (ed.), *Human Sexuality: A Comparative and Developmental Perspective*, pp. 51–80. Berkeley: Univ. California Press.

Lancaster, J.B. and Lee, R.B. (1965). The annual reproductive cycle in monkeys and apes. In I. DeVore (ed.), *Primate Behavior: Field Studies of Monkeys and Apes*, pp. 486–513. New York: Holt, Rinehart and Winston.

Langton, J. (1979). Darwinism and the behavioral theory of sociocultural evolution: An analysis. *Am. J. Sociol.* 85:288–309.

Larkin, J., McDermott, J., Simon, D.P., and Simon, H.A. (1980). Expert and novice performance in solving physics problems. *Science* 208:1335–1342.

Lawton, J.H. (1979). Optimality in evolution. *Science* 204:165–166.

Lehrman, D.S. (1953). A critique of Konrad Lorenz's theory of instinctive behavior. *Q. Rev. Biol.* 28:337–363.

LeMagnen, J. (1967). Habits and food intake. In C.F. Code (ed.), *Handbook of Physiology, Section 6, Alimentary Canal. Vol. 1, Control of Food and Water Intake*, pp. 11–30. Washington, D.C.: Am. Physiol. Soc.

Leresche, L.A. (1976). Dyadic play in hamadryas baboons. *Behaviour* 57:190–205.

Lethmate, J. (1977). Versuche zum Schlagstockverfahren mit zwei jungen Orang-Utans. *Zool. Amz., Jena* 199:209–226.

Leuba, C. and Friedlander, B.Z. (1968). Effects of controlled audio-visual reinforcement on infants' manipulative play in the home. *J. Exp. Child Psychol.* 6:87–99.

Lever, J. (1976). Sex differences in the games children play. *Soc. Problems* 23:478–487.

Levitsky, D.A. and Barnes, R.H. (1972). Nutritional and environmental interactions in the behavioral development of the rat: Long-term effects. *Science* 176:68–71.

Lewis, M. and Rosenblum, L.A. (1974). *The Effect of the Infant on its Caregiver*. New York: Wiley.

Lewontin, R. (1974). *The Genetic Basis of Evolutionary Change*. New York: Columbia Univ. Press.

Lewontin, R. (1978). Adaptation. *Sci. Am.* 239(3):213–230.

Lewontin, R. (1979). Sociobiology as an adaptionist program. *Behav. Sci.* 24:5–14.

Lindburg, D.G. (1969). Rhesus monkeys: Mating season mobility of adult males. *Science* 166:1176–1178.

Lindburg, D.G. (1971). The rhesus monkey in North India: An ecological and behavioral study. In L.A. Rosenblum (ed.), *Primate Behavior: Developments in Field and Laboratory Research*, Vol. 2, pp. 1–106. New York: Academic Press.

Lindsley, D.B. (1951). Emotion. In S.S. Stevens (ed.), *Handbook of Experimental Psychology*, pp. 473–516. New York: Wiley.

Lindsley, D.B. (1961). Common factors in sensory deprivation, sensory distortion, and sensory overload. In P. Solomon, P.E. Kubzansky, P.H. Leiderman, J. Mendelson, and D. Wexler (eds.), *Sensory Deprivation*, pp. 174–194. Cambridge: Harvard Univ. Press.

Loizos, C. (1967). Play behaviour in higher primates: A review. In D. Morris (ed.), *Primate Ethology*, pp. 176–218. London: Weidenfeld and Nicolson.

Long, J.O. and Cooper, R.W. (1968). Physical growth and dental eruption in captive-bred squirrel monkeys, *Saimiri sciureus* (Leticia, Colombia). In L.A. Rosenblum and R.W. Cooper (eds.), *The Squirrel Monkey*, pp. 193–205. New York: Academic Press.

Lorenz, K. (1937a). Über die Bildung des Instinktbegriffes. *Naturwiss.* 25:289–300, 307–318, 324–331.

Lorenz, K. (1937b). The companion in the bird's world. *Auk* 54:245–273.

Lorenz, K. (1956). Play and vacuum activities. In *L'Instinct dans le Comportement des Animaux et de l'Homme*, pp. 633–638. Paris: Masson et Cie Editeurs.

Lorenz, K. (1963). *On Aggression*. New York: Harcourt, Brace and World.

Lorenz, K. (1965). *Evolution and Modification of Behavior*. Chicago: Univ. Chicago Press.

Lorenz, K. (1970). *Studies in Animal and Human Behavior*, Vol. 1, Cambridge: Harvard Univ. Press.

Lorenz, K. (1974). Analogy as a source of knowledge. *Science* 185:229–233.

Lorenz, K. (1977). *Behind the Mirror*. New York: Harcourt Brace Jovanovich.

Lovinger, S.L. (1974). Socio-dramatic play and language development in preschool disadvantaged children. *Psychol. Sch.* 11:313–320.

Loy, J. (1970). Behavioral responses of free-ranging rhesus monkeys to food shortage. *Am. J. Phys. Anthrop.* 33:263–272.

MacKinnon, J. (1971). The orang-utan in Sabah today. *Oryx* 11:141–191.

Maddi, S.R. (1968). *Personality Theories: A Comparative Analysis*. Homewood, Illinois: Dorsey.

Mahoney, M.J. (1974). *Cognition and Behavior Modification*. Cambridge, Mass.: Ballinger Publishing.

Mahoney, M.J. (1975). The sensitive scientist and empirical humanism. *Am. Psychol.* 30:864–867.

Maier, R.A. and Maier, B.M. (1973). *Comparative Psychology*. Monterey, California: Brooks/Cole.

Maltzman, I. (1960). On the training of originality. *Psychol. Rev.* 67:229–242.

Maple, T. and Zucker, E.L. (1978). Ethological studies of play behavior in captive great apes. In E.O. Smith (ed.), *Social Play in Primates*, pp. 113–142. New York: Academic Press.

Marler, P. (1968). Aggregation and dispersal: Two functions in primate communication. In P.C. Jay (ed.), *Primates: Studies in Adaption and Variability*, pp. 420–438. New York: Holt, Rinehart and Winston.

Marler, P. (1976). On animal aggression: The roles of strangeness and familiarity. *Am. Psychol.* 31:239–246.

Marler, P. and Gordon, A. (1968). The social environment of infant macaques. In D.C. Glass (ed.), *Environmental Influences*, pp. 113–128. New York: Rockefeller Univ. Press.

Marsden, H.M. (1968). Agonistic behaviour of young rhesus monkeys after changes induced in social rank of their mothers. *Anim. Behav.* 16:38–44.

Marsh, C.W. (1979). Female transference and mate choice among Tana River red colobus. *Nature* 281:568–569.

Martineau, W.H. (1972). A model of the social functions of humor. In J.H. goldstein and P.E. McGhee (eds.), *The Psychology of Humor*, pp. 116–119. New York: Academic Press.

Mason, W.A. (1960). The effects of social restriction on the behavior of rhesus monkeys: I. Free social behavior. *J. Comp. Physiol. Psychol.* 53:582–589.

Mason, W.A. (1965a). The social development of monkeys and apes. In I. DeVore (ed.), *Primate Behavior: Field Studies of Monkeys and Apes*, pp. 514–543. New York: Holt, Rinehart and Winston.

Mason, W.A. (1965b). Determinants of social behavior in young chimpanzees. In A.M. Schrier, H.F. Harlow, and F. Stollnitz, *Behavior of Nonhuman Primates*, Vol. 2, pp. 335–364. New York: Academic Press.

Mason, W.A. (1968). Early social deprivation in the nonhuman primates: Implications for human behavior. In D. Glass (ed.), *Environmental Influences*, pp. 70–101. New York: Rockefeller Univ. Press.

Mason, W.A. and Harlow, H.F. (1959). Initial responses of infant rhesus monkeys to solid foods. *Psychol. Rep.* 5:193–199.

Mason, W.A., Hill, S.D., and Thomsen, C.E. (1974). Perceptual aspects of filial attachment in monkeys. In N.F. White (ed.), *Ethology and Psychiatry*, pp. 84–93. Toronto: Univ. Toronto Press.

Mason, W.A. and Kenney, M.D. (1974). Redirection of filial attachments in rhesus monkeys: Dogs as mother surrogates. *Science* 183:1209–1211.

Massey, A. (1977). Agonistic aids and kinship in a group of pigtail macaques. *Behav. Ecol. Sociobiol.* 2:31–40.

Masters, R.D. (1976). Functional approaches to analogical comparison between species. In M. von Cranach (ed.), *Methods of Inference from Animal to Human Behavior*, pp. 73–102. Chicago: Aldine.

Mathews, D.K. and Fox, E.L. (1976). *The Physiological Basis of Physical Education and Athletics* (2nd ed.). Philadelphia: W.B. Saunders.

Maynard Smith, J. (1976). Group selection. *Q. Rev. Biol.* 51:277–283.

Mayr, E. (1972). The nature of the Darwinian revolution. *Science* 176:981–989.

Mayr, E. (1978). Evolution. *Sci. Am.* 239(3):47–55.

Mazur, A. and Robertson, L.S. (1972). *Biology and Social Behavior*. New York: Free Press.

McDougall, W. (1908). *An Introduction to Social Psychology*. London: Methuen.

McFarland, D.J. (1976). Form and function in the temporal organization of behaviour. In P.P.G. Bateson and R.A. Hinde (eds.), *Growing Points in Ethology*, pp. 55–93. Cambridge: Cambridge Univ. Press.

McGhee, P.E. (1979). *Humor: Its Origin and Development*. San Francisco: Freeman.

McGrew, W.E. (1977). Socialization and object manipulation of wild chimpanzees. In S. Chevalier-Skolnikoff and F.E. Poirier (eds.), *Primate Bio-Social Development*. pp. 261–288. New York: Garland.

McKearney, J.W. (1969). Fixed-interval schedules of electric shock presentation: Extinction and recovery of performance under different shock intensities and fixed-interval durations. *J. Exp. Anal. Behav.* 12:301–313.

McKenna, J.J. (1978). Biosocial functions of grooming behavior among the common Indian langur monkey (*Presbytis entellus*). *Am. J. Phys. Anthrop.* 48:503–510.

Mead, G.H. (1934). *Mind, Self and Society*. Chicago: Univ. Chicago Press.

Mead, G.H. (1936). *Movements of Thought in the Nineteenth Century* (Merritt H. Moore, ed.) Chicago: Univ. Chicago Press.

Meichenbaum, D. and Cameron, R. (1974). The clinical potential of modifying what clients say to themselves. In M.J. Mahoney and C.E. Thoresen (eds.), *Self-control: Power to the Person*, pp. 263–290. Monterey, California: Brooks/Cole.

Meier, G.W. and Devanney, V.D. (1974). The ontogeny of play within a society: Preliminary analysis. *Am. Zool.* 14:289–294.

Menzel, E.W., Jr. (1969). Chimpanzee utilization of space and responsiveness to objects: Age differences and comparison with macaques. *Proc. 2nd Int. Congr. Primat.*, Vol. 1, pp. 72–80. Basel: Karger.

Menzel, E.W., Jr. (1972). Spontaneous invention of ladders in a group of young chimpanzees. *Folia Primat.* 17:87–106.

Menzel, E.W., Jr. (1973). Chimpanzee spatial memory organization. *Science* 182:943–945.

Menzel, E.W., Jr. (1974). A group of young chimpanzees in a one-acre field. In

A.M. Schrier and F. Stollnitz (eds.), *Behavior of Nonhuman Primates*, Vol. 5, pp. 83–153. New York: Academic Press.

Michael, R.P., Bonsall, R.W., and Zumpe, D. (1978). Consort bonding and operant behavior by female rhesus monkeys. *J. Comp. Physiol. Psychol.* 92:837–845.

Michael, R.P. and Keverne, E.B. (1968). Pheromones in the communication of sexual status in primates. *Nature* 218:746–749.

Miles, R.C. (1965). Discrimination-learning sets. In A.M. Schrier, H.F. Harlow, and F. Stollnitz (eds.), *Behavior of Nonhuman Primates*, Vol. 1, pp. 51–95. New York: Academic Press.

Miller, D.B. (1979). Review of *Sociobiology and Human Nature*. *Am. Sci.* 67:477.

Miller, L.G. (1976a). Fated genes. *J. Hist. Behav. Sci.*, April, pp. 183–190.

Miller, L.G. (1976b). Philosophy, dichotomies, and sociobiology. Hastings Center Report (Oct. 25, 1976), pp. 20–25.

Miller, N.E. (1948). Studies of fear as an acquirable drive: I. Fear as motivation and fear-reduction as reinforcement in the learning of new responses. *J. Exp. Psychol.* 38:89–101.

Miller, N.E. (1969). Learning of visceral and glandular responses. *Science* 163:434–445.

Miller, R.E., Caul, W.F., and Mirsky, I.A. (1967). Communication of affects between feral and socially isolated monkeys. *J. Pers. Soc. Psychol.* 7:231–239.

Miller, S. (1973). Ends, means, and galumphing: Some leitmotifs of play. *Am. Anthrop.* 75:87–98.

Milton, K. (1977). The foraging strategy of the howler monkey in the tropical forest of Barro Colorado Island, Panama. Doct. diss., New York Univ.

Milton, K. and May, M.L. (1976). Body weight, diet and home range area in primates. *Nature* 259:459–462.

Missakian, E.A. (1969). Effects of social deprivation on the development of patterns of social behavior. *Proc. 2nd Int. Congr. Primat.*, Vol. 2, pp. 50–55. Basel: Karger.

Mitchell, G. (1977). Paternal behavior in nonhuman primates. In J. Money and H. Musaph (eds.), *Handbook of Sexology*, pp. 749–759. New York: Elsevier.

Mitchell, G.D., Ruppenthal, G.C., Raymond, E.J., and Harlow, H.F. (1966). Long-term effects of multiparous and primiparous monkey mother rearing. *Child Dev.* 37:781–791.

Mitchell, G. and Schroers, L. (1973). Birth order and parental experience in monkeys and man. In H. Reese (ed.), *Advances in Child Development and Behavior*, Vol. 13, pp. 159–184. New York: Academic Press.

Mitchell, G. and Stevens, C.W. (1968). Primiparous and multiparous monkey mothers in a mildly stressful social situation: First three months. *Dev. Psychobiol.* 1:280–286.

Mitchell, G. and Tokunaga, D.H. (1976). Sex differences in nonhuman primate grooming. *Behav. Processes* 1:335–345.

Montagu, M.F.A. (1968). *Man and Aggression*. New York: Oxford Univ. Press.

Moore, R. and Goldiamond, I. (1964). Errorless establishment of visual discrimination using fading procedures. *J. Exp. Anal. Behav.* 7:269–272.

Morgan, C.L. (1894). *Introduction to Comparative Psychology* (2nd ed. 1906). New York: Scribner's.

Mori, A. (1977). Intra-troop spacing mechanism of the wild Japanese monkeys of the Koshima troop. *Primates* 18:331–357.

Mori, U. (1979). Development of sociability and social status. In M. Kawai (ed.), *Ecological and Sociological Studies of Gelada Baboons*, pp. 125–154. Basel: Karger.

Morris, D. (1964). The response of animals to a restricted environment. *Symp. Zool. Soc. Lond.* 13:99–118.

Morris, D. (1967). *The Naked Ape*. New York: McGraw-Hill.

Mowrer, O.H. (1960). *Learning Theory and Behavior*. New York: Wiley.

Moynihan, M. (1976). *The New World Primates*. Princeton, N.J.: Princeton Univ. Press.

Murphy, J.V., Miller, R.E., and Mirsky, I.A. (1955). Interanimal conditioning in the monkey, *J. Comp. Physiol. Psychol.* 48:211–214.

Mussen, P. and Eisenberg-Berg, N. (1977). *Roots of Caring, Sharing and Helping*. San Francisco: Freeman.

Nadler, R.D. (1976). Sexual behavior of captive lowland gorillas. *Arch. Sex. Behav.* 5:487–502.

Nadler, R. and Braggio, J. (1974). Sex and species differences in captive-reared juvenile chimpanzees and orang-utans. *J. Hum. Evol.* 3:541–550.

Nash, L.T. (1978a). The development of the mother-infant relationship in wild baboons (*Papio anubis*). *Anim. Behav.* 26:746–759.

Nash, L.T. (1978b). Kin preference in the behavior of young baboons. In D.J. Chivers and J. Herbert (eds.), *Recent Advances in Primatology*, Vol. 1, pp. 71–83. New York: Academic Press.

Neville, M. (1968a). A free-ranging rhesus monkey troop lacking adult males. *J. Mammal.* 49:771–773.

Neville, M. (1968b). Ecology and activity of Himalayan foothill rhesus monkeys (*Macaca mulatta*). *Ecology* 49:110–123.

Nevin, J.A. (1971a). Stimulus control. In J.A. Nevin and G.S. Reynolds (eds.), *The Study of Behavior*, pp. 114–152. Glenview, Ill.: Scott, Foresman.

Nevin, J.A. (1971b). Conditioned reinforcement. In J.A. Nevin and G.S. Reynolds (eds.), *The Study of Behavior*, pp. 154–198. Glenview, Ill.: Scott, Foresman.

Nevin, J.A. and Reynolds, G.S. (1971). *The Study of Behavior*. Glenview, Ill.: Scott, Foresman.

Nicolson, N.A. (1977). A comparison of early behavioral development in wild and captive chimpanzees. In S. Chevalier-Skolnikoff and F.E. Poirier (eds.), *Primate Bio-Social Development*, pp. 529–560. New York: Garland.

Nishida, T. (1966). A sociological study of solitary male monkeys. *Primates* 7:141–204.

Nishida, T. and Kawanaka, K. (1972). Inter-unit-group relationship among wild chimpanzees of the Mahali Mountains. *Kyoto Univ. Afr. Stud.* 7:131–169.

Nishimura, A. (1973). Age changes of the vocalization in free-ranging Japanese monkeys. *Symp. 4th Int. Congr. Primat.*, Vol. 1, pp. 76–87. Basel: Karger.

Norikoshi, K. and Koyama, N. (1975). Group shifting and social organization among Japanese monkeys. *Symp. 5th Congr. Int'l. Primat. Soc.*, pp. 43–61. Tokyo: Science Press.

Novak, M.A. (1979). Social recovery of monkeys isolated for the first year of life: I. Long-term assessment. *Dev. Psychol.* 15:50–61.

Oakley, F.B. and Reynolds, P.C. (1976). Differing responses to social play deprivation in two species of macaque. In D.F. Lancy and B.A. Tindall (eds.), *The Anthropological Study of Play: Problems and Perspectives*, pp. 179–188. Cornwall, N.Y.: Leisure Press.

Ohta, T. and Kimura, M. (1975). Theoretical analysis of electrophoretically detectable polymorphisms: Models of very slightly deleterious mutations. *Am. Nat.* 109:137–145.

Opie, I. and Opie, P. (1959). *The Lore and Language of School Children*. Oxford: Oxford Univ. Press.

Oppenheimer, J.R. (1977). *Presbytis entellus*, the hanuman langur. In Prince Rainier III and G.H. Bourne (eds.), *Primate Conservation*, pp. 469–512. New York: Academic Press.

Oster, G.F. and Wilson, E.O. (1978). *Caste and Ecology in the Social Insects*. Princeton, N.J.: Princeton Univ. Press.

Packer, C. (1975). Male transfer in olive baboons. *Nature* 255:219–220.

Packer, C. and Pusey, A.E. (1979). Female aggression and male membership in troops of Japanese macaques and olive baboons. *Folia Primat.* 31:212–218.

Parker, C.E. (1973). Manipulatory behavior and responsiveness. In D.M. Rumbaugh (ed.), *Gibbon and Siamang*, Vol. 2, pp. 185–207. Basel: Karger.

Parker, C.E. (1974). Behavioral diversity in ten species of nonhuman primates. *J. Comp. Physiol. Psychol.* 87:930–937.

Parker, C.E. (1978). Opportunism and the rise of intelligence. *J. Hum. Evol.* 7:597–608.

Paterson, J.D. (1973). Ecologically differentiated patterns of aggressive and sexual behavior in two troops of Ugandan baboons, *Papio anubis*. *Am. J. Phys. Anthrop.* 38:641–647.

Patterson, B. (1974). Musical dynamics. *Sci. Am.* 231(5):78–95.

Patterson, F.G. (1978a). The gestures of a gorilla: Language acquisition in another pongid. *Brain Lang.* 12:72–97.

Patterson, F.G. (1978b). Conversations with a gorilla. *Nat. Geogr.* 154:438–465.

Patton, H.D. and Ruch, T.C. (1944). Preference thresholds for quinine hydrochloride in chimpanzee, monkey and rat. *J. Comp. Psychol.* 37:35–49.

Pavlov, I.P. (1927). *Conditioned Reflexes*. Oxford: Oxford Univ. Press.

Perin, C.T. (1943). A quantitative investigation of the delay-of-reinforcement gradient. *J. Exp. Psychol.* 32:37–51.

Peterson, B.W., Franck, J.I., Pitts, N.G., and Daunton, N.G. (1976). Changes in responses of medial pontomedullary reticular neurons during repetitive cutaneous, vestibular, cortical, and tectal stimulation. *J. Neurophysiol.* 39:564–581.

Pitcairn, T.K. (1976). Attention and social structure in *Macaca fascicularis*. In M.R.A. Chance and R.R. Larsen (eds.), *The Social Structure of Attention*, pp. 51–81. New York: Wiley.

Platt, J.R. (1961). Beauty: Pattern and change. In D.W. Fiske and S.R. Maddi (eds.), *Functions of Varied Experience*, pp. 402–430. Homewood, Ill.: Dorsey.

Ploog, D., Hopf, S., und Winter, P. (1967). Ontogenese des Verhaltens von Totenkopfaffen (*Saimiri sciureus*). *Psychol. Forsch.* 31:1–41.

Poirier, F.E. (1969). Behavioral flexibility and intertroop variation among Nilgiri langurs (*Presbytis johnii*) in South India. *Folia Primat.* 11:119–133.

Poirier, F.E. (1970). Nilgiri langur ecology and social behavior. In L.A. Rosenblum (ed.), *Primate Behavior: Developments in Field and Laboratory Research*, pp. 251–383. New York: Academic Press.

Poirier, F.E. (1972a). Introduction. In F.E. Poirier (ed.), *Primate Socialization*, pp. 3–28. New York: Random House.

Poirier, F.E. (1972b). The St. Kitts green monkey (*Cercopithecus aethiops sabaeus*): Ecology, population dynamics, and selected behavioral traits. *Folia Primat.* 17:20–55.

Poirier, F.E., Bellisari, A., and Haines, L. (1978). Functions of primate play behavior. In E.O. Smith (ed.), *Social Play in Primates*, pp. 143–168. New York: Academic Press.

Poirier, F.E. and Smith, E.O. (1974). Socializing functions of primate play behavior. *Am. Zool.* 14:275–287.

Premack, D. (1971). On the assessment of language competence in the chimpanzee. In A.M. Schrier and F. Stollnitz (eds.), *Behavior of Nonhuman Primates*, Vol. 4, pp. 185–228. New York: Academic Press.

Premack, D. and Woodruff, G. (1978). Chimpanzee problem-solving: A test for comprehension. *Science* 202:532–535.

Pryor, K., Haag, R., and O'Reilly, J. (1969). The creative porpoise: Training for novel behavior. *J. Exp. Anal. Behav.* 12:653–661.

Pycraft, W.P. (1912). *The Infancy of Animals*. London: Hutchinson.

Quadagno, J.S. (1979). Paradigms in evolutionary theory: The sociobiological model of natural selection. *Am. Soc. Rev.* 44:100–109.

Rachlin, H. (1976). *Introduction to Modern Behaviorism* (2nd ed.). San Francisco: Freeman.

Ransom, T.W. (1971). Ecology and behaviour of the baboon, *Papio anubis*, at the Gombe Stream National Park Tanzania. Doct. diss., Univ. California, Berkeley.

Ransom, T.W. and Rowell, T.E. (1972). Early social development of feral baboons. In F.E. Poirier (ed.), *Primate Socialization*, pp. 105–144. New York: Random House.

Redican, W.K. (1975). Facial expression in nonhuman primates. In L.A. Rosenblum (ed.), *Primate Behavior: Developments in Field and Laboratory Research*, Vol. 4, pp. 104–194. New York: Academic Press.

Redican, W.K. (1976). Adult male-infant interactions in nonhuman primates. In M.E. Lamb (ed.), *The Role of the Father in Child Development*, pp. 345–385. New York: Wiley.

Redican, W.K., Kellicutt, M.H., and Mitchell, G. (1971). Preferences for facial expressions in juvenile rhesus monkeys (*Macaca mulatta*). *Dev. Psychol.* 5:539.

Redl, F. (1959). The impact of game ingredients on children's play behavior. In B. Schaffner (ed.), *Group Processes*, pp. 33–81. New York: Joshiah Macy, Jr. Foundation.

Reed, E. (1978). *Sexism and Science*. New York: Pathfinder Press.

Reese, E. (1972). *The Analysis of Human Operant Behavior*. Dubuque, Iowa: Wm. C. Brown.

Reite, M., Seiler, C., and Short, R. (1978). Loss of your mother is more than loss of a mother. *Am. J. Psychiatr.* 135:370–371.

Revusky, S.H. and Garcia, J. (1970). Learned associations over long delays. In G.H. Bower (ed.), *The Psychology of Learning and Motivation*, Vol. 4, pp. 1–84. New York: Academic Press.

Reynolds, V. (1976). *The Biology of Human Action.* San Francisco: Freeman.

Rheingold, H.L. and Eckerman, C.O. (1970). The infant separates himself from his mother. *Science* 168:78–90.

Rheingold, H.L., Stanley, W.C., and Cooley, J.A. (1962). Method for studying exploratory behavior in infants. *Science* 136:1054–1055.

Rhine, R.J. (1975). The order of movement of yellow baboons (*Papio cynocephalus*). *Folia Primat.* 23:72–104.

Rhine, R.J. and Hendy-Nelly, H. (1978). Social development of stumptail macaques (*Macaca arctoides*): Synchrony of changes in mother-infant interactions and individual behaviors during the first 60 days of life. *Primates* 19:681–692.

Rhine, R.J. and Westlund, B.J. (1978). The nature of a primary feeding habit in different age-sex classes of yellow baboons (*Papio cynocephalus*). *Folia Primat.* 30:64–79.

Richard, A. (1974). Intra-specific variation in the social organization and ecology of *Propithecus verreauxi*. *Folia Primat.* 22:178–207.

Richerson, P.J. and Boyd, R. (1978). A dual inheritance model of the human evolutionary process. I: Basic postulates and a simple model. *J. Soc. Biol. Struct.* 1:127–154.

Richter, C.P. (1954). Behavioral regulators of carbohydrate homeostasis. *Acta Neuroveg.* 9:247–259.

Riesen, A.H. (1961). Stimulation as a requirement for growth and function in behavioral development. In D.W. Fiske and S.R. Maddi (eds.), *Functions of Varied Experience*, pp. 57–80. Homewood, Ill.: Dorsey.

Riesen, A.H. (1965). Effects of early deprivation of photic stimulation. In S.F. Olser and R.E. Cooke (eds.), *The Biosocial Basis of Mental Retardation*, pp. 61–85. Baltimore: Johns Hopkins Univ. Press.

Rilling, M. (1977). Stimulus control and inhibitory processes. In W.K. Honig and J.E.R. Staddon (eds.), *Handbook of Operant Behavior*, pp. 432–480. Englewood Cliffs, N.J.: Prentice-Hall.

Riss, D. and Goodall, J. (1977). The recent rise to the alpha-rank in a population of free living chimpanzees. *Folia Primat.* 27:134–151.

Roberts, J.M., Arth, M.J., and Bush, R.R. (1959). Games in culture. *Am. Anthrop.* 61:597–605.

Roberts, J.M. and Sutton-Smith, B. (1962). Child training and game involvement. *Ethnology* 1:166–185.

Roberts, J.M., Sutton-Smith, B., and Kendon, A. (1963). Strategy in games and folk tales. *J. Soc. Psychol.* 61:185–199.

Roberts, W.W., Dember, W.N., and Brodwick, M. (1962). Alternation and exploration in rats with hippocampal lesions. *J. Comp. Physiol. Psychol.* 55:695–700.

Robinson, J.A. and Bridson, W.E. (1978). Neonatal hormone patterns in the macaque: I. Steroids. *Biol. of Reprod.* 19:773–778.

Robson, K.S. (1967). The role of eye-contact in attachment. *J. Child Psychol. Psychiatr.* 8:13–25.

Rogers, C.M. (1973). Implications of a primate early rearing experiment for the concepts of culture. *Symp. 4th Int. Congr. Primat.* Vol. 1, pp. 185–191. Basel: Karger.

Rogers, C.M. and Davenport, R.K. (1969). Sexual behavior of differentially-reared chimpanzees. *Recent Advances in Primatology*, Vol. 1, pp. 173–177. New York: Academic Press.

Rogers, C.M. and Davenport, R.K. (1970). Chimpanzee maternal behavior. In G.H. Bourne (ed.), *The Chimpanzee*, Vol. 3, pp. 361–368. Basel: Karger.

Rose, M.D. (1977). Interspecific play between free ranging guerezas (*Colobus guereza*) and vervet monkeys (*Cercopithecus aethiops*). *Primates* 18:957–964.

Rosenblum, L.A. (1971a). Kinship interaction patterns in pigtail and bonnet macaques. *Proc. 3rd Int. Congr. Primat.*, Vol. 3, pp. 79–84. Basel: Karger.

Rosenblum, L.A. (1971b). The ontogeny of mother-infant relations in macaques. In H. Moltz (ed.), *Ontogeny of Vertebrate Behavior*, pp. 315–367. New York: Academic Press.

Rosenblum, L.A. (1974a). Sex differences in mother-infant attachment in monkeys. In R.C. Friedman, R.M. Richart, and R.L. Vande Wiele (eds.), *Sex Differences in Behavior*, pp. 123–141. New York: Wiley.

Rosenblum, L.A. (1974b). Sex differences, environmental complexity, and mother-infant relations. *Arch. Sex. Behav.* 3:117–128.

Rosenblum, L.A. and Alpert, S. (1977). Response to mother and stranger: A first step in socialization. In S. Chevalier-Skolnikoff and F.E. Poirier (eds.), *Primate Bio-Social Development*, pp. 463–477. New York: Garland.

Rosenblum, L.A. and Cross, H.A. (1963). Performance of neonatal monkeys in the visual-cliff situation. *Am. J. Psychol.* 76:318–320.

Rosenblum, L.A. and Kaufman, I.C. (1967). Laboratory observations of early mother-infant relations in pigtail and bonnet macaques. In S.A. Altmann (ed.), *Social Communication among Primates*, pp. 33–41. Chicago: Univ. Chicago Press.

Rosenblum, L.A. and Lowe, A. (1971). The influence of familiarity during rearing on subsequent partner preferences in squirrel monkeys. *Psychon. Sci.* 23:35–37.

Rosenthal, T.L. and Zimmerman, B.J. (1978). *Social Learning and Cognition*. New York: Academic Press.

Rosenzweig, M.R. (1976). Effects of environment on brain and behavior in animals. In E. Schopler and R.J. Reichler (ed.), *Psychopathology and Child Development*, pp. 33–49. New York: Plenum.

Rowell, T.E. (1966a). Forest living baboons in Uganda. *Proc. Zool. Soc. Lond.* 149:344–364.

Rowell, T.E. (1966b). Hierarchy in the organization of a captive baboon group. *Anim. Behav.* 14:430–443.

Rowell, T.E. (1969). Long-term changes in a population of Ugandan baboons. *Folia Primat.* 11:241–254.

Rowell, T.E. (1972). *The Social Behaviour of Monkeys*. Baltimore: Penguin.

Rowell, T.E. (1974a). Contrasting adult male roles in different species of non-human primates. *Arch. Sex. Behav.* 3:143–149.

Rowell, T.E. (1974b). The concept of social dominance. *Behav. Biol.* 11:131–154.

Rowell, T.E. (1979). How would we know if social organization were *not* adaptive? In I.S. Bernstein and E.O. Smith (eds.), *Primate Ecology and Human Origins: Ecological Influences on Social Organization*, pp. 1–22. New York: Garland.

Rowell, T.E. and Dixson, A.F. (1975). Changes in social organization during the breeding season of wild talapoin monkeys. *J. Reprod. Fertil.* 43:419–434.

Roy, D.F. (1959–60). "Banana time"—job satisfaction and informal interaction. *Hum. Organ.* 18:158–168.

Rumbaugh, D.M. (1970). Learning skills of anthropoids. In L.A. Rosenblum (ed.), *Primate Behavior: Developments in Field and Laboratory* Research, Vol. 1, pp. 1–70. New York: Academic Press.

Rumbaugh, D.M. (1974). Comparative primate learning and its contributions to understanding development, play, intelligence and language. In A.B. Chiarelli (ed.), *Perspectives in Primate Biology*, Vol. 9, pp. 253–281. New York: Plenum.

Rumbaugh, D.M., Gill, T.V. and Wright, S.C. (1973). Readiness to attend to visual foreground cues. *J. Hum. Evol.* 2:181–188.

Rumbaugh, D.M., Riesen, A.H., and Wright, S. (1972). Creative responsiveness to objects: A report of a pilot study with young apes. *Folia Primat.* 17:397–403.

Ruse, M. (1978). Sociobiology: A philosophical analysis. In A.L. Caplan (ed.), *The Sociobiology Debate*, pp. 355–375. New York: Harper & Row.

Rutter, D.R. and Stephenson, G.M. (1979). The functions of looking: Effects of friendship on gaze. *Br. J. Soc. Clin. Psychol.* 18:203–205.

Ruyle, E.E. (1973). Genetic and cultural pools: Some suggestions for a unified theory of biosocial evolution. *Hum. Ecol.* 1:201–215.

Saayman, G.S. (1971). Behaviour of the adult males in a troop of free-ranging chacma baboons (*Papio ursinus*). *Folia Primat.* 15:36–57.

Sackett, G.P. (1966). Monkeys reared in visual isolation with pictures as visual input: Evidence for an innate releasing mechanism. *Science* 154:1468–1472.

Sackett, G.P. (1971). Isolation rearing in monkeys: Diffuse and specific effects on later behavior. *Colloq. Int. Cent. Nat. Rech. Sci.* 198:61–110.

Sackett, G.P. (1972). Exploratory behavior of rhesus monkeys as a function of rearing experiences and sex. *Dev. Psychol.* 6:260–270.

Sackett, G.P. and Ruppenthal, G.C. (1973). Development of monkeys after varied experience during infancy. In S.A. Barnett (ed.), *Ethology and Development*, pp. 52–87. London: Spastics Int. Med. Publ.

Sade, D.S. (1965). Some aspects of parent-offspring and sibling relations in a group of rhesus monkeys, with a discussion of grooming. *Am. J. Phys. Anthrop.* 23:1–17.

Sade, D.S. (1967). Determinants of dominance in a group of free-ranging rhesus monkeys. In S.A. Altmann (ed.), *Social Communication among Primates*, pp. 99–114. Chicago: Univ. Chicago Press.

Sade, D.S. (1972). A longitudinal study of social behavior of rhesus monkeys. In R. Tuttle (ed.), *The Functional and Evolutionary Biology of Primates*, pp. 378–398. Chicago: Aldine-Atherton.

Sahlins, M. (1976). *The Use and Abuse of Biology: An Anthropological Critique of Sociobiology*. Ann Arbor: Univ. Michigan Press.

Salzen, E.A. (1966). The interaction of experience, stimulus characteristics and exogenous androgen in the behaviour of domestic chicks. *Behaviour* 26:286–322.

Salzen, E.A. and Meyer, C.C. (1968). Reversibility of imprinting. *J. Comp. Physiol. Psychol.* 66:269–275.

Samuels, I. (1959). Reticular mechanisms and behavior. *Psychol. Bull.* 56:1–25.

Sato, M., Hiji, Y., Ito, H., and Imoto, T. (1977a). Sweet taste sensitivity in Japanese macaques. In M.R. Kare and O. Maller (eds.), *The Chemical Senses and Nutrition*, pp. 327–341. New York: Academic Press.

Sato, M., Hiji, Y., and Ito, H. (1977b). Taste discrimination in the monkey. *Olfaction Taste, Proc. Int. Symp., 6th,* Vol. 6, pp. 233–240. Washington, D.C.: Information Retrieval.

Savage-Rumbaugh, E.S. and Wilkerson, B.J. (1978). Socio-sexual behavior in *Pan paniscus* and *Pan troglodytes*: A comparative study. *J. Hum. Evol.* 7:327–344.

Schaller, G.B. (1963). *The Mountain Gorilla*. Chicago: Univ. Chicago Press.

Schaller, G.B. (1972). *The Serengeti Lion*. Chicago: Univ. Chicago Press.

Schiff, W. (1965). Perception of impending collision: A study of visually directed avoidant behavior. *Psychol. Monogr.* 79(11):1–26.

Schiller, P.H. (1957). Innate motor action as a basis of learning: Manipulative patterns in the chimpanzee. In C. Schiller (ed.), *Instinctive Behavior*, pp. 264–287. New York: International Universities Press.

Schneirla, T.C. (1956). The interrelationships of the "innate" and the "acquired" in instinctive behavior. In P.-P. Grassé (ed.), *L'Instinct dans le Comportement des Animaux et de l'Homme*, pp. 387–452. Paris: Masson.

Schneirla, T.C. (1959). An evolutionary and developmental theory of biphasic processes underlying approach and withdrawal. In M.R. Jones (ed.), *Nebraska Symposium on Motivation*, pp. 1–42. Lincoln: Univ. Nebraska Press.

Scholtz, G. and Ellis, M. (1975). Repeated exposure to objects and peers in a play setting. *J. Exp. Child Psychol.* 19:448–455.

Schrank, R. (1978). *Ten Thousand Working Days*. Cambridge, Mass.: MIT Press.

Schusterman, R.J. and Sjoberg, A. (1969). Early behavior patterns of squirrel monkeys (*Saimiri sciureus*). *Proc. 2nd Int. Congr. Primat.*, Vol. 1, pp. 194–203. Basel: Karger.

Seay, B. (1966). Maternal behavior in primiparous and multiparous rhesus monkeys. *Folia Primat.* 4:146–168.

Seligman, M.E.P. (1970). On the generality of the laws of learning. *Psychol. Rev.* 77:406–418.

Seligman, M.E.P. and Hager, J. (1972). *The Biological Boundaries of Learning*. New York: Appleton-Century-Crofts.

Segundo, J.P., Takenaka, T. and Encabo, H. (1967). Somatic sensory properties of bulbar reticular neurons. *J. Neurophysiol.* 30:1221–1238.

Seyfarth, R.M. (1976). Social relationships among adult female baboons. *Anim. Behav.* 24:917–938.

Seyfarth, R.M. (1977). A model of social grooming among adult female monkeys. *J. Theor. Biol.* 65:671–698.

Sidman, M. (1966). Avoidance behavior. In W.K. Honig (ed.), *Operant Behavior*, pp. 448–498. New York: Appleton-Century-Crofts.

Siegel, J.M. and McGinty, D.J. (1977). Pontine reticular formation neurons: Relationship of discharge to motor activity. *Science* 196:678–680.

Simonds, P.E. (1965). The bonnet macaque in south India. In I. DeVore (ed.),

Primate Behavior: Field Studies of Monkeys and Apes, pp. 175–196. New York: Holt, Rinehart and Winston.

Simonds, P.E. (1974a). Sex differences in bonnet macaque networks and social structure. *Arch. Sex. Behav.* 3:151–166.

Simonds, P.E. (1974b). *The Social Primates*. New York: Harper and Row.

Singer, J.L. (1973). *The Child's World of Make-Believe*. New York: Academic Press.

Singh, R.K. and Sen, N.N. (1977–78). A note on adoption of two rhesus juveniles by a langur group. *J. Sci. Res. Banaras Hindu Univ.* 281:135–138.

Singh, S.D. (1968). Social interactions between the rural and urban monkeys, *Macaca mulatta*. *Primates* 9:69–74.

Singh, S.D. (1969). Urban monkeys. *Sci. Am.* 221(1):108–115.

Sipes, R.G. (1973). War, sports and aggression: An empirical test of two rival theories. *Am. Anthrop.* 75:64–86.

Smilansky, S. (1968). *The Effects of Sociodramatic Play on Disadvantaged Preschool Children*. New York: Wiley.

Southwick, C.H. (1963). Challenging aspects of the behavioral ecology of howling monkeys. In C.H. Southwick (ed.), *Primate Social Behavior*, pp. 185–191. Princeton, N.J.: Van Nostrand.

Southwick, C.H. (1972). Aggression among nonhuman primates. *Addison-Wesley Module in Anthropology*, 23:1–23. Reading, Mass.: Addison-Wesley.

Southwick, C.H., Beg, M.A., and Siddiqi, M.R. (1965). Rhesus monkeys in north India. In I. DeVore (ed.), *Primate Behavior: Field Studies of Monkeys and Apes*, pp. 111–159. New York: Holt, Rinehart and Winston.

Spence, K.W. (1938). Gradual versus sudden solution of discrimination problems by chimpanzees. *J. Comp. Psychol.* 25:213–222.

Spencer-Booth, Y. (1968). The behaviour of group companions towards rhesus monkey infants. *Anim. Behav.* 16:541–557.

Spuhler, J.N. and Jorde, L.B. (1975). Primate phylogeny, ecology and social behavior. *J. Anthrop. Res.* 31:376–405.

Staats, A.W. (1963). *Complex Human Behavior*. New York: Holt, Rinehart and Winston.

Staats, A.W. (1968). *Learning, Language and Cognition*. New York: Holt, Rinehart and Winston.

Staats, A.W. (1975). *Social Behaviorism*. Homewood, Ill.: Dorsey.

Steiner, J. (1970). Observing responses and uncertainty reduction, II: The effect of varying the probability of reinforcement. *Q. J. Exp. Psychol.* 22:592–599.

Stern, D.N. (1974). Mother and infant at play: The dyadic interaction involving facial, vocal, and gaze behaviors. In M. Lewis and L.A. Rosenblum (eds.), *The Effect of the Infant on its Caregiver*, pp. 187–213. New York: Wiley.

Stern, D. (1977). *The First Relationship: Mother and Infant*. Cambridge, Mass.: Harvard Univ. Press.

Stevenson-Hinde, J. and Zunz, M. (1978). Subjective assessment of individual rhesus monkeys. *Primates* 19:473–482.

Stoffer, G.R. and Stoffer, J.E. (1976). Stress and aversive behavior in non-human primates: A retrospective bibliography (1914–1974) indexed by type of primate, aversive event, and topical area. *Primates* 17:547–578.

Stoltz, L.P. and Saayman, G.S. (1970). Ecology and behavior of baboons in northern Transvaal. *Ann. Transvaal Mus.* 26(5):99–143, pps. 10–17.

Strayer, F.F. and Harris, P.J. (1979). Social cohesion among captive squirrel monkeys (*Saimiri sciureus*). *Behav. Ecol. Sociobiol.* 5:93–110.

Stretch, R., Orloff, E.R., and Dalrymple, S.D. (1968). Maintenance of responding by fixed-interval schedule of electric shock presentation in squirrel monkeys. *Science* 162:583–586.

Struhsaker, T.T. (1967a). Social structure among vervet monkeys (*Cercopithecus aethiops*). *Behaviour* 29:83–121.

Struhsaker, T.T. (1967b). Ecology of vervet monkeys (*Cercopithecus aethiops*) in the Masai-Amboseli Game Reserve, Kenya. *Ecology* 48:891–904.

Stumpf, C. (1965). The fast component in the electrical activity of the rabbit's hippocampus. *Electroencephalogr. Clin. Neurophysiol.* 18:477–486.

Sugiyama, Y. (1967). Social organization of hanuman langurs. In S.A. Altmann (ed.), *Social Communication among Primates*, pp. 221–236. Chicago: Univ. Chicago Press.

Sugiyama, Y. (1968). Social organization of chimpanzees in the Budongo Forest, Uganda. *Primates* 9:225–258.

Sugiyama, Y. (1969). Social behavior of chimpanzees in the Budongo Forest, Uganda. *Primates* 10:197–225.

Sugiyama, Y. (1976). Characteristics of the ecology of the Himalayan langurs. *J. Hum. Evol.* 5:249–277.

Sugiyama, Y. and Koman, H. (1979). Social structure and dynamics of wild chimpanzees at Bossou, Guinea. *Primates* 20:323–339.

Suomi, S.J. (1977). Adult male-infant interactions among monkeys living in nuclear families. *Child Dev.* 48:1255–1270.

Suomi, S.J. and Harlow, H.F. (1971). Monkeys at play. *Nat. Hist.* 80(10):72–75. December, 1971.

Sussman, R.W. (1977). Socialization, social structure, and ecology of two sympatric species of *Lemur*. In S. Chevalier-Skolnikoff and F.E. Poirier (eds.), *Primate Bio-Social Development*, pp. 515–528. New York: Garland.

Sutton-Smith, B. and Rosenberg, B.G. (1961). Sixty years of historical change in the game preferences of American children. *J. Am. Folklore* 74:17–46.

Suzuki, A. (1969). An ecological study of chimpanzees in a savanna woodland. *Primates* 10:103–148.

Suzuki, A. (1979). The variation and adaptation of social groups of chimpanzees and black and white colobus monkeys. In I.S. Bernstein and E.O. Smith (eds.), *Primate Ecology and Human Origins: Ecological Influences on Social Organization*, pp. 153–173. New York: Garland.

Symons, D. (1978). *Play and Aggression: A Study of Rhesus Monkeys*. New York: Columbia Univ. Press.

Szacki, J. (1979). *History of Sociological Thought*. Westwood, Conn.: Greenwood Press.

Tartabini, A. and Dienske, H. (1979). Social play and rank order in rhesus monkeys (*Macaca mulatta*). *Behav. Processes* 4:375–383.

Tartabini, A., Genta, M.L., and Bertacchini, P.A. (1980). Mother-infant interaction and rank order in rhesus monkeys (*Macaca mulatta*). *J. Hum. Evol.* 9:139–146.

Teitelbaum, P. (1977). Levels of integration of the operant. In W.K. Honig and J.E.R. Staddon (eds.), *Handbook of Operant Behavior*, pp. 7–27. Englewood Cliffs, N.J.: Prentice-Hall.

Teleki, G. (1973). *The Predatory Behavior of Wild Chimpanzees*. Lewisberg, Pa.: Bucknell Univ. Press.

Teleki, G., Hunt, E.E., Jr., and Pfifferling, J.H. (1976). Demographic observations (1963–1973) on the chimpanzees of Gombe National Park, Tanzania. *J. Hum. Evol.* 5:559–598.

Terrace, H.S. (1971). Classical conditioning. In J.A. Nevin and G.S. Reynolds (eds.), *The Study of Behavior*, pp. 70–112. Glenview, Ill.: Scott, Foresman.

Testa, T.J. and Mack, D. (1977). The effects of social isolation on sexual behavior in *Macaca fascicularis*. In S. Chevalier-Skolnikoff and F.E. Poirier (eds.), *Primate Bio-Social Development*, pp. 407–438. New York: Garland.

Thibaut, J.W. and Kelley, H.H. (1959). *The Social Psychology of Groups*. New York: Wiley.

Thorington, R.W., Jr. (1967). Feeding and activity of *Cebus* and *Saimiri* in a Colombian forest. In D. Starck, R. Schneider, and H.-J. Kuhn (eds.), *Neue Ergebnisse der Primatologie*, pp. 180–184. Stuttgart: Gustav Fischer Verlag.

Thorington, R.W., Jr. (1968). Observations of squirrel monkeys in a Colombian forest. In L.A. Rosenblum and R.W. Cooper (eds.), *The Squirrel Monkey*, pp. 69–85. New York: Academic Press.

Tiger, L. (1969). *Men in Groups*, New York: Random House.

Tiger, L. and Fox, R. (1971). *The Imperial Animal*. New York: Holt, Rinehart and Winston.

Tinbergen, N. (1951). *The Study of Instinct*. New York: Oxford Univ. Press.

Tinbergen, N. (1963a). On aims and methods of ethology. *Z. Tierpsychol.* 20:410–429.

Tinbergen, N. (1963b). *The Herring Gull's World*. London: Collins.

Tinbergen, N. (1973). *The Animal in its World*. Cambridge, Mass.: Harvard Univ. Press.

Trivers, R.L. (1971). The evolution of reciprocal altruism. *Q. Rev. Biol.* 46:35–57.

Trivers, R.L. (1972). Parental investment and sexual selection. In B. Campbell (ed.), *Sexual Selection and the Descent of Man, 1871–1971*, pp. 136–179. Chicago: Aldine.

Trivers, R.L. (1974). Parent-offspring conflict. *Am. Zool.* 14:249–264.

Tsumori, A. (1967). Newly acquired behavior and social interactions of Japanese monkeys. In S.A. Altmann (ed.), *Social Communication among Primates*, pp. 207–219. Chicago: Univ. Chicago Press.

Vacha, E.F. (1976). Children's culture and child socialization. Doct. diss., Univ. California, Santa Barbara.

Vandenbergh, J.G. (1967). The development of social structure in free-ranging rhesus monkeys. *Behaviour* 29:179–194.

van den Berghe, P.L. (1975). *Man in Society*. New York: Elsevier.

van Hooff, J. (1967). The facial displays in the catarrhine monkeys and apes. In D. Morris (ed.), *Primate Ethology*, pp. 7–68. London: Weidenfeld and Nicolson.

van Hooff, J. (1972). A comparative approach to the phylogeny of laughter and smiling. In R.A. Hinde (ed.), *Non-Verbal Communication*, pp. 209–423. Cambridge: Cambridge Univ. Press.

van Lawick-Goodall, J. (1967a). Mother-offspring relationships in free-ranging chimpanzees. In D. Morris (ed.), *Primate Ethology*, pp. 287–346. London: Weidenfeld and Nicolson.

van Lawick-Goodall, J. (1967b). *My Friends the Wild Chimpanzees*. Washington, D.C.: National Geographic Society.

van Lawick-Goodall, J. (1968). The behavior of free-living chimpanzees in the Gombe Stream area. *Anim. Behav. Monogr.* 1:161–311.

van Lawick-Goodall, J. (1970). Tool-using in primates and other vertebrates. In D.S. Lehrman, R.A. Hinde, and E. Shaw (eds.), *Advances in the Study of Behavior*, pp. 195–249. New York: Academic Press.

van Lawick-Goodall, J. (1973a). Cultural elements in a chimpanzee community. *Symp. 4th Int. Congr. Primat.* Vol. 1, pp. 144–184. Basel: Karger.

van Lawick-Goodall, J. (1973b). Behavior of chimpanzees in their natural habitat. *Am. J. Psychiatr.* 130:1–12.

Vilensky, J.A. (1979). Masses, centers-of-gravity, and moments-of-inertia of the body segments of the rhesus monkey (*Macaca mulatta*). *Am. J. Phys. Anthrop.* 50:57–66.

Virgo, H.B. and Waterhouse, M.J. (1969). The emergence of attention structure amongst rhesus macaques. *Man* 4:85–93.

Vitz, P.C. (1966). Affect as a function of stimulus variation. *J. Exp. Psychol.* 71:74–79.

Volkmar, F.R. and Greenough, W.T. (1972). Rearing complexity affects branching of dentrites in the visual cortex of the rat. *Science* 176:1445–1447.

von Cranach, M. (1976). *Methods of Inference from Animal to Human Behavior*. Chicago: Aldine.

Waddington, C.H. (1975). Mindless societies. *The New York Review of Books*. Aug. 7, 1975.

Walk, R.D. (1965). The study of visual depth and distance perception in animals. In D.S. Lehrman, R.A. Hinde, and E. Shaw (eds.), *Advances in the Study of Behavior*, Vol. 1, pp. 99–154. New York: Academic Press.

Walk, R.D. and Gibson, E.J. (1961). A comparative and analytical study of visual depth perception. *Psychol. Monogr.* 75(15):1–44.

Wallace, I. (1977). Self-control techniques of famous novelists. *J. Appl. Behav. Anal.* 10:515–525.

Wallen, K., Bielert, C., and Slimp, J. (1977). Foot clasp mounting in the prepubertal rhesus monkey: Social and hormonal influences. In S. Chevalier-Skolnikoff and F.E. Poirier (eds.), *Primate Bio-Social Development*, pp. 439–461. New York: Garland.

Walters, G.C. and Grusec, J.F. (1977). *Punishment*. San Francisco: Freeman.

Washburn, S.L. (1978). Animal behavior and social anthropology. In M.S. Gregory, A. Silvers, and D. Sutch (eds.), *Sociobiology and Human Values*, pp. 53–74. San Francisco: Jossey-Bass.

Washburn, S.L. and DeVore, I. (1961). The social life of baboons. *Sci. Am.* 204(6):62–71.

Washburn, S.L. and Hamburg, D.A. (1965). The implications of primate research. In, I. DeVore (ed.), *Primate Behavior: Field Studies of Monkeys and Apes*, pp. 607–622. New York: Holt, Rinehart and Winston.

Watson, J.B. (1924). *Behaviorism*. Norton: New York.

Watson, J.S. (1966). The development and generalization of "contingency awareness" in early infancy: Some hypotheses. *Merrill-Palmer Q.* 12:123–135.

Weber, I. and Vogel, C. (1970). Sozialverhalten in ein- und zweigeschlechtigen Langurgruppen. *Homo* 21:73–80.

Wechkin, S. (1970). Social relationships and social facilitation of object manipulation in *Macaca mulatta*. *J. Comp. Physiol. Psychol.* 73:456–460.

Weiner, H. (1965). Conditioning history and maladaptive human operant behavior. *Psychol. Rep.* 17:935–942.

Weiner, H. (1969). Controlling human fixed-interval performance. *J. Exp. Anal. Behav.* 12:349–373.

Welker, C. (1976). Fishing behaviour in *Galago crassicaudatus* E. Geoffroy, 1812 (Prosimiae; Lorisiformes; Galagidae). *Folia Primat.* 26:284–291.

Welker, W.I. (1961). An analysis of exploratory and play behavior in animals. In D.W. Fiske and S.R. Maddi (eds.), *Functions of Varied Experience*, pp. 175–226. Homewood, Ill.: Dorsey.

Welker, W.I. (1971). Ontogeny of play and exploratory behaviors: A definition of problems and a search for new conceptual solutions. In H. Moltz (ed.), *The Ontogeny of Vertebrate Behavior*, pp. 171–228. New York: Academic Press.

White, R.W. (1961). Motivation reconsidered: The concept of competence. In D.W. Fiske and S.R. Maddi (eds.), *Functions of Varied Experience*, pp. 278–325. Homewood, Ill.: Dorsey.

Wilcoxon, H.C., Dragoin, W.B., and Kral, P.A. (1971). Illness-induced aversions in rat and quail: Relative salience of visual and gustatory cues. *Science* 171:826–828.

Wilcoxon, H.C., Meier, G.W., Orlando, R., and Paulson, D.G. (1969). Visual self-stimulation in socially-living rhesus monkeys. *Proc. 2nd Int. Congr. Primat.* Vol. 1, pp. 261–266. Basel: Karger.

Williams, G.C. (1966). *Adaptation and Natural Selection*. Princeton, N.J.: Princeton Univ. Press.

Williams, T.R. (1972). *Introduction to Socialization: Human Culture Transmitted*. St. Louis: C.V. Mosby.

Wilmore, J.H. (1975). Inferiority of female athletes: Myth or reality. *J. Sports Med.* 3(1):1–6.

Wilmore, J.H. (1977). *Athletic training and physical fitness*. Boston: Allyn and Bacon.

Wilson, A.P. and Vessey, S.H. (1968). Behavior of free-ranging castrated rhesus monkeys. *Folia Primat.* 9:1–14.

Wilson, E.O. (1975). *Sociobiology: The New Synthesis*. Cambridge, Mass.: Harvard Univ. Press.

Wilson, E.O. (1978). *On Human Nature*. Cambridge, Mass.: Harvard Univ. Press.

Winick, M. (1979). *Hunger Disease: Studies by the Jewish Physicians in the Warsaw Ghetto*. New York: Wiley.

Wolfe, J.B. (1936). Effectiveness of token-rewards for chimpanzees. *Comp. Psychol. Monogr.* 12:1–72.

Wolfe, L. (1978). Age and sexual behavior of Japanese macaques (*Macaca fuscata*). *Arch. Sex. Behav.* 7:55–68.

Wolfheim, J.H. (1977a). A quantitative analysis of the organization of a group of captive talapoin monkeys (*Miopithecus talapoin*). *Folia Primat.* 27:1–27.

Wolfheim, J.H. (1977b). Sex differences in behavior in a group of captive juvenile talapoin monkeys (*Miopithecus talapoin*). *Behaviour* 63:110–128.

Wrangham, R.W. (1974). Artificial feeding of chimpanzees and baboons in their natural habitat. *Anim. Behav.* 22:83–93.

Wynne-Edwards, V.C. (1962). *Animal Dispersion in Relation to Social Behaviour*. Edinburgh and London: Oliver and Boyd.

Yamada, M. (1963). A study of blood-relationship in the natural society of the Japanese macaque. *Primates* 4:43–65.

Yamada, M. (1971). Five natural troops of Japanese monkeys on Shodoshima Island: II. A comparison of social structure. *Primates* 12:125–150.

Yerkes, R.M. and Dodson, J.D. (1908). The relation of strength of stimulus to rapidity of habit formation. *J. Comp. Neurolog. Psychol.* 18:459–482.

Yoshiba, K. (1968). Local and intertroop variability in ecology and social behavior of common Indian langurs. In P.C. Jay (ed.), *Primates: Studies in Adaptation and Variability*, pp. 217–242. New York: Holt, Rinehart and Winston.

Young, G.H. and Bramblett, C.A. (1977). Gender and environment as determinants of behavior in infant common baboons (*Papio cynocephalus*). *Arch. Sex. Behav.* 6:365–385.

Zaltman, G., Duncan, R., and Holbek, J. (1973a). *Innovations and Organizations*. New York: Wiley.

Zaltman, G., et al. (1973b). *Processes and Phenomena of Social Change*. New York: Wiley.

Zaltman, G. and Duncan, R. (1977). *Strategies for Planned Change*. New York: Wiley.

Zuckerman, M. (1978). Sensation seeking. In H. London and J. Exner, Jr. (eds.), *Dimensions of Personality*, pp. 487–559. New York: Wiley.

Zuckerman, S. (1932). *The Social Life of Monkeys and Apes*. London: Routledge.

Zurif, E.B. and Blumstein, S.E. (1978). Language and the brain. In M. Halle, J. Bresnan, and G.A. Miller (eds.), *Linguistic Theory and Psychological Reality*, pp. 229–245. Boston: MIT Press.

GLOSSARY

Adaptive behavior (operant) Any behavior that helps an individual attain reinforcers and avoid punishers is defined as adaptive in the learning literature. Maladaptive behavior is behavior that fails to produce normal levels of reinforcement or leads to unnecessary punishment.

Adaptive trait (evolution) Any characteristic that increases an individual's fitness—i.e., the ability to successfully leave descendents—is defined as adaptive in evolutionary theory. Such characteristics can be called adaptations.

Allele One of the several possible forms of a given gene. For example, there might be several different alleles for canine tooth length in a baboon population (page 28).

Analogy A similarity that is based on the natural selection of similar traits, but not on common ancestry. For example, primate analogies can be found in the patterns of aggression seen in insects and mammals. (Compare with homology.)

Balanced biosocial theory Any theory that incorporates an empirically defensible balance of causal variables from all explanatory levels: evolution and adaptation, physiological mechanisms, constructive and destructive proximal inputs, and natural learning. (See pages 16–19.)

Carnivore An animal that eats the flesh of other animals.

Cerebral cortex The area of the brain that has become highly developed in advanced species and allows complex learning.

Conspecific A member of the same species.

Contingencies of reinforcement The contingent relationship between antecedent stimuli (S^D's), behavior, and reinforcement. The analysis of operant conditioning requires that one know all three of these conditions of reinforcement: when and where a behavior may be reinforced; what behavior is suited to those conditions; and the nature and frequency of the reinforcement.

CS Conditioned stimulus. A CS can elicit a conditioned response due to Pavlovian conditioning. (See page 82.)

Differential reinforcement The reinforcement of some responses but not others.

Differential reproduction Different rates of reproduction, such that some individuals leave more offspring than do others.

Discrimination The act or incidence of responding differently to different stimuli. This differential responsiveness to stimuli is sometimes innate (hence the result of differential reproduction), but in primates it is largely acquired by learning (hence the result of differential reinforcement or differential exposure to positive and negative stimuli).

Distal   Distant. Distal causes are the distant causes that explain the effects of natural selection on a trait or behavior. (Compare with proximal.)

Dorsal   Of or pertaining to the back.

Ethology   Ethology—the biology of behavior—was the first discipline to study behavior from the biological perspective. Ethologists emphasized the importance of studying behavior in the natural environment in order to understand evolutionary adaptation. (See pages 46–48.)

Extinction (evolution)   The dying out of a species.

Extinction (operant)   The discontinuation of reinforcement or punishment. Usually, any behavioral effects that had been produced by the reinforcement or punishment begin to disappear during extinction.

Extinction (Pavlovian)   The discontinuation of Pavlovian conditioning. Usually, a CS loses its ability to elicit reflexive responses once it is no longer paired with other reflexes.

Fitness   A measure of the ability of an individual to leave descendents. Any characteristic that increases an individual's capacity to leave descendents increases its personal fitness. Characteristics that increase the survival and reproduction of kin who carry similar genes increases its inclusive fitness.

Fixed action pattern   A term used by ethologists to describe "instinctive movements" or innate motor patterns.

Generalization   The act or process by which an individual responds to similar stimuli in the same way.

Genotype   The genetic inheritance of an organism. (Contrast with phenotype.)

Habituation   The type of learning in which an individual stops responding to irrelevant stimuli after repeated experience with them. (See pages 33–34.)

Herbivore   An animal that eats plants but not animals.

Home range   The geographic area typically used by an animal or a group. It need not be defended against invading conspecifics. (Compare with territory.)

Homology   A similarity that can be traced to common ancestry. For example, the canine teeth of different primate species are homologous, even though they are much larger in some species than in others.

Imprinting   The type of learning in which an individual (usually a young animal) forms a strong attachment to a given stimulus (usually its mother). (See pages 103–104.)

Induction   Any process by which new variations on operant behavior appear and provide the raw material for the shaping of new operant performances. Induction provides the raw material for shaping of new operants much as mutation provides the raw material for the evolution of new genotypes. (See pages 37–38.)

Lamarckian theory   The theory that organisms have an urge for perfections that helps adjust them to their environment and that these self-accomplished adaptations can be transmitted to the offspring, via the inheritance of acquired characteristics.

Multiparous   Having given birth more than once.

Mutation   Any change in the genes. Mutations provide the raw material for the production of new evolutionary forms through differential reproduction. Mutations that increase fitness tend to become more common in later generations. (Compare with induction.)

Natural learning   Learning as it takes place in the natural environment, influenced by both the proximal and distal determinants of learning.

Natural selection   The process by which the environment favors the survival and reproduction of some individuals more than others in the same population.

Neonate   A newborn animal. Neonatal is the adjectival form: of or pertaining to the newborn individual.

Observational learning   Learning that occurs by observing the behavior of another individual.

Omnivore   An animal that eats all types of food—both plant and animal.

Ontogenetic   Relating to the individual's own unique history of development since conception.

Operant conditioning   The type of learning in which behavior is modified by its consequences. Behavior that is followed by reinforcers becomes more frequent and comes under the control of any antecedent stimuli (S^D's) that correlate with reinforcement. Behavior that is followed by nonreinforcement or punishment becomes less frequent and comes under the control of any antecedent stimuli (S^Δ's) that correlate with nonreinforcement or punishment.

Pavlovian conditioning   The type of learning in which a neutral stimulus is paired with the unconditioned stimulus (US) of a reflex and eventually becomes a conditioned stimulus (CS) that is capable of eliciting reflexive responses. Higher order conditioning occurs when a neutral stimulus is paired with a CS (rather than a US) and becomes a CS, too.

Phenotype   The observable traits and behaviors of an organism. The phenotype is always a product of nature and nurture: i.e., the interaction of genes and proximal environmental inputs. Therefore neither nature alone nor nurture alone can ever provide an adequate explanation of phenotypes.

Phylogenetic   Relating to the evolutionary history of a given species.

Phylogenetic inertia   The genetic inheritance of a species that increases or decreases the likelihood of future evolutionary changes.

Primiparous   Having given birth only once.

Proximal   Close. Nearby. Proximal causes are the environmental inputs that influence the physiological mechanisms and behavior of an individual during its own lifetime.

Punisher   Any stimulus that can cause operant behavior to become less frequent. Unconditioned punishers ($^-$US's) include cuts, hard blows, bad food in the stomach, loud noise, and extreme temperatures. Conditioned punishers ($^-$CS's) are created when neutral stimuli are paired with $^-$US's. (See pages 75–90.)

Reinforcer   Any stimulus that can cause operant behavior to become more frequent. Unconditioned reinforcers ($^+$US's) include food, sex, water, optimal levels of warmth, and optimal levels of sensory stimulation. Conditioned reinforcers ($^+$CS's) are created when neutral stimuli are paired with $^+$US's. (See pages 74–90.)

Reticular formation   A structure in the brain stem that is involved in measuring the amount of stimulation in the central nervous system. (See pages 193–197.)

Satiation   The state of being full of or overexposed to a given positive reinforcer to the point where the reinforcer loses its ability to reinforce behavior.

S^D *and* S^Δ Discriminitive stimuli. S^D's are antecedent stimuli that signal that a behavior has been followed by reinforcers in the past. S^Δ's are antecedent stimuli that signal that a behavior has been followed by nonreinforcement or punishment in the past.

Sociobiology   A recent discipline that uses modern evolutionary theory as the central principle for explaining behavior. (See pages 2–5.)

Sociogram   A map or diagram of social relationships. Sociograms may portray general social patterns or depict only specific types of relations, such as grooming, aggression, or spacing.

Stimulus-seeking behavior   Any behavior that increases the chances that an individual will be exposed to increasing levels of stimulus input. Exploration, play, and creativity are three common types of stimulus-seeking behaviors.

Strategy   Sociobiologists and other biologists often use the word strategy as a metaphor that helps them discuss optimal methods of adaptation. They do not intend to infer conscious self-adaptation to organisms, but the term can encourage genetic idealism. (See page 64, note 33.)

Territory   A geographic area that is used by an animal or a group and defended to prevent invasion by conspecifics.

Type II error   Accepting a hypothesis that should not have been accepted. (A Type I error involves rejecting a hypothesis that should not have been rejected.)

US   Unconditioned stimulus. A US can elicit an unconditioned response without prior learning being involved.

Ventrum   The underside—abdomen or chest—of an animal.

AUTHOR INDEX

SUBJECT INDEX

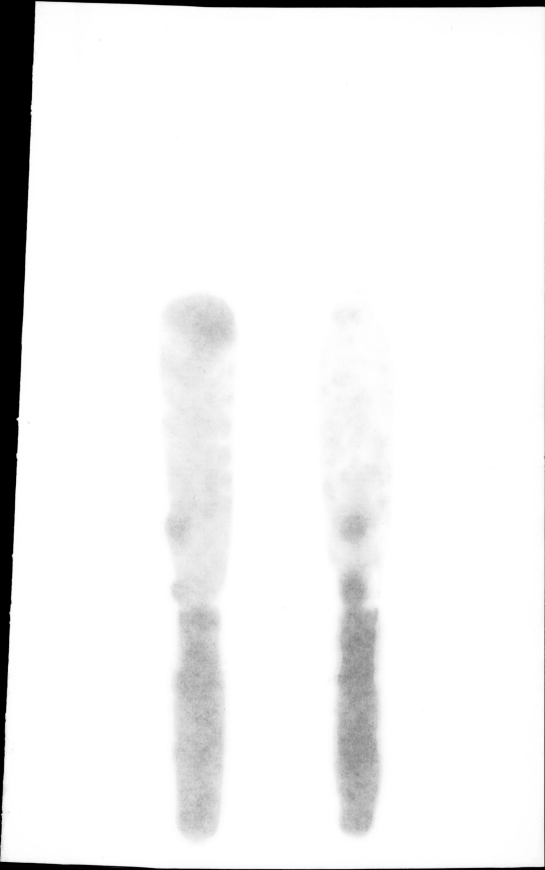